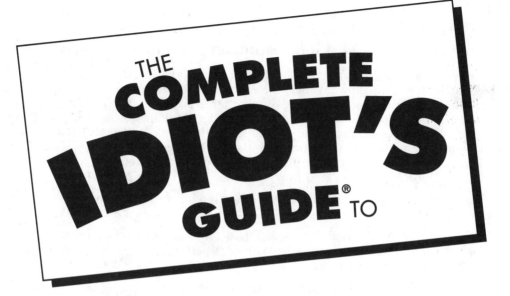

THE COMPLETE IDIOT'S GUIDE® TO

the Bible

by Stan Campbell and
James S. Bell, Jr.

alpha books

A Division of Macmillan General Reference
A Simon & Schuster Macmillan Company
1633 Broadway, New York, NY 10019-6785

I, Jim, would like to dedicate this book to my son, Brendan Bell, a full-time student at Bible College—stay serious, it will pay great dividends in your daily life.

Copyright © 1999 by Stan Campbell and James S. Bell, Jr.

Macmillan Publishing books may be purchased for business or sales promotional use. For information please write: Special Markets Department, Macmillan Publishing USA, 1633 Broadway, New York, NY 10019.

International Standard Book Number: 0-02862728-8
Library of Congress Catalog Card: information available on request

00   8 7

Interpretation of the printing code: the rightmost number of the first series of numbers is the year of the book's printing; the rightmost number of the second series of numbers is the number of the book's printing. For example, a printing code of 98-1 shows that the first printing occurred in 1998.

Printed in the United States of America

The Complete Idiot's Reference Card

Books of the Bible

Old Testament	New Testament
Genesis	Matthew
Exodus	Mark
Leviticus	Luke
Numbers	John
Deuteronomy	Acts
Joshua	Romans
Judges	1 Corinthians
Ruth	2 Corinthians
1 Samuel	Galatians
2 Samuel	Ephesians
1 Kings	Philippians
2 Kings	Colossians
1 Chronicles	1 Thessalonians
2 Chronicles	2 Thessalonians
Ezra	1 Timothy
Nehemiah	2 Timothy
Esther	Titus
Job	Philemon
Psalms	Hebrews
Proverbs	James
Ecclesiastes	1 Peter
Song of Songs	2 Peter
Isaiah	1 John
Jeremiah	2 John
Lamentations	3 John
Ezekiel	Jude
Daniel	Revelation
Hosea	
Joel	
Amos	
Obadiah	
Jonah	
Micah	
Nahum	
Habakkuk	
Zephaniah	
Haggai	
Zechariah	
Malachi	

alpha
books

Where to Find Some Favorite Stories and Passages

Old Testament

Creation/Adam and Eve (Genesis 1–3)

Noah and the ark (Genesis 6–9)

The tower of Babel (Genesis 11:1–9)

Abraham offers Isaac (Genesis 22:1–19)

Jacob's ladder (Genesis 28:10–22)

Joseph and his coat (Genesis 37:1–11)

Moses and the burning bush
(Exodus 3–4)

The plagues on Egypt (Exodus 7–11)

Moses parts the Red Sea (Exodus 14)

The Ten Commandments
(Exodus 20:1–17)

Spies enter Promised Land (Numbers 13)

The battle of Jericho (Joshua 6)

Gideon's fleece and battles (Judges 6–7)

Samson and Delilah (Judges 16)

Ruth marries Boaz (Book of Ruth)

The boy Samuel hears God's voice
(1 Samuel 3)

David and Goliath (1 Samuel 17)

David and Jonathan (1 Samuel 20)

David and Bathsheba (2 Samuel 11)

Solomon's wisdom (1 Kings 3; 4:29–34)

The Queen of Sheba (1 Kings 10:1–13)

Elijah calls down fire (1 Kings 18:16–46)

Elisha heals Naaman's leprosy (2 Kings 5)

Rebuilding Jerusalem's walls
(Nehemiah 1–6)

A queen saves her people (Book of
Esther)

Job's trials and rewards (Job 1–2; 42)

"The Lord is my Shepherd" (Psalm 23)

A noble woman described
(Proverbs 31:10–31)

To everything a season
(Ecclesiastes 3:1–8)

"To us a child is born" (Isaiah 9:6–7)

A prophet in the pits (Jeremiah 38)

Dry bones come back to life
(Ezekiel 37:1–14)

Daniel in the lions' den (Daniel 6)

Jonah and the big fish (Jonah 1–2)

New Testament

The birth of Jesus (Matthew 2; Luke 2)

Jesus' temptations (Matthew 4:1–11)

The Lord's prayer (Matthew 6:9–13)

The golden rule (Matthew 7:12)

The greatest commandment
(Mark 12:28–34)

Jesus walks on water (Matthew 14:22–33)

Jesus calms a storm (Mark 4:35–41)

Jesus' transfiguration (Luke 9:28–36)

The good Samaritan (Luke 10:25–37)

The prodigal son (Luke 15:11–32)

Jesus changes water to wine
(John 2:1–11)

The woman at the well (John 4:1–42)

Jesus feeds 5,000 (John 6:1–15)

The resurrection of Lazarus
(John 11:1–44)

Jesus' triumphal entry (Matthew 21:1–11)

Jesus' crucifixion (Matthew 26:36–27:66)

Jesus' resurrection (John 20)

Jesus ascends into heaven (Acts 1:1–11)

The Holy Spirit comes at Pentecost
(Acts 2)

Stephen is martyred (Acts 6:8–7:60)

Paul's conversion (Acts 9:1–31)

An angel frees Peter from prison
(Acts 12:1–19)

The "love chapter" (1 Corinthians 13)

Paul's sufferings (2 Corinthians 11:16–33)

The fruit of the Spirit (Galatians 5:22–23)

The armor of God (Ephesians 6:10–18)

The ultimate in humility
(Philippians 2:1–11)

The "Faith Hall of Fame" (Hebrews 11)

Taming the tongue (James 3:1–12)

God is love (1 John 3–4)

Alpha Development Team

Publisher
Kathy Nebenhaus

Editorial Director
Gary M. Krebs

Managing Editor
Bob Shuman

Marketing Brand Manager
Felice Primeau

Editor
Jessica Faust

Development Editors
Phil Kitchel
Amy Zavatto

Production Team

Development Editor
Kate Layzer

Production Editor
Suzanne Snyder

Copy Editor
Krista Hansing

Cover Designer
Mike Freeland

Photo Editor
Richard H. Fox

Illustrator
Jody P. Schaeffer

Designer
Nathan Clement

Indexer
Nadia Ibrahim

Layout/Proofreading
Angela Calvert
Mary Hunt
Julie Trippetti

Contents at a Glance

Part 1: Before You Begin   **1**

1 The B-I-B-L-E, Is That a Book for Me?   3
*Taking the "fear and trembling" out of approaching the
Bible, a few basic benefits of Bible reading, how we got our
Bible from a bunch of manuscripts, how to choose a Bible
translation that's right for you.*

2 Claims and Disclaimers   15
*Why people view the same Bible so differently, what the
Bible says about its own authority, what noted people have
said about the Bible, understanding the Bible's layout,
getting the most from what you read.*

Part 2: The Old Testament   **23**

3 In the Beginning   25
*(Genesis 1–11) God creates the world, Adam and Eve romp
around naked until they're tossed out of Eden, Cain kills
Abel, Noah builds an ark, and people (partially) build the
Tower of Babel.*

4 Abraham: A Not-So-Accidental Tourist   35
*(Genesis 12–23) Abraham receives some promises, moves
his family, separates from Lot, gives up his wife a couple of
times, witnesses the destruction of Sodom and Gomorrah,
and comes within a second of killing his son.*

5 Isaac and Jacob: Lessons in Family Dysfunction   45
*(Genesis 24–36) Isaac gets a long-distance bride, their sons
Jacob and Esau don't get along at all, Jacob leaves home
and starts a family of his own, Jacob has a couple of
encounters with God—one of which leaves him limping,
but with a new name.*

6 Joseph: Not Your Average Joe   57
*(Genesis 37–50) Joseph is the little brother nobody likes, is
sold into slavery, ends up in Egypt where he is imprisoned
on rape charges, is released to become second in command
of Egypt, and is eventually reunited with his family.*

7 Moses: God's Reluctant Hero   67
*(Exodus, Leviticus, Numbers, Deuteronomy) The life of
Moses from a baby on the Nile, to the burning bush in the
desert, to the plagues before Pharoah, across the Red Sea,
up Mount Sinai, and through the wilderness.*

8 The Good, the Bad, and the Lovely 81
(Joshua, Judges, and Ruth) Joshua takes over for Moses, including his famous battle at Jericho and making the sun stand still; the judges (including Gideon and Samson) take over; Ruth adds some romance to the Old Testament.

9 That's Saul, Folks! 93
(1 Samuel –15; portions of Chronicles) The Israelites demand a king; Saul is crowned but doesn't exactly shine as a leader; David rises to power after a little confrontation with a giant named Goliath.

10 David: Now for Some King Completely Different 105
(1 Samuel 16–2 Samuel; portions of Chronicles) David becomes king and strengthens Israel into a formidable nation, but then has an affair with Bathsheba and watches everything go downhill from there.

11 The Riches-to-Rags Story of Israel and Judah 117
(1 & 2 Kings; portions of Chronicles) Solomon becomes king and is unsurpassed in wealth and wisdom; the kingdom splits into Israel and Judah; a long series of kings provided very few positive examples of worthwhile leadership; foreign nations conquer both Israel and Judah.

12 Making the Best of a Bad Situation 133
(Ezra, Nehemiah, Esther, Job) Ezra and Nehemiah return from captivity to repair Jerusalem; Esther boldly goes where no Jewish woman has gone before; Job sees his good life fall apart and wonders why.

13 Old Testament Lit. 101 145
(Psalms, Proverbs, Ecclesiastes, Song of Songs) Wisdom comes in many forms, including songs and proverbs; a look into the mind-set of the guy who has everything; and proof that passion has its place among God's people.

14 Tell-a-Vision Personalities 157
(Isaiah through Malachi) God's message to humankind is forwarded to us by the prophets who found themselves in some of the strangest places—heaven, fish stomachs, lions' den, mud pits, and more.

Part 3: The New Testament **171**

15 God's Baby Gift 173
(The Birth, Early Life, and Relationships of Jesus) The four centuries between testaments is a trying time for God's people, after which Jesus is born and begins to introduce some new perspective on religion as they know it.

16 We're Going to Need to See Some I.D.   187
    *(The Miracles of Jesus) Jesus astounds people by walking
    around healing the sick, casting out evil spirits, telling
    nature what to do, and even raising the dead.*

17 Did I Hear That Right?   199
    *(The Teachings of Jesus) Whether teaching in parables or
    saying exactly what he means, Jesus' teachings raise a lot
    of questions and discussion among his listeners.*

18 Arose by Any Other Name...   213
    *(Jesus' Death, Burial, and Resurrection) Jesus' enemies
    determine to stop him at any cost, resulting in his crucifix-
    ion, but his death is followed by a resurrection that
    surprises even his closest followers.*

19 The Church Hits the Road   225
    *(Acts) Jesus' disciples carry on where he left off and a new
    leader is called to include the Gentiles in the message of
    salvation, all resulting in the spread of Christian teachings
    from Jerusalem throughout the world.*

20 You've Got Mail!   237
    *(Paul's Letters, Part 1) The epistles of Paul begin with
    three lengthy letters that provide clarity of Christian
    doctrines, rules for church order, some personal sharing
    from Paul's heart, and more.*

21 More of the Apostle's Epistles   253
    *(Paul's Letters, Part 2) Paul's other epistles include numer-
    ous instructions and encouragement, including warnings
    about false teachers, insight into the second coming of
    Jesus, and some mentoring comments.*

22 Still More People Doing the Write Thing   265
    *(Hebrews through Jude) We hear from other epistle writers,
    including Peter, James, John, and Jude on a variety of
    topics.*

23 It's the End of the World As We Know It   279
    *(Revelation) John records an amazing vision of heaven,
    angels, churches, horsemen, beasts, and much, much more
    that is likely to keep people confused about the end of the
    world until it gets here.*

Appendices

A The Books of the Bible   293

B Where Can You Go from Here?   297

C Reading the Bible in One Year   301

   Index   315

Contents

Part 1: Before You Begin   **1**

1 The B-I-B-L-E, Is That a Book for Me?   **3**

Check Your Bible IQ 4
What's In It for Me? 6
   Bible Knowledge Can Make You a More Literate Person 7
   *Bible Knowledge Can Make You a More
     Authoritative Person* 7
   Bible Knowledge Can Make You a More Virtuous Person 8
   Bible Knowledge Can Make You a More Spiritual Person 8
Has Bible Content Changed over the Years? 9
How Did We Get Our Bible from a Bunch of Manuscripts? . 9
Choosing the Best Bible from All the Good Books 11
   Translation versus Paraphrase 11
   Familiarity versus Contemporary Feel 11
   Basic Bible versus Study Bible 11
   Other Factors 12
   Go Shopping! 12

2 Claims and Disclaimers   **15**

Seeing the Whole Elephant 15
   The Cultural Problem 16
   The Religion Problem 17
   The Language Problem 17
   The Pronoun/Gender Issue 18
   On a Personal Note 18
Why Put Up with All These Problems? 19
The Layout of the Bible 19
   A Little of Everything 20
   What's with All the Numbers? 20
Stocking Your Bible Toolbox 21
   A Dictionary 21
   A Bible Dictionary 21
   A Bible Atlas 21
   Bible Commentaries 21
   Concordance 21
   Cross-References 22

Part 2: The Old Testament 23

3 In the Beginning 25

What Was Before the Beginning? (Genesis 1:1) 25
A Good Day's Work (Genesis 1:1–2:3) 26
Adam and Eve in a Brave Nude World
  (Genesis 2:4–25) 27
Fall Comes to Eden (Genesis 3) 27
Brother Against Brother (Genesis 4:1–16) 29
A Population Explosion (Genesis 4:17–5) 30
Looks Like Rain (Genesis 6–7) 31
Rain, Rain, Go Away (Genesis 8:1–9:17) 32
What Do You Do with a Drunken Ex-Sailor?
  (Genesis 9:18–29) 32
No Comprende: Conversations at the Tower
  of Babel (Genesis 10–11) 33

4 Abraham: A Not-So-Accidental Tourist 35

Go West, Old Man (Genesis 11:27–12:9) 36
Take My Wife—I Mean, Sister…Please!
  (Genesis 12:10–20) 37
Lots of Trouble from Lot and His Lot (Genesis 13–14) 37
Gone Today, Heir Tomorrow (Genesis 15) 38
Sarah Problem Here? (Genesis 16) 39
The Sign of (Ouch!) Faith (Genesis 17) 39
Let's Make a Deal (Genesis 18) 40
Hot Time in the Cities (Genesis 19:1–29) 41
A Family Affair (Genesis 19:23–29) 42
All I Want Is the Heir That I Breed (Genesis 20–22) 43

5 Isaac and Jacob: Lessons in Family Dysfunction 45

Isaac's Mail-Order Bride (Genesis 23–25:18) 45
Birthright Gumbo (Genesis 25:19–34) 46
Like Father, Like Son (Genesis 26) 47
The Old Man and Deceit (Genesis 27–28:9) 48
Stairway to Heaven (Genesis 28:10–22) 49
The Wrong "Honey" on the Honeymoon
  (Genesis 29:1–30) 50
Baby, Baby, Baby, Etc. (Genesis 29:31–30:23) 51

An Early Experiment in Genetic Engineering
(Genesis 30:25–43) 52
On the Road Again (Genesis 31) 53
Getting All Out of Joint (Genesis 32) 54
He Saw Esau (Genesis 33; 35–36) 55

6 Joseph: Not Your Average Joe   57

Dream a Little Dream of Me (Genesis 37:1–11) 57
Ten Angry Men (Genesis 37:12–36) 58
"Mrs. Potiphar, I'm a Joe—Not a John" (Genesis 39) 59
A Baker, a Cupbearer, and a Hangman (Genesis 40) 59
Dreaming of the Cows 'n' the Corn (Genesis 41:1–40) 60
From Ex-Con to CEO (Genesis 41:41–57) 61
I Never Forget a Face—Much Less 10 of Them
(Genesis 42) 61
Ben There, Done That (Genesis 43–44) 62
Family Reunion (Genesis 45–47:12) 63
A Fair Deal from Pharaoh? (Genesis 47:13–26) 64
The Last of the Patriarchs (Genesis 47:28–50:26) 65

7 Moses: God's Reluctant Hero   67

Four Centuries of Decline, from Joe to Moe (Exodus 1) 67
Rollin' on the River (Exodus 2:1–10) 68
Hit and Run (Exodus 2:11–25) 68
You Can't Beat the Bush (Exodus 3–4) 69
Bricks Without Straw (Exodus 5–6) 70
The Plague's the Thing (Exodus 7–11) 71
The First Passover (Exodus 11–12:30) 72
An Order of 600,000 Israelite Families—to Go!
(Exodus 12:31–13) 72
Stalk Like an Egyptian (Exodus 14–15:21) 73
Hey Manna, Manna (Exodus 15:22–17:7) 74
Smoke on the Mountain, and Fire in the Sky
(Exodus 19–31) 75
Unholy Cow! (Exodus 32–34) 76
The Group Regroups (Exodus 35–40) 77
Spy versus Spy (Numbers 13–14) 78
Generation Next (Numbers 27–35) 79

8 The Good, the Bad, and the Lovely   **81**

Next in Command (Joshua 1) 81
Help from Unexpected Quarters (Joshua 2) 82
The Miraculous Water Crossing You Hardly Ever Hear
   About (Joshua 3–5:12) 83
Joshua Fought the Battle of Jericho—But First, Some Laps
   (Joshua 5:13–8) 83
If You Can't Beat Them, Psyche Them Out
   (Joshua 9–12) 85
Movin' In (Joshua 13–24) 86
The Apathy of Defeat (Judges 1–2) 86
Here Come the Judges! (Judges 3–16) 86
   Ehud (Judges 3:12–30) 87
   Deborah (Judges 4–5) 87
   Gideon (Judges 6–8) 88
   Samson (Judges 13–16) 89
No Longer Ruthless (Ruth 1–4) 90

9 That's Saul, Folks!   **93**

Prayer? So That's Where Babies Come From!
   (1 Sam. 1–2:11) 93
Problems with the Priest Hoods (1 Sam. 2:12–26) 94
Speak Three Times from the Ceiling If You Want Me
   (1 Sam. 3) 94
Raiders of the Lord's Ark (1 Sam. 4–7) 95
King Me! (1 Sam. 8–12) 95
Who Is This "Phyllis Stein," and Why Are There So Many
   of Her? (1 Sam. 13–14) 97
The Bleat Goes On (1 Sam. 15) 98
Touching His Harp Strings (1 Sam. 16–17) 98
Fee-Fi-Foe-Fight, I Want the Blood of an Israelite
   (1 Sam. 17) 99
Banned, On the Run (1 Sam. 18–23) 100
A Little Longer Live the King! (1 Sam. 24–26) 102
A Short Ghost Story (1 Sam. 27–31) 102

10 David: Now for Some King Completely Different   **105**

Here Comes the New Boss, Not Like the Old Boss
   (2 Sam. 1–4) 105
King at Last! (2 Sam. 5) 107

Disembarking the Ark (2 Sam. 6) 108
Israel: Growing by Leaps and Boundaries (2 Sam. 8–10) .. 109
My Kingdom for a House (2 Sam. 7) 109
Splish, Splash, I Was Taking a Bath (2 Sam. 11) 110
Uriah Is In a Heap (2 Sam. 12) 111
Rape, Revenge, and Regrets (2 Sam. 13)........................... 112
The Hair Apparent (2 Sam. 14–16:14) 112
Plants, Plots, and Perverse Pleasures
   (2 Sam. 16:15–17:29) 114
A Really, *Really* Bad Hair Day (2 Sam. 18) 114
Back in Business (2 Sam. 19:9–21) 115

11 The Riches-to-Rags Story of Israel and Judah   117

Solomon's Successful Succession (1 Kings 1) 117
Wisdom? In Your Dreams! (1 Kings 2–4) 118
Temple Temps (1 Kings 5–9) 120
Queen for a Stay (1 Kings 10) 121
The Odds Against Success Are About a Thousand to One
   (1 Kings 11) 121
Split Decision (1 Kings 12) 122
   The Kings of Israel 124
   The Kings of Judah 126
Down Come the Ravens, Up Goes the Chariot
   (1 Kings 17–19; 2 Kings 1–2) 130
Miracles In All Shapes and Sizes (1 Kings 19:19–21;
   2 Kings 2–8:15) 130

12 Making the Best of a Bad Situation   133

The Long Walk Home (Ezra 1–2) 134
   *Got No Church; Got No Steeple; All We've Got is a Bunch
     of People (Ezra 3)* 134
   A Temple of Doom? (Ezra 4–6) 135
   And Then Along Came Ezra (Ezra 7–8) 135
   *Next on Jeremiah Springer: Idol Worshipers and the Priests
     Who Marry Them! (Ezra 9–10)* 135
Sayonara, Nehemiah (Nehemiah 1–2:10) 136
   Stalling the Walling (Nehemiah 2:11–6:14) 137
   Wall-to-Wall Carpentry (Nehemiah 6:15–13) 137
If You Knew Susa Like Esther Knew Susa
   (Esther 1–2:18) 138

The Plot Thickens (Esther 2:19–4) 139

Queen Saves the Godly (Esther 5–7) 140

A Good Job Description (Job 1:1–4) 141

Take This Job and Shove Him (Job 1:5–2:10) 141

With Friends Like These… (Job 3–37) 143

Another Voice Heard (Job 38–41) 143

Another Happy Ending (Job 42) 144

13 Old Testament Lit. 101   145

Psing Us a Psong, You're the Psalmist 145

Simile When You Say That 146

Be Honest 147

Solomon Says 149

Now Listen Up! 149

Ecclesiastes: The Book of Meaning—and
Meaninglessness 152

The Song of Songs (Parental Warning: Explicit Lyrics) 155

14 Tell-a-Vision Personalities   157

Isaiah: Hot Lips, Warm Heart 157

Bad News, Good News 158

Rebels, Rebels Everywhere 158

Don't Cry for Me, Jeremiah 159

If You Can't Say Something Nice 160

They're Clay in My Hands 160

How Deserted Lies the City 161

Ezekiel: This Wheel's on Fire 162

A Face Like an Angel 162

God and Ezekiel Down by the Boneyard 163

Staying Cool Under Pressure 164

A Beastly King…Or the King of Beasts 166

Spending Some Time in the Minors 167

Hosea 167

Joel 168

Amos 168

Obadiah 168

Jonah 168

Micah 169

Nahum 169

Habakkuk 169

Zephaniah *169*
Haggai *169*
Zechariah *169*
Malachi *170*

Part 3: The New Testament   **171**

15 God's Baby Gift   **173**

Where Are We Going? 173
What Have We Missed? 174
Unplanned Parenthood (Luke 1) 175
   If You Don't Mind My Asking 176
   "You're WHAT?" 176
It's Beginning to Look a Lot Like Christmas
   (Matthew 2; Luke 2) 177
   "We've Been Expecting You" 178
   Some Kid! 178
   And the Word Became Flesh (John 1:1–18) 179
How John Became "the Baptist" (Matthew 3; Luke 3;
   John 1:29–34) 179
The Devil Couldn't Make Him Do It (Matthew 4:1–11) ... 180
The Dusty Dozen (Matthew 4:18–22; 9:9; Luke 10:2–4;
   John 1:35–51) 181
One Reason Why You Can't Go Home Again
   (Luke 4:14–30) 182
Nic at Night (John 3:1–21) 183
A Chat Around the Water Cooler (John 4:1–42) 183
Can Someone Get This Lady a Robe? (John 8:1–11) 184

16 We're Going to Need to See Some I.D.   **187**

Demons, Diseases, and Disabilities 187
   Jesus Heals a Ceiling Fan (Mark 2:1–2) 188
   Nothing Up His Sleeve… 188
   Here's Mud in Your Eye 189
It's Not Hard to Rule Mother Nature 190
   Six Huge Bottles of Wine on the Floor (John 2:1–11) 190
   The Ones That Didn't Quite Get Away (Luke 5:1–11) 191
   When Nature Calls, Call Back (Matthew 8:23–27;
   14:22–33) *191*

We're Trying to Divide This Food, but It Keeps
Multiplying (Matthew 14:13–21) 192
Straight from the Fish's Mouth (Matthew 17:24–27) 193
The Tree That Didn't Give a Fig (Mark 11:12–14,
19–25) 193
I Was Dead for a While, but I'm Much Better Now
(Mark 5:21–43) 194
Another Stinking Resurrection (John 11) 194
Some Relationships Require a Miracle 195
A Drop in the Miracle Bucket 196

17 Did I Hear That Right?   **199**

Higher Education (Matthew 5–7) 200
The Spirit of the Law 201
Don't Worry, Be Holy 201
Coming Down with a Code 202
Parables of the Kingdom 203
A Parable for Every Occasion 204
The Good Samaritan (Luke 10:25–37) 205
The Prodigal Son and Other Lost Things (Luke 15) 206
Hellfire and Damnation 207
New Wine and Hard Teachings 209
Jesus' Not-So-Secret Identity 210
The Loved One That Got Away (Mark 10:17–23) 212

18 Arose by Any Other Name...   **213**

The Big Question 214
Glow (but Don't Tell It) on the Mountain
(Luke 9:28–36) 214
An Entrance Fit for a King (Luke 19:28–44) 215
Jesus the Bouncer (Mark 11:15–18) 215
Final Countdown 215
A Meal Worthy of a DaVinci Painting 216
Disciples Squabble, Then They All Fall Down 217
Trial, Trial Again 218
Cross Purposes 220
Friends in High Places 221
Alive Again 222
Getting the Story Straight 223
For Pete's (and Thom's) Sake 223

19 The Church Hits the Road   **225**

Onward and Upward (Acts 1) 225
On a Wind and a Prayer (Acts 2:1–41) 226
Peter Principal (Acts 2:42–5) 227
The Subordinate Seven (Acts 6–8) 228
Blinded by the Light (Acts 9:1–31) 229
Peter, Peter, Reptile Eater (Acts 9:21–12) 230
Road Trip #1 (Acts 13–15:35) 231
Road Trip #2 (Acts 15:36–21:36) 232
   Derbe/Lystra (Acts 16:1–5) 232
   Philippi (Acts 16:6–40) 232
   Thessalonica/Berea (Acts 17:1–15) 233
   Athens (Acts 17:16–34) 233
   Corinth (Acts 18) 233
   Ephesus (Acts 19) 233
   Troas (Acts 20:1–12) 234
   Miletus (Acts 20:13–38) 234
   Home to Jerusalem (Acts 21:1–36) 234
Road Trip #3 (Acts 21:37–28) 235

20 You've Got Mail!   **237**

Buón Giorno, Roma (Romans 1–3) 238
   Abraham, Adam, and Jesus (Romans 4–5) 239
   Everything Old Is New Again (Romans 6–7) 240
   The Benefit Plan (Romans 8) 240
The Choice of a New Generation (Romans 9–11) 241
   Altar Egos (Romans 12–16) 242
1,000 Prostitutes—No Waiting (1 Cor. 1:1–8) 242
   Whom Do You Love? (1 Cor. 1:10–4) 242
   Incest and Outplacement (1 Cor. 5–6:11) 243
   The Wonderful World of Sex (1 Cor. 6:12–7) 244
   Taking the Heat for the Meat That You Eat (1 Cor. 8) 244
   Order in the Church! (1 Cor. 10–11) 245
Five Intelligible Words (1 Cor. 14) 247
All Rise (1 Cor. 15–16) 248
Same Church, Different Problems (2 Cor. 1–5) 248
   Tidings of Contusions and Joy (2 Cor. 6–9) 248
Paul versus the Super-Apostles: A Grudge Match
(2 Cor. 10–13) 249
   Same As It Ever Was 250

21   More of the Apostle's Epistles   253

Galatian Salutations 253
An Emphasis on Ephesus 255
Philippians: Don't Worry, Be Joyful 257
Colossians: Who's Number One? 258
One and Two Thessalonians: Guess Who's Coming
   (Back) to See Us? 259
Paul as Mentor (1 and 2 Timothy; Titus) 260
   2 Timothy 262
   Titus 263
Philemon: A Runaway Slave Makes A Round Trip 263

22   Still More People Doing the Write Thing   265

Hebrews: Everything Old Is New Again 265
James: Uncommonly Common Sense 268
   No Wonder Mom Liked Big Brother Better 268
   Bible, Bible on the Wall 269
   It's Hard to Lick Your Own Tongue 270
Peter's Priority Mail 271
   An Invitation to Join the Priesthood 271
   Imitating the Savior's Behavior 272
   Just a Second Peter 273
Dear John Letters 274
Jude Says Hey 276
Yours Truly 276

23   It's the End of the World As We Know It   279

Club Med Meets Century One (Rev. 1) 280
Rate-a-Church (Rev. 2–3)... 280
Up, Up and Away (Rev. 4–5) 282
Scroll with the Punches (Rev. 6–7)................................... 283
The Trumpet Septet You Never Want to Hear
   (Rev. 8–9) 284
God's Witness Protection Program (Rev. 10–11:14) 285
The Seventh Trumpet (Rev. 11:15–14) 286
Bowled Over (Revelation 16–18) 287
Rider on the Storm (Rev. 19–20) 288
Trying to Make Sense of It All 289
Heaven: New and Improved (Rev. 21–22) 290
The End? Or Just the Beginning? 292

Appendices

A The Books of the Bible 293

THE OLD TESTAMENT 293
  Law 293
  Histories 293
  Writings 293
  Prophets 293
THE NEW TESTAMENT 294
  Gospels 294
  History 294
  Epistles 294
  Apocalypse 294

B Where Can You Go from Here? 297

Bibles: 297
Bible Translation Abbreviations: 298
Resources: 298

C Reading the Bible in One Year 301

Index 315

Foreword

Technology has made the world a neighborhood but not a brotherhood. We can push a few buttons or click a mouse and connect instantly with someone continents away, but it may take months for opposing governments just to begin communicating with each other. More than one PC and several phones may get used to the max in a household where lines of interpersonal communication have broken down. While living in a free society, many of us lock our doors, engage our security systems, and watch nightly news reports of kidnappings, murders, drive-by shootings, hate crimes, drug deals gone bad, and international terrorism. Graphic pictures of bloodshed bombard our senses and assault our respect for the sanctity of human life. We long for a system of beliefs and values that will help us cope with injustice, affirm human dignity, hope for a brighter future, and navigate a safe and satisfying course through life.

Perhaps it is this fragile and uncertain aspect of post-modern existence that has prompted so many to turn to the Bible for help. In significant numbers, Generation-Xers, Silent Generation seniors, Baby Busters, and Baby Boomers are discovering the Bible and identifying it as their ultimate source of wisdom, peace, and fulfillment. For such people, who are just discovering the Bible (or rediscovering it), the *Complete Idiot's Guide to the Bible* can be an important and useful aid to understanding. Authors Stan Campbell and James S. Bell, Jr. have done a masterful job of introducing readers to the Bible's structure and message and illuminating its significance. Their conversational, contemporary writing style entertains and informs while escorting readers on a journey through the Bible. Significant passages, stories, and events highlight the journey and leave readers with a desire to keep coming back to the Bible again and again for a closer look.

If you are concerned that the authors' interpretation of the Bible may differ from that of your own denomination or church, you needn't be. Campbell and Bell present what's in the Bible, not their interpretations of the Bible. Also included are some practical tips on selecting a Bible that's right for you—and even how to shop for it at the best price.

Consider this book your ticket to adventure. While it doesn't pretend to be a substitute for the Bible, it will make your Bible reading a less perplexing, more enjoyable experience. As you explore, you can expect to discover timeless and valuable truths along the way, and more than a few surprises—some of which can enrich your life for time and eternity.

—James T. Dyet is managing editor for Scripture Press Publications and Accent Publications. He has written more than 30 Bible study courses for children and adults and has authored several books, *including Out of the Rough—Meditations for Golfers* (Thomas Nelson Publishers). He has extensive pastoral experience and is a frequent guest speaker at Colorado churches. He and his wife, Gloria, live in Colorado Springs.

Introduction

How the Bible Came to Be

Ever wonder how our Bible came to exist? Was it dropped to Earth by aliens? Was it patched together like a community cookbook?

Not quite. The truth is more interesting.

Actually, the Bible is a collection of 66 books divided in two sections, the Old and New Testaments. To write these scriptures, God chose and inspired people, gathered from all walks of life from many different eras, and employed various literary styles, such as poetry, prophecy, history, love songs, and biography.

The Old Testament, written in Hebrew and Aramaic, portrays God's dealings with His chosen people, the Jews, who were the human bloodline of Jesus. He is the grand centerpiece of the entire Bible. Over the centuries the books of the Old Testament were collected by unknown Jewish holy men and finally categorized in divisions called Law, Prophets, and Writings.

After a 400-year interval, the New Testament begins—revealing the life, death, and resurrection of Jesus the Messiah (the "anointed one") and later the burgeoning of the first churches in Greece, Italy, and Asia Minor. It was written in Koine Greek, the common language of the day, as opposed to Classical Greek, which was the language of philosophy and formal business transactions.

Much of the New Testament was originally written as letters (or epistles) to churches. These, combined with the Gospels detailing the life of Christ (Matthew, Mark, Luke, and John) and Acts, a history of the early church, were used to educate and encourage Christian congregations. For their Old Testament studies these believers used the Septuagint, a Greek translation of the Hebrew.

Other books in circulation were claiming divine inspiration, some of them decidedly different in their teaching, and by the early 2nd century the church hierarchy was forced to resolve the issue of which writings were from God and which were not. For the next hundred years councils met periodically to discuss which writings were part of the "canon," the process for determining a book's biblical worthiness. Did the earliest disciples and apostles consider this writing fully from God? Was its theology sound? Were its facts accurate?

By the middle of the 4th century the matter was settled. The important people agreed on all the writings—which were in and which were out. The canon was closed.

As missionaries spread the gospel, it became necessary to translate the scriptures. A Latin version of the Bible called the Vulgate was brought to England from Rome.

In the 14th century an Oxford scholar named John Wycliffe translated the whole Bible from Latin into English. But, because he questioned Catholic practices, he was mercilessly persecuted. Long after his death, the Roman Catholic Church exhumed his body, burned it, and proclaimed him a heretic.

In 1525, another Oxford scholar named William Tyndale attempted a translation using Hebrew and Greek instead of Latin. But he, too, was harassed by the church authorities, and in 1536 he was arrested and burned at the stake. Others secretly completed his project in 1537.

Consulting Tyndale's work, John Rogers attempted yet another version, in time called The Great Bible. But Mary, Queen of Scots, violently anti-Protestant, captured and executed many Christians, including Rogers and his courageous colleagues.

To avoid persecution, masses of English Christians fled to Geneva, Switzerland, where they produced a translation called The Geneva Bible, disliked by the Church of England for its biased, uncomplimentary textual notes.

In 1568, the Church of England published its own revision of The Great Bible, called The Bishop's Bible. It was widely read until 1611, when King James commanded his most learned men to develop a new version, using The Bishop's Bible as its foundation. Eventually they produced the most elegant and influential translation in the English-speaking world, the King James version of the Bible. Since then scores of versions have been published.

Emperor Menelik II was an African ruler who defeated the Italian army at Adwa in 1896 and established the nation of Ethiopia. He believed the Bible had power to cure illness, and he would eat a few pages of it any time he felt sick. He suffered a stroke in 1913, after which he ate the entire Book of Kings. As a result, his bowels become obstructed and he died of related complications (*from The Emperor Who Ate the Bible,* © 1991 Scot Morris, published by Doubleday).

The authors would like to suggest some different options to help you benefit from the Bible. You won't find any recipes in this book, but we hope your life will be enriched in numerous other ways. Whether you want to read the Bible in search of help for what's ailing you, or whether just out of curiosity you want to know more about it, this guide is a starting point to help direct you in your search.

You probably know more about the Bible than you realize. Most people know some of the basic Old Testament stories, a few of the Ten Commandments, many of the things Jesus said and did, and which verse the guy in the funny wig holds up at football games. In addition, the Bible's influence on our culture is reflected in our everyday conversation. Here are just a few of the Bible-originated words and phrases we toss around:

➤ "Do unto others as you would have them do unto you."

➤ "The skin of one's teeth."

➤ "Born again."

➤ "The root of all evil."

➤ "Armageddon" and "the coming Apocalypse."

➤ "Doubting Thomas."

➤ "The belly of the beast."

Other similar figures of speech are more metaphorical:

➤ "Getting those day-care kids to behave is like trying to turn water into wine."

➤ "My boss thinks he can walk on water."

➤ "Presenting that proposal was like going into the lions' den."

➤ "Finishing this crossword puzzle would take the wisdom of Solomon."

➤ "I can see the writing on the wall."

Yet in spite of how much or how little we know about the Bible, most of us realize there is much, much more we don't know. Unlike other books, the Bible can be quite intimidating in several ways: its length, its language, the unfamiliarity of the people and places it describes, and its variety of writing styles. Even when we think we're clear about what it's saying, there are parts where the content itself can make us uncomfortable.

This book was written to reduce the intimidation factor of the Bible. Because you already know *something*, the challenge of improving your familiarity with the Bible is simply a matter of gradually adding small bits of new information. You'll be surprised at how quickly you can develop a basic understanding of the Bible as a whole.

How to Get the Most from This Book

This guide is intended to be a supplement to Bible reading, not a substitute for it. We can by no means cover the topics of each chapter in depth. Instead, we will try to direct your attention to significant passages, stories, and people. The real rewards will come as you interact with the Bible itself—not this book. (If you don't have a Bible, Chapter 1, "The B-I-B-L-E, Is That a Book for Me," offers some practical suggestions for selecting one.)

Nor will we attempt to do much in the way of interpretation. Our goal is to help you see clearly what the Bible *says*; it won't always be completely clear what the Bible *means*. Many passages are open to various interpretations. We'll try to provide a balanced analysis for the more controversial portions, but we won't be able to explain what everybody thinks about every point. We will try to be as objective as possible and let the Bible speak for itself, but you can expect that our conclusions won't always agree with your own. (Chapter 2, "Claims and Disclaimers," addresses a list of problems you can expect as you approach Bible reading.)

Where you see quotations from the Bible, they are from the *New International Version*, unless otherwise noted.

Practice Makes Closer to Perfect

No matter how much you read the Bible, you'll never get it *all* figured out. You'll still have unanswered questions—and perhaps even a few doubts. People who have devoted their lives to Bible study are the first to answer "I don't know" to difficult questions.

Much can be discovered with a simple, basic reading of the Bible. Yet the more thought you put into understanding the key people and concepts, the better you'll start connecting running themes and discovering previously hidden insights.

Chapters 1 and 2 provide some background about the Bible before you start. But if you're in a big hurry to get to what's *in* the Bible, go to Chapter 3, "In the Beginning," which starts with Genesis. Either way, you're off to a good beginning.

Extras

As you go through this guide, look for the following sidebars that (we hope) will be helpful in better understanding the material.

Snapshots

We are attempting to present the "big picture" of the Bible in our running text. But sometimes space gets tight and there's only room for a "Snapshot." These will refer you to fascinating stories or passages that you can delve into on your own.

Look for these sidebars beginning in Chapter 3. The first two chapters are things you need to know before starting to read through the Bible.

Manna from Heaven

The first time people saw manna (their daily supply of food for 40 years), they called it by the expression in their language meaning "What's it?" Our "Manna from Heaven" pops up in spots where you may need further explanation of who, what, or where something or someone is.

Potent Quotables

Jeopardy has its Potent Potables category; our Potent Quotables will focus on familiar biblical quotes or especially significant passages. (Chapters 1 and 2 contain quotes *about* the Bible. All others will be quotations *from* the Bible.)

What Saith Thou?

In other words, "Whatcha think about this?" We've tried to answer frequently asked questions as we come to them. Some such questions are favorites of Bible skeptics; others are included simply for clarity. "Saith," by the way, is an archaic but standard spelling for "sayeth."

Acknowledgements

The Book of Ecclesiastes provides insight into the publishing industry: "Of making many books there is no end, and much study wearies the body" (12:12). This book would certainly have had no end had it not been for a dynamic editorial team who overcame weary bodies (and minds) to get the job done. Thanks to Bob Shuman and Nancy Mikhail who got the ball rolling, and Krista Hansing who fine-tuned the manuscript. Special thanks, however, are due Kate Layzer and Suzanne Snyder who did the lionesses' share of editing. While the authors wrote from a conservative Christian background, our editors challenged us to view the same Bible from a more liberal Christian perspective, as well as a Messianic Jewish one. With two authors, two editors, and too much copy for one book, it can safely be said that no one got everything exactly the way he or she might have wanted it. But after all the editing process, we trust the end result is a much stronger book—to the ultimate benefit of the reader.

We also would not want to forget Scott Waxman, our literary agent, who introduced us to the world of the idiot guides; moreover, we appreciate the talents of designers and artists who contributed to this book, as well as the authors of other titles in the series who inspired us with their creativity. We are especially grateful to the people throughout our lives who have taught us the truths of the Bible and helped us see their importance in very real and relevant ways. We also would like to thank family members for their considerable patience in doing without our presence.

Special Thanks to Our Technical Reviewers

The Complete Idiot's Guide to the Bible was written because of the authors' love of the topic and their personal experience with Bible study and teaching. However, as neither author had extensive formal Bible training, we therefore asked two additional pairs of well-trained eyes to examine our manuscript: Richard L. Schultz, Associate Professor of Old Testament at Wheaton College (M.Div. from Trinity Evangelical Divinity School, Ph.D [in Old Testament] from Yale University); and Jane M. Vogel, writer and editor (M.C.E. from Calvin Theological Seminary).

We are immensely grateful for the expertise these readers brought to the project, and for their willingness to come down to "Idiot level" and ensure the academic accuracy of what we wrote.

We are told that, "God is not the author of confusion, but of peace" (1 Corinthians 14:33, KJV). As you read this book, we hope you'll be able to say the same about the authors and editors of this guide.

Part 1
Before You Begin

With any major project, the most difficult step is getting started. If you want to take a lengthy vacation, for example, you probably don't just hop in the car and start driving. You need a general idea of where you're going, the climate, the road conditions, the availability of housing, and so on. The success of the trip frequently depends on the extent of the planning you put into it—even though the planning is more work than you might like.

Before we begin our "trip" through the Bible, we'll start with just a bit of background. These first two chapters provide some insight as to how we got the Bible, why it's such a significant book, why so many people consider it authoritative, and how it can benefit you. You'll also find some warnings about problems you might encounter as you begin looking into the Bible.

Perhaps you've picked up a Bible at a yard sale or in a hotel room and started reading, only to be overwhelmed by a feeling of being in an alien landscape. And truly, parts of the Bible are intimidating. This Guide should help you pole-vault across the drier, more forbidding sections and keep you involved where the action is.

Meanwhile, you've already taken the hardest step: You've gotten started! Now it's just a matter of turning the page, maintaining your momentum, and enjoying the trip.

Chapter 1

The B-I-B-L-E, Is That a Book for Me?

In This Chapter

➤ A Bible IQ Quiz

➤ How the Bible can benefit us in practical ways

➤ How the Bible went from a bunch of manuscripts to a bunch of different modern translations

➤ Some factors to consider when selecting a Bible

Most homes have one or more copies of the Bible. It's the best-selling book of all time, so those copies have to be going somewhere besides hotel room drawers. Yet although the cover says *Holy Bible*, most people admit that when it comes to knowing what's between those covers, their comprehension is, well, *holey*. They know bits and pieces. They're pretty sure about some of the stories, and they *think* other things they have come to believe might be in there somewhere. But then, those things could have come from *Aesop's Fables* or some bit of mythology they've picked up along the way.

For people who dare approach the Bible to learn more about what's there, sometimes the challenge seems overwhelming. Genesis and Exodus read pretty well, but that next Leviticus/Numbers/Deuteronomy stretch is enough to bring even the best-intentioned Bible readers to their knees.

Our goal in this guide is to help you discover what's *really* in the Bible—and what isn't. We want to help you plug the gaps in your holey perspective so you will soon become more wholly informed. We'll try to condense the longer, drier passages and let you spend more time focused on the narratives, the people, and the action that makes the Bible probably the most beloved book ever printed.

Check Your Bible IQ

But before we go too far, let's see how much you *do* know. Below is a short quiz to test your knowledge about how we got the Bible, as well as a bit of what's in it. Some of the multiple-choice questions may have more than one correct answer.

1. We got our word *Bible* from:

    ___ A.   A variation of Babylon, which had extensive libraries

    ___ B.   The Hebrew word *biblius,* meaning "scroll that has no ending"

    ___ C.   The Greek word *biblion,* meaning "roll" or "book"

    ___ D.   An acronym for "<u>B</u>oy, <u>I</u>t's <u>B</u>ig, <u>L</u>eather, and <u>E</u>xpansive"

2. The original language(s) of the Bible are:

    ___ A.   Hebrew, Greek, and Latin

    ___ B.   Hebrew, Greek, and Aramaic

    ___ C.   Hebrew, Latin, and Assyrian

    ___ D.   100 percent King James English

3. Which of the following are *not* books of the Bible?

    ___ A.   Haggai and Philemon

    ___ B.   Zephaniah and Zechariah

    ___ C.   2 Chronicles and 3 John

    ___ D.   Guacamole and Minestrone

4. *Canon* refers to:

    ___ A.   An overweight 1970s detective played by William Conrad

    ___ B.   Civil war weaponry

    ___ C.   A Greek word for a measuring device

    ___ D.   Writings that are accepted as authentic and inspired scripture

5. The *Apocrypha* is:

    ___ A.   A group of writings purported to be scripture but not accepted as such in every tradition

    ___ B.   A British term for drugstore

    ___ C.   A hill in Greece where the Parthenon was built

    ___ D.   A reference to the "four horsemen" in Revelation

Match correct numbers to the appropriate statements:

6. Total number of books in the Bible _____   1
7. Number of Old Testament books _____   2
8. Number of New Testament books _____   1,500
9. Approximate number of Bible book authors _____   27
10. The Bible was written over a period of about _____ years.   176
11. Number of verses in the shortest chapter in the Bible _____   39
12. Number of verses in the longest chapter in the Bible _____   66
13. The book with the most chapter divisions has _____ of them.   40
14. Of all the books ever written, the Bible is _____ of a kind.   150

Finally, see if you can identify which of the following events are really found in the Bible and which are made up.

For Real	No Way		
_____	_____	15.	After the flood, Noah gets drunk and naked.
_____	_____	16.	A guy named Balaam has an unsettling conversation with his talking donkey.
_____	_____	17.	A dead man touches Elisha's bones and comes back to life.
_____	_____	18.	Elijah calls down fire from heaven and then outruns a chariot down a mountain.
_____	_____	19.	Isaiah sees God on a throne surrounded by hovering, six-winged angels.
_____	_____	20.	Queen Jezebel is eaten by dogs.
_____	_____	21.	After surviving his big fish, a worm gets the better of Jonah.
_____	_____	22.	Uzzah touches the Ark of the Covenant and a year later his wife delivers septuplets.
_____	_____	23.	Wanting to prolong a victorious battle, Joshua commands the sun to stand still—and it does!
_____	_____	24.	God causes a shadow to move backward, to prove the truth of Isaiah's message.
_____	_____	25.	In the course of a single night, Aaron's staff buds, blossoms, and produces almonds.
_____	_____	26.	Lot's daughters take turns getting him drunk and having sex with him so they can have children.
_____	_____	27.	King Herod takes credit for being a god and is struck down immediately and eaten by worms.

continues

continued

For Real	No Way		
_____	_____	28.	After their sister is raped, some of Jacob's sons convince the family of the offender to be circumcised and then kill them while they are incapacitated.
_____	_____	29.	Moses spends so much time with God that his head begins to glow.
_____	_____	30.	King Solomon's famous wisdom fails him when he gets involved with a thousand women.
_____	_____	31.	During the decline of Israel, things get so bad that people are reduced to eating donkey heads—and each other.
_____	_____	32.	Paul dies when bitten by a deadly viper, but comes back to life.
_____	_____	33.	A woman named Jael hammers the head of an enemy general to the ground with a tent peg.
_____	_____	34.	Jesus brings three dead people back to life.
_____	_____	35.	Paul and Barnabas are mistaken for the gods Zeus and Hermes.

Potent Quotables

It is impossible to rightly govern the world without God and the Bible.

—George Washington

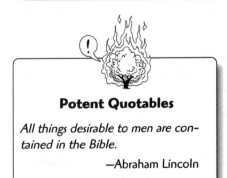

Potent Quotables

All things desirable to men are contained in the Bible.

—Abraham Lincoln

This is one of those tests where you probably have a good idea how well you did as soon as it's over. If you've had a bit of Bible background, you may have zipped through the questions with little problem. But don't be alarmed if you didn't have a clue about many of the questions. That's why this book was written. By the time you finish, you'll have all these answers—and many more. But if you can't wait, the quiz answers are provided at the end of this chapter.

What's In It for Me?

Of course, the stories and events are only a small portion of what's in the Bible. The big picture shows how God has interacted with people throughout history. The accounts of God's justice and judgment are there, as some people like to point out. But so are the numerous examples of God's love, mercy, and forgiveness. Until we view the Bible as a whole, it's difficult to develop a valid perspective. If we start with what we *want* to believe, it's not usually too much trouble to find a few verses to back up our opinion. Taking a verse or two out of context, however, doesn't necessarily lend validity to a shaky premise.

It is far better to approach the Bible objectively, read it thoroughly, and refrain from forming strong opinions until we've seen it in its entirety. If we stay in the Old Testament, for example, we're much more likely to have an eye-for-an-eye mentality about justice. But if we add the teachings of the New Testament, we are challenged to "raise the bar" in our interactions with others. It is more of a challenge to attempt a basic comprehension of the entire Bible, but it's better than continually emphasizing certain portions of the Bible while ignoring the rest.

When it comes to reading the Bible, some people approach it as completely true, inspired, and authoritative. It is literally "God's Word," God's message to humankind. Such people read the Bible to find guidance, wisdom, promises to cling to, comfort through trying times, and hope for the future. Even those who doubt that the Bible is divinely inspired will agree that it is an important and influential book.

Bible Knowledge Can Make You a More Literate Person

The Bible has been a cultural influence for hundreds of years and is reflected in art, literature, and music. Whether you're reading *Pilgrim's Progress* (published in 1678), listening to Handel's *Messiah* (written in 1741), or attending the latest production of Andrew Lloyd Webber's *Joseph and the Amazing Technicolor Dreamcoat*, you'll get more out of the experience if you're familiar with the original source. People can ignore the Bible's teachings if they wish, but its stories, parables, and poetry will always be part of our cultural heritage. We lose out if we ignore such a treasury.

Bible Knowledge Can Make You a More Authoritative Person

The Bible may or may not be the most quoted book, but it's almost certainly the most misquoted one. How many times have you listened to a discussion of politics, abortion, homosexuality, gender roles, or some other hot topic, only to hear one of the participants raise his voice and say, "Well, doesn't the Bible say..."? Very frequently, the answer is a resounding no! Using the Bible as a last-ditch defense for one's latest whim isn't very impressive.

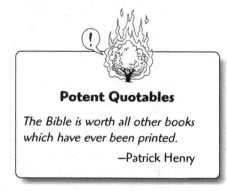

Potent Quotables

The Bible is worth all other books which have ever been printed.

—Patrick Henry

On the other hand, the ability to cite a specific quote or an applicable example goes a long way to support an opinion. An awareness of what's in the Bible helps us speak with authority rather than settling for off-the-top-of-the-head speculation.

Bible Knowledge Can Make You a More Virtuous Person

The Bible is filled with good and practical instruction:

➤ Do unto others as you would have them do unto you.

➤ Turn the other cheek when someone strikes you.

➤ Share with those in need.

➤ Care about the "overlooked" people in society: children, widows, orphans, the sick and hungry, those in prison, and so on.

➤ Drop the facade of hypocrisy and be authentic.

➤ Respect others—even bosses and government leaders.

➤ Don't hold grudges.

➤ Be slow to become angry.

Not only will taking such advice make you more virtuous, but you'll very likely be happier and healthier as well.

Bible Knowledge Can Make You a More Spiritual Person

The search for spirituality is as intense today as it has been in years. Eastern philosophies and New Age religions promise enlightenment and have attracted numerous seekers, many of whom—assuming they know what's in the Bible—overlook or reject Judaism and Christianity. It's too bad that scripture has so often been used to support unloving, judgmental, and condemning attitudes and actions. A thoughtful reading of the Bible offers a much more complete and balanced picture of God—as well as Jewish and Christian teachings.

Reading the Bible will stretch your mind and expand your thinking. It offers profound insight into the realm of the invisible and the unseen. It helps us separate truth from mythology. We come to see God less as a tyrant and more as a loving parent, counselor, and friend.

And the Bible helps us see ourselves more clearly as well. We discover that our shortcomings have been shared by many others—some of them great "heroes" of faith. We won't even get out of Genesis before we witness murder, deceit, betrayal, rape, incest, gang violence, drunken escapades, seduction, and numerous other dysfunctions. Part of the greatness of the Bible is its willingness to show the darker side of humanity, as well as our potential for godliness.

The Bible teaches that we have value. We have God-given abilities. The better we understand how to relate to the Bible, the more we can learn to benefit from its teachings instead of remaining resistant or apprehensive.

Has Bible Content Changed over the Years?

The Bible has come down to us across the millennia surprisingly intact. Copies of the entire New Testament have been found that date within 250 years of writing. If equitable standards of authenticity are used, the reliability of New Testament writings is less questionable than most secular works of the same era.

As for the Old Testament, the discovery of the Dead Sea Scrolls in 1947 uncovered manuscripts of Old Testament books that predated existing copies by 1,000 years or more. And when the existing Hebrew manuscripts were checked against the earlier ones, the faithfulness of the text was confirmed. That's pretty amazing!

How Did We Get Our Bible from a Bunch of Manuscripts?

When you walk into a bookstore and pick up a Bible, what exactly are you buying? The words are neat, easy to read, and contained within nice, even margins. It's hard to imagine the original work that the 40 or so Bible authors put into their original writing, followed by generations of faithful people making copy after copy by hand until the words could be reproduced mechanically. Below is a timeline that shows some of the steps to illustrate how these texts got from their hands into yours. Some of the dates are approximate.

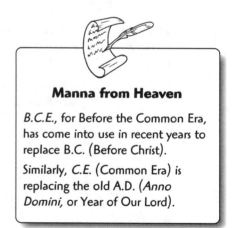

Potent Quotables

It is impossible to enslave mentally or socially a Bible-reading people. The principles of the Bible are the groundwork of human freedom.

—Horace Greeley

1400 to 400 B.C.E. This was the period during which the Old Testament writers lived and worked. Documents were written on leather or papyrus, which aren't exactly conducive to a long shelf life. Traditionally, the Jews held such respect for the text that they would bury copies that had aged to the point of impaired legibility. The original manuscripts were copied with meticulous care, as were those copies. A system of checking was devised to count characters and sections. As with all literature of this time period, the originals are long gone. But with scripture, the transfer from copy to copy was made with exacting care and precision.

Manna from Heaven

B.C.E., for Before the Common Era, has come into use in recent years to replace B.C. (Before Christ).

Similarly, C.E. (Common Era) is replacing the old A.D. (*Anno Domini,* or Year of Our Lord).

285 B.C.E. The Hebrew (Old Testament) scriptures were translated into Greek. One legend says that 72 scholars got the job done in 72 days, but it actually took much longer. The completed translation is known as the "Septuagint," from the Latin word for 70. This version was very popular with the early church as well as the Jews outside of Palestine, who no longer spoke Hebrew.

50 to 90 C.E. The New Testament was written during this time period.

95 C.E. The historian Josephus identified the Old Testament canon (works officially accepted as scripture) as the 39 books we have now. Some people believe Ezra had collected them all as early as the fifth century B.C.E.

397 C.E. A meeting of church leaders known as the Council of Carthage acknowledged the 27 books of the New Testament as we know them. Most of the books had already been treated as scripture for many years, but a half dozen or so warranted further discussion and final approval.

400 C.E. The entire Bible was translated into Latin, primarily by Saint Jerome. This version is known as the "Vulgate," meaning, "written in the language of the people." (In the West, Latin *was* the language of the people!)

The Early and High Middle Ages (the fifth through the fourteenth centuries). Intense scholarship and study took place during this time, but little in the way of Bible translation. The Bible of the Christian Church was still the Vulgate.

1380 C.E. An English theologian named John Wycliffe began a translation of the Bible into English. The project was completed by friends after his death.

1456 C.E. The Gutenberg Bible was printed. It was an edition of the Vulgate, significant as the first major work printed with movable type.

1525 to 1530 C.E. William Tyndale, a scholar involved in the reform movement, translated the New Testament and the Pentateuch (the first five books of the Old Testament) into English despite persecution. He was martyred before he could complete the Old Testament.

1548 C.E. Members of the Council of Trent voted to accept the 12 books of the Apocrypha as part of the biblical canon—a decision that was rejected by the reform movement.

1611 C.E. King James I of England commissioned a translation of the Bible that would become the primary Bible of English-speaking people for more than 300 years.

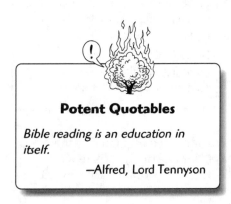

Potent Quotables

Bible reading is an education in itself.

—Alfred, Lord Tennyson

1782 C.E. The first English Bible was printed in America. It was known as the Aitken Bible.

1881–1884 C.E. A group of English and American scholars assembled to translate *The Revised Version* of the Bible, using manuscripts that had not been available at the printing of the King James Bible.

1900–1901 C.E. The *American Standard Version* of the Bible was translated.

1978 C.E. *The New International Version* of the Bible was completed.

These are only a few of the highlights in the history of Bible publishing. In recent years, a proliferation of Bible versions has hit the shelves. Not long ago your choices were confined to two or three versions with a couple of color options. These days, however, choosing a Bible that's right for you can be a major, time-intensive project.

Choosing the Best Bible from All the Good Books

Selecting a Bible depends on how you're going to use it. Bibles can be very expensive or quite affordable. And as in most things, you tend to get what you pay for.

Translation versus Paraphrase

If you're looking for authenticity, it's best to make sure you have a translation rather than a paraphrase. Some of the most common translations are the *King James Version* (KJV), the *New King James Version* (NKJV), the *New Revised Standard Version* (NRSV), the *New American Standard Version* (NAS), and the *New International Version* (NIV).

Translations take great care to give you a precise interpretation from the original texts, and some of the more current ones are quite readable. But if you're looking purely for "a good read," you may want to go with a paraphrase, such as *The Living Bible* (TLB). Because paraphrases aren't quite as true to the original, they can update certain phrases, throw in a little slang now and then, and generally provide a looser, more familiar writing style. Inevitably, they also bring perspective to the texts that may not have been present originally.

Familiarity versus Contemporary Feel

Some people grew up hearing frequent quotes from the *King James Version*, and they may even recall certain passages from memory. If they come back to the Bible after several years and use a more contemporary version, those same passages may not sound familiar at all.

If you're looking to take up where you left off, the *King James Version* might be the only translation that provides the familiarity you seek. More recent versions have their advantages and use more contemporary language, but they may not sound right at first. And for some people who have always used the *King James Version*, nothing else ever seems to "feel" right.

Potent Quotables

The Bible is an inexhaustible fountain of all truths. The existence of the Bible is the greatest blessing which humanity ever experienced.
—Immanuel Kant

Basic Bible versus Study Bible

If your goal is simply to read through the Bible and see what's there, you can get a copy without any "bells and whistles"—simply straight text from

Genesis to Revelation. But if you are a curious type who is likely to have questions as you go through, you may want to consider getting a study Bible. Such Bibles come in any of the translations or paraphrases you wish, but the added feature is a plethora of footnotes, maps, charts, and other aids to your Bible reading. A good study Bible saves a lot of trips to the dictionary, atlas, concordance, and so forth when you get to a confusing passage. In addition, many study Bibles are targeted to a specific demographic (students, men, women, and so on) or topic (prophecy, end times, praise, and so on). The drawbacks of study Bibles are cost (they're usually considerably more expensive) and size (all those notes take up space and add weight to the Bible).

Other Factors

If you tend to travel a lot and think you'll want to do your Bible reading on the road, you might consider a travel Bible. They're a little harder to find, so you might have to ask around. But you can find very compact New Testaments or entire Bibles that don't take up a lot of space. Some even have fold-around snaps to protect the Bible from getting too banged up.

If eyesight is a consideration, you can find large-print Bibles. Even standard Bibles have a variety of type sizes and fonts, so be sure to look at several options before you buy one.

Most Bibles have a soft-cover (paperback) version that is considerably cheaper. However, even with moderate use many of these tend to tear and deteriorate relatively easily. It may be well worth the extra cost to acquire a hard cover or leather cover if you plan an ongoing commitment to Bible reading.

Another consideration is the size of the margins. Some people treat the Bible as if the book itself is sacred. Others take the view that it's what we internalize from the Bible that changes lives. They do whatever helps them get to know the Bible better—underlining, taking notes in the margins, highlighting, or whatever. Some Bibles are printed in loose-leaf form and/or with extra-wide margins just for this purpose.

Go Shopping!

If you have a copy of the *King James Version* lying around and it just doesn't make any sense to you, remember that you have other options. Get out and see what else is available, and take your time in making a choice. Read the same passage in several different versions, and see what hits your fancy. Go to more than one store and look around. Because so many kinds of Bibles are available, no bookstore is likely to have a complete selection. Don't be afraid to ask for what you want. If it's not there, it can probably be ordered.

When it comes to Bible shopping, you will probably benefit by seeking out a Christian/family bookstore rather than the nearest big chain. The selection is likely to be much more diverse, and store personnel can probably answer more questions and offer better advice. When you find exactly what you want, you can always shop around for the best price. Many mail-order catalogs offer attractive prices on Bibles as well. (And if price is your *primary* concern, your local library is likely to have a good assortment of Bibles.)

When you get your hands on a Bible you like, get ready to put your heart into it. In Chapter 3, "In the Beginning," we're going to dive into Genesis, and we won't come up for air until we get through Revelation. Expect a lot of surprises along the way. It's likely to be a trip you won't forget. First, however, Chapter 2, "Claims and Disclaimers," explains how your Bible is laid out and prepares you for some of the problems you might encounter as you begin to acquire a basic knowledge of the Bible.

But before we get out of this chapter, here are the quiz answers we promised you:

1. C
2. B—Aramaic was probably the colloquial language of Palestine and the primary language of Jesus. It was used occasionally in both the Old and New Testaments.
3. D
4. C and D
5. A—The other responses refer to *apothecary*, *Acropolis*, and *apocalypse*.
6. 66
7. 39
8. 27
9. 40
10. 1,500
11. 2
12. 176
13. 150
14. 1

15.–35. The events described in #22 and #32 have been altered, so they are untrue. But all the others are found in the Bible, as we will see as we go through this guide.

The Least You Need to Know

➤ In spite of its stodgy reputation, the Bible is actually a pretty cool book.

➤ Knowledge of the Bible has a number of benefits—spiritual, intellectual, and moral.

➤ In spite of the antiquity of biblical writings, they remain trustworthy because of the care with which they have been transmitted.

➤ Choosing the right Bible can make a significant difference in Bible reading.

Chapter 2

Claims and Disclaimers

In This Chapter

➤ Difficulties to expect while going through the Bible

➤ Why there are so many interpretations of biblical "truth"

➤ How the Bible is organized

It seems as if it should be a simple matter to work our way through the Bible and come to some mutual conclusions. However, history suggests that this will not be the case. Don't be surprised if the conclusions you draw are somewhat different from those of the authors. In this chapter, we'll be looking at some of the challenges of reading the Bible, such as changing culture, changing approaches to religion, and varying ways of understanding sacred writing.

Seeing the Whole Elephant

Looking back across time, it seems that coming to agreement about what the Bible means has been quite a difficult task. Otherwise, we would have only a handful of Jewish and Christian denominations instead of the dozens that currently exist. The Catholics would never have split from the Orthodox. The Protestants would never have split from the Catholics. The Baptists, Episcopalians, and African Methodist Church members would all be worshipping side by side. All seem to agree that the Bible provides God's truth for our lives, but how to interpret that truth is another question.

So who is "correct" amid all the segregation and segmentation? Perhaps we all are. When the five blind men examined the elephant, each was completely convinced that he had the correct perception. The elephant was indeed much like a tree (around the leg), a rope (at the tail), a fan (at the ear), a hose (at the trunk), and a wall (on the side). Each man was absolutely correct in the extent of his knowledge. The problem was that none of them had grasped the animal in its entirety. They preferred to argue about what little they *did* know.

People approach the Bible from different points and arrive at a number of various beliefs and interpretations. In most cases, the differences are not huge, yet they tend to be significant enough to divide rather than unite.

For the authors, the privilege of introducing the Bible to new readers is balanced by the knowledge that for every opinion we express, there are likely to be hordes of dissenting opinions. Our challenge (and our intent) is to help you interact with the whole "animal." After a lifetime of study, we have arrived at our own beliefs. These beliefs, to be realistic, aren't likely to intersect with yours at every single point. We certainly honor your right to disagree with us, and we hope you'll understand if we occasionally write something that doesn't exactly set well with you.

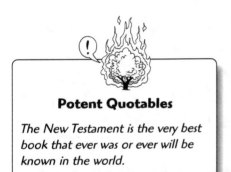

Potent Quotables

The New Testament is the very best book that ever was or ever will be known in the world.

—Charles Dickens

We're going to try, to the best of our ability, to present what's in the Bible rather than our own interpretations. Yet even that approach presents certain challenges. Let's take a closer look at a few of the problems we might expect as we start through the Bible.

The Cultural Problem

As we in the twenty-first century flash back thousands of years, we must be aware that the world was quite a different place in biblical times. For one thing, women weren't exactly on an equal level with their male peers. (Some would say we still haven't come too far in this area.) In the next chapter, you will see that God created "man" as both male and female. They started out equal. Yet as cultures and societies developed, the male became dominant. So when we tell you that Abraham passed his wife off as his sister and allowed her to enter the harem of a foreign king, we're just reporting the facts. Any wrath you feel should be directed toward Abe, not the authors.

Even in New Testament times, women were admonished to show up for church with long (but covered) hair, and to keep silent once they got there. Hospitality included washing your guests' feet. Slavery was a fact of life. Most of the civilized world was under the authority of the Roman Empire.

Biblical instructions are provided for how to live in such a world, and some such instructions don't tend to translate clearly across centuries. For example, some people have tried to use the Bible to justify modern-day slavery, simply because the first-century world included slaves. Some good people feel that the biblical rules about clothing, hair styles, and worship procedure should remain in effect today. Other good people think we've moved on, that these sorts of biblical instructions were written for the culture of the time and were not meant to apply to all times and places.

The Religion Problem

Another major difference between our times and Bible times concerns the idea of freedom of religion. We enjoy such a freedom, but the ancient land of Israel did not. They had one choice and were expected to adhere to it. God's rule was a theocracy—government by immediate divine guidance, mediated through priests, prophets, and kings. Penalties were sometimes severe for rebellion or disobedience. The severity seems more extreme to us because we've come to expect that "anything goes" in our society. But ancient Israelites knew what to expect if they defied the religious regulations of their day. They never had the defense of saying, "Hey, it's a free country, isn't it?"

We *do* have the right to believe, reject, and interpret what the Bible says, at least as far as our government is concerned. The Bible says that God created human beings, but you have the right to believe in a theory of random evolution instead. When the Bible recounts that God caused something to happen, you may choose to believe it never happened, or perhaps that it happened by pure coincidence. It is not our intent in this book to force any beliefs on anyone. We simply want to point out what the Bible says. How you respond is your choice. Yet because the Bible is very firm on certain points, the authors will tend to come across that way, too. Our intent, however, is merely to help you understand and process the biblical material—not to tell you what to think.

The Language Problem

One reason you need to check out the Bible on your own, rather than limiting your knowledge to what we tell you, is that people vary in their opinions of what is to be taken literally and what is figurative or symbolic. We all tend to draw those lines in different places, and it's no simple matter to say that one person is right and another is wrong.

For instance, when Jesus says to cut off any body part that causes us to sin (Matthew 5:27–30), people are in almost total agreement that he's speaking in a symbolic sense. Otherwise the world would be filled with self-mutilated Christians. But when it comes to prophecy, church order, customs, and other topics, opinions are more diverse. What one person clings to as literal, another sees as figurative.

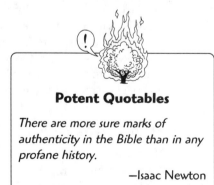

Potent Quotables

There are more sure marks of authenticity in the Bible than in any profane history.

—Isaac Newton

For example, God tells believers to remain separate from unbelievers (Isaiah 52:11; 2 Corinthians 6:14–18). Most people see this as a spiritual issue to be taken somewhat figuratively. Historically, however, groups such as the Amish have interpreted this command literally, to the point of actually living apart from the secular world. It's a legitimate concern for them.

In other cases, the biblical texts themselves seem to allow for some diversity of opinion. When capital punishment becomes an issue, proponents may point to Old Testament law, which is clear: "Anyone who [deliberately] strikes a man and kills him shall surely be put to death" (Exodus 21:12). Opponents point to the example of Jesus, who had the opportunity and legal right to endorse the stoning of a woman caught in the act of adultery, yet told her accusers: "If any one of you is without sin, let him be the first to throw a stone at her" (John 8:7). This woman was given a second chance for rehabilitation. When both sides of an argument can cite the Bible for their authority, it's not easy to reach agreement.

Many Christians oppose homosexuality, remarriage after divorce, and other practices on the basis of certain biblical texts. Others emphasize the broader concepts of grace, mercy, and forgiveness. We will attempt to present a broad enough spectrum of scripture to help you come to your own informed conclusions.

The Pronoun/Gender Issue

The Bible uses male pronouns for God, so we will, too. We realize that many people would rather find a way around this practice, and we agree that the fullness of God lacks nothing in positive qualities—either male or female. The Bible provides images of God as a mother hen (Psalm 91:4; Luke 13:34) and even as a woman in labor (Isaiah 42:14), as well as a forgiving father (Luke 15:11–32). All these images, and many more, are true and biblical. But for the sake of editorial simplicity, we will adopt the Bible's use of male pronouns when referring to God.

The motto of Richard Baxter, a seventeenth-century theologian, has been endorsed by many Christians, including the authors: "In necessary things, unity; in doubtful things, liberty; in all things, charity." In other words, as we look at the Bible, we all need to agree on a few things. Yet we also ought to provide others the liberty to disagree with us on certain points and form their own opinions. And in all things, we need to foster an attitude of charity (love) toward one another. When someone disagrees with us, we don't assume that person is less virtuous or sincere than we are. There's a time and place to be serious about reading and applying the Bible. And maybe, just maybe, there's a time and place to lighten up.

On a Personal Note

The authors both have an immense respect for the Bible. It is the basis upon which we have built our religious beliefs and our moral code. The wisdom it contains influences our lives on a daily basis. However, we realize this is not the case for everyone. Therefore, this guide is by no means a traditional Bible commentary. We have made every effort to explain the Bible without editorializing on it. We have attempted to be honest about the parts that appear harsh or confusing. We have brought to light portions that make many religious people squirm at times. Regardless of whether you believe the Bible is divinely inspired, we hope you may still regard it as a book of influence and wisdom, and that we can help you in your search— whatever you're seeking.

This book is a quick once-over of the Bible. We'll give you the Genesis-to-Revelation tour and point out numerous points of interest. But after you watch the sights whiz by and begin to accumulate information, we hope you'll return and dwell on the portions that interest you. When you finish this book, don't expect to be finished with the Bible. If we've done our job properly, we will have only whetted your appetite for further reading on your own.

Potent Quotables

I know the Bible is inspired because it finds me at a greater depth of my being than any other book.

—Samuel Taylor Coleridge

Why Put Up with All These Problems?

With all the difficulty and confusion that reading the Bible involves, the logical question might be, "Why bother?" Why take the trouble to try and separate the cultural from the contemporary instructions, the literal from the symbolic language? Why sweat it?

Simply put, the benefits of Bible study greatly outweigh the difficulties. Yes, parts will be confusing, but much of what you read will be clear and easy to comprehend. If the more difficult portions are perceived as challenges rather than annoyances, Bible reading can become a satisfying and informative source of spiritual and intellectual growth.

Perhaps we can adopt the viewpoint of an old man who once told famous English preacher, Charles Spurgeon: "For a long period I puzzled myself about the difficulties of Scripture, until at last I came to the resolution that reading the Bible was like eating fish. When I find a difficulty I lay it aside and call it a bone. Why should I choke on the bone when there is so much nutritious meat for me? Someday, perhaps, I may find that even the bone may afford me nourishment."

Potent Quotables

Make it the first morning business of your life to understand some part of the Bible clearly, and make it your daily business to obey it in all that you do understand.

—John Ruskin

The Layout of the Bible

So let's turn our attention to a few more things you need to know in order to get to the "meat" of the Bible—and maybe even deal with some of the "bones." First let's consider all the numbers and weird headings you see as you leaf through a Bible. If you don't know what those mean, you're likely to become confused quite quickly.

A Little of Everything

The Bible may look like a single book, but within its covers lies an entire library. Both the Old and New Testaments contain books of history, writing (instruction), and prophecy. The Old Testament starts out with five books that make up "the Law of Moses," followed by several books of history. But if law and history are the subjects you tried to dodge in college, don't be too concerned. Within these books are some of the most familiar and fascinating stories of scripture.

After the history comes the literature section, known as the Writings, which includes a variety of stories, songs, and poetry. Finally, a large section of the Old Testament is prophecy: a few major prophets with a lot to say, and a dozen or so minor prophets with shorter books.

The New Testament begins with four gospels, called "good news" in Greek, about the life of Jesus. The New Testament has only one book of history, followed by numerous short epistles, or letters, by the Apostle Paul and others. The New Testament also concludes with prophecy—the Book of Revelation.

Rather than attempting to give each of the books equal attention, we will focus on the story line running through the Bible. Because space is limited, this means spending less time on the Writings and prophecy to spend more time with the people and stories.

What's with All the Numbers?

Perhaps you've heard people refer to knowing something so well they could cite "chapter and verse." This phrase comes from the way the Bible is divided into smaller sections. Originally, the books of the Bible were straightforward accounts from beginning to end, with no breaks. Jewish synagogues continue to revere the Torah—a collection of written (and sometimes oral) laws preserved in the original Hebrew, handwritten on parchment scrolls. The content varies little from the first five books of the Old Testament, but the format is quite distinctive.

But for purposes of finding and referencing specific sections, chapter breaks and verses within the chapters were added, leading to the Bible format now familiar to Protestants and Catholics. Where you see two numbers separated by a colon or period, the first number is the chapter and the second is the verse. So, to find John 3:16 (also written John 3.16), you would look in the third chapter of the book of John and find verse 16. (The verses are designated by the tiny numbers within the text.)

Potent Quotables

I study my Bible as I gather apples. First, I shake the whole tree that the ripest may fall. Then I shake each limb, and when I have shaken each limb I shake every branch and every twig. Then I look under every leaf.

—Martin Luther

In some cases, long books were even divided into shorter, separate books. For example, Samuel, Kings, and Chronicles were originally unified books. Each, however, was too long to be written on a single scroll, so scribes had to write them on two scrolls. For this reason, tradition divides them into two parts: 1 and 2 Samuel (say *"First and Second Samuel"*), 1 and 2 Kings, and 1 and 2 Chronicles—six books instead of three.

Stocking Your Bible Toolbox

As you begin to read through the 1,189 chapters and 31,173 verses in the Bible, you may run upon a place or two where you could use a bit of help. We've tried to do as much as possible in this guide to help you out, but we certainly won't answer *all* your questions. As with any other venture, the right tools can make all the difference when it comes to Bible reading. If you can get your hands on one or more of these, don't hesitate to use them. Many of these tools have electronic counterparts as well.

A Dictionary

Sometimes Noah Webster is the only authority you need to answer a biblical question. Many strange biblical words are well interpreted in modern dictionaries.

A Bible Dictionary

If, however, you have a dictionary that pertains exclusively to Bible artifacts, customs, and culture, it will likely give you an even better grasp about the subject. Bible dictionaries often provide pictures and lists of other Bible references to the same topic.

A Bible Atlas

Only a few of the place names in the Bible have lasted into current times. Even today the geographic boundaries in the Middle East seem to change faster than mapmakers can keep up with them. A Bible atlas provides maps of all the relevant eras of biblical history, helping you to pinpoint various locations—even if the same location goes by several different names during the course of history.

Bible Commentaries

Commentaries are some person's (or organization's) comments about what's in the Bible. Many good ones are available, some general, some quite specific. Do some spot-checking as to writing style and depth of content before choosing one for yourself.

Concordance

If you want to find something in the Bible but don't know where to look, a concordance contains a list of key words that will help you narrow your search. Many Bibles contain an abridged concordance in the back. You can also find complete ("exhaustive") concordances, but they tend to be pretty hefty. Be sure your concordance is based on the same Bible translation you are using, or the words won't always match up. Concordances are also useful for conducting "word studies," where you can quickly accumulate a fairly comprehensive understanding of key themes: forgiveness, repentance, salvation, prayer, hope, and so on.

Cross-References

Many Bibles contain cross-references within the text. The tiny little letters interspersed next to key words or names are supposed to match up to the same letter in the margins, which direct you to other places in the Bible where the person or thing pops up.

Obviously, the more tools you try to use, the more time will be required for your Bible reading. However, the Bible is not exactly a whodunit, where you're eager to get to the last page and be done with it. If you use one or more of these tools, your comprehension level will be significantly higher. If your goal is to get *through* the Bible, don't fool with the tools. But if you'd rather get *into* the Bible and increase your understanding, these tools can help.

So, without further ado, let's turn our attention to what the Bible has to say. The next chapter begins at a logical place—the beginning.

The Least You Need to Know

➤ Although people may agree that the Bible is a divinely inspired and/or essential religious text, not everyone will arrive at the same conclusions about its teachings.

➤ Applying biblical teaching to contemporary life can be challenging when culture, language, and other variants are taken into account.

➤ When other people's opinions vary with our own, we need to be charitable and respect them as people.

➤ Numerous resources are available to add depth to Bible reading.

Part 2
The Old Testament

We call it the Old Testament, but to be quite honest, much of it is new to most readers. We tend to be satisfied as long as we know the key stories: Adam and Eve, Noah, Abraham, Moses, David, Jonah, Daniel, and such. Yet these are only the major veins of the Old Testament mine. Also to be uncovered are numerous strange and wonderful accounts: an unexpected resurrection in a graveyard, a talking donkey, incredible battle strategies, behind-the-scenes secrets of royalty, a prophet fed by ravens, visions of the future that would astound even the best science fiction writers, and much, much more.

We should never consider the Old Testament "old" in the sense of useless or used up. It is old in contrast to the new covenant initiated by Jesus, yet it should be considered old in the same sense as "Old Ironsides," "Old Glory," or "Old Smokey." This part of the Bible has weathered the test of time and endured numerous trials—and still continues to thrive and to inspire.

In fact, the better you get to know the Old Testament, the more relevant some of the stories will seem. In a male-dominated society, several examples are provided of women whose character far outshone that of their male peers. In a context where God was usually perceived with fear and trembling, we see humans who "walked with God" or were deemed to be "after God's own heart."

If anything, the Old Testament shows us the drawbacks of having a crowd mentality—and the possibilities that exist if we can break free of such mental limitations. For many of us, that is a new revelation indeed. So as you begin your trek through the next several chapters, here's hoping you have a good "old" time!

Chapter 3

In the Beginning

In This Chapter

➤ Creation and the Garden of Eden: How everything started out well but got messed up

➤ God's response to disobedience

➤ Cain and Abel, Noah's ark, and the Tower of Babel

When you begin a big project, it's good to start from scratch, from "Ground Zero," from the very beginning. Yet no sooner do we begin our excursion into reading and understanding the Bible than we run into a question. The first four words of Genesis are "In the beginning, God...." But what, inquiring minds might wonder, about *God's* beginning?

What Was Before the Beginning? (Genesis 1:1)

The Bible takes us back to the beginning of life as we know it, but it never suggests that *God* had a beginning. The concept of eternity is going to be important as we get into the basic teachings and doctrines of the Bible. Believers hope in eternal life with God. Because there is no *end* to this time, we should not expect that God's "time" had a *beginning* either. This is a hard concept to wrap your mind around. Scientists have recently tried to expand our thinking to grasp concepts of billions of years, but it's more challenging still to comprehend something that has always existed and will never end. Yet the Bible makes that claim about God—the one who, in turn, sees to the creation of everything else.

A Good Day's Work (Genesis 1:1—2:3)

The story of creation follows a logical progression. The Bible suggests that humankind was God's greatest achievement. (Who are we to disagree?) Yet that's not where the creation starts. Why make people first if there is no dry land to park them on, or while it is still dark and they could bump into something and hurt themselves?

Just as a sculptor begins with rough forms before concentrating on finer details, God began the work of creation by separating and shaping. The farther along God went, the more defined creation became. Notice the practical sequence of the days of creation.

Day 1 (Gen. 1:3–5)	Light is created and is separated from darkness to designate day and night.
Day 2 (Gen. 1:6–8)	God structures an expanse called "sky" to separate the water on earth from the water above.
Day 3 (Gen. 1:9–13)	The water on earth is gathered to form seas distinct from land. Vegetation is created with the capability of reproducing from seeds.
Day 4 (Gen. 1:14–19)	Heavenly bodies (sun, moon, and stars) are created to provide light and mark seasons.
Day 5 (Gen. 1:20–23)	Birds and sea creatures are formed with the capability of reproducing "according to their kinds."
Day 6 (Gen. 1:24–2:1)	God turns his attention to land creatures, completing his work with the creation of humankind—both male and female.
Day 7 (Gen. 2:2–3)	God rests.

What Saith Thou?

Were the days of creation literal, 24-hour days?

Those who say yes believe in a "young earth" that is thousands, rather than billions, of years old. Others accept scientific evidence such as fossil records and carbon dating and view the "days" of creation as time periods of undetermined length. (After all, the sun wasn't even present to determine "days" until Day 4.)

The Genesis account of creation describes God as speaking each day's work into existence. We are repeatedly told that God saw that his work was good. But when it was over and the totality of creation was evaluated, he knew it was *very* good (Gen. 1:31).

When the time came to create humans, God said, "Let *us* make man in *our* image" (Gen. 1:26). The use of the first-person plural pronoun suggests to some scholars that ancient Israelites believed God to be surrounded by angelic members of a heavenly court, much as the kings on earth were surrounded by courtiers. Others interpret the "we" to mean that God's being comprises a "three in one" Holy Trinity of God the Father, God the Son, and God the Holy Spirit. (More about the Trinity when we get to the New Testament.)

One more question before we move on. Why did God rest? (Gen. 2:2)

Although an omnipotent God cannot, by definition, become tired, the God of the Bible sometimes models what he wants people to do. In this case, the pattern is established from the beginning of time to set aside one day of the week for renewal and spiritual reflection.

Adam and Eve in a Brave Nude World (Genesis 2:4–25)

The first chapter of Genesis is essentially the overview of creation. Genesis 2 backs up a bit to provide a closer look at the creation of human beings. This is an intensely personal and intimate description. In the Bible, human life begins as a relationship—not simply a chance occurrence involving slimy primordial ooze.

According to the Genesis narrative, God formed dirt into the shape of a man and performed a kind of heavenly CPR to breathe life into him. He then placed the man in a green paradise known as the Garden of Eden, filled with trees, rivers, and food. The Bible says that the garden was a place where four rivers converge, including the Tigris and the Euphrates. (In today's world, its location would probably be southern Iraq.) At the center were two significant trees: the Tree of Life and the Tree of the Knowledge of Good and Evil. God gave Adam almost unlimited freedom, plus a fulfilling job naming animals and overseeing the garden. The one restriction was that Adam had to avoid eating from the Tree of the Knowledge of Good and Evil.

As Adam went through the process of naming animals, he probably couldn't help noticing peculiar behavior among the birds and the bees. Adam was singular, a one-of-a-kind creature, when he surely longed to be two-of-a-kind. So God caused him to fall into a deep sleep, during which God took a rib (or "part of the man's side") and created woman. "For this reason," the story continues, "a man will leave his father and mother and be united to his wife, and they will become one flesh" (Genesis 2:24). You hear this verse recited at many weddings, and it is quoted in the New Testament by both Jesus (Matt. 19:5) and Paul (1 Cor. 6:16). But isn't it interesting that the "two becoming one" principle is established in this context when Adam and Eve didn't even have a mother or father?

Adam and Eve were both naked, the narrative concludes, "and they felt no shame."

Fall Comes to Eden (Genesis 3)

We don't know how many blissful years (or decades or centuries) Adam and Eve spent in Eden. The next account we have is when things go sour for them. Although Satan is not mentioned in this narrative, tradition holds that the serpent who figures so largely in this episode was none other than the Temptor himself, the Devil, taking the form of the serpent to tempt Eve. In the book of Revelation, Satan is designated "that ancient serpent" (Rev. 20:2).

What Saith Thou?

Why would God place a potentially lethal tree in Eden? Didn't he know what would happen?

Here's one way of looking at it. Parents want their children to love them by choice, not as a result of parental manipulation or authority. Similarly, God surely wanted Adam's devotion and loyalty to be voluntary. The tree of the knowledge of good and evil allowed Adam (and later Eve) the freedom to obey or disobey God.

Potent Quotables

I will put enmity between you and the woman, and between your offspring and hers; he will crush your head, and you will strike his heel. (Gen. 3:15)

This verse is often considered the first prophecy in the Bible. Speaking to the serpent (Satan), God makes it clear that this isn't the last time they will oppose one another. Satan will "strike the heel" of the woman's offspring—usually interpreted to refer to the death of Jesus—but in the ultimate victory, this same offspring will crush the "serpent" with a fatal blow.

The serpent's strategy is crafty. He doesn't oppose anything God has said or done—at least, not overtly. Instead, he asks an innocent-sounding question that causes Eve to doubt what she has been told. Before she has time to think clearly, he follows up with an even more venomous suggestion that perhaps God has an ulterior motive. Is Eve going to let herself be duped? "For God knows that when you eat of [the forbidden fruit], your eyes will be opened, and you will be like God, knowing good and evil" (Genesis 3:5). The Satan-serpent has succeeded in directing Eve's attention from the vast expanse of paradise to the single forbidden tree and the luscious, ripe fruit hanging there. (The Bible doesn't specify the kind of fruit that was forbidden.)

The fruit looked delicious. Eve grabbed a piece, took a bite, and handed some to Adam so he could share the experience. He, too, ate some of the fruit. Things changed, all right. We don't know what kind of wisdom they were expecting, but the first recorded result of eating the forbidden fruit was something to the effect of, "Hey, turn your head! I'm buck naked!" Adam and Eve took to the bushes and didn't come out until they had sewed some fig leaves together to cover themselves.

They must not have become *very* smart, because after who knows how long of being naked and unashamed, they suddenly decided to try to hide from God. When they finally came out, they were wearing the latest fig fashions. God knew what was going on. "Who told you that you were naked? Have you eaten from the tree that I commanded you not to eat from?" (3:11)

Adam blamed Eve. Eve blamed the serpent. But neither the man nor the woman had any idea what the disastrous effects of their disobedience would be. In fact, as the Bible explains it, Adam and Eve had moved from a state of perfection and innocence to one of sin and death. That is why this biblical account is frequently referred to as "the Fall." Although they didn't die immediately, death did come to them in time, and to every one of their descendants, too.

God did not let the human beings' disobedience pass unpunished. Adam and his descendants were sentenced to endure "painful toil" for their livelihood. Eve and her descendants would have greatly increased pains in childbirth, and in addition, her desire for her husband would somewhat diminish the more equitable status she had enjoyed in the garden.

Stronger still was the curse God placed upon the serpent: It was doomed to "crawl on [its] belly" and "eat dust" (3:14).

The ground was also cursed: From now on it would produce thorns and thistles to interfere with the "easy pickings" Adam had previously enjoyed. Then Adam and Eve were evicted from Eden.

The serpent had been right: Having tasted the fruit, the humans now knew the difference between good and evil—and, as the saying goes, ignorance turned out to have been bliss. To protect them from eating from the Tree of Life, which would doom them to live forever in their new, imperfect state, God placed an angel with a flaming sword to prevent their return to Eden.

Yet God had not ceased to care about human beings. Before they left Eden, he replaced their figgy clothing with more practical animal skins (the first suggestion of death in the Bible).

Brother Against Brother (Genesis 4:1-16)

Dramatic as it was, the sudden downward mobility of Adam and Eve did not prevent them from getting on with their lives. As they adapted to their new lifestyle, they began a family. Cain, their older son, became a farmer. Abel, the younger son, raised flocks.

One day, Cain and Abel decided to make an offering to God. Cain brought some of the fruits of his farming, while Abel offered God some of the firstborn of his flock. In ancient Israelite culture and religion, the firstborn was the most valued offspring, whether animal or human. However, as we shall see, in biblical narratives God makes frequent exceptions to this rule.

God was pleased with Abel's offering, but rejected Cain's. Why? The narrative does not explain. In the days of temple sacrifice, farm animals, grain, oil, and flour were all perfectly acceptable sacrifices, so the nature of the offering doesn't seem to be at issue. The New Testament perspective on this event suggests the problem was one of attitude: Abel's offering was sincere; Cain's wasn't (Heb. 11:4; 1 John 3:12).

Whatever the reason, Cain was very unhappy. Ignoring God's stern warning that "sin is crouching at your door" (Genesis 4:7), he lured Abel into a field and killed him. The first instance of sibling rivalry in the Bible ended disastrously.

When God questioned Cain about Abel's disappearance, Cain replied, "I don't know. Am I my brother's keeper?" (Genesis 4:9). People who have heard this question quoted in various contexts may not have realized that originally it was a rather inept defense for fratricide.

This time it was Cain's turn to be cast out. He was sentenced to quit farming and become a "restless wanderer" upon the earth. At that point, Cain suddenly developed a passion for life—his own life. He feared that someone would kill *him*. So God provided some kind of mark for Cain's protection.

A Population Explosion (Genesis 4:17–5)

After Adam, Eve, Cain, and Abel, the next major figure in the Bible is Noah. But tucked away between these accounts is a genealogy and some significant comments regarding the increase of humankind on earth. People lived for a long time back then, apparently. Adam lived to be 930 years old, and that, according to the Bible, was nothing unusual.

As humankind grew in numbers, civilization began to take shape. Cities were built. Various vocations were established. The arts began to be important.

We are told, "At that time men began to call on the name of the Lord" (Gen. 4:26). But it soon becomes clear that not everyone is overly concerned about God's wishes. A strange passage tells us, "The sons of God saw that the daughters of men were beautiful, and they married any of them they chose" (Gen. 6:2). Some speculate that the "sons of God" were heavenly beings who intermarried with human women. Others suggest "sons of God" were righteous men who married sinful "daughters of men." Or perhaps the "sons of God" were royal leaders trying to estab-lish harems. The interpretation is unclear, but there is little confusion about the results —wickedness was spreading on the earth.

This union, whatever it was, resulted in the *nephilim*—a large and mighty people, according to a later reference. Here they are called "the heroes of old, men of renown" (6:4), but the Hebrew word *nephilim* could mean "fallen ones."

Snapshots

This portion of Genesis records several people who remain somewhat obscure, yet deserve to be remembered:

The first man noted for marrying more than one wife (4:19);

The first musician we know about (4:21);

The next recorded child of Adam and Eve (5:3);

A man remembered because he didn't die (instead, "God took him away") (5:24); and

The oldest recorded person in the Bible (5:27).

In any event, humankind had grown so wicked that God's "heart was filled with pain" (6:6). He was grieved that he had ever made human beings. He decided to deal with their wickedness in a widespread way, by wiping them all off the earth. The glowing exception was a righteous man named Noah.

Looks Like Rain (Genesis 6–7)

God confided His plan to Noah and told him to prepare for what was coming by building an ark. He was to gather two of each kind of living creature, one male and one female. In the case of "clean" animals (those suitable for offerings and for food), Noah was to take seven each. He also took seven of each kind of bird, so sending out the dove later was not too much of a risk. When the ark was built, we are told the animals came to Noah in pairs (7:8–9, 15). Noah, his three sons, and their wives also came on board, for a total of eight people. Once inside, God shut them in (7:16).

Manna from Heaven

Many of the pictures we see of the ark show a kind of cramped floating zoo, with animals hanging over the side. But the ark was at least 450 feet long, 75 feet wide, and 45 feet high—perhaps a bit larger. Each of its three decks was the size of one and a half football fields—plenty of room for people and animals.

It started to rain. Most of us know it rained for 40 days and 40 nights, but in addition we are told that "all the springs of the great deep burst forth" (7:11). Talk about water, water everywhere! According to the Bible, the flood was a world-wide cataclysm. "All the high mountains under the entire heavens were covered," (7:19) and "every living thing that moved on the earth perished" (7:21). In fact, it took much longer for the waters to recede than it had to cover the earth. When we compare the date of the flood (7:11) with the date of Noah's departure from the ark (8:13-16), we realize that he and his family were in the ark for more than a year.

Rain, Rain, Go Away (Genesis 8:1–9:17)

At last the ark settled on the mountains of Ararat in Armenia, near modern Turkey— 500 miles or more from where Noah had set sail.

When the mountaintops began to come into view, Noah used his birds to do occasional weather reports for him. First he sent out a raven. It flew around until the water receded and it could settle safely. Next he sent out a dove, but it had no success in finding a home and returned to the ark. Seven days later he tried the dove again, and this time it returned with a freshly plucked olive branch. (Olive trees cannot grow at high altitudes.) Seven days later, Noah sent the dove out a third time; this time it did not return—a sure sign that the land was inhabitable again.

Still, Noah didn't disembark until God gave the all-clear signal. And the first thing Noah did after landing was build an altar and make an offering to God. Pleased with Noah's righteous attitude and action, God promised never again to make the earth suffer such devastation (8:21). As a sign of this promise, God placed a rainbow in the sky (9:14–15).

At this moment of new beginnings, God told Noah to "be fruitful and increase in number and fill the earth" (9:1). Interestingly, the Bible also recounts that it was at this time that human beings became meat eaters, feared by all other creatures (9:2–4).

What Do You Do with a Drunken Ex-Sailor? (Genesis 9:18–29)

Although Noah is remembered primarily for his boat-building and sailing feats, after the flood he became a farmer. His vineyard produced grapes from which he made wine, and one day he got drunk and slept naked inside his tent. His son, Ham, found him and seemed to think the situation was worthy of a joke. But when he told his brothers, Shem and Japheth, they took it seriously and entered Noah's tent backward, carrying a garment between them so they could cover Dad without seeing him *au naturel*. Later, after Noah discovered what had happened, he chewed out Ham with a curse, and blessed God because of Shem and Japheth.

Names shed some light on this story of Noah and his sons. The descendants of Ham are said to have became the Canaanites, taking the name of Ham's son, Canaan. The descendants of Shem were known as Shemites for a while, but came to be known as Semites. The Semites (including the Israelites) eventually took over the land of Canaan —a fulfillment of Noah's curse. Meanwhile, according to the Bible, the descendants of Japheth expanded until they came to dominate much of the world.

No Comprende: Conversations at the Tower of Babel (Genesis 10–11)

These genealogies are laid out in Genesis 10. What happens next echoes the aftermath of Cain's fratricide. As people spread out and populated the earth, wickedness increased. Humans became quite smug about themselves and their abilities. Needless to say, nothing drives out the awareness of God like self-pride. One group decided to work together and construct a tower that reached into the heavens, "so that we may make a name for ourselves and not be scattered over the face of the whole earth" (11:4). In focusing on their own glory, they had become ambitious and untrustworthy, without any sense of reasonable limits. God had promised not to unleash another major flood, so instead he splintered their common language into many dialects. Soon they could no longer communicate. They gave up building the tower and the city and began to spread out. The place became known as Babel, which sounds like the Hebrew word for *confused*.

Babel is also the Hebrew name for Babylon, where the story of the tower is thought to have taken place. The land that is today the country of Iraq, near the intersection of the Tigris and Euphrates rivers, would continue to play a significant role in biblical history.

Following the story of the Tower of Babel is another genealogy, this one of the family of Terah, Abraham, Sarah, and Lot. These people will be the focus of the next chapter.

Manna from Heaven

Though the word isn't used in the Bible, the Tower of Babel was probably like other towers of that time known as *ziggurats*. These towering buildings had square foundations and steps up the sides, usually leading to a shrine on top to honor the people's gods.

The Least You Need to Know

➤ God is not only eternal, he's creative, too.

➤ When Adam and Eve disobeyed, they distanced themselves (and humankind) from their creator. However, God promised to do something to remedy the problem.

➤ We humans have a long history of turning good into evil.

➤ Even in the midst of widespread wickedness, God recognizes and rewards righteousness. For example, the account of Noah's ark begins as a story of judgment but ends as one of salvation.

Chapter 4

Abraham: A Not-So-Accidental Tourist

In This Chapter

➤ How Israel became the Hebrew "Promised Land"

➤ Why three major religions claim Abraham as a founding father

➤ How just a few righteous people can have a major influence on society

➤ Abraham and Sarah, Lot and his wife (Ms. Pillar of Salt), Sodom and Gomorrah, Abraham's (near-) sacrifice of Isaac, and a couple of embarrassing failures for a so-called man of faith

---

As people get on in life, they tend to want to settle down—especially if they have the means to do so comfortably. Whether we prefer a cabin by the lake, a lodge in the mountains, or a condo on the beach, we tend to get more sedate as age creeps up on us; we become content to slow down and let the younger generations fret about what's wrong with the world.

When we first meet Abraham in the Bible, he is about 75 years old. Life expectancies have already decreased dramatically. Abraham lived to be 175, but he's not like Noah, who did most of his ark building while in his 500s. Indeed, it seemed that Abraham had settled down for good in a place called Ur of the Chaldeans. His family was there. He had herds and servants. He could have lived quite comfortably. But one day he got a call.

Go West, Old Man (Genesis 11:27–12:9)

God told Abraham to pack up and leave his cushy home. Instead of enjoying a comfortable retirement, Abe was going to be more like one of those people who cash everything in and take to the open road in a Winnebago. Most of us know what it's like to take long trips with older family members. Add the complication of flocks, servants, and the need to find a nightly water supply for everyone, and you'll get some idea of the kind of commitment this trip would require.

That's probably why they took the scenic route to Canaan. If you look on a map, you'll see that Canaan—the land in and around modern-day Israel—is almost due-west from Ur, which is in the region Iraq occupies today. A direct route, however, would take them through 600-plus miles of desert. That's probably why they made an extended pit stop in Haran, which was considerably farther north than they needed to go. They followed the Euphrates River and then came back south near the coastline of the Mediterranean Sea.

What would motivate a person to pack up and make such a journey? For Abraham, it seems it was enough that God said so. Besides that, God had made him a few promises:

"The Lord had said to Abram [Abraham], Leave your country, your people and your father's household and go to the land I will show you. I will make you a great nation and I will bless you; I will make your name great, and you will be a blessing. I will bless those who bless you, and whoever curses you I will curse; and all the peoples on earth will be blessed through you" (Genesis 12:1–3).

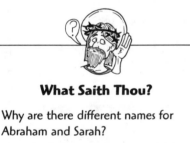

What Saith Thou?

Why are there different names for Abraham and Sarah?

If you're following along in a Bible, you'll see that the main characters begin life as "Abram" and "Sarai." Their names change later. To avoid confusion, we'll use their more familiar names throughout the story.

It sounded fine as far as it went, but most lawyers today would hang their heads in shame to close such a deal on behalf of a client. Where was the promise of financial security? A place to live? An escape clause in case things didn't work out? Yet Abraham set off anyway, with none of these assurances.

In Haran, Abraham's father died. Abraham traveled on with his wife, Sarah, his nephew, Lot, and their servants. (Abraham and Sarah were childless.) At last they arrived in Canaan and began to look around. Only then did God promise to give the land to Abe's descendants. This pattern will be repeated in many other Bible stories: First comes the faith and later comes the reward. God doesn't do a lot of arm-twisting in these stories, but obedience is always rewarded.

Take My Wife—I Mean, Sister...Please! (Genesis 12:10–20)

Yet for a so-called man of faith, Abraham soon proved to be a pretty wimpy husband. A famine in Canaan sent people south to Egypt for food. Though his family had probably been well established in Ur, now they were simply nomads. With no place to call home, Abraham knew he would be vulnerable when he came into contact with the native Egyptians.

Now Sarah was a babe. (That's an approximate translation from Hebrew to English.) She was 65 years old but still very beautiful. In fact, one of the Dead Sea Scrolls contains a description of Sarah's beauty. Abraham feared they would meet lusty Egyptians who would conk him on the head and take his wife and property. So to keep them from *taking* her, he came up with a brilliant plan to say she was his sister and *give her away* if they ran into trouble. She happened to be his half-sister on his father's side, as a matter of fact—but that didn't make his plan any more palatable.

Sure enough, it wasn't long before some Egyptian officials started checking Sarah out and telling Pharaoh about her. Before long, they were treating Abraham with great respect, hoping to arrange a trade. Abraham did pretty well, getting sheep, cattle, donkeys, camels, and servants in the trade. Sarah, on the other hand, was simply added to the list of Pharaoh's women.

This could have been a terrible story if God hadn't gotten involved. But soon Pharaoh's household was suffering from a rash of serious diseases, and somehow Pharaoh knew that Abraham was responsible. He arranged another meeting where Abraham confessed what he had done. The irony was that Pharaoh seemed shocked that Abraham had sunk so low. He asked, "Why didn't you tell me she was your wife?" (12:18). Abraham and Sarah were released without repercussions, and were even allowed to keep the Pharoah's gifts.

Do you think Abraham learned a valuable lesson from this experience? You'll hear more about that at the end of this chapter.

Lots of Trouble from Lot and His Lot (Genesis 13–14)

Meanwhile, even as a nomad, Abraham was prospering. In addition to silver and gold, he had plentiful livestock—an important measure of success at that time. In fact, he and his nephew Lot were doing so well that their combined herds became too large for the land to support. Soon their herdsmen started competing with each other and quarreling.

To solve the problem, Abraham suggested they part company, and he gave Lot the first choice of where to settle. When Lot started looking around, it was clear that the land around the Jordan River was considerably greener than the surrounding countryside—and that's where he chose to go; it gave him the luxury of settling down in one place. Abraham was left with the dust and the necessity of traveling from place to place for sustenance.

But Lot wasn't the only one who had his eyes on easy living. The cities of Sodom and Gomorrah, thought to have been located south or southeast of the Dead Sea, had a nasty reputation for worse-than-average wickedness. Could a righteous man live among such people without becoming corrupt? We shall see.

Lot soon had more pressing concerns. A coalition of foreign kings invaded the local group of allied leaders, among them the kings of Sodom and Gomorrah. The foreign kings won the ensuing battle and carried off Lot and his family as part of the spoils. When this news reached Abraham, he put together an army of his own. A total of 318 "trained men" from his entourage went in pursuit. They attacked during the night, routing the foreign army and reclaiming the plunder that had been stolen—including Lot and the other people who had been taken.

The king of Sodom wanted Abraham to keep the spoils for himself, but he refused. His loyalty was to God, and he didn't want it said that he owed a debt of loyalty to some corrupt political leader for making him wealthy (14:21-24). But before he gave the spoil back, Abraham gave 10 percent of everything to a local priest named Melchizedek, who represented the true God.

The sudden appearance of this Melchizedek guy is a bit strange. His identification as "king of Salem" (14:18) is an early reference to the area eventually to become Jerusalem. And because he represented "God Most High" as both king and priest, Jesus is later compared to him in terms of title, job description, and worthiness to receive personal offerings (Hebrews 7:11-28).

Gone Today, Heir Tomorrow (Genesis 15)

During all this time, the Bible tells us that Abraham had been "calling on the name of the Lord" (12:8; 13:4). Now God called on Abraham, promising to be his "very great reward" (15:1). In essence, Abraham replied that God had already given him everything he needed—except a child. Abraham had resigned himself to leaving his fortune to one of his servants. Not so, God told him. Abraham would soon have a son of his own (15:4). God directed Abraham's eyes to the night sky and promised him offspring as numerous as the stars.

God made a covenant with Abraham—a binding contract to keep his promises of land and offspring. Strikingly, this was an unconditional covenant. God did not ask Abraham to reciprocate with promises about faithfulness, as in later agreements. Whatever Abraham did or did not do from then on, God intended to keep his word.

God's covenant with Abraham was confirmed in a solemn ceremony. Animals were cut in two and separated to form an aisle—a common practice in the Ancient Near East.

(You've heard of cutting a deal; well, this ceremony was called "cutting a covenant." Normally two parties would negotiate a deal and both would "walk the aisle." In this case, however, God initiated the promises, (see Jeremiah 34:18, for example) so Abraham's presence in the ceremony was unnecessary.) Along with the promises God had already made to Abraham, the covenant defined the boundaries of the land promised to Abraham's descendants (15:18-21). As Abraham fell into a troubled sleep, God warned him that his descendants would someday be carried off and enslaved, but promised that it would all turn out for the best. (Remember that when we get to Chapter 7, "Moses: God's Reluctant Hero"). Then God passed between the animal parts in the form of smoke and fire.

Potent Quotables

Abram believed the Lord, and [God] credited it to him as righteousness. (Genesis 15:6)

This verse is often quoted to remind believers of the validity of a faith motivated more by the person's personal relationship with God than mere adherence to a lot of religious do's and don'ts.

Sarah Problem Here? (Genesis 16)

As you read about Abraham, perhaps you can sense his frustration and impatience. He had received all kinds of dazzling promises based on having a child, but he had yet to receive that child. It is likely Sarah was feeling the pressure more than Abraham. She was unable to conceive in a culture where child-bearing was the primary source of a woman's fulfillment and self-esteem—and fertility clinics weren't yet an option.

So Sarah came up with a plan. A custom of the society allowed the husband of a barren woman to bear a child through a servant and raise it as his legal heir. Sarah offered Abraham her Egyptian attendant, Hagar. But as soon as Hagar became pregnant, the interpersonal dynamics changed drastically. Hagar, feeling superior, began to make Sarah's life miserable. Sarah complained to Abraham, who told her she could do as she liked; he wouldn't interfere. Then Sarah began to mistreat Hagar, and Hagar ran away.

An angel confronted Hagar near a spring in the desert and convinced her to return, naming her child-to-be Ishmael ("God hears") and promising her innumerable descendants. Hagar returned and gave birth to Ishmael. At 86, Abraham finally became a father, but Sarah was still not a mother.

The Sign of (Ouch!) Faith (Genesis 17)

Thirteen years later—Abraham was now 99—God appeared to him again to confirm the previous covenant. This time God provided some new names. Abram ("exalted father") became Abraham ("father of many"). Sarai's name was changed to Sarah, an honorary change, perhaps, because both words mean "princess."

To his previous promises, God added two more: "everlasting possession" of the whole land of Canaan, and a son to be conceived by Sarah and born within a year. Abraham had a very spiritual response to this latest bit of news—he fell on the ground laughing (17:17).

Abraham would have been happy for Ishmael to be his heir, but God had other plans. And just so Abraham wouldn't forget this exchange, God proclaimed that Abraham's son should be named Isaac ("he laughs"). To close the deal, God established circumcision as the sign by which his people would be identified.

You'd think that if God wanted a sign by which his people could identify themselves, he could have thought of something besides slicing off the foreskin of the penis. (Matching jewelry or color-coordinated clothing might have made a nice alternative.) But the symbolism of circumcision is suggested in Genesis 17:14: Those who don't conform to God's wise and loving guidance will ultimately be "cut off." The willingness to be circumcised also demonstrates a somewhat higher level of commitment than, say, a handshake or a loyalty oath.

Abraham didn't waste any time. On that very day, he, Ishmael, and all the males in his household were circumcised. Abraham was 99; Ishmael was 13. For future Hebrew males, God designated that circumcision should take place at eight days old (17:12). Arab people, who by tradition are descendants of Ishmael, tend to prefer age 13 for their circumcision ritual.

What Saith Thou?

Can people change God's mind?

If the answer to this question is no, then the next question is, "Why bother praying about anything?" Abraham's intervention on behalf of Sodom didn't change the outcome. That city was doomed by its own wickedness. But in some cases, the intercession of God's people has spared civilizations (Exodus 32:9–14), saved entire cities from extinction (Jonah 3), and extended personal life expectancy (2 Kings 20:1–11). Prayer allows God's people to get involved with his plans and his outreach. Indeed, it is often said that prayer is more for our benefit than God's.

Let's Make a Deal (Genesis 18)

Not long after Abraham's circumcision, he received three rather important visitors. Two of them were clearly angels; the third appears to have been God. All three appeared in human form. Although he did not recognize them as divine, Abraham gave the full measure of Middle-Eastern hospitality, bowing, washing their feet, preparing food, and so forth. The visitors asked about Sarah and promised that she would have a son within a year. Perhaps at this moment Abraham realized whom he was entertaining. But inside the tent, out of sight (in that society, a woman's job was to serve the guests, not socialize with them), Sarah overheard what was said. Her first response was just what Abraham's had been: She laughed! It was ludicrous. She was 89 years old, for goodness' sake. Who would know better than she that she was past childbearing age?

The visitor identified as "the Lord" asked why Sarah had laughed. She tried to deny it, but God knew what she had done. She didn't know it yet, but God would have the last laugh—and his name would be Isaac.

The two angels left, but God stayed to talk further with Abraham. Because of God's great respect for Abraham, and because of the covenant between them, God decided to share some of his future plans. It seems that God was on his way to check out the cities of Sodom and Gomorrah, to see whether the terrible things people were saying about them were true. He already knew what was going on in the twin cities of wickedness, of course, but this step would make clear that any judgment was not the result of a hasty decision.

But before God could say a word about judgment, Abraham began pleading for the inhabitants of Sodom (because that's where Lot was living). "Will you sweep away the righteous with the wicked? What if there are fifty righteous people in the city?" (18:23-24). God promised to spare the city if 50 righteous people were found there. Abraham didn't stop there. Boldly he lowered the target number to 45, then 40, 30, 20, and finally 10. You would think that—counting Lot and his family—there would be at least 10 decent people in the city of Sodom. It turned out not to be true.

Hot Time in the Cities (Genesis 19:1-29)

Meanwhile, the two other angels had already reached Sodom. It seems that Lot had done quite well for himself, because there he was, "sitting in the gateway of the city" (19:1)—the place where important city officials usually hung out. It's unclear whether Lot knew the visitors were angels. His behavior, however, conveyed to them that Sodom was not a nice place to visit, even though he wanted to live there.

What he did was invite them to stay at his home. At first they declined, saying they would spend the night in the public square. Then Lot *insisted* they come home with him.

Lot had good reason for concern. Shortly after supper the men of Sodom surrounded his home yelling, "Where are the men who came to you tonight? Bring them out to us so that we can have sex with them" (19:5). Lot went out and tried to reason with the crowd, even offering them his two virgin daughters so they could "do what you like with them." But the townsmen began to threaten Lot as well and stormed forward to knock down his door.

We have no insight into Lot's motivations and very little more into his character. The New Testament refers to Lot as "a righteous man" (2 Peter 2:7), but it's hard to tell that from this account. In Lot's defense, however, social etiquette required that he protect anyone "under the protection of (his) roof" (Gen. 19:8). He may have suspected that his visitors were more than ordinary men, and therefore took extreme measures to try and protect their safety. In addition, the story reflects the harsh reality that in the ancient Near East, females were simply much less valuable than males. The angels then took charge. First they pulled Lot back inside to safety. Then they inflicted blindness on the crowd, preventing them from finding the door. Then they told Lot to gather his household together and go. Sodom was about to be destroyed.

What Saith Thou?

One of the most sensitive issues in the church (and in society) today is the debate as to whether homosexuality is to be considered a sin. Some people defend a gay lifestyle on the grounds that our culture has changed since biblical times. However, others are adamant that the Bible clearly identifies homosexuality as a sin (citing examples such as Leviticus 18:22 and Romans 1:27).

The topic will come up again in the context of other passages. However, at this point it should be noted that homosexuality was by no means the only problem behavior exhibited by the people of Sodom. They clearly demonstrated lust, rage, unprovoked violence, covetousness, and complete disregard for God and other people. God was judging the totality of their sin. Any attempt to lay the problem on one single sin is to belittle the complexity and depth of their wickedness.

Lot told his prospective sons-in-law what was about to happen, but they laughed it off as a joke. As dawn approached, the list of potential evacuees was down to Lot, his wife, and his two daughters. And even they were so reluctant to leave that the angels had to pull them out of the city by their arms, like whining kids in a supermarket. When the angels told them to run for the hills or be killed, Lot pleaded to be allowed to take refuge in the smaller city of Zoar instead. The angels agreed, but they told Lot to hurry, and they gave explicit warnings not to stop along the way or to look back.

No sooner had Lot reached Zoar than God began to rain burning sulfur on Sodom and Gomorrah. Watching from a distance, Abraham saw smoke rising "like smoke from a furnace" as the cities were destroyed. Although the newer Bible translations use the phrase "burning sulfur," the older versions referred to "brimstone and fire," a phrase which has become synonymous with God's judgment.

A Family Affair (Genesis 19:23–29)

Lot's wife hadn't even made it to Zoar. All we're told is that she "looked back, and she became a pillar of salt" (19:26). It is usually thought that she just couldn't let go of her devotion to her old lifestyle. Jesus later uses her as an object lesson as he teaches his disciples about the last days and warns them to stay focused on the essential things in life (Luke 17:28–33).

Even those of Lot's family who escaped were in no healthy state of mind. First they left the city of Zoar and ended up living in a cave in the mountains. With no one else around, Lot's daughters feared they would never have husbands, but they didn't let that stop them from having children. They took turns getting Lot drunk and sleeping with him. Both daughters became pregnant and had children by their own father.

The children of Lot's daughters were named Moab and Ben-Ammi. These may not seem to be big names in the Bible, but they had a lot of significance for the Israelites. The offspring of those children became the *Moabites* and the *Ammonites*, two major groups that provoked and competed with the Israelites for generations to come.

All I Want Is the Heir That I Breed (Genesis 20–22)

Meanwhile, Abraham had *again* tried to pass off Sarah as his sister while in a foreign culture. And again God had to intervene to prevent damage to health, reputation, or his plan for their lives. By this time Abraham was a hundred years old. Sarah was 90. They had spent the past 25 years on the road, trying to do what God had commanded them. Now, at long last, God's promise was fulfilled: They had a son. They named him Isaac, as they had been told, and circumcised him at eight days old.

As you might expect, the birth of Isaac intensified the conflict between Sarah and Hagar. When Sarah saw Ishmael playing with little Isaac, she got upset. She didn't want Ishmael, her servant's child, to be on equal footing with Isaac, to grow up with him and share his inheritance. To Abraham's distress, Sarah demanded that Hagar and Ishmael be cast out, sent away unprotected. Abraham was caught squarely in the middle. But God told him to do what Sarah wanted. God would look after the refugees. Moreover, God assured Abraham, Ishmael would not be forgotten. He was Abraham's son as well as Isaac, and he, too, would be blessed with many descendants.

Abraham furnished Hagar and Ishmael with provisions and sent them into the wilderness on their own. When their water ran out, Hagar left Ishmael beneath a bush and walked a little way off so she wouldn't have to see him die. She heard him crying, though, and so did God. He spoke to Hagar, reassuring her and showing her a spring of water. We're told that "God was with [Ishmael] as he grew up" (21:20). It is said that Ishmael's descendants became the Arab people. Indeed, Muslims, like Jews and Christians, revere Abraham as their spiritual forefather.

Meanwhile, Abraham was coping with the usual hassles of life (21:22–34) and watching Isaac grow up. Then, one day, something utterly unexpected happened. Out of the blue, God told him to take Isaac to a particular mountain and offer him as a burnt offering. Isaac was a boy at the time, old enough to talk, reason, and carry wood. The Bible says that God did this to test Abraham.

God referred to Isaac as "your son, your only son, Isaac, whom you love" (22:2). Why "only"? It was not just because Hagar and Ishmael could no longer be part of Abraham's life. Isaac was the promised one, the heir through whom God's other promises would be fulfilled.

What Saith Thou?

Is there a difference between a "test" and a "temptation"?

The Bible makes it clear that God never *tempts* anyone to do anything wrong (James 1:13). Yet He sometimes *tests* His people for the same reason teachers test students—to allow them to see how much they have been learning, or what they *still* need to learn.

What Saith Thou?

Why would God tell someone to kill a child?

This is a tough question. Although other religions practiced child sacrifice, the Israelites never did. Some say that God's command gave Abraham the opportunity to show that he was just as devoted to his God as those others were to their cruel idols. Or perhaps God had so much respect for Abraham that He allowed him to empathize with the feelings involved in sacrificing an innocent son. More than anyone else who ever lived, Abraham must know best what it felt like for God to sacrifice his own beloved Son, Jesus.

And now Abraham was to offer Isaac up to God. Though his heart must have been breaking, he didn't argue. We're told that "early the next morning" he cut the wood and set out for the specified location—a three days' journey. When they reached the place, he left his servants at the foot of the mountain, and he and Isaac ascended. On the way up the mountain, Isaac noticed they were missing a lamb for the sacrifice. Abraham replied, "God himself will provide the lamb for the burnt offering" (22:8).

At the top of the mountain, Abraham built an altar, tied Isaac to it, and stacked the wood around it. He raised his knife to kill his son. It was then, at the last possible moment, that an angel, speaking for God, called out to him to stop. Abraham was directed to a ram caught by its horns in the bushes. He offered the ram in Isaac's place and returned home with his son. (The New Testament suggests that Abraham had so much faith that although no one had ever witnessed a resurrection, he believed Isaac would come back from the dead if that's what it took for God to honor his promises [Hebrews 11:17-19].)

From this point on, the focus is more on Isaac than Abraham. Yet it was Abraham's great faith that allowed God's blessings to be handed down to Isaac, Jacob, and future generations. Abraham's willingness to obey God has stood as a motivating example of faith for centuries.

The Least You Need to Know

➤ Abraham is honored as a forefather of three religions: Judaism, Islam, and Christianity.

➤ Abraham was the first to receive most of the promises inherited by the generations of Israelites who followed him.

➤ The life of Abraham shows us that patience is an important part of faith.

➤ Even though Abraham is held up as a great model of faith, he had shortcomings just like everyone else.

Chapter 5

Isaac and Jacob: Lessons in Family Dysfunction

In This Chapter

➤ God's promises to Abraham, extended to two more generations

➤ An unlikely candidate in Abraham's line of succession

➤ The beginning of the 12 tribes of Israel

➤ Isaac and Rebekah, Jacob and Esau, Jacob's ladder and wrestling match

They say you can choose your friends but that you're pretty much stuck with your family. Abraham had his faults, of course, but overall he was a reasonably stable guy. As we move on into successive generations, however, you have to wonder about some of his progeny.

Isaac's Mail-Order Bride (Genesis 23–25:18)

When we last saw Isaac, he was coming off Mount Moriah, breathing a deep sigh of relief. He had lived to tell the tale of almost being sacrificed. Sarah, his mother, however, died not long afterward. (Jewish folklore says that she never recovered from seeing her husband take their child away to be sacrificed.) Abraham bought a piece of land containing the cave of Machpelah, which became his family burial plot.

Abraham was quite old himself, and before he died he wanted to ensure that his son had a good wife. After all, the only character we've seen in the whole land of Canaan who claimed to serve the true God was Melchizedek, the king/priest. So Abraham decided to import a wife from his homeland who would make Isaac a worthy bride. He sent a faithful servant all the way back to Mesopotamia to scout out prospects.

In a drama that affirmed God's active participation, the servant found a woman named Rebekah among Abraham's kinfolk, and she agreed to return with him and become Isaac's wife.

Snapshots

A handsome and wealthy protagonist...a beautiful young girl...a wise old messenger bearing gifts...a wedding...and even the camels go home happy. If you enjoy a good romance, Genesis 24 has all the details.

What Saith Thou?

Why not choose a Canaanite woman for Isaac as long as she was willing to convert to his religion?

Throughout the Old Testament you will see an emphasis on avoiding intermarriage with peoples who served other gods. In the land of Canaan native religions were based on a pantheon of traditional gods such as Ba'al, the storm god, who were called upon to help with weather, fertility, and other down-to-earth concerns. Such religions worshipped graven images of the gods—something the Israelite religion abhorred. Abraham seemed to be aware of the potential dangers and insisted on finding a woman for Isaac who shared his faith in the true God.

When Abraham died, Isaac inherited everything. Abraham had remarried and had numerous other children, but he took care of them while he was alive and made sure they laid no claim to what had been promised to Isaac. When Abraham died, Ishmael returned to help Isaac with the burial.

Birthright Gumbo (Genesis 25:19–34)

At first Rebekah was unable to have children. But rather than repeat the mistake of his father (remember the story of Hagar in Chapter 4, "Abraham, a Not-So-Accidental Tourist"), Isaac prayed about it. And after a time, God answered his prayer—with twins. (Talk about double or nothing!)

Isaac and Rebekah had been married 20 years when she finally became pregnant. But when she did, she could feel what seemed to be an intense struggle in her womb. This caused *her* to turn to prayer. God replied that she was carrying two "nations" within her. He told her they wouldn't get along any better after they were born, and that the older one would end up serving the younger.

They say all babies are cute, but Rebekah's first child might have been an exception. It is recorded that he was red and "his whole body was like a hairy garment." They named him Esau (which might have meant *hairy*). The second twin was born right on the heels of Esau—literally. As Esau was born, Jacob's hand was grabbing his heel.

As they grew, perhaps no two brothers have been more different. Esau was a skilled hunter who was drawn to the outdoors. Jacob was quiet and tended to stay "among the tents." Consequently, Isaac was partial to Esau, while Rebekah liked Jacob better. As for the brothers, they didn't seem to get along at all.

For example, one day Esau came in after an ex-tended time away, and he was very hungry. Jacob just happened to be in the kitchen (to the extent that tents have kitchens), whipping up a little something to eat. The soup of the day was a delicious lentil stew, and Esau immediately asked for some. Jacob looked at his famished brother, thought of the strong brotherly ties between them as twins, and with a heart filled with love (no doubt), said, "First sell me your birthright."

Except for the hand-on-the-heel delivery, this is the first glimpse we have into Jacob's character, but it won't be the last. Jacob was a schemer, a trickster always looking for an advantage. In this case, Esau figured his birthright wouldn't do him any good if he dropped dead from hunger. So in a hasty decision, he agreed to the deal. It was a foolish impulse, but Esau was never known for his smarts.

Manna from Heaven

In ancient Israelite culture, a *birth-right* was the entitlement bestowed on the firstborn son. Privileges included a double portion of the father's inheritance. Esau had been born mere seconds before Jacob, but the birthright was still his—until Jacob got through with him.

Like Father, Like Son (Genesis 26)

The next account looks back to a time before Jacob and Esau were born to highlight what exactly Esau was giving up. It should also sound very familiar to anyone who remembers the story of Abraham from Chapter 4 of this book. A famine in the land drove Isaac and Rebekah to the land of the Philistines, where a king named Abimelech was in charge. (You'll be reading much more about the Philistines in later chapters.) Here God appeared to Isaac and repeated the terms of His previous agreement with Abraham: God's blessing, the promise to inherit the land, and the assurance of numerous descendants.

You may remember that a couple of times Abraham had allowed foreign leaders to believe that Sarah was his sister (Genesis 12:10–20; 20:1–18). Now the same sad story is repeated, with Isaac and Rebekah as the co-complicitors. Things go well for a while as they live among the Philistines as "brother" and "sister." Then one day King Abimelech (not the same leader Abraham had encountered in Genesis 20) looks out the window and sees Isaac and Rebekah kissing in a not-very-sibling-like manner.

Isaac is summoned, and the truth is finally revealed. The king orders the death penalty for anyone harming either Isaac or Rebekah.

While Isaac was in the land of the Philistines, God blessed him. His crops yielded an abundant increase; his flocks and herds grew quickly. Soon he was the envy of everyone around, until eventually Abimelech asked him to leave. Even then, Abimelech's men gave him grief every time he tried to settle down. Finally, Isaac found a place where they left him alone. By this time, Abimelech had figured out that opposing Isaac meant going up against his God as well, and that was a situation he wanted to avoid. Abimelech paid Isaac a visit, reminded him that he had done everything in his power to keep him from being harmed, and asked the same favor in return. They swore an oath of peace to each other, and Isaac moved on. As Isaac was preparing to depart, God appeared to him again and once more affirmed his previous covenant. And we are told that "Isaac built an altar there and called on the name of the Lord" (26:25).

These reminders of God's covenant promises, so close to the story of Esau's birthright, recall what Esau traded for a bowl of lentil soup. And when the story returns to Esau, he makes another bad decision in taking wives from the local area—which caused his parents grief.

The Old Man and Deceit (Genesis 27–28:9)

When next we see Isaac, he is old and has lost his eyesight. On the other hand, his appetite is still good, it seems, because he got a hankering for a certain kind of cooked meat that Esau, the hunter, sometimes prepared for him. Isaac asked Esau to go shoot him some game and make the dish, in return for which he would bless him—an act that would formally designate Esau to receive the inheritance that should go to the older son.

For some reason, Esau didn't pipe up and explain that he had traded away that asset. (Surely it hadn't slipped his mind!) Instead, he grabbed his bow and set out for the open country. Rebekah, however, had overheard Isaac and went to Jacob with a plan. If he could pass himself off as Esau, his blind father might be fooled into giving him the blessing instead.

In a scene straight out of *Mission Impossible*, mother and son went into action. They killed a couple of young goats to prepare the meal Isaac had requested. Rebekah pulled out some of her older son's clothes for Jacob to wear so he would have that special *eau d'Esau* scent in Isaac's presence. And because Jacob was follicly challenged in comparison to Esau, Rebekah used the goatskins left over from the meal to prepare toupees for the neck, hands, and forearms, of her smooth-skinned younger son.

Isaac was blind, but he wasn't completely stupid. The dialogue in Isaac's tent is a little like that scene in *Little Red Riding Hood*, where the wolf pretends to be the granny—except with the positions reversed. Isaac was suspicious from the get-go. How had "Esau" acquired the food so quickly? Jacob said, "The Lord your God gave me success" (27:20). Isaac told "Esau" to come nearer. The voice was Jacob's, Isaac observed, but the hands were like Esau's. Isaac then asked directly: "Are you really my son Esau?" Jacob lied again and said yes. Finally, Isaac ate the food and told "Esau" to come and kiss him. As Jacob leaned over to do so, Isaac smelled the clothes and at last gave him his blessing. He had been deceived with taste, with touch, and with smell.

No sooner had Jacob left the room than Esau returned from hunting, bringing the food his father had requested. When he told Isaac to sit up, eat, and give him the blessing, imagine his shock when Isaac replied, "Who are you?" When Esau discovered what had happened, "he burst out with a loud and bitter cry" (v. 34). He, too, wanted a blessing. But the blessing given to Jacob had already made Jacob lord over his brother and ensured God's continual provision. There was little left to bestow to Esau.

Esau was more than a little upset with Jacob. As long as his parents were around, he could bide his time. But he made up his mind then and there to kill Jacob eventually.

Rebekah learned of Esau's plans and decided to remove Jacob from harm's way. She sent Jacob to live with her brother for a while in distant Mesopotamia, where Abraham's servant had found her. She would send word when Esau had cooled down and/or forgotten about the incident. Rebekah's plan had worked in getting what she wanted for Jacob, but the price she paid was that this was the last time she would ever see her younger son.

Jacob departed with Isaac's blessing (and a warning not to marry a Canaanite woman), and off he headed to Uncle Laban's to find a suitable cousin to take for a wife. When Esau saw how much his Canaanite wives had disturbed his parents, he went out and married yet another wife—a daughter of his Uncle Ishmael.

What Saith Thou?

Why didn't Isaac correct his mistake when he discovered the truth?

For one thing, it wasn't exactly a mistake. God had already chosen Jacob to receive the blessing (25:23). Besides, official verbal statements such as Isaac's were as legally binding as written contracts are today.

Stairway to Heaven (Genesis 28:10–22)

Jacob stopped for the night when it got dark, and as he slept, he dreamed he saw a stairway extending from earth to heaven. Angels were traveling up and down the stairway, and the voice of God came from above, promising Jacob the same things he had promised Abraham and Isaac. God also promised to watch over Jacob while he was gone and bring him back to the land he was currently leaving.

Manna from Heaven

This passage is the source of our references to "Jacob's ladder." Older Bible versions refer to a *ladder* with angels going up and down, but a more accurate translation is *stairway* (providing an even greater challenge for those of us who mastered the "Jacob's Ladder" string creation as children).

Jacob was amazed at this encounter. Previously, he had referred to the Lord as *"your God"* (27:20); now he realized that he, too, was going to have God to reckon with. It must have come as a surprise to realize that Esau wasn't the only force driving his life. Boldly, Jacob announced that he would claim the Lord as his God—*if* God came through on all his promises. It was a step in the right direction, but he still has a long road ahead of him.

The Wrong "Honey" on the Honeymoon (Genesis 29:1–30)

Jacob finally arrived at the home of Rebekah's brother, Laban. And what do you know? While he was standing there asking directions from a group of shepherds, Laban's daughter Rachel approached. Jacob helped her water the sheep by single-handedly rolling a huge stone from the mouth of the well. (Not bad for a guy who liked to hang around the tents.) Then Jacob told Rachel who he was, and she ran home to tell her father the news.

Laban went out to meet Jacob, and Jacob became his guest. Later he hired Jacob to work for him. When asked what his wages should be, Jacob said he would take Rachel, the younger of Laban's two daughters. The other daughter was named Leah, and apparently this Leah was no princess. Her name meant "cow." (After all, Laban was a herdsman.) All we know of Leah is that she had "weak eyes"—or the Hebrew could mean "delicate eyes." Either way, it is clear that as far as Jacob was concerned, Rachel was the looker in the family.

Jacob and Laban agreed that Jacob would work seven years in exchange for Rachel. And these seven years "seemed like only a few days to [Jacob] because of his love for her" (29:20). At the end of seven years, the wedding took place amid great celebration. When night fell, Jacob and his bride retired to the nuptial tent—the bride, of course, still modestly swathed in veils. Surprise! In the morning, Jacob discovered not Rachel beside him, but her sister Leah. How dare someone have the audacity to deceive him like that! Laban was turning out to be a competant con man as well. He explained that local custom required him to marry off his older child first. Of course, if Jacob wanted Rachel, too, he could sign on for another seven years of labor. Jacob had little choice. The honeymoon night had pretty much sealed the deal with Leah, but she would never be Jacob's one and only love. Jacob went ahead and married Rachel, agreeing to stay and work for Laban.

Irony upon irony. The younger son who schemed to pass himself off as the elder had been fooled into taking the older daughter in place of the younger. And the son who took advantage of his father's blindness had himself been blinded (and blindsided) in the darkness of the wedding tent.

Baby, Baby, Baby, Etc. (Genesis 29:31–30:23)

Jacob suddenly went from being a runaway little brother to a husband with a significant household. In addition to wives Rachel and Leah, he also had two servants named Bilhah and Zilpah—Laban's wedding gifts to his daughters. It was clear from the beginning that Jacob loved Rachel more than Leah. But God looks out for the overlooked. While Rachel was unable to have children, Leah was a baby machine. She had four sons in succession, naming them Reuben, Simeon, Levi, and Judah.

Tormented by her inability to conceive, Rachel resorted to Sarah's tactic: She told Jacob to sleep with Bilhah, her maidservant. Bilhah bore two sons for Jacob—Dan and Naphtali. By this time it was Leah who was not getting pregnant. She encouraged Jacob to sleep with Zilpah, producing Gad, then Asher.

The way the women in this family were beginning to act, you'd think there was a scoreboard in the bedroom. In fact, Rachel and Leah had side deals going for who would spend the night with Jacob. One day, for example, Reuben found some mandrakes—believed to be an aid to conception. Rachel was just desperate enough to trade a night with Jacob in exchange for the mandrakes. She lived to regret it, however, when Leah conceived again, bearing a fifth son, Issachar, and afterward a sixth, Zebulun. Some time later Leah finally had a girl, whom she named Dinah.

Finally "God remembered Rachel; he listened to her and opened her womb" (Genesis 30:22). She had a son of her own and named him Joseph.

The women of Jacob's household and their children

Leah	Bilhah	Zilpah	Rachel
Reuben "He has seen my misery")	**Dan** "He has vindicated"	**Gad** Can mean "good fortune" or "a troop"	**Joseph** "May he add"
Simeon "One who hears"	**Naphtali** "My struggle"	**Asher** "Happy"	
Levi "Attached"			
Judah "Praise"			
Issachar "Reward"			
Zebulun "Gift" or "Honor"			
Dinah "Justified"			

So let's check back to the previous table to see how the tally has come out for the four women of Jacob's household. Notice the meanings of the sons' names; they go with the story of each one's birth. Several of these may seem a little odd, but get used to them because many of them will be popping up again.

An Early Experiment in Genetic Engineering (Genesis 30:25–43)

Obviously, Jacob had been busy. While all his offspring were being born, he had paid off his debt to Laban and was now ready to head back toward his own home with his new family. Laban, however, was reluctant to let him go. He had figured out that his prosperity was largely due to Jacob. It seems that whatever Jacob did, God blessed it. If Jacob left, what would happen to Laban?

Laban told Jacob he could name his price if he would just stay a little longer. So Jacob proposed a deal. Laban would give him the present and future animals from the herds that were dark, speckled, and spotted. These were few compared to the traditional white animals; in fact, they were considered good omens. The remaining goats and sheep would be Laban's.

It sounded like a no-risk deal for the old herdsman. But Laban was greedy. That very day he removed all the dark, spotted, and speckled animals from his herds. Giving them to his sons, he sent them far enough away that they would never intermingle with his son-in-law's herds. Jacob was left with essentially nothing to begin with. But Jacob still had a trick or two up his sleeve.

He collected fresh tree branches and peeled back some of the bark, exposing white strips on the wood. He then set the branches in front of the animals' watering troughs. As the animals came for water, apparently the white strips had the same effect as dim lights and soft music for providing a romantic mood. They mated in front of the branches and had numerous offspring. But Jacob would only set up the strips when the stronger animals came to water. He also separated the streaked and dark-colored animals into a separate flock so they would be more likely to bear similar offspring. In a period of six years he grew very wealthy with large flocks, camels, donkeys, and a number of servants.

Jacob was certainly clever and innovative. However, it seems that the extent of his success caused him to realize that he was not completely responsible for such over-whelming results. He later confessed that God had to be the One responsible for the results of his experiment (31:9).

On the Road Again (Genesis 31)

Jacob's success was hard to take for someone like Laban, who was used to getting the upper hand in all his business agreements, and Laban's sons resented it even more. Jacob was accumulating what they deemed should be their inheritance. So at this point God told Jacob it was time to pack up and head for home.

By now Jacob had enough of an entourage to form his own caravan. He hoisted the family onto camels, while he and his servants drove the livestock. He left quietly and without saying anything to Laban. But what Jacob didn't know is that Rachel had stolen her father's household gods, and brought them along.

The whole point of Jacob traveling to Laban's house was to find a wife who worshiped the true God. Yet Laban's family members believed in the magical power of mandrakes (30:14), had idols in the home (31:19), and practiced divination—an attempt to use some method (sleeping in a sacred place, casting lots, astrology, reading omens, etc.) to determine secret knowledge. Such practices would be strictly forbidden when the Hebrew law was given.

It took Laban three days to discover that Jacob and his daughters were gone, and another seven to catch up with them. When he did, he demanded to know why Jacob had snuck off with Rachel and Leah as if they were prisoners of war. He would have given them a big going-away party, he said, if Jacob had bothered to share his plans. And he seemed quite concerned that they had taken his gods.

Jacob, who didn't know that Rachel had snatched her father's household idols, denied taking anything of Laban's. Anyone found with the gods, he declared, would be put to death. A search was made from tent to tent. Rachel had hidden the idols beneath her saddle, and when Laban came to search her stuff, she told him she was having her period and couldn't stand up. (She's catching on. She deceived Jacob by not telling him what she had done, and Laban with a bluff he would never call.)

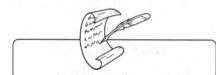

Manna from Heaven

Teraphim, statues or figurines representing household gods, were common in Syria and Palestine in Jacob's day. They had superstitious, religious, and legal significance; in fact, the ones in this story may even have functioned as the deed to Laban's estate.

In his ignorance, Jacob was angry that Laban would question his integrity. He emphasized the hard work he had done for his uncle and questioned Laban's honesty and motives during the past twenty years. Laban, on the other hand, explained that he saw everything of Jacob's as his own to some extent—his daughters, his grandchildren, and his flocks. Jacob had the right to them, to be sure, but it could all be traced back to Laban. But rather than escalate the argument, Laban and Jacob built a monument as a boundary and agreed to stay on their respective sides. Jacob made a sacrifice and prepared a family meal. The next morning Laban kissed and blessed his children and grandchildren. Then he returned home, as Jacob and crew continued on their way.

Getting All Out of Joint (Genesis 32)

Cutting himself loose from Laban must have given Jacob a sense of relief. But the farther away he got from Laban, the closer he got to Esau. And the last time they had been together, Esau had murder on the mind.

Along the way, Jacob was met by a number of angels—a reminder that God was still watching out for him. Jacob sent messengers ahead to tell Esau that he was on his way home. In response, the news came back that Esau was coming out to meet him with a group of 400 men.

Jacob responded to the news "in great fear and distress." And, as usual, his first instinct was to come up with a plan. He split his family and herds into two separate groups, hoping to give one group the opportunity to escape if Esau's men attacked the other.

But then to Jacob's credit, he stopped to pray. For once, he sounded sincere. Now that Jacob had a family to care for, he had to be concerned for their welfare as well as his own.

What Saith Thou?

If this stranger was really God, why couldn't he defeat Jacob easily?

He could have, of course, but more was at stake here than the score of a wrestling match. Perhaps God wanted to demonstrate the futility of wrestling with him, as Jacob had been doing symbolically throughout his life. Perhaps their literal struggle represented Jacob's inner struggle— Jacob the trickster wrestling with Jacob the man of God. When dawn broke and Jacob received his new name, it was clear that Israel the man of God would henceforth have the upper hand.

Then he set about preparing a magnificent peace offering for his brother. He selected an impressive gift assortment of animals: 220 goats, 220 sheep, 30 camels, 50 cattle, and 30 donkeys. He then divided the animals into groups and commissioned servants to take them out to meet Esau, staggering their departure. As each person and group of animals met Esau along the way, the servant was to say, "They belong to your servant Jacob. They are a gift sent to my lord Esau, and he is coming behind us" (Genesis 32:18). Jacob hoped that by the time the last servants came along, driving their flocks, Esau would be too floored to stay angry. This done, Jacob sent his family and possessions across a stream. After doing everything he could to avert a bloodbath, he prepared to spend the night by himself.

But a stranger came and wrestled with Jacob all night. Daybreak came, and they were still wrestling. Then the man touched the socket of Jacob's hip, wrenching it and putting it out of joint. "Let me go," the man said, but Jacob wouldn't until the man blessed him. "What is your name?" the man asked. When Jacob told him, the man replied that his new name would be Israel, which means "he struggles with God." Then Jacob asked the stranger's name. "Why do you ask?" the stranger replied, and he blessed Jacob and went away. Jacob named the place Peniel, which means "face of God." Jacob grasped that he had seen God up close and personal, and he was left with a limp to remind him of this extraordinary event.

He Saw Esau (Genesis 33; 35–36)

As soon as the wrestling match ended, Esau and his men came into sight. Jacob approached him and bowed seven times, demonstrating complete submission. But after 20 years, Esau was ready to make up. He had done well for himself during Jacob's absence and was eager to let bygones be bygones. He didn't even want to accept his brother's gift, but Jacob talked him into it. Esau turned back and went home, and Jacob set up camp nearby.

Snapshots

As if Jacob didn't have enough on his mind, his daughter, Dinah, found herself in the midst of a horrific family feud. This obscure story contains rape, the use of circumcision as a battle ploy, cold-blooded deceit, and mass murder. The details are in Genesis 34.

God told Jacob to return to Bethel ("house of God"), the place where Jacob had dreamt about the angels on the staircase. Before they left, Jacob instructed everyone with him to purify themselves, to get rid of their foreign gods and even to change their clothes. It was time for a fresh start.

At Bethel, God again appeared to Jacob and blessed him, reiterating that his name would be Israel and that kings and nations would come from him. Jacob commemorated the appearance with a stone pillar and an offering to God.

Rachel died while giving birth to a second son, whom Jacob named Benjamin. Isaac also died, leaving Jacob (Israel) as the family patriarch. The next chapter covers the life of Jacob and his sons.

The Least You Need to Know

➤ The promises God made to Abraham were handed down to Isaac and then to Jacob, although Jacob was the younger of two sons.

➤ Jacob had a life-long reputation as a schemer and deceiver, yet he was the person chosen by God and was blessed.

➤ Even though Jacob was chosen by God, his family had jealousy, anger, deceit, and other "issues."

➤ Jacob's name was changed to Israel, and his sons became the originators of the tribes of the nation of Israel.

Chapter 6

Joseph: Not Your Average Joe

In This Chapter

➤ The continuing saga of the family of Abraham, Isaac, and Jacob (Israel)

➤ More examples of how God works in mysterious ways

➤ How the Israelites ended up in Egypt

➤ Joseph's dreams, his coat of many colors, his fall, and his rise to power

---

One of the standard Smothers Brothers' bits was the accusation the two used to level at each other that "Momma always loved you more." We've already seen how this problem of family favorites caused trouble for Jacob and Esau. Their sufferings pale, however, compared to those of Jacob's son Joseph. As we will see, Joseph spent his entire life trying to overcome the aftermath of being his father's favorite.

Dream a Little Dream of Me (Genesis 37:1–11)

When first we encounter Joseph, he is 17 and something of a tattle-tale. The Bible says that he was tending flocks with his brothers and "brought their father a bad report about them." To make matters worse, Jacob (now called Israel) loved Joseph more than the rest of his sons, and the others knew it. Joseph, you may remember from Chapter 5, "Isaac and Jacob: Lessons in Family Dysfunction," was the 11th of 12 sons—but he was the first son of Israel's beloved wife Rachel. Perhaps he even resembled his mother in some ways. Israel displayed his preference for Joseph openly by giving him a richly

Manna from Heaven

A *cistern* was a large hole or tank created to store rain and spring water. Such tanks were numerous in this arid land. When cisterns were empty, they made ideal makeshift prisons because they were up to 100 feet deep and had covers that could be placed over the top.

ornamented robe—frequently referred to as his "coat of many colors." Joseph's 10 older brothers hated Joseph; they couldn't even bring themselves to speak in a civil manner to him.

As we have already seen, Joseph didn't exactly excel in tact and diplomacy. Things came to a head when he shared some unusual dreams he had been having with his family. Once he dreamed they were all binding sheaves of grain. His sheaf stood up and the other sheaves bowed down to it. Another night he dreamed that the sun, moon, and 11 stars were bowing down to him. As you might imagine, these dreams didn't sit well with Joseph's brothers. Even his father scolded him for his insensitivity. However, the Bible says, Jacob "kept the matter in mind."

Ten Angry Men (Genesis 37:12–36)

Indeed, Jacob did little to ease the family unrest. One day, while his older sons were out tending to the flocks, he sent Joseph to check on them. The brothers looked up and saw Joseph coming a long way off, and there and then they hatched a plot to kill him. Some of them speculated it would be a simple matter to toss him into a nearby cistern, leave him to die, and tell their father a wild animal had eaten him.

Fortunately, not all the brothers were equally intent on doing away with Joseph. Although Reuben, the oldest, agreed to the plan of sticking him in a cistern, he argued against killing him. In fact, Reuben intended to come back and rescue Joseph. So the brothers laid hold of Joseph, took off his ornamented robe, tossed him in the cistern, and sat down to eat a nice meal. It was right about then that a caravan of Ishmaelites passed by on the way from Gilead to Egypt.

Manna from Heaven

Gilead was southeast of the Sea of Galilee. "Balm of Gilead" was an oil highly prized for its medicinal value, and the **Ishmaelites** (the descendants of Ishmael) were taking it to Egypt to sell or trade.

Seeing the traders gave Judah an idea. Why kill Joseph when they could sell him into slavery and make a nice profit? So they pulled him up out of the cistern and sold him to the Ishmaelites for 20 shekels (about 8 ounces) of silver. Apparently Reuben wasn't present for the transaction, because he was very upset when he returned to the cistern and Joseph wasn't there.

To cover their shameful actions, the brothers slaughtered a goat and smeared Joseph's ornamented robe with its blood. Then they returned to their father with the bloody robe and told him they had found it. Jacob assumed that a wild animal had torn Joseph to pieces.

He mourned for many days and refused to be comforted. Meanwhile, the Ishmaelites arrived in Egypt and sold Joseph to one of Pharaoh's officials, a man named Potiphar.

Snapshots

When Judah gets a bit too sanctimonious, a huge skeleton comes tumbling out of his closet. It's a great story (but for mature audiences only) in Genesis 38.

"Mrs. Potiphar, I'm a Joe—Not a John" (Genesis 39)

Joseph may have been a bratty little brother, but he was special to God. Although his position had dropped from favored son to personal servant, everything he did prospered. Even Potiphar could see that God was with Joseph, and he gave him control of the whole household. From then on, Potiphar enjoyed tremendous success. He didn't have to worry about anything except what to have for dinner that night.

Potiphar's wife was also taken with Joseph, but in a different way. Seeing how handsome he was, she waited until her husband was out of the house and then tried one of those subtle Egyptian pick-up lines: "Come to bed with me!" (39:7) Politely, Joseph pointed out that if he did that, he would be betraying Potiphar and sinning against God. In other words, "No." Every day Potiphar's wife made the same offer, and every day Joseph declined. One day when no one was around, she finally grabbed Joseph and tried to force him into action. He got away, but his cloak stayed behind. Potiphar's wife came up with a spiteful plan. Calling loudly for the household servants, she showed the cloak and said that Joseph had made advances, then had run away when she screamed for help. When her husband got home, she told him the same story.

And you thought the Bible was dull!

Joseph didn't get much of a hearing. Furious, Potiphar threw him into prison. But God was with Joseph even in jail. Before long, he was essentially running the place for the warden.

A Baker, a Cupbearer, and a Hangman (Genesis 40)

It must not have been too difficult to wind up in prison in ancient Egypt. While Joseph was serving his time, Pharaoh became upset with his chief cupbearer and chief baker. He had them tossed into prison, where they were assigned to Joseph's care.

On the same night, the king's two officials had a dream. Both were disturbed because they didn't know what their dreams meant. Joseph volunteered to help: The power to interpret dreams, he said, comes from God.

Manna from Heaven

A *cupbearer* was responsible for tasting the food and wine to make sure it wasn't poisoned—an important position in a king's household.

The baker and cupbearer related their dreams to Joseph, and he interpreted them. The good news was that in three days the cupbearer would get his job back and be restored to Pharaoh's good graces. The bad news was that in three days the baker would be hanged from a tree for the birds to eat. Joseph asked the cupbearer to put in a good word for him to Pharaoh. He did not bother asking the baker.

As it turned out, the third day was Pharaoh's birthday, and things happened just as Joseph had said they would. The baker was hanged, and the chief cupbearer got his job back. But with jail behind him, the cupbearer also forgot all about Joseph.

Dreaming of the Cows 'n' the Corn (Genesis 41:1–40)

A year passed, and another year. One night, Pharaoh was troubled by weird dreams. He saw cows grazing beside the Nile; then seven scrawny cows walked up and ate seven healthy, fat cows. Next he dreamed that seven full, healthy heads of grain were swallowed up by seven thin and scorched heads of grain. Both dreams disturbed him enough to wake him up.

Pharaoh was worried. It didn't take a certified counselor to point out that the dreams had something in common, and that they were probably quite significant. He called in the best magicians and wise men of Egypt, but none of them could help him.

Suddenly the chief cupbearer remembered Joseph. The Bible doesn't actually say he smacked his palm to his forehead, but he might well have. He told Pharaoh about this Hebrew guy he had met in prison who was pretty good at interpreting dreams. You guessed it: Pharaoh called for Joseph.

Was it true that Joseph knew what dreams meant? Pharaoh asked. Joseph answered that he only repeated what God gave him to say. So Pharaoh recounted his dreams, and Joseph interpreted them. They meant the same thing. Seven years of good, abundant harvests (fat cows) would be followed by seven years of drought and famine (thin cows). Joseph advised Pharaoh to hire a storage consultant to direct grain collection for the next seven years, laying aside enough to sustain the nation when the famine struck. And because Joseph had just proven himself more knowledgeable than all the wise men in Egypt, that's who Pharaoh chose to head Operation Famine.

From Ex-Con to CEO (Genesis 41:41–57)

Just like that, Joseph was out of prison and serving as second in command over all of Egypt. Pharaoh took off his personal signet ring and gave it to Joseph, along with fine linen robes and a gold chain. Joseph got his own chariot and men to clear the way for him. To top it all off, Pharaoh gave him a wife from a good family.

During the seven years of abundance, more grain was produced than the Egyptians could even count. It was "like the sand of the sea"—eventually they had to stop keeping records. Joseph built large storehouses in all the cities.

Meanwhile, he had become the father of two sons, Manassah and Ephraim. *Manassah* means "forget": God was helping Joseph forget the injustices of his past. *Ephraim* means "fruitful": God had blessed Joseph richly in Egypt.

After seven years of abundance, a severe famine hit, just as Joseph had foretold. Joseph opened up his storehouses and began to sell the grain. Soon people were coming not only from Egypt but from all over the world.

I Never Forget a Face—Much Less 10 of Them (Genesis 42)

Joseph was 17 when we first saw him; now he was 37. Twenty years had passed since his brothers had sold him into slavery. Wouldn't it be ironic if the famine hit the folks back home and the brothers had to go down to search for food in Egypt, where Joseph was all-powerful?

Well, guess what. The famine did hit the land of Canaan, and Jacob sent his 10 older sons to Egypt to stock up. His youngest, Benjamin, he kept at home. Besides Joseph, Benjamin was Rachel's only son. Perhaps Jacob treated him with the same kind of favoritism he had previously shown Joseph.

When the gang arrived in Egypt, they stood before Joseph without recognizing him. He knew them, all right—but he didn't let on. The brothers bowed down, just as in Joseph's boyhood dreams. But Joseph accused them of being spies and put them all in custody for three days.

As panic set in, the brothers started telling Joseph their whole story, how they were 12 brothers with one still at home in the land of Canaan and one who "is no more." Joseph acted stony-faced. He demanded that one of them remain in Egypt while the others return and fetch the brother who

What Saith Thou?

Why didn't Joseph's brothers recognize him?

Joseph had adopted Egyptian dress and customs. He had even shaved, which nomadic men don't do. He was speaking Egyptian like a pro and using an interpreter to "translate" what his brothers were saying. Besides, who would ever expect to find someone they had sold into slavery running an empire two decades later?

remained in Canaan. (Perhaps Joseph was concerned that Benjamin was receiving treatment similar to what he had suffered at the hands of the ten older brothers.)

The brothers started bickering among themselves, convinced that God was finally punishing them for abandoning their little brother two decades ago. Joseph understood every word they said, though they didn't realize it. Overcome, he left the room and wept. Then, resuming his somber facade, he had Simeon tied up in front of the others to languish in prison while they returned to Canaan.

Before they left he supplied them with provisions for the journey and had his servants fill the grain bags the brothers had brought with them. Then, unbeknownst to them, he had each brother's grain money hidden in his newly purchased sack of grain. Imagine their consternation when one of the brothers discovered this on the way home. They began to tremble. What could it mean? God must certainly have it in for them. And when they got home and found that *everyone's* silver was in the bags, they really got scared. Jacob was beside himself. "Joseph is no more and Simeon is no more, and now you want to take Benjamin!" And he refused to hear of their going back.

Ben There, Done That (Genesis 43–44)

After a while, however, they began to run out of food again. Egypt was still the only take-out place around, and the brothers knew they could never get food there without complying with the Egyptian fellow's demands. It was Judah who finally persuaded Jacob that he must let them take Benjamin, or the whole family would starve, little children and all. Judah took the responsibility for Benjamin's safety upon himself.

What Saith Thou?

Why didn't Joseph eat with his brothers?

Egyptians were pretty picky about whom they socialized with. For one thing, they didn't care at all for shepherds (46:34). In addition, there might have been some significant religious/cultural biases that caused them to look down on Hebrews. In any case, Joseph was playing to the hilt his role as an Egyptian "stranger."

Poor Jacob had no choice. He assembled a large gift basket of Canaan's finest products and made sure the sons took double the silver—to return the first payment and to pay for the new shipment of grain.

When Joseph saw Benjamin with his brothers, he had them all taken to his own house, where a meal was prepared. This did nothing to comfort the brothers. They feared he would hold them accountable for not paying for the grain they had previously taken, and possibly even seize them and their possessions as restitution. They tried to explain their plight to Joseph's steward, but he told them not to worry. He said their payment had been received; perhaps their God had rewarded them with the silver in their sacks.

When Joseph got home, the brothers gave him the gifts they had brought. He inquired about their father and then turned his attention to Benjamin. At the sight of his little brother, Joseph once again had to leave the room to hide his tears. When he had composed himself, he ordered the food to be served.

When the food came out, Joseph saw to it that Benjamin's share was five times what the others received. Later, as he loaded up their donkeys with grain and prepared to send them on their way, he gave secret instructions that his own silver drinking cup be placed in Benjamin's bag. The brothers rode off early in the morning. They were hardly out of the city, however, when Joseph's steward came up behind in hot pursuit, demanding to know why Joseph's cup had been stolen after he had been so kind to them.

The brothers vigorously denied taking anything of Joseph's. They told the steward that if it was found on them, he could kill whoever had it and the rest of them would become his slaves. A search was conducted beginning with the oldest and ending with the youngest. And as Benjamin's sack was opened, out tumbled Joseph's cup!

Distraught, they packed up the donkeys again and returned to Joseph's home, where they offered to become his slaves. No, no, Joseph said, only the guilty party would have to stay. The others were free to leave. Of course, this was all an elaborate test. Joseph wanted to know what his brothers would do. Would they abandon Benjamin, as they had abandoned Joseph, or had they learned their lesson? The extra food allotted to Benjamin was probably intended to see if the others might be harboring jealousy toward Benjamin, Rachel's other son. Now they had an excuse to leave him behind. Would they act upon it?

The brothers passed the test. Humbly, Judah pleaded with Joseph for his little brother, telling of Jacob's special love for Benjamin, and how he had already lost one beloved son. The loss of the youngest would kill his father, and it would be all their doing. Judah could not bear to bring such suffering on his father. He urged Joseph to take him as a slave instead, saying that he had pledged himself to see that Benjamin returned safely.

Family Reunion (Genesis 45–47:12)

At this, Joseph could no longer keep up his charade. He sent all the other Egyptians out of the room, and all they could hear was his loud crying. Then Joseph told his brothers who he was.

The brothers were terrified. Years ago they had abused the power that came with age, strength, and numbers. Now Joseph was the one with all the power. He could have them killed, sold, or imprisoned for life, and no one could stop him. Joseph's brothers stood speechless, unable to answer him.

But Joseph wasn't angry with them. He wanted no revenge. He saw now that God had brought these events about to save the region from starvation.

He told his brothers to hurry home and return with their father. There were still five years of famine to go: Better for everyone to relocate near Joseph in Egypt than to keep making trips back and forth. Having told them what to do, he embraced each one of them and wept with them. Then they all talked together as family for the first time in 20 years.

When Pharaoh heard the story of how Joseph had been reunited with his brothers, he insisted on picking up the bill for their move to Egypt. He gave them the best land in the area to settle in. He provided Egyptian-made carts to move them. And he told them not to worry about moving their belongings: He would provide them with Egyptian goods when they arrived.

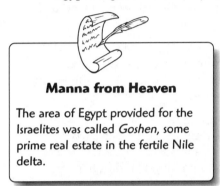

Manna from Heaven

The area of Egypt provided for the Israelites was called *Goshen*, some prime real estate in the fertile Nile delta.

Joseph gave all his brothers new clothes. He sent his father 10 donkeys loaded with Egyptian souvenirs and 10 more with grain, food, and other provisions for his trip.

Jacob was stunned to discover that Joseph was not only alive, but also second-in-command over all of Egypt. He was eager to move, but he was careful to stop along the way and offer sacrifices to God. In response, God appeared to Jacob in a vision, told him not to worry about moving to Egypt, and promised to eventually return his family members to the land of Canaan again.

In all, about 70 Israelite families relocated to Egypt. It was a potentially embarrassing situation for Joseph; Egyptians had absolutely no respect for shepherds. But Pharaoh was gracious and even offered to let them tend his own livestock. At his request, he was introduced to Jacob, the patriarch of whom he had heard so much. This meeting of the head of the Egyptian empire and the head of the Israelite family might have seemed a little one-sided to onlookers, and so it was; Pharaoh was being gracious. However, the story of the Hebrew sojourn in Egypt was only just beginning.

A Fair Deal from Pharaoh? (Genesis 47:13–26)

Joseph didn't let family matters interfere with his job. With five years of famine yet to go, people were willing to do almost anything for food. At first they paid for grain, but their money eventually ran out. When all the money had been transferred to Pharaoh's treasury, the people paid Joseph in livestock instead. That lasted about a year, and then Pharaoh had all the livestock. When the people again grew hungry, all they had left was themselves and their land, so Joseph bought their land for Pharaoh with additional food supplies, and the people became slaves—serfs, to be precise. What a guy.

Even after Pharaoh possessed the money, livestock, and land, the people grew hungry again. Joseph then instituted a program to provide people with seed to grow more food. The only expectation was that they give back one-fifth to Pharoah when the crops came in. This agreement became law in Egypt, and the people didn't seem to mind because Joseph had saved their lives.

The Last of the Patriarchs (Genesis 47:28–50:26)

Jacob was 130 when he moved to Egypt and lived there seventeen years before he died. He made Joseph promise not to bury him there because he wanted to be buried with his own ancestors.

When Jacob started getting ill, he gave his blessing to Joseph's sons, Manassah and Ephraim, promising to consider them equal to his own children. As the old man reached to lay his hands on the heads of his grandchildren to bless them, Joseph placed Manassah, the older, on Jacob's right so that his right hand would be on Manassah's head, signifying the greater share of blessing. But Jacob crossed his hands, placing his right hand on Ephraim's head and his left hand on Manassah's. Joseph tried to correct him, but Jacob explained that although both sons would become great, the younger of the two would become more prominent.

In the culture of ancient Israel, the firstborn in families were supposedly the more important ones. Yet in just a few generations we've seen Isaac chosen over Ishmael, Jacob chosen over Esau, Joseph (the second-youngest) chosen over his brothers, and now Ephraim chosen over Manassah. As we'll see as we go through the Bible, though people may follow certain rules, God is not constrained by our traditions and expectations.

Having blessed Ephraim and Manassah, Jacob called for his 12 sons, to bless and to withhold blessing, depending on their deeds. The oldest son, Reuben, he castigated for sleeping with his father's concubine—a symbolic (but somewhat premature) gesture of taking his father's place (see 35:22). For this misdeed Jacob deprived him of his place of honor as eldest. Simeon and Levi, the second and third sons, he blasted for massacring the people of Shechem in retaliation for the rape of their sister, Dinah (Genesis 34). They, too, would go without blessing.

The blessing of the oldest son thus fell upon Judah, fourth in number but destined for leadership. He had already stepped into the role in his dealings with Jacob and Joseph. References to "the lion of Judah" begin here and continue throughout the Bible. King David and his descendants (including Jesus) will come from the tribe of Judah.

What Saith Thou?

Doesn't Jacob's blessing seem arbitrary and unfair? Couldn't he just let bygones be bygones?

Any attempt to determine "fairness" by our standards is difficult in certain Bible texts. For example, Judah was the one who slept with his daughter-in-law because he thought she was a prostitute. And it was his big idea to cash in Joseph's freedom for a bit of spending money. Yet he is the one blessed by Jacob and who takes a leading role among his siblings.

However, because Jacob had accepted responsibility for both of Joseph's sons, Manassah and Ephraim, it is Joseph who receives the double portion that frequently went to the oldest son. And although Jacob was addressing individuals, his blessing was applied to the tribes that would eventually descend from them.

Jacob died not long after blessing his sons, and Joseph returned his body to his homeland to be buried, as he had promised his father he would. The Egyptians formed a large processional of chariots and horsemen to accompany him. Then everyone returned to settle in Egypt.

With Jacob dead, Joseph's brothers once again worried that Joseph might decide to retaliate. They sent him a message begging forgiveness, then went to see him in person, offering to become his servants. Joseph reiterated his forgiveness and his assurance that he would do nothing to harm them.

Joseph lived to be 110. When the time came for him to die, he made an unusual request. He knew God would return the descendants of Jacob (Israel) to the land promised to Abraham. Desiring to be buried with the rest of his family in Canaan, he left instructions for his bones to accompany the people when they returned. The Book of Genesis ends with Joseph dying, being embalmed, and being placed in a coffin in Egypt.

We've taken four whole chapters to get through the first book of the Bible, but these have been foundational stories. You'll need to be familiar with this part of the Bible before you can understand much of the rest. From this point on, we'll be covering more material, perhaps in a bit less depth, but with more momentum and at a much quicker pace. Next comes the not-so-ordinary life of a pretty ordinary guy—Moses.

Potent Quotables

"Don't be afraid. Am I in the place of God? You intended to harm me, but God intended it for good to accomplish what is now being done, the saving of many lives" (Genesis 50:19–20).

Joseph's words to his brothers reveal a level of spiritual maturity that allowed him to see the pitfalls of life from God's perspective, not just his own. Joseph's innocent suffering could have led him to retaliate, but he responded with love and refused to hold grudges. It could be said the rest of Israelite history rested on that single choice.

The Least You Need to Know

➤ With Joseph, yet another younger sibling in Abraham's line was chosen over an older one.

➤ Thanks to God's faithfulness to Joseph after Joseph being sold, his family survived the famine and was given a place to live in Egypt.

➤ The patriarchs of Israel were an earthy bunch whose dedication to God exceeded their faults as individuals.

➤ Joseph is a good example of hope for all people reared in dysfunctional families.

Chapter 7

Moses: God's Reluctant Hero

In This Chapter

➤ God calls a leader to deliver the Israelites from Egyptian bondage

➤ How people tend to prefer known slavery to unknown freedom

➤ The Israelites return to their Promised Land

➤ The burning bush, the plagues, the exodus, crossing the Red Sea, the Ten Commandments, the golden calf, the tabernacle, rules and regulations

It is said that some people have leadership thrust upon them. Perhaps no one has been more reluctant than Moses to accept the leadership role to which God called him. Yet after he accepted the responsibility, Moses established a standard of leadership that few others have ever come close to equaling.

Four Centuries of Decline, from Joe to Moe (Exodus 1)

When Jacob moved his family from Canaan to Egypt, they had the best of everything. They settled on the most fertile land, they were in Pharaoh's good favor, and the entire nation owed Joseph a debt of gratitude. That's how the Book of Genesis ends. But as we move into the Book of Exodus, time has passed. Pharaohs have come and gone. The Israelites have flourished and are very numerous. A Pharaoh has come to power who knows nothing about Joseph—and doesn't care to find out. This Pharaoh is more concerned about the great numbers of foreigners (Israelites) cluttering up Egypt. He

How could Joseph be forgotten after saving the entire Egyptian empire?

By the time the Israelites left Egypt, they had been there for 430 years (Exodus 12:40). Even with all the modern advancements in history-recording resources, how much do you know about the music, culture, or key figures of the mid-1500s? No doubt Joseph's accomplishments were forgotten over time—or perhaps attributed to legend rather than literal truth.

feared that if Egypt went to war, these Canaanite settlers might side with the enemy and overthrow their hosts.

This new Pharaoh's solution was to enslave the Israelites. The Egyptians put slave masters over them and forced them to build cities. But the worse the Egyptians treated them, the more the Israelites seemed to multiply. Soon a bitter rivalry developed between Egyptians and Israelites. It got so bad that Pharaoh commanded the Hebrew midwives to kill all the male children they delivered. The midwives refused to carry out this order. They told Pharaoh that the strong Hebrew women were giving birth before the midwives could get there. So Pharaoh demanded that every newborn Hebrew boy be thrown into the Nile River.

Rollin' on the River (Exodus 2:1–10)

Moses was born under this death sentence. His mother kept his birth secret as long as possible, but after three months she could hide him no longer. She made a papyrus basket, coated it with tar, placed her baby in the basket, and launched the basket onto the Nile. Then her daughter stationed herself at a distance to see what happened.

It just so happened that Pharaoh's daughter had gone to the Nile for bath time. She saw a basket in the reeds and found a crying Hebrew baby inside. She adopted the baby, but at three months old he still needed more than she could offer. Moses' sister "happened by" and asked Pharaoh's daughter if she would like one of the Hebrew women to nurse the baby until he got older. Of course she did! She named the baby Moses ("drew out") because she had drawn him out of the water. Then she paid Moses' own mother to raise him until he was old enough to live with her.

Hit and Run (Exodus 2:11–25)

So Moses grew up in Pharaoh's palace as an Egyptian. Yet as he saw the hard labor imposed on the Israelites, it seems that Moses continued to identify with them. One day he came across an Egyptian beating a Hebrew worker. Looking around and seeing no one, Moses killed the Egyptian and hid his body in the sand. The next day he saw two Hebrews fighting and tried to break it up. One of them asked, "Are you thinking of killing me as you killed the Egyptian?" (Exodus 2:14).

Moses thought his crime had been a secret. But now that it was out in the open, he had to run or else Pharaoh would have killed *him*. He fled to Midian, where he soon found himself in another fight. Seven women were trying to water some sheep, but a group of trouble-making shepherds were giving them a hard time. Moses ran off the shepherds and watered the flock for the women.

The Midianite women invited Moses to their home to meet their father, Reuel ("friend of God") also called Jethro ("his excellency"). Moses ended up staying with the family, marrying one of the daughters, Zipporah, and having a son. Time passed. The Pharaoh who had tried to kill Moses died. But the Israelites continued to suffer at the hands of the Egyptians.

You Can't Beat the Bush (Exodus 3–4)

Manna from Heaven

Midian the person was a son of Abraham by his second wife, Keturah (Genesis 25:1–2). The *land of Midian* during the time of Moses was east of the Jordan River and the Dead Sea, and extended southward into the Sinai Peninsula.

One day, while he was tending Jethro's flock, something caught Moses' eye. How strange: a bush that appeared to be on fire, yet didn't burn up. As he went in for a closer look, suddenly he heard the voice of God calling him by name and telling him to remove his shoes because this was holy ground. Moses was scared, but he obeyed. The voice identified himself: "I am the God of your father, the God of Abraham, the God of Isaac and the God of Jacob" (Exodus 3:6). God explained He was aware of the sufferings of the Israelites and that it was time to do something about it. Therefore, he wanted Moses to go tell Pharaoh to let the people leave Egypt. We discover later that, "Moses was a very humble man, more humble than anyone else on the face of the earth" (Numbers 12:3). He was quite reluctant to step into the job description God was suggesting. Consequently, he used a number of excuses to try to avoid this assignment. Who am I, he asked, a man "slow of speech and tongue," to go before Pharaoh and lead the Israelites? Can't someone else do this?

To each of Moses' objections, God gave the same assurance: He would be with Moses every step of the way. But Moses was not convinced. He was having a hard time picturing himself going back to Egypt and telling people that God had sent him to confront Pharoah. "Suppose I go to the Israelites," he said, "and say to them, 'The God of your fathers has sent me to you,' and they ask me, 'What is his

Manna from Heaven

God's name for himself was "YHWH" (probably pronounced *Yahweh)*. The exact meaning is shrouded in mystery, evoking presence and power. Of all the names and titles for God in the Old Testament, this one is the most personal. Over time, the Jewish people came to hold the name in such respect that, to this day, they will not speak or write it for fear of profaning it in some way.

Another name for God is "Adonai," which means "my great Lord." This title is used frequently in the Bible and is translated as "the Lord." The name *Jehovah* is a composite of YHWH and *Adonai.*

name?' what shall I tell them?" God said, "I AM WHO I AM. This is what you are to say to the Israelites: 'I AM has sent me to you.'"

God also told Moses to take his brother, Aaron, along as spokesperson.

Snapshots

Blood. Snakes. Leprosy. God gave Moses some impressive signs to prove his authority (Exodus 4:1–9).

So Moses set off for Egypt with his family. But on the journey, something happened that the Bible does not attempt to explain. We are told that "The Lord met Moses and was about to kill him" (4:24). We don't know how. All we know is how Zipporah responded: She immediately circumcised their son. Perhaps Moses' wife wasn't fond of the Hebrew rite of circumcision and had resisted it. And perhaps Moses had contracted an incapacitating disease that almost killed him, leaving his wife to do what was necessary. We can't be sure. Later we learn that Zipporah was back at home with her father and her two sons. Conceivably, they might have turned around at this point, leaving Moses to continue his assignment alone for a while.

Whatever happened, Moses got well, met up with Aaron, and performed the signs God had given him for the Israelites. They believed him and worshipped God.

Bricks Without Straw (Exodus 5–6)

But Moses wasn't nearly as persuasive when he met with Pharaoh. He repeated exactly what God told him, but Pharaoh had no respect for Moses—or Moses' God, for that matter. To teach the Hebrews a lesson, Pharaoh ordered the Egyptian slave drivers to stop providing them with straw. From now on they were to gather their own straw, while maintaining their regular quota of bricks.

God had warned Moses that Pharaoh would be resistant. But that didn't make it any easier when his own people accused him of making their lives more miserable than before. God wanted the Israelites to see that he was essentially going to do the impossible to free them, leading them out of Egypt and making them his people (6:6–8). But the people couldn't see beyond their immediate suffering (6:9).

The Plague's the Thing (Exodus 7–11)

Moses needed a pep talk after his first failure with Pharaoh. God assured him that all was going according to plan, and he sent Moses and Aaron back for another round. This time Aaron threw down his staff and it became a snake. Pharaoh called for his magicians, and they did the same thing. Aaron's snake ate the other ones. And so the contest escalated. One after another, as Pharaoh refused to relent, God brought a series of full-scale plagues on Egypt.

1. The Nile River (their primary water source) was turned to blood.

2. Frogs, frogs, frogs appeared—in beds, in ovens, and just about everywhere a frog could go.

3. "All the dust throughout the land of Egypt became gnats." People and animals were swatting like crazy.

4. Dense swarms of flies appeared—there were no screens in Egypt.

5. A massive plague killed most of the Egyptian livestock.

6. The people and remaining animals broke out in awful festering boils.

7. The worst storm in the history of Egypt produced devastating hail stones that destroyed their crops.

8. Locusts covered the ground and ate what was left.

9. A thick, spooky darkness covered Egypt for three days.

Needless to say, Egypt was having a difficult year. After the fourth plague, when things got unbearable, Pharaoh began promising to let the Israelites go out to the wilderness and worship, provided they came right back. But as soon as the plague had been lifted, he would go back on his promises.

What Saith Thou?

Why didn't Pharaoh's magicians do something to prevent or negate the plagues?

The Bible says that the power of Moses and Aaron came from God, yet Pharaoh's magicians used "secret arts" to emulate many of the same miracles. They successfully accomplished the staff-to-snake transformation, the water-to-blood change, and the appearance of frogs. (It is debated whether their magic was real or sleight of hand.)

Yet, from that point on, even the magicians believed that what Moses commanded came from "the finger of God" (8:19). (When the boils hit, even they were too sore to stand before Moses.) And if they were really on the ball, surely they would have changed the blood back to water and gotten rid of the frogs rather than making matters worse.

God's displeasure became even more emphatic when the plagues began to hit only where the Egyptians lived. The land of Goshen, where the Israelites resided, had good weather, growing crops, healthy people and animals, and light. Even the Egyptian people could see that Moses knew what he was doing. When he predicted hail, for example, many of the Egyptians hurried to shelter their animals and crops. So even though Pharaoh could be pigheaded, the Egyptian citizens were beginning to respond to Moses.

The First Passover (Exodus 11–12:30)

Then came the 10th and final plague. Moses brought God's terrible message to Pharaoh: Relent, or God would kill the firstborn of every family in Egypt, humans and animals alike. Pharaoh would not listen. His heart was completely hardened.

This time the Israelites were told to prepare so that the devastation would not fall upon them as well. Every family was to choose a lamb for a sacrifice: a year-old male with no defects. They were to set it apart and care for it for four days, after which it was to be slaughtered, roasted, and eaten. The lamb's blood was to be smeared on the sides and top of their door frames. Any home without this protection would be hit by the coming plague; those marked in blood would be *passed over*.

Manna from Heaven

The term *Passover* was instituted to remember and celebrate how God had "passed over" homes with the blood sacrifice.

The Passover meal was to be prepared and eaten in haste, in preparation for a journey. The people were to dress in sandals and a cloak and, with staff in hand, eat unleavened (quickly baked, unraised) bread. What was about to happen would be regarded by Jewish people ever after as the greatest event of their history.

At midnight on the designated night, God struck down the firstborn of every family in Egypt, from the family of Pharaoh to the families of imprisoned felons. Pharaoh didn't even wait until morning. He summoned Moses and Aaron and told them to take the Israelites and leave. Pharaoh was so shaken that he even asked for a blessing for himself.

An Order of 600,000 Israelite Families—to Go! (Exodus 12:31–13)

The Egyptians were so eager to get rid of the Israelites that they gave them anything they needed or requested. So in the middle of the night, a group of 600,000 families departed from the place they had lived for the past 430 years.

God realized this was a stressful time for the Israelites. Rather than put them on a course straight for the Promised Land, God guided them on a route that would allow them to avoid many of their enemies. A skirmish right away would be likely to drive them back into the relative security of Egyptian slavery. As they fell in and began their march beside the Red Sea, among the things they were carrying were the bones of Joseph, who had asked to be buried in the Promised Land with his ancestors.

God went before them in a cloudy pillar during the day and a pillar of fire after dark, bright enough so they could travel at night if they wished. One or the other of these two representations of God's presence was always before the people. As they went along, God explained to Moses that he was going to take the people to a place where Pharaoh would think they were vulnerable and would come after them.

Stalk Like an Egyptian (Exodus 14–15:21)

Meanwhile, back at the pyramids, Pharaoh was having second thoughts. After all, he had just allowed a slave force of more than half a million men to simply walk away. Downsizing may have its benefits, but this was a tad extreme. Pharaoh decided to organize an enormous posse.

The Israelites were traveling on foot—men, women, children—all carrying their belongings. Pharaoh came after them with full military might: "all Pharaoh's horses and chariots, horsemen and troops" (Exodus 14:9). The Israelites had camped beside the Red Sea, probably gazing out over the peaceful waters. When they turned around and looked the other way, they saw the army of the Egyptian empire coming right at them.

Terrified, the Israelites asked Moses whether he didn't think that living as slaves in Egypt would be preferable to dying in the desert. Moses told them to stand firm and see God's deliverance.

The pillar of cloud that rose before the Israelites moved behind them, providing light on the Israelite side and darkness for the Egyptians. Moses stretched out his hand toward the sea, and a powerful wind divided the water so that it rose up on either side, leaving a path in the middle. So long as Moses kept stretching out his hand, the sea remained like this all night long, as the Israelites made their way to the other side. When the Egyptians showed signs of closing in, God caused their chariot wheels to fall off and an atmosphere of confusion to drift over the entire Egyptian army.

Once across the sea, Moses turned back and stretched out his hand again. This time the waters came crashing down on the stranded Egyptian army. We are told that "not one of them survived" (14:28). The Israelites sang a song of victory to God as Miriam, Moses' sister, led a tambourine band, singing and dancing in celebration.

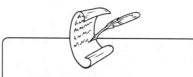

Manna from Heaven

Where was the *Red Sea?* It was once thought to be what is now the Gulf of Suez, between Egypt and the Sinai Peninsula. But another translation is *"Reed"* Sea—and reeds don't grow in salt water! For this and other reasons, many people now think that the "Red (Reed) Sea" was probably one of the larger freshwater lakes on the eastern side of the Nile delta.

Hey Manna, Manna (Exodus 15:22–17:7)

The Israelites were a free people again. However, the real test was just beginning. Before long, they were in the desert without water. The water they did find was bitter and undrinkable. These people had been slaves all their lives. They had never had to make decisions or solve their own problems; their Egyptian overseers had done that for them. Now, confronted with the real world, they reacted just like children. They whined.

It was a pattern they were to follow for 40 years. Things got tough, they blamed Moses, Moses turned to God, and God came to the rescue. First it was the thirst problem; then it was the hunger problem. The people were longing openly for the good old days of slavery, when at least they had food available. So God sent a flock of quail that covered the camp. The next morning a strange dew settled on the ground, evaporating to leave frost-like flakes on the ground. Moses told the people this would be each day's allotment of bread which they were to gather. The exception was that the stuff wouldn't be available on the Sabbath, so the day before each Sabbath they were to gather two days' worth. Otherwise, they were to take only what they needed for each day. People who tried to store it found the remainder became stinky and filled with maggots. Since they had never seen anything like this before, they called it *manna*, meaning, "What is it?"

Apparently manna was not only convenient but tasty. It tasted like wafers made with honey. For forty years God used this method of providing daily bread for his people.

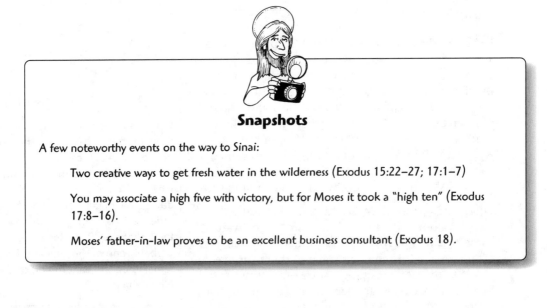

Snapshots

A few noteworthy events on the way to Sinai:

> Two creative ways to get fresh water in the wilderness (Exodus 15:22–27; 17:1–7)
>
> You may associate a high five with victory, but for Moses it took a "high ten" (Exodus 17:8–16).
>
> Moses' father-in-law proves to be an excellent business consultant (Exodus 18).

Smoke on the Mountain, and Fire in the Sky (Exodus 19–31)

Three months after leaving Egypt, the Israelites arrived in the Desert of Sinai, which is toward the southern tip of the Sinai Peninsula. There God "called a meeting" with Moses on top of Mount Sinai. To everyone else, the mountain was strictly off-limits. This was going to be a momentous occasion, and the sanctity of the site was to be respected.

At the appointed time, a thick cloud settled over the mountain. Lightning flashed, thunder rolled, and there came the sound of a loud trumpet blast. Smoke billowed up until the whole mountain was covered. The people trembled; the trumpet sound got louder. And when Moses spoke to God, the voice of God answered him.

The Bible says that "God descended to the top of Mount Sinai and called Moses to the top of the mountain" (19:20). There God gave Moses the Ten Commandments, as well as other laws to help the Israelites govern their relationships, possessions, social interaction, and every other area of life. God promised to guard his people as they continued into the Promised Land, and he warned them not to get involved with any foreign gods they might encounter along the way.

How many of the Ten Commandments can you name? Here they are:

1. You shall have no other gods before God.

2. You shall not make for yourself an idol.

3. You shall not misuse the name of the Lord your God.

4. Remember the Sabbath day by keeping it holy.

5. Honor your father and your mother.

6. You shall not murder.

7. You shall not commit adultery.

8. You shall not steal.

9. You shall not give false testimony against your neighbor.

10. You shall not covet.

After some of the initial laws were established, Moses went down and reported to the people, reading them what had been recorded so far. The Israelites agreed to everything and worshipped God with offerings.

Unholy Cow! (Exodus 32–34)

But the next time Moses went up the mountain, he stayed much longer—forty days, in fact. Moses was witnessing some incredible sights (Exodus 24:9–18), but it seemed like an eternity to the people waiting for him to return. They had seen him ascend a trembling, smoke-covered mountain, and they had no guarantee that he was even still alive. At last they decided to move on. Without Moses, however, they weren't sure how they were going to bring God's guidance with them. They implored Aaron to create some gods that would go before them to lead them. More than likely, this was a request for tangible symbols of God, not substitute gods. Aaron had the Israelites bring him their golden earrings, which he melted down and reformed into the shape of a calf.

In a disturbingly ironic scene, God and Moses are atop Sinai literally "carving in stone" the rules for the Israelites to live by. Meanwhile, at the foot of the mountain, the people were making offerings to God at an altar in front of the golden calf. They were also eating, drinking, and "running wild." Angrily, God told Moses what was going on at the foot of the mountain. He threatened to wipe out all those "stiff-necked people" and start over with a new nation that could make Moses proud. But Moses interceded on behalf of his people. Then he took the tablets and headed down the mountain.

But when he saw the scene with his own eyes, he was furious. He threw down the tablets, shattering them to pieces. Then he ground the golden calf into powder, threw the powder into the water supply, and made the people drink it. In the aftermath of this event, about 3,000 people died and God struck the camp with a plague.

Moses went back for another 40 days and made new tablets, by which time his face glowed so brightly from being in God's presence that he had to wear a veil to keep from blinding people.

Moses set up a "tent of meeting" outside the camp. When Moses went into this tent, the pillar of cloud would position itself at the entrance. The Israelites would watch from their own tents and worship God. We are told that "The Lord would speak to Moses face to face, as a man speaks with his friend" (33:11).

What Saith Thou?

Why choose a calf, of all things, to be a god?

Most early cultures held the bull in high esteem, or even revered it as sacred. The Egyptians had a bull-god named Apis, but it is unlikely Aaron had this foreign deity in mind, even though the people had just come from there. More likely, the bull was chosen to represent the true God because it symbolized fertility, vitality, and strength.

The Group Regroups (Exodus 35–40)

The period of time after Moses returned from Sinai was dedicated to constructing and furnishing the tabernacle, the portable place of worship as the Israelites traveled through the wilderness. Aaron was designated by God to serve as high priest. He was assisted by his sons (Exodus 28:1–13).

Snapshots

The details involved in the planning and construction of the tabernacle are numerous. Read about the furnishings, floor plan, building materials, and even the two gifted "tool men" who were put in charge. It's all in Exodus 25–31 and 35–40.

When it was finally completed, Moses inspected it and blessed the people for completing the work just as God had commanded. In an elaborate and portable chest known as the Ark of the Covenant, Moses placed the Ten Commandments. The Ark was kept in the Most Holy Place (also known as the Holy of Holies), the most sacred part of the tabernacle. When everything was in place, the cloud that symbolized God's presence filled the tabernacle. From this point on, when the cloud lifted from the tabernacle, the people knew it was time to move on. Otherwise, they would stay and camp.

Snapshots

Did you know Miriam, Moses' sister, once got a severe case of temporary leprosy for slandering the man who was "more humble than anyone else on the face of the earth"? It's true! See for yourself in Numbers 12.

Spy versus Spy (Numbers 13–14)

After mistakes, rebellions, and hardships, the people finally arrived at the boundary of the Promised Land. But do you think they just waltzed in and pitched their tents? Afraid not. The land, you see, was already inhabited. So a leader from each tribe was sent to spy it out and bring back a report. When the spies returned, they brought pomegranates, figs, and a single cluster of grapes so huge it was carried on a pole between two of them. It was a sure sign that, yes, the land was fruitful and productive.

However, the cities in the land were large and well-protected. The people themselves seemed huge. The Israelite men had felt "like grasshoppers" beside them (13:33). The majority of the spies (ten of the twelve) felt there was no way to overpower the people living there. But Joshua and Caleb protested and reminded the people that God had led them to this point, so they should have faith and move forward. But as the opposing factions continued the heated debate, the majority of Israelites eventually prepared to stone Joshua and Caleb, fire Moses, and elect a new leader to take them back to Egypt.

Snapshots

Make sure these terrific stories don't get lost in the wilderness as the Israelites are wandering around:

An earthquake swallows a group of rebels alive—and fire falls from heaven to finish off the rest (Numbers 16).

Aaron's staff goes through a growth spurt (Numbers 17).

Moses cracks under the pressure to appease his whining people—and discovers even he isn't exempt from God's discipline (Numbers 20:1–13).

A bronze serpent negates the deadly effects of some very real venomous snakes (Numbers 21:4–9).

And now a few words from our donkey—the strange tale of Balaam (Numbers 22).

A messy way to end an orgy (Numbers 25:1–9).

Zelophehad's daughters take a stand for Old Testament women's rights—and succeed (Numbers 27:1–11; 36).

Again God was ready to wipe out the whole bunch, and again Moses interceded. God forgave the people, but he refused to reward them for such obstinacy. They would have to wander in the wilderness as nomads for another 40 years, until everyone over the age of 20 had died. The only exceptions were to be Joshua and Caleb, who had demonstrated strong faith. Naturally, the Israelites didn't particularly enjoy this news of what was about to happen. They *then* determined to go ahead and enter the Promised Land—no matter what God had just told them. Moses warned that God was not with them, but they wouldn't listen. As a result, they were severely routed.

Generation Next (Numbers 27–35)

During the wanderings in the desert, Aaron and Miriam (Moses' brother and sister) eventually died. God appointed Joshua to lead the people the rest of the way into the Promised Land. Already some cities were being designated for the Levites (the priests), others as cities of refuge for those who had killed someone unintentionally. The rest of the land was parceled out among the other tribes. All that was left to do was go into the land and possess it, which is where the next chapter begins.

Before we move on, however, let's notice what we skipped by focusing on the narrative. The books of Leviticus, Numbers, and Deuteronomy are filled with rules, laws, and ceremonies. For example, in Leviticus you will find these:

➤ Descriptions for the various kinds of offerings (Chapters 1–7)

➤ Ordination ceremonies for the priests (Chapters 8–9)

➤ The procedure for the "Day of Atonement," the most holy day of the Jewish year—and the source of our word "scapegoat" (Chapter 16)

➤ A description of various Hebrew feasts to be held regularly (Chapter 23)

In Numbers, you will find this information:

➤ A census of the Israelites (Chapter 1)

➤ Camp assignments by tribe (Chapter 2)

➤ Priestly information (Chapters 3–8)

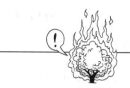

Potent Quotables

"If the Lord is pleased with us, he will lead us into that land, a land flowing with milk and honey, and will give it to us. Only do not rebel against the Lord. And do not be afraid of the people of the land, because we will swallow them up. Their protection is gone, but the Lord is with us." (Numbers 14:8–9)

The faith of Joshua and Caleb was sure and certain. Too bad they were in the minority.

Deuteronomy is essentially a collection of Moses' speeches, ending with Moses blessing the tribes just before his death. After this speech of blessing, Moses climbed Mount Nebo and looked into the Promised Land. Moses died on the mountain and was buried by God, no one ever knew exactly where. The last three verses of Deuteronomy provide a fitting epitaph for this man of God:

Since then, no prophet has risen in Israel like Moses, whom the Lord knew face to face, who did all those miraculous signs and wonders the Lord sent him to do in Egypt—to Pharaoh and to all his officials and to his whole land. For no one has ever shown the mighty power or performed the awesome deeds that Moses did in the sight of Israel.

The Least You Need to Know

➤ Moses was reluctant to represent God at first, but he turned out to be an excellent leader.

➤ Aaron, Moses' brother, was chosen as the first high priest. All subsequent priests came from their tribe (Levi).

➤ Although God performed miracle after miracle to transport the Israelites safely from Egypt to the Promised Land, the people seldom stopped complaining and rebelling. Consequently, they spent 40 additional years in the wilderness, dying off and being replaced by a more faithful generation.

➤ During this time, the worship of God became more formalized as the tabernacle was set up and laws were provided to let people know exactly what was expected of them.

Chapter 8

The Good, the Bad, and the Lovely

Leadership is a delicate skill. Any number of organizations and institutions can tell of the trouble they went through after a change in leadership. Even when the organization contains the same people, the same mission, and the same structure, the leader may have a dramatic impact on the group. One leader can inspire and succeed, but another may take the whole shebang down the tubes.

Next in Command (Joshua 1)

Joshua was the leader chosen by God to replace Moses, and he had some big sandals to fill. The Israelites had grumbled under Moses, but there was little doubt that he had spoken with the authority of God. Now Joshua was expecting the people to do something they wouldn't even do for Moses: enter the Promised Land and do battle with the hostile natives.

But Joshua had a couple of things going for him. First, the grumpy Israelites had all died in the wilderness during the 40 years of wandering. The younger generation was both more willing and more faithful than its parents. Second, as with Moses, God had promised Joshua victory. Three times in the opening chapter, God urges Joshua to "be strong and courageous" (v. 6, 7, 9). The Israelites picked up this phrase as they prepared to move forward (v. 4).

Help from Unexpected Quarters (Joshua 2)

Just as Moses had sent spies ahead to investigate the Promised Land, so did Joshua. But Joshua was more interested in military information, particularly concerning the heavily fortified city of Jericho. Probably wanting to avoid being conspicuous, Joshua sent only a couple of men.

Once inside the great walled city, the spies hid in the house of a prostitute named Rahab—not a bad choice, if you think about it. A couple more strangers shouldn't have seemed unusual. Yet somehow they were seen and immediately identified as spies.

Rahab covered for them—literally!—by concealing them under bundles of flax. She told the searchers that the spies had come and gone—they'd just missed them, as a matter of fact. As the men hurried off, Rahab told the spies that the people in Jericho were scared to death of the Israelites. The miraculous crossing of the Red Sea had made the news, as had Israel's military victories in the wilderness.

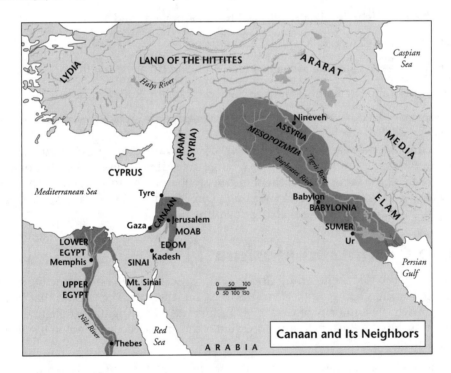

Canaan and Its Neighbors

Rahab fully believed that the Israelites would overpower Jericho, she offered to help the spies escape if they could promise that she and her family would be protected when the time came. The spies agreed. They told her to tie a scarlet cord in her window as a sign, and to stay inside. Rahab opened her back window and lowered the Israelites down the city wall by a rope. The spies hid in the hills for three days until the search for them had been called off.

The Miraculous Water Crossing You Hardly Ever Hear About (Joshua 3–5:12)

Encouraged by the spies' report, Joshua began to ready the people. The Ark of the Covenant would go before them. To enter the Promised Land, the people needed to cross the Jordan River while it was at flood stage. But as soon as the feet of the priests carrying the Ark touched the water, the river stopped flowing and the waters walled up. The priests remained in the dry river bed while the Israelites crossed. To commemorate this event, Joshua instructed a volunteer from each tribe to take a stone from the river bed. He then used the stones to make a monument so that, whenever the Israelites saw the pile of stones, they would remember how God had provided for them on this day. Like moon rocks, the significance of these stones would be where they came from.

Manna from Heaven

Crossing the Jordan has become a euphemism for dying: The act may be something of a chore, but on the other side awaits the Promised Land.

Before moving on, Joshua set up camp long enough to take care of some unfinished business. The ritual of circumcision and celebration of Passover had largely been ignored in the wilderness, so both were observed at this opportune time. The next day, the people ate food that came from the Promised Land, and from that day on the supply of manna stopped. Now that they had reached the place where God had led them, they would be expected to provide for themselves from what the land produced.

Joshua Fought the Battle of Jericho—But First, Some Laps (Joshua 5:13–8)

To enter the Promised Land, the Israelites had to get past the stronghold of Jericho. As they approached it, Joshua was confronted by a mysterious soldier who identified himself as "commander of the army of the Lord." The heavenly warrior gave Joshua a strategy for taking Jericho, and a strange plan it was.

What Saith Thou?

Why should the sin of one person affect others who did nothing wrong?

It certainly doesn't seem fair for 36 people to die because of one selfish lout. Yet we, too, live in a world where we're sometimes at the mercy of people who make bad choices. Drunk drivers, Internet stalkers, abusive relatives—there are many ways that one person's sinful actions can destroy the innocence of others.

What Saith Thou?

Why would God allow the killing of women and children in raids like the one on Ai?

It seems cruel to make "innocent" people suffer. And indeed, the New Testament mentions loving our enemies and praying for those who persecute us. But the Israelites were incapable of coexisting with the Canaanites without falling into their idolatry, immorality, and sinful lifestyle. And as we have just seen with Achan, even *Israelites* who threatened to pollute the spiritual purity of the nation were put to death.

Once a day for six days, the Israelite army was to march around the city as the priests played trumpets of rams' horn. On the seventh day the army was to march around the city seven times. Then the priests would blow their trumpets, and everyone would give a loud shout.

It's hard to tell if this plan would be more stressful for the Israelites or the citizens of Jericho. But the Israelites obediently did their laps. And after the seventh lap on the seventh day...after the trumpet blast...after the mighty shout...the walls came tumblin' down.

Joshua had given a couple of explicit instructions. One was that Rahab and her family be kept alive. The other was that the Israelites were to take none of the spoils for themselves. The city of Jericho was to be dedicated to God, and anything acquired as a result was to go into God's treasury.

Everything seemed to go according to plan, and Joshua placed a curse on anyone who dared rebuild Jericho. But not long after that, the Israelites attacked the walled city of Ai, which should have been no problem compared to Jericho. Yet The Canaanites routed the Israelites and chased them away, killing 36. After the stunning victory over Jericho, losing this skirmish was all it took to knock all the confidence out of the Israelites. Now that everyone knew that Israel was "beatable," it would be much harder to take over the territory.

Joshua couldn't understand what had gone wrong, and asked God. It turned out that one man among the Israelites had disobeyed the command to give everything to God and had hidden some valuables for himself. The man, Achan, and his family were stoned to death. Everything they owned was burned—including the robe and the 5 or 6 pounds of gold and silver he had swiped from Jericho. Today we could call such a sentence "a policy of zero toleration." After Achan's sin had been uncovered, the Israelites took the city of Ai with ease.

Joshua built an altar and offered sacrifices to God after the victory. Then he read the entire Book of the Law that Moses had recorded.

Snapshots

If you have an interest in military battle strategies, the conquest of Ai (Joshua 8:1–29) demonstrates Joshua's skill as a commander.

If You Can't Beat Them, Psyche Them Out (Joshua 9–12)

When the rest of the Canaanites saw that Jericho and Ai had been defeated so handily, they began banding together so that their armies would have a fighting chance. A tribe called the Gibeonites, however, tried another strategy.

They pulled out their oldest clothes, sacks, and wineskins. They wore tattered sandals and loaded up with dry and moldy bread. Then they went to Joshua, saying they had come from a distant country and asking to make a treaty with him. The Israelites examined the group and their belongings; their story seemed to check out. Yet the Bible makes the observation that "they did not inquire of the Lord" (9:14). Joshua agreed to make a treaty with the Gibeonites, allowing them to live. Three days later, he discovered they were not foreigners at all, but neighbors.

Because of the oath Joshua had taken, he could not have them killed. Yet because of their deception, he mandated that they become the water carriers and woodcutters for all of Israel. The Gibeonites quickly agreed. They knew they *should* have been on the list for obliteration. Neither side was completely happy with the deal, but they both agreed to abide by it.

Snapshots

Did you ever have one of those days where everything was going so well you didn't want it to end? So did Joshua (even though all hail was breaking loose). See what he did to create some immediate daylight savings time (Joshua 10:1–15).

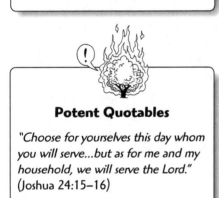

Movin' In (Joshua 13–24)

The rest of the Book of Joshua details the settlement of the Promised Land. Canaanites still living in remote areas had to be chased out, but that responsibility would belong to the individual tribes who settled there. God had already designated through Moses what portions of the land each tribe should receive as an inheritance. Joshua exhorted the tribal leaders to carry on the fight, and then sent the people on their way.

Joshua died at 110 and was buried in the Promised Land, as were the bones of Joseph that had been brought out of Egypt. In his farewell address to the people, Joshua urged them to remain faithful to God and do all that they had been instructed. Any alliance with the native tribes would lead to severe trouble.

The Apathy of Defeat (Judges 1–2)

The optimism of Joshua's conquests and spiritual reforms carries into the Book of Judges, but not for long.

As the book of Judges opens, the people ask God which tribe will be the first to take possession of the land. God answers, "Judah" (which happened to be the tribe of Caleb, the faithful spy). The Judahites got *almost* all their area cleared out—including, most significantly, the city of Jerusalem.

After their victories, however, there are very few success stories. Tribe after tribe of Israelites failed to drive out the people who resided there. As a result, God declared that the Canaanites would continue to be "thorns in your sides" (2:3). Rather than peace in the land, there would be continual struggle.

Here Come the Judges! (Judges 3–16)

With this arrangement, it didn't take long for the Israelites to find themselves adapting to the customs of the local people. The next generation after Joshua was already immersed in worship of other gods, and a pattern soon emerged. The Israelites dabbled in other religions. God responded by refusing to help them in battle. The Israelites, finding themselves at the mercy of their enemies, began to call on God again. God would raise up a leader to get them out of trouble, and soon after the people would revert to idolatry. This cycle continued for many years. The people God called as leaders were known as the judges, but they functioned as military leaders.

Ehud (Judges 3:12–30)

Very little is said about many of the judges: Othniel (Caleb's relative), Shamgar, Tola, Jair, Ibzan, Elon, and Abdon—to name a few. Even those with good stories have remained in relative obscurity. Take Ehud, for instance. After Israel had been subject to the king of Moab for 18 years, the people sent Ehud to deliver tribute money. But Ehud had a double-edged sword strapped to his right thigh beneath his robe. He offered the tribute and also said he had a secret message, so the king sent everyone out of the room. As the king stood to hear Ehud's "message from God," Ehud plunged the sword into his stomach. The king of Moab must have been built like Santa Claus, because the sword was eighteen inches long, but his fat closed over it. (Of course, part of the blade was sticking out his back.) Ehud sneaked out of the palace, locking the doors behind him. When the servants called for the king and received no answer, they assumed he was in the bathroom. But after they "waited to the point of embarrassment," they entered and found him dead. Meanwhile, Ehud escaped, rallied the Israelites, and defeated Moab, providing peace in the land for 80 years.

Deborah (Judges 4–5)

Deborah was a prophetess who engineered the defeat of a Canaanite army when a male counterpart balked at leadership. She also foretold the downfall of Sisera, its commander, at the hand of a woman.

Sisera's 900 iron chariots were impressive, but were no match for God. The Israelite troops routed the

What Saith Thou?

How did people "ask God" (Judges 1:1) without a clear leader?

Up to this point, God had frequently communicated directly with the person in charge, whether Abraham, Jacob, Moses, or Joshua. Now Israel was divided into tribes with no single leader. However, the very clothing of the high priest had a built-in method of determining God's will. Two special stones, "the Urim and the Thummim," were contained in his breastpiece "(Exodus 28:15-30). Somehow, by casting lots, the priest could always determine what God wanted the people to do. Perhaps this was the method used in Judges 1.

Manna from Heaven

The chore of *pitching tents* was frequently "woman's work" in this culture. No wonder Jael swung a mean hammer.

Canaanites and killed all but Sisera, who fled on foot and took refuge at the tent of Jael, a woman whose husband he had befriended. Jael gave Sisera some milk, covered him up, and agreed to stand guard while he got some rest. When he was asleep, she picked up a hammer and tent peg and quietly nailed his head to the ground. After Sisera's death, Israel had another 40 years of peace and quiet.

Gideon (Judges 6–8)

But before long, trouble arose with the Midianites—a fierce and cruel people. In fact, when we first see Gideon, he is threshing wheat in a winepress so the Midianites won't steal what little he has. Yet the angel of the Lord appeared and said, "The Lord is with you, mighty warrior."

Snapshots

It took Gideon a while to become absolutely sure he was the person God wanted in charge. His insecurities are described in Judges 6—and it's where we get the literary allusion to "putting out a fleece."

God wanted Gideon and Israel to know that he was responsible for their victories, so he asked Gideon to reduce the size of Israel's army. Gideon started out with 32,000 men, but when he told all the chicken-hearted soldiers to go home, he was left with only 10,000. Still, that was too many. God told Gideon to take the remaining army to the water and watch them drink. Those who dropped their weapons and lay down to drink directly from the water were to be eliminated. In contrast, Gideon was to single out those who knelt and lapped the water, hand to mouth. These would be the more alert and battle-worthy soldiers, but only 300 men did so. Yet, sure enough, these 300 were able to defeat the Midianites. (Don't miss all the details in Judges 7.)

Snapshots

Two more unusual stories about judges:

Abimelech, a self-appointed judge, learns the hard way not to stand under a tower holding feisty women (Judges 9).

Jephthah wins a battle but must sacrifice his only child as a result (Judges 11).

Samson (Judges 13–16)

Best known of the judges, Samson is also the last in this book of the Bible. Even before he was born an angel showed up to let his parents know he would be special and should be raised as a Nazirite—a person set apart for God. Nazirites were to avoid getting haircuts, partaking of wine (or anything related to grapes), or coming into contact with dead bodies (Numbers 6:1–21).

Samson could have been the poster boy for the "big stupid male" stereotype. Nobody could stop him from doing what he wanted to do, and what he wanted to do was rarely based on good sense. For example, he sought out a Philistine bride rather than an Israelite woman. This choice was OK with God, however, because the Philistines had been oppressing Israel for 40 years. God would use this marriage to strike the first blow against the Philistines through Samson.

On the way to set up the engagement, a lion attacked him. Samson killed the lion with his bare hands. On a return trip, he noticed bees had nested in the lion's carcass, and he scooped out some honey and ate it. No one had seen him kill the lion, so he bet his 30 bridegrooms a set of clothes apiece that they couldn't figure out the answer to this riddle: "Out of the eater, something to eat; out of the strong, something sweet." He was right. They couldn't. So they threatened his fiancée with death if she didn't coax the answer out of Samson. She cried and whined for the entire seven days of the wedding feast until Samson finally cracked and told her at the last minute. She quickly told the men, who repeated the answer to Samson.

Samson was furious because even he could figure out what must have happened. He told them, "If you had not plowed with my heifer, you would not have solved my riddle." Then he left and beat up 30 Philistines, taking their clothes to pay off his bet. He did not return to claim his bride, so her father gave her to one of the groomsmen.

Some time later, when Samson returned, he was not allowed to see her. Samson caught 300 foxes, tied them in pairs by their tails, tied a torch to each pair, and turned them loose in the Philistine fields, destroying their grain, vineyards, and olives.

After this, tension intensified between Samson and the Philistines. It didn't help, of course, that he would sleep with their prostitutes, rip up and carry off their city gates, and kill 1,000 of them at a time with any old donkey jawbone that happened to be lying around. But the Philistines saw an opportunity for revenge when Samson fell in love with a woman named Delilah. The Philistine leaders promised her a large reward if she could determine the source of Samson's strength. So she set about trying. At first his answers were simply made up, but finally he gave in and told her the truth: His strength was in his long hair. The same day, while he was asleep, Delilah had someone shave his head. When he awoke, he was helpless. The Philistines blinded him, placed him in bronze shackles, and put him to work grinding grain in prison.

Some time later, the Philistines were celebrating their capture of Samson and fgiving their god the credit. As part of the festivities, they brought Samson out to "perform for them." What they didn't notice was that his hair had begun to grow back out. Samson asked to be propped against the pillars of the Philistine temple, where he prayed to God for one last surge of strength. Pushing against the pillars, he literally brought the house down. With the temple filled with Philistine leaders and 3,000 more people on the roof, Samson killed many more Philistines with this single act than he had previously.

The rest of the Book of Judges (17–21) is disheartening—a sequence of grim stories about the moral state of Israel during the era of the judges. All in all, the Book of Judges is aptly summed up by the last verse: "In those days Israel had no king; everyone did as he saw fit."

No Longer Ruthless (Ruth 1–4)

Joshua was the good, and the era of the judges was the bad—so Ruth must be the lovely. Indeed, after the repeated cycles of sin and total mayhem in Judges, the Book of Ruth stands out like a jewel in a pile of manure—and Ruth wasn't even an Israelite. She was a Moabitess who married into an Israelite family. Her mother-in-law, Naomi, and Naomi's husband and two sons had come to Moab fleeing famine. But then Naomi's husband and sons died, leaving her in a foreign country with two childless daughters-in-law. Naomi decided to go back home, telling Ruth and Orpah, her other daughter-in-law, to remain in their homeland. Orpah reluctantly agreed, but Ruth refused to leave Naomi's side.

When they got back to Israel, barley harvest was underway. Ruth set out to do what other poor people of her time did. As the barley was bound into sheaves, she was allowed to follow behind, picking up what was left—a process called *gleaning*. She found work in the field of a man named Boaz, who demonstrated great kindness to her. He gave her food and water and told her to stay with his servant girls, where she would be safe. He instructed his men not to touch her and to purposely leave behind grain for her to pick up.

Ruth returned to Naomi with quite a haul. Naomi was amazed at the "coincidence": Boaz was a relative of Naomi's. After a few days, Naomi realized that Ruth and Boaz would be a good match, and she knew the proper procedure. She had Ruth take a bath and put on perfume and her best clothes. At night she was to slip out, find where Boaz was sleeping, uncover his feet, and lie down nearby. Ruth followed all these instructions. When Boaz woke up around midnight, he was quite startled. Ruth told him who she was, and asked him to spread his cloak over her, "for you are next of kin." To us this sounds like an attempt at seduction—and not a very subtle one—but in that culture it was a request for marriage. By placing the covering over Ruth, Boaz would be symbolically committing to care for her.

Boaz was quite flattered by Ruth's interest in him. He also affirmed that she was a "woman of noble character" (v. 11), indicating that nothing improper took place. But by law, he was not the closest relative. One other family member had first crack at Naomi's property. Boaz made sure Ruth left before anyone could see her and get the wrong idea, and he gave her a gift of grain as she went. The next day Boaz looked up the other potential kinsman-redeemer. The man was interested in the family inheritance—but not if a wife went with it. He told Boaz to go ahead and acquire Naomi's husband's property, if he wanted to, and to marry Ruth. Notarizing an action was done by passing along a sandal, so Boaz received the other man's sandal as an official sanction.

Potent Quotables

"Where you go I will go, and where you stay I will stay. Your people will be my people and your God my God." (Ruth 1:16)

A favorite at a lot of weddings, this verse exemplifies the Moabite Ruth's wholehearted devotion to her Israelite mother-in-law, Naomi.

Manna from Heaven

Boaz is referred to as Naomi's *kinsman-redeemer*. This was a person qualified to redeem something or someone. Primarily, this person had the responsibility of marrying a widow (such as a brother's wife) to ensure that she had a husband and/ or children to care for her.

Ruth's love and loyalty toward Naomi paid off in unexpected ways. Not only did she get a home and husband from the deal, but she also got a son. She named him Obed, which doesn't mean much to most people. But Obed's son was Jesse, and Jesse's son was David. So the story of Ruth and Boaz is more than a sentimental love story—it is part of the genealogy of king David, and later of Jesus himself. So something good did come out of the period of the judges after all.

And by the way, the worst is not yet passed. If you think the era of the judges was bad, just wait till we get to some of the kings!

The Least You Need to Know

➤ Joshua took over as leader after Moses, defeating the Canaanite strongholds and settling the Israelites in the Promised Land.

➤ After the death of Joshua, the Israelites fell into regular periods of religious apostasy, only to be dominated by their enemies. A series of judges would deliver them from time to time, but never with lasting success.

➤ The stories of Deborah, Jael, Ruth, and Naomi highlight some positive female role models—both at home and on the field of battle.

Chapter 9

That's Saul, Folks!

In This Chapter

➤ Israel demands a king

➤ Samuel becomes a prominent figure in the spiritual development of Israel

➤ Saul's shortcomings lead to David's rise to power

➤ Samuel's voices in the night; Saul, Israel's first king; David and Goliath; David and Jonathan; David versus Saul

In a 1588 speech to her troops, Elizabeth I said, "I know I have the body of a weak and feeble woman, but I have the heart and stomach of a king." As we're about to see, King Saul was just the opposite. He had the body of a king, standing head and shoulders taller than most of the other Israelite men. He had the support of his people and the endorsement of God. But when it came to heart and courage—the "innards" of a good king—he just didn't have what it takes to succeed.

Prayer? So *That's* Where Babies Come From! (1 Sam. 1–2:11)

Before we get to Saul, we meet a couple named Hannah and Elkanah. Actually, we meet a trio, because Elkanah had another wife. His other wife had given him children, but so far Hannah had been unable to conceive. Although Elkanah treated Hannah well, the other wife provoked her on a regular basis.

We've seen biblical women deal with the issue of infertility in different ways. Sarah loaned her handmaiden to Abraham. Rachel bartered with Leah for aphrodisiacs and husband "time shares." Lot's daughters got him drunk and slept with him. But Hannah stands out. She went to the house of God and prayed. She promised that if she could have a son, she would give him back to God for a lifetime of service. She was so fervent in her praying that Eli, the priest, thought she was drunk and reprimanded her. But when she explained, he gave her his blessing.

In time, God honored Hannah's request with a son, whom she named Samuel ("heard of God"). Hannah kept him until he was weaned, which, in that culture, meant until he was about 3 years old. Then she took him to live with Eli the priest. Every year when she brought her annual offering she would visit Samuel and give him a new robe. And in the years that followed, Hannah had three sons and two daughters.

Problems with the Priest Hoods (1 Sam. 2:12–26)

It's a good thing Eli had Samuel to work with, because his own sons had turned out to be self-centered, immoral, sacrilegious thugs. They had no respect for the offerings the people brought. They were allowed to take a portion as it was offered to God, but they would demand their cut before they would make the offering in the first place. They even slept with the women who served in the worship area.

Eli scolded them, but he did not take stern measures. Holding him responsible for the way his sons had turned out, God passed judgment on Eli and his family. Eli's sons would die on the same day, ending the priestly succession from Eli's family, and a faithful priest would be chosen elsewhere.

Speak Three Times from the Ceiling If You Want Me (1 Sam. 3)

So it was that one night, when everyone had gone to bed, Samuel heard God call his name. Samuel did not know it was God calling, however. He assumed the voice was that of Eli, who was old and almost blind. So Samuel ran over to see what Eli wanted, and Eli told him he hadn't called—to go back and lie down. This happened two more times. Finally Eli figured out what was going on and told Samuel to reply, "Speak, Lord, for your servant is listening" (1 Samuel 3:9).

So Samuel did. God told Samuel that he planned to bring Eli's house to an end. The next morning, when Eli asked what God had said, it must have been difficult for a young boy to convey such a message to his mentor. But Eli already knew God's intentions and accepted them. From that time on, God spoke to Samuel on a regular basis. Everything Samuel said came to pass, and the people realized he was a true prophet.

Raiders of the Lord's Ark (1 Sam. 4–7)

Now disaster befell the Israelites. After losing a battle with the Philistines, they carried their most sacred object, the Ark of the Covenant, into the next skirmish, hoping with its help to be victorious. Instead, Israel was routed. Eli's sons were killed, and the Philistines carried off the Ark. When Eli heard this, he fell over backward. Being an old and heavy man, the fall broke his neck and he died.

Meanwhile, the Philistines placed the Ark in their temple with their god, Dagon, who was sometimes represented with the form of a fish. But the next morning, the statue of Dagon was on its face before the Ark. They stood him up again, but the next day the statue had fallen again, this time breaking off its head and hands.

The Philistine people weren't having it any better than their idol. Those who lived near the Ark were afflicted with "tumors." And to make matters even worse, the plague was accompanied by an outbreak of rats—perhaps responsible for spreading the disease. The original language suggests the primary location of these tumors was the groin/rectal area. That would tend to take the fight out of a warlike people!

A few months of this was all the Philistines could take. They put the Ark in a wagon pulled by cattle and sent it back to Israel (along with a tribute of rats and tumors, both made of gold), where it was received with great joy. But the holy object was not to be treated casually. Seventy Israelites died after peeking into the Ark to see what it looked like inside. After that the Ark was carried to a nearby home and put under guard for 20 years. Samuel used this opportunity to challenge the Israelites to destroy their idols and recommit themselves to God. They had a ceremony of repentance which drew many people to the same location. When the Philistines saw the crowd, they assembled to attack. Samuel turned to God on Israel's behalf, and God used thunder to disorient and panic the Philistines. As they fled, the Israelites followed and chased them away. And from that time on, throughout the life of Samuel, the Philistines ceased to be a major threat.

What Saith Thou?

Why would God allow a defeat with the Ark in front of the people?

Apparently the Israelites made the same mistake as the Nazis in the movie *Raiders of the Lost Ark*. The Ark of the Covenant was never intended to be a "lucky charm." It was tempting for the Israelites to think they could carry God's power around in a box, but God doesn't work that way. In this case, God was not leading the Israelites to victory, and not even their most holy religious artifact could make a difference.

King Me! (1 Sam. 8–12)

Samuel was a wise and upright leader. Unfortunately, as he got older and began to set his sons in the roles of judges, they were no better than Eli's sons had been. They took bribes and perverted justice to suit their own wishes. Before long, the leaders of Israel asked Samuel to end the line of judges and find them a king instead so they could be like all the other nations. Samuel was upset. Israel wasn't supposed to be like all the other nations. Their king was God, who could appoint human judges as he wished. God told him not to take it so personally. After all, it was God the people were rejecting, not Samuel.

Samuel let the people know what the downside of having a king would be. They would be forced to serve in his armies, to labor in his fields, to give up the best of their flocks and produce for the use of the king and his officials. Israel was determined, however. "We will be like all the other nations, with a king to lead us and to go out before us and fight our battles" (1 Samuel 8:20). God told Samuel to give the people what they wanted.

God's choice was Saul, from the tribe of Benjamin, "an impressive young man without equal among the Israelites—a head taller than any of the others" (1 Samuel 9:2). Saul could hardly believe he would be considered as a leader because he came from an insignificant clan in the smallest tribe of Israel. Samuel anointed Saul and then told him precisely what would happen to him in the immediate future. He also told Saul to meet him in seven days when Samuel would offer sacrifices to God and give him additional instructions.

Samuel called out all the people of Israel by tribe to allow God to designate who the new king would be, through the ritual of casting lots. Sure enough, Saul was chosen. But when it came time for the big ta-da, Saul was nowhere to be found. God let the people know that Saul was hiding "among the baggage" (10:22). If modesty is a useful trait for kingship, Saul was off to a great start. He was brought out and the people cheered, but the joy was not unanimous. Some of the Israelites made spiteful comments and refused to give him gifts, but Saul ignored them for the time being.

Manna from Heaven

Anointing with oil was a way of dedicating someone to God. Prophets, priests, and kings were anointed, although the phrase "the anointed of the Lord" eventually came to be a synonym for God's chosen king.

Anointing was also done for personal reasons (fragrant oil was used like perfume) and medical reasons (as balm to treat a wound).

Not long afterward, Saul got a chance to prove himself when an Israelite town was threatened by ferocious Ammonites. Gathering an army of 330,000 men, he won a decisive victory and became an instant hero. All doubts about his qualifications were dispelled. Immediately after the battle the people wanted to find the guys who had insulted Saul and do some more killing. But Saul instructed everyone to focus on the victory God had given them and forget about the previous offense. While the people were celebrating, Samuel gathered everyone to publicly confirm Saul as their king.

Samuel used this opportunity to give a farewell speech. He reminded the assembled people that God had always provided Israel with capable leaders. So long as the people remained faithful to God, their lives had run smoothly—and would continue to do so if both king and citizens followed God, their true king. Otherwise, they would be in for trouble.

Who Is This "Phyllis Stein," and Why Are There So Many of Her? (1 Sam. 13–14)

Now the threat from the Philistines was renewed. Saul again gathered an army for battle. But where was Samuel? The Israelites could not go out to fight without making sacrifices to God. Samuel was to meet them there in seven days, but when the time came and went without any sign of him, the Israelites began to quake with fear and go into hiding. In desperation, Saul made the sacrifices himself—at which point Samuel showed up, none too pleased. He told Saul that this would be the beginning of the end for Saul's kingdom. Because Saul had overstepped his authority, his line would never inherit the throne.

Despite that inauspicious beginning, the battle went well for the Israelites, largely with the help of Saul's courageous and faithful son Jonathan. By the end of the day, however, the soldiers were feeling tired and famished. With characteristic impulsiveness, Saul had sworn a binding oath that no one could eat "before I have avenged myself on my enemies!" Between fasting and fighting, the army was not exactly in top shape.

Meanwhile, Jonathan hadn't heard about the fast. Finding honey in the woods, he ate some of it before anyone could stop him. Because of this, when Saul wanted to inquire of God about his next military move, he received no answer. Guessing that there had been some major sin among his officers, he threatened death to the offender, "even if it lies with my son Jonathan" (1 Samuel 14:39). Sure enough, Jonathan was identified by the casting of lots. Saul was determined to have Jonathan put to death, but the men interceded.

Potent Quotables

"But now your kingdom will not endure; the Lord has sought out a man after his own heart and appointed him leader of his people, because you have not kept the Lord's command." (1 Samuel 13:14)

Though not mentioned by name, David will be the person honored to be known as a man after God's own heart. As we shall see, David's popularity will increase as Saul's influence declines.

Manna from Heaven

It's for good reason that we've adopted the term "Philistine" to describe a merciless or uncouth person. The Philistines weren't exactly noble when it came to conflict:

Peace treaties required having enemies' eyes gouged out (1 Samuel 11:1–11).

They tended to "stack the deck" in their favor in terms of numbers and armament (1 Samuel 13:5–7).

They had a forced monopoly on blacksmiths, so Israel had very few metal weapons (13:19–22).

They realized that God had clearly used Jonathan to rout the Philistines. They refused to back Saul in killing a hero who had inadvertently broken an oath he knew nothing about. So Jonathan's life was spared and the fighting was ended as the Philistines retreated to their own land.

With the Philistines out of the way, Saul continued to deal with other enemies surrounding Israel—the Moabites, Ammonites, Edomites, and others. Saul had many victories, largely because of his habit of drafting everyone he saw who was "a mighty or brave man" (v. 52).

The Bleat Goes On (1 Sam. 15)

Next God told Saul to do battle with Israel's old enemies, the Amalekites—the ones who had plagued God's people in the wilderness during the exodus (Exodus 17:8–16). Because they were wicked people who had shown no respect toward God or mercy toward God's people, God was going to eliminate them as a threat. Through Samuel, God told Saul to attack the Amalekites and destroy them completely—"men and women, children and infants, cattle and sheep, camels and donkeys" (1 Samuel 15:3). Saul followed these instructions, but imperfectly. He spared the life of the king, and he saved the best of the fat cattle and sheep. God told Samuel privately that he was sorry he had made Saul king, and Samuel was troubled as well. When he went to confront Saul, he was told the king had set up a monument in his own honor.

When Samuel finally caught up with Saul, the king claimed to have carried out God's instructions. Samuel replied, "What then is this bleating of sheep in my ears? What is this lowing of cattle that I hear?" (Samuel may have been a good man of God, but it seems he was also capable of a bit of sarcasm.)

Saul was defensive. He claimed to have saved the animals to offer them to God, but Samuel wasn't buying it. Saul had had his instructions, and he didn't follow them.

Bitter words followed. As Samuel turned to leave, Saul grabbed for him and tore the prophet's robe. In the same way, the prophet responded, God would soon tear away the kingdom from Saul and give it to someone else. Then Samuel himself killed the king of the Amalekites. From that day on, Samuel mourned for Saul but never went to see him again. And although Saul continued to reign for a while, his popularity almost immediately began to decline.

Touching His Harp Strings (1 Sam. 16–17)

Indeed, Samuel's next assignment was to anoint Saul's successor. All he knew was that it would be one of the sons of a man of Judah named Jesse, which narrowed it down to only eight people. Samuel went to the house of Jesse and asked to see his sons. One by one, they came before him, and each time Samuel thought, "Surely this one is kingly stock." But seven sons later, God still hadn't given any of them the OK. Samuel sent for the youngest, David, who was tending the sheep. When young David arrived, God told Samuel to anoint him. We learn that "from that day on the Spirit of the Lord came upon David in power" (16:13) and that "the Spirit of the Lord had departed from Saul, and an evil spirit from the Lord tormented him" (v. 14). In fact, it seems that God used this evil spirit to bring Saul and David together.

As it happened, in addition to being a shepherd, David played a mean harp. Someone told Saul about him, and before long he was summoned to the royal camp to play his harp for the king, in hopes that it would soothe him. So David played, and Saul felt better. Saul grew so fond of David that he gave him the position of armor-bearer.

Potent Quotables

"The Lord does not look at the things man looks at. Man looks at the outward appearance, but the Lord looks at the heart." (1 Samuel 16:7)

This statement of God to Samuel is often quoted as a reminder that God has a different set of standards than we do in determining the worth of a person.

Fee-Fi-Foe-Fight, I Want the Blood of an Israelite (1 Sam. 17)

David still commuted between Saul's camp and his father's home, where he helped tend the flocks, but his three oldest brothers were full-time soldiers for Saul. One day, while David was taking them provisions, a Philistine showed up and the entire Israelite army ran away.

We need to mention, however, that this was no ordinary Philistine. His name was Goliath, and he was more than 9 feet tall. He was walking around in 125 pounds of armor; the tip of his spear alone weighed 15 pounds. For 40 days he had been coming out every morning and every evening, challenging anyone in Israel to fight him one-on-one. It would be a winner-take-all bout, with the loser's people agreeing to serve the winner's.

Saul promised great glory to anyone who would kill Goliath—wealth, his daughter in marriage, and a family-wide tax exemption. David was disturbed that no one had stood up to Goliath, but when he asked about it, his brothers told him not to be so uppity. So David went straight to Saul and volunteered to fight the giant. Saul felt David was much too young and inexperienced, but David insisted. His training had come while tending sheep. He gave God credit, but explained that he had already killed a lion and a bear in the line of duty. He didn't see the problem with Goliath as any worse.

Manna from Heaven

It may seem a shade ludicrous for David to go after Goliath with only a *sling*. However, his sling was nothing like the slingshot toys we might envision. Slings were deadly weapons. The Book of Judges speaks of 700 soldiers "each of whom could sling a stone at a hair and not miss" (Judges 20:16).

Saul finally relented and dressed David for battle, but David wasn't comfortable in armor. Instead, he went down to the stream and selected five smooth rocks for his own sling. He and Goliath walked toward each other. But Goliath became insulted and ticked off. He wanted to face the best Israel could throw at him—not the young and unarmored "boy" he saw coming toward him. Goliath swore and let loose with a bunch of "trash talk" involving how the birds and beasts would soon be feeding off David's body. David replied that the birds' meal would be much larger—not only Goliath's ugly carcass, but also most of the Philistine army. In addition, David explained that God was going to demonstrate that victory didn't require a sword or spear.

Goliath closed in to attack, and David ran straight toward him. As the opponents neared each other, David reached into his bag, pulled out a stone, and slung it. It sank deep in Goliath's forehead—the only part of the giant that wasn't covered with armor. That's all it took. The great giant fell face down. David cut off Goliath's head with the giant's own sword. Goliath's weapons he kept for himself.

Taken by surprise, the Philistines turned and ran, and the Israelites ran after them. It was a great day for Israel. David became a full-time soldier. He had success in every assignment Saul gave him and soon had a high rank in the army.

Banned, On the Run (1 Sam. 18–23)

But Saul wasn't the only one impressed with David's achievement. By the time the army came marching back into Israel, the women were dancing and singing David's praises. The lyrics went, "Saul has slain his thousands, and David his tens of thousands." In Hebrew poetry, this might simply mean that David and Saul together had killed a bunch of enemies—not necessarily that David was ten times better than Saul. Still, Saul took offense that David had been elevated to his level in the minds and songs of the people. He didn't mind letting David take on the difficult assignments, but he didn't like it one bit when David proved himself an equal. The next day, Saul's evil spirit was back. David tried to soothe the king with his harp, but instead of being soothed, Saul hurled a spear at David. Evidently David had come to seem like the problem, not the solution. Saul missed, so he sent David off to battle hoping to get rid of him, but David was again a success. It was a no-win situation for Saul. He was intensely jealous when David was in his presence, but every time he sent him on a dangerous mission, David became even more famous and popular.

Saul later offered David his older daughter in marriage, but then married her to someone else. When he learned that another daughter of his, Michal, was in love with David, Saul thought he was off the hook. Besides, he used it as an opportunity to collect a "dowry" of sorts from David—100 Philistine foreskins. Now, the foreskin is what's left over after a circumcision, a procedure the Philistines were not likely to submit to voluntarily. Saul fully expected David to die while trying to accomplish this feat.

But David and killed 200 Philistines and brought their foreskins to Saul. The king was dismayed. God was clearly on David's side. Meanwhile, his whole household seemed to have fallen head over heels for David. Michal became his wife, and Saul's son, Jonathan, became his best friend. The two protected David more than once from Saul's attempts on his life. It seemed wise for David to take a leave of absence and see if Saul calmed down. Jonathan promised to keep David posted and to signal David if Saul appeared serious about wanting David dead.

Snapshots

Saul's futile attempts to kill or capture David make good reading. See 1 Samuel 19.

When David was a no-show at the next royal festival, Saul turned on Jonathan, accused him of disloyalty, and tried to kill *him* with a spear. It's clear that if Saul's aim had been better, his household would have been littered with bodies. Jonathan excused himself from the table and went to signal David to clear out. But before David left, the two friends cried and said their farewells.

Now a wanted man, David went to see the priest at a city called Nob, perhaps to try to discern what God would have him do during this period of exile. There he asked for food and was given bread that had been consecrated to God. Goliath's sword happened to be there, too. David took it with him when he left.

From Nob, David went to Gath, a Philistine city. No one in Israel would look for him there, yet he wasn't exactly high on the list of the Philistines' desired guests. He faked insanity by doodling on doorways and slobbering into his beard. Some cultures considered insane people to be suffering at the hands of the gods, therefore they were generally left alone for fear that the gods' wrath would spread to anyone who interfered. From Gath he moved on to a cave (or stronghold) in Judah. By now, Robin Hood-style, he had attracted a loyal following of about 400 men. But he also had his enemies. One of these enemies, an Edomite named Doeg, had seen David with the priests in Nob and informed Saul, who went to Nob. When the priests tried to tell Saul that David was still loyal to him, Saul wouldn't hear of it. He commanded that the priests be killed, but his soldiers refused. Doeg, however, had no qualms about such dirty work. He killed 85 priests as well as the men, women, children, and livestock of Nob. One priest escaped and joined up with David's men. His name was Abiathar, and he took with him the ephod used by the priests to discern God's will. (See Exodus 28:6–14.)

Abiathar was a big help to David. Through him, David inquired of God and learned Saul's plans. David was able to rescue a town from the Philistines and clear out before Saul could get there. Now numbering 600, David's men went from place to place in the desert as God helped them avoid king Saul. At one point David's men and Saul's men were on opposite sides of the same mountain with Saul closing in. But just then the Philistines attacked Israel and Saul had to leave to fight them.

What Saith Thou?

Why David's reluctance to kill Saul? Didn't he have every right to do so?

While it is true that David had already been anointed king, Saul was also anointed. It was God who had ordained both anointings, so in David's mind it would have to be God who determined when to make the change in leadership. David respected Saul in spite of all his hostile actions because Saul remained "the Lord's anointed" until the Lord determined otherwise. In the meantime, David was trusting God to look out for him.

A Little Longer Live the King! (1 Sam. 24–26)

David and Saul were playing by different rules. Saul wanted David dead. David had no particular malice toward Saul; he just wanted to stay alive. In fact, David twice was close enough to personally kill Saul. The first time, Saul went into a cave "to relieve himself." It just so happened that David and his men were hiding in that very cave. David crept up and cut off a piece of Saul's robe, but was later remorseful that he had even done that much. Yet when he called out to Saul and told him what he *could* have done, Saul wept, apologized, and left.

Still, it wasn't long before Saul changed his mind and took up the pursuit of David again. Saul's army numbered 3,000 compared to David's 600, but one night God placed Saul's army in a deep sleep. David and another guy named Abishai crept up to where the king was sleeping. Abishai wanted to pin Saul to the ground. Instead, David left with the king's spear and water jug. Again, David called out to prove that he could have killed Saul, yet hadn't. And again, Saul went home while David went on his way.

A Short Ghost Story (1 Sam. 27–31)

Samuel died during this time, and the nation mourned. Meanwhile, David and his men took up residence in the land of the Philistines, who now regarded him as safe because he had become Saul's Public Enemy No. 1. During his sojourn there, David went out and fought enemies of Israel, telling the Philistine king that he was fighting against Israelite outposts. The king trusted David, looking on him as the perfect guest.

But when the Philistines gathered to fight against Israel, David found himself in a predicament. The Philistine king expected David to join his forces, which he did, bringing up the rear. Would David actually have to fight against his own people? Fortunately, the other Philistines didn't trust David as much as the king, who apologized and sent David back home.

Snapshots

More of David's exploits:

A rich snob gets what's coming to him—and David gets his wife (1 Samuel 25).

David's small band of men reclaim their captured wives and possessions (1 Samuel 30).

As the Philistines camped around Israel, Saul was terrified. He tried to get help from God, "but the Lord did not answer him by dreams or Urim [the stones in the priest's ephod] or prophets" (28:7). In desperation, Saul sought help from a psychic. As king, he himself had decreed that all psychics be expelled from the land, but his servants knew of one at a place called Endor. Saul went to her in disguise and asked her to summon Samuel. When the prophet actually appeared, no one was more surprised than the psychic. At that point she screamed and realized her client was none other than King Saul.

In the conversation that followed, Samuel reminded Saul about the torn robe. Not only was Saul about to lose his kingdom, he told the king, but "tomorrow you and your sons will be with me" (v. 19). If Saul had been terrified before, it was nothing compared to the way he felt now—and with good cause. During the battle that followed, Saul watched his army flee before the Philistines. His sons were killed, and he was critically wounded. Fearing a humiliating death at the hands of the enemy, he asked his armor-bearer to finish him off, but the man refused. So Saul fell on his own sword, killing himself. The armor-bearer followed suit.

But the Philistines weren't finished. They found the bodies of Saul and his sons, cut off Saul's head, put his armor in their temple, and attached the bodies to the wall of one of their cities. However a number of valiant Israelites from the city of Jabesh Gilead came in the night. (Jabesh Gilead was a city Saul had previously rescued when the Ammonites had wanted to put out the right eye of everyone there [1 Samuel 11].) They removed the bodies of Saul and his sons, and took them back to their city for a proper burial.

Saul hadn't been an evil leader, but he had been an impulsive one, quick to defend his own interests, incapable of negotiating, and somehow always on the wrong side of God. Now it will be David's turn to rule. Yet David's transition to leadership wasn't an easy one, as we will see in the next chapter.

The Least You Need to Know

➤ Samuel was a faithful man of God who helped the nation during the leadership transition from judges to kings.

➤ Saul, the first king, started out well. However, he allowed personal fears and faults to distract him from God's clear directions, leading to his eventual downfall.

➤ David was chosen by God to be the second king. Like Saul, he seemed an unlikely candidate—Saul because he came from a minor tribe, David because he was a youngest son.

➤ The combination of Saul's early successes, David's fighting skills, and Samuel's religious leadership helped Israel hold her own against her enemies during this period.

Chapter 10

David: Now for Some King Completely Different

In This Chapter

➤ David becomes king and unites a divided nation

➤ Israel becomes a significant world power

➤ David sins and is forgiven, but the effects continue

➤ David and Bathsheba, Absalom's revolt, turmoil in Israel

Periods of transition are seldom easy. Perhaps you've been in a job where a tyrannical boss was replaced by a much nicer one. Still, it is likely that you experienced periods of tension when the new person started changing the way you were accustomed to doing things. And if changing bosses can be traumatic, try to imagine what it might be like changing *kings*.

Here Comes the New Boss, Not Like the Old Boss (2 Sam. 1–4)

Years after David had been anointed king, Saul, his predecessor, continued to reign. Following Saul's death, tension continued between those who had followed David and those who had supported Saul.

Manna from Heaven

The books of *1 and 2 Samuel* in the Bible were originally a single narrative, so 2 Samuel picks up right where 1 Samuel left off.

Potent Quotables

"How the mighty have fallen!" (2 Samuel 1:19, 27)

Twice used by David in reference to Saul and Jonathan, this phrase continues to come to mind when powerful people meet a quick and/or unexpected demise.

Three days after Saul's death, a messenger arrived in David's camp with the news that Saul and his sons were all dead. In fact, he claimed to have killed Saul himself. Actually, as we know, Saul had committed suicide; the man was probably hoping for a reward from Saul's opponent. If so, he was sorely disappointed. David had the man killed for daring "to lift your hand to destroy the Lord's anointed" (2 Samuel 1:14).

David had the accomplishments of Saul written in the Book of Jashar ("Book of the Upright"), a record of Israel's military history. Jonathan, too, was remembered for his courage, strength, and love for David.

Then, following God's direction, David returned to Judah, where he was proclaimed king. One of David's first public acts was to praise the men of Jabesh Gilead, in the territory of Benjamin, who had sneaked up on the Philistines and stolen back the bodies of Saul and his sons. It's clear that David's move was partly political: He hoped to make an alliance with a territory that had been fiercely loyal to Saul.

Saul's influence continued to be felt. The leader of Saul's army had been his nephew, a man named Abner. One of Saul's sons, named Ish-Bosheth (also translated Ishbaal), had apparently survived. Abner crowned Ish-Bosheth as king of Israel, putting him at odds with David, as well as with the Philistines who continued to inhabit much of the surrounding territory.

David's army was led by a man named Joab. Abner and Joab met to negotiate a test of strength between the two forces—a test that soon escalated to full-scale battle. Joab's brother, Asahel, who was "as fleet-footed as a wild gazelle" (2:18), went after Abner on foot. Abner pleaded with him to give up the pursuit, or at least to turn his attention to someone else, but Asahel refused. So Abner turned around and killed him by thrusting the butt end of his spear into the young man's stomach. The impact was so intense that the weapon came out Asahel's back.

Then Joab picked up the pursuit of Abner. Again Abner suggested a truce. This time Joab signaled his troops with a trumpet and everyone went home. But Joab did not forget.

Meanwhile, David's forces had won the battle. Though the conflict was far from settled, over time David grew stronger while Ish-Bosheth's forces waned.

The sudden defection of Abner to David's camp brought a decisive shift to the balance of power. It seems that Abner had slept with one of King Saul's concubines—a way to enhance a man's standing in the eyes of his peers. Ish-Bosheth was threatened by this bold move, and Abner responded with a message to David, offering his services. David offered him a job if he would see that David's former wife, Michal, was returned to him. (Out of anger, Saul had given Michal to another man [1 Samuel 25:44].) David's request was probably more political than personal. Reclaiming Saul's daughter as his wife would establish David as Saul's son-in-law. Abner complied, but Michal's husband followed her all the way, brokenhearted and weeping.

Abner suggested that he was in an excellent position to win Israel over to David. David agreed. But when Joab discovered that the man who had killed his brother was about to become one of his allies, he tracked Abner down without David's knowledge. Pretending to desire a private conversation, Joab called Abner aside and stabbed him to death.

David was outraged when he learned of Joab's actions. Joab's brother Asahel had died in battle; Joab's vengeance was simply murder. Worse, it had been committed in Hebron, a city of refuge where such retribution should not have occurred. David cursed the house of Joab and undertook a period of mourning and fasting. The Bible says that people were pleased to see David's sincere grief, realizing he had played no part in the killing of Abner.

Abner had been Ish-Bosheth's number-one soldier. The news of his defection and murder was taken hard. Ish-Bosheth lost his courage, and the entire nation was alarmed. At this moment of weakness and confusion, two men sneaked into the king's quarters, assassinated him, and carried his head to David, who rewarded them as he had the Amalekite at the beginning of this chapter: with death. In spite of the unavoidable conflict between David and Saul, it seemed that David always had genuine respect for Saul and his family.

Potent Quotables

May Joab's house never be without someone who has a running sore or leprosy or who leans on a crutch or who falls by the sword or who lacks food. (2 Samuel 3:29)

How's that for a curse?

King at Last! (2 Sam. 5)

With Ish-Bosheth out of the way, however, all of Israel was prepared to unite under David's leadership. Samuel had anointed David king over Judah while he was just a young shepherd. He had been made king over Judah seven and a half years ago. Now he was finally anointed as king over all the tribes of Israel—and he was only 37 years old.

A masterful politician as always, David did not try to rule from either Judah (in the south) or Israel (in the north). Instead he looked for a city on the border, one inhabited by non-Israelites. David chose Jerusalem, a city that had been around for centuries. Jerusalem was so well fortified that its inhabitants sneered at the suggestion that it could be defeated. They told David, "You will not get in here; even the blind and the lame can ward you off" (2 Samuel 5:6). They were wrong. David took Jerusalem, known ever after as "the City of David."

With his headquarters established, David began to assume the duties of a world ruler. A Phoenician king sent a crew with materials to build David a palace, shoring up a friendship on which Phoenicia's seaport trade depended. David also began to take on more wives and concubines, fortifying his political alliances and providing him with numerous children. And he renewed Israel's campaign against the Philistines, with great success. Thereafter these people would never pose much of a threat to Israel.

Disembarking the Ark (2 Sam. 6)

High on David's to-do list was bringing the Ark of the Covenant to Jerusalem. You may remember that after the Philistines had captured and returned the Ark, it went into storage in the home of a man named Abinadab. David wanted to restore it to a more prominent place, and the transfer was a time of rejoicing. The sons of Abinadab walked behind and before, while crowds walked with them, singing and playing their instruments. The Israelites were carrying the Ark on a new cart, as the Philistines had done. But the Ark had been designed to be carried on the shoulders of the priests using poles that went through attached rings (Exodus 25:10–16). As the cart rolled across a threshing floor, the oxen stumbled, jeopardizing the security of the Ark. Instinctively, the person closest to the Ark, a man named

What Saith Thou?

Wasn't God's punishment of Uzzah a little harsh?

As much as anything else, the Ark of the Covenant represented God's presence among His people. In a tabernacle setting, the high priest was the only person permitted to see the Ark, much less touch it. Even then, special clothes and specific sin offerings were required before he could enter the Most Holy Place (Leviticus 16). There is little doubt that Uzzah acted in good faith and intended to be helpful, but the Ark was such a holy object that no excuse was sufficient for touching it. You might step off a steep precipice accidentally, but the fall is just as fatal. Uzzah's death was a lesson not of God's cruelty, but rather his holiness.

Uzzah, reached out to steady it. But respecting the holiness of the Ark was imperative. Because Uzzah touched it, even for good reason, he died on the spot.

David was angry and not a little alarmed by this incident. He took the Ark to another nearby home and left it there, unwilling to transport it further. When the presence of the Ark in the home resulted in God's blessing for the family, however, David decided to try again. This time the priests carried the poles that supported the Ark, and they began the journey with a sacrifice to God.

As the Ark made its way to Jerusalem, David celebrated. Stripping down to a linen ephod—an undergarment of about hip-length—he leaped and danced in praise of God "with all his might" to the sound of trumpets and the shouts of the people.

Watching him from her window, his wife Michal was incensed, and told him so when she saw him. Why was the king making a fool of himself in front of everybody, dancing with slave girls? It is also suggested that David's active dancing, combined with the limited coverage of his linen undergarment, might have revealed certain kingly characteristics that his wife felt should have been for her eyes only. David defended his actions as legitimate celebration before God. As a result of her unjustified criticism, Michal remained childless throughout her lifetime.

Israel: Growing by Leaps and Boundaries (2 Sam. 8–10)

David's military successes against the Moabites and the Ammonites brought Israel territory and wealth, while his political astuteness continued to strengthen his position. David learned that Saul's son Jonathan had fathered a son named Mephibosheth, who had not been killed during the wars but whose nurse had dropped him in her haste to escape, leaving him crippled in both feet. Mephibosheth now had a son of his own. Where another ruler might have invented an excuse to kill any and all descendants of Saul, David sought peace. He gave Mephibosheth the estate that had belonged to Saul and provided an open invitation for Mephibosheth and his family to eat at the king's table.

Snapshots

Warfare causes people to act strangely—and Old Testament warfare was no different. David used string to determine which of his prisoners of war would live and which would die (2 Samuel 8:1–3). And his enemies came up with some "revealing" ways to humiliate the Israelites (2 Samuel 10).

My Kingdom for a House (2 Sam. 7)

When David brought the Ark to Jerusalem, he had hoped to erect a permanent house for God in place of the traditional tabernacle. After all, God's people were no longer the wanderers they had once been. David consulted a prophet named Nathan about constructing a temple. The idea sounded good to Nathan, and he endorsed it heartily. But when he got around to consulting God, the prophet discovered God didn't want

David to be the one to build the house of worship. In fact, God promised to build a house for David in the form of a line that would have no end. Saul's line of succession had been taken away, but, ultimately, David's never would. God's house would be constructed, but it would be by someone else from David's house.

Splish, Splash, I Was Taking a Bath... (2 Sam. 11)

Up until this point, David was a pretty good role model. He was modest, brave, honorable, thoughtful, and a valiant warrior—not to mention a gifted musician and poet. No one is perfect, however, and David eventually made a colossal blunder in judgment. Giant Philistines and hostile armies hadn't been able to defeat David. But one naked woman and a moment of weakness was all it took for David to self-destruct.

It was a lovely spring evening. David was strolling around his palace roof thinking about his army, which was off at war fighting Canaanites. As he looked out over his kingdom, David suddenly realized he was also looking out over a beautiful woman taking a bath. Now, he might have turned around. He might have closed his eyes or gone back inside. Instead, David sent someone to find out who she was. The woman's name was Bathsheba, and she was married to one of David's soldiers. Her husband, Uriah, wasn't home because he was out fighting David's enemies.

What Saith Thou?

Why would David be up on the roof?

Most houses had flat roofs with easy access. Homes were rather small, and the roof provided much-needed additional space for anything from storage to extra beds. The roof was also the coolest part of the house, which is probably why David was hanging out there.

David sent for Bathsheba, and they slept together. The Bible doesn't tell us how Bathsheba felt about it. Was she frightened? Angry? Flattered? Had she planned her bathtime to coincide with David's rooftop schedule? All we know is that some time later she sent word back to David that she was pregnant. With Uriah away, there could be no doubt that the child was David's. The king set about trying to cover up what he had done.

He immediately sent for Uriah under the pretense of getting a report from the front lines. He then sent Uriah home, assuming he and Bathsheba would have sex. After Uriah returned to the battle, it would be no surprise if he heard that he had fathered a child.

The trouble was that Uriah was an intensely loyal soldier. He refused to go home, sleeping at the palace with the other servants instead. He considered himself still on the job, as were all his peers back on the battle lines. He did consent to eat with David, who used the opportunity to get him drunk. But even in his inebriated condition, Uriah refused to enjoy the luxuries of his home while other soldiers were still away.

When subtle deceit didn't work, David changed his strategy. He wrote a note to his field commander, Joab, and sent it by Uriah. In essence, it was a sealed death warrant, carried by the doomed man himself, instructing Joab to send Uriah to the front lines as the rest of the army retreated. The plan worked as designed. The fierce fighting resulted in the deaths of several of David's men, including Uriah. Joab was somewhat concerned that David would be angry because of the losses sustained in the battle, so with the news he also sent specific word that Uriah was dead. David understood exactly, and told Joab he could now go ahead and take the city.

Bathsheba underwent a time of mourning, after which she married David and they had their son. It seemed that no one was the wiser to what they had done, but the notation is made that "the thing David had done displeased the Lord" (11:27). This comes as no surprise. Since David had coveted, committed adultery (and essentially murder), and lied to cover it up, he was shattering commandments left and right.

Uriah Is In a Heap (2 Sam. 12)

God sent Nathan the prophet to confront David. Nathan chose his words carefully. He told the king a story about two men living in David's kingdom. One was wealthy beyond need, with vast flocks. The other was poor, owning only one little ewe lamb, which he had raised as a pet and loved like one of his own children. One day the rich man had a visitor. He was too stingy to serve up one of his own sheep for the meal, so he took the poor man's young lamb and turned it into mutton.

When David heard this story, he burned with anger. The man deserved to die. At the very least he must pay back four times what he had taken. Nathan let him finish. Then he said, "You are the man!"

Nathan reminded David of everything God had done for him to this point. David already had wives, children, wealth, power, prestige, and more. Yet in God's eyes he "struck down Uriah the Hittite with the sword and took his wife" (12:10). David was as guilty of Uriah's death as if he had personally plunged the sword into the poor guy's heart. The act was inexcusable. Yet in God's mercy, it was forgivable.

David confessed his sin. And though he would receive forgiveness, there would be consequences. For one thing, Nathan foretold that "the sword will never depart from your house" (v. 10). For another, David would be on the receiving end of the same sin he had committed as someone close to him would publicly sleep with David's wives. And the worst blow was that the child David and Bathsheba had conceived would die.

Potent Quotables

"While the child was alive, I fasted and wept; for I said, Who knows? The Lord may be gracious to me, and the child may live. But now he is dead; why should I fast? Can I bring him back again? I shall go to him, but he will not return to me." (2 Samuel 12:22–23)

This statement of David's helps explain his attitude toward his son's death. He realized the common bond shared by all people is death. Though his son would not return from the grave, David would go to meet him some day. Some people believe David's statement suggests an expectation that father and son would someday be united in a heavenly, eternal realm—not just that David would join his son in death.

Soon the baby became seriously ill. David pleaded with God for the child's life. He went into solitude and fasted. His staff had no success in rousing him or getting him to eat. After seven days the baby died, and everyone was scared to give David the news. But he wasn't stupid and could tell from their whispering that something had happened. He asked if the child was dead, and they confirmed it. Only then did David get up, take a bath, go to worship at the house of God, and return home to eat.

The servants were perplexed at David's actions. He grieved while the child was alive, and stopped as soon as it actually died. But David was only being practical. He explained that he had hoped God would relent on His judgment. But when the baby died, David accepted it and prepared to get on with his life. He knew he could do nothing else. However, it wasn't long before David and Bathsheba had another child, and they named him Solomon.

Rape, Revenge, and Regrets (2 Sam. 13)

Nathan's prophecy of turmoil in David's family didn't take long to be fulfilled. In this blended family with various children by various wives, one of the sons (Amnon) fell in love with one of the daughters (Tamar), his half-sister. Amnon's crush on Tamar soon became an obsession, until he literally made himself sick. On the advice of a friend, he feigned illness to lure Tamar to his room, then raped her. Afterward, filled with disgust, he sent her away and bolted the door behind her. Tamar put ashes on her head, tore her robe, and went away weeping.

Absalom, Tamar's full brother, took her into his house, "a desolate woman" (v. 20). Then he bided his time. David was furious when he found out what Amnon had done, though we are told of no actions taken on the king's part. Absalom, in contrast, simply avoided Amnon, saying nothing to him, good or bad.

But Absalom wasn't finished with his half-brother. For two years he waited, filled with hate, until Amnon was completely unsuspecting. Then he invited all his brothers over for a meal, gave Amnon plenty of wine, and with a word to his servants, murdered him in the sight of all.

Absalom went into exile, living with his grandfather in a distant land. Soon David's grief for Amnon subsided, but he continued to mourn for Absalom. In a single evening, David had lost his two oldest sons—one to death and another to self-imposed banishment.

The Hair Apparent (2 Sam. 14–16:14)

Three years passed. David still wished to reunite with Absalom, but he could not bring himself to offer amnesty to Amnon's murderer. At last Joab intervened, hiring an actress to pose as a widow with a story about two sons. As with Nathan's story of the man with the ewe lamb, David saw his situation differently when he looked at it through others' eyes. David allowed Absalom to return to Jerusalem, but he would not see him. Absalom set up residence in a house of his own and waited, but two more years passed, and he was still barred from his father's presence. Even Joab refused to meet with him, until Absalom set his barley field on fire. That got Joab to Absalom's door. Absalom told Joab he would rather be found guilty and killed than go on this way. A second time Joab intervened with the king, and this time David forgave Absalom entirely.

Manna from Heaven

Hairiness seems to have been associated with manliness and strength in biblical times. Here, Absalom's luxuriant hair is part of his striking appearance. In the next chapter you'll see that Elisha was ridiculed for his baldness.

It is doubtful, however, whether Absalom's intentions were entirely sincere. The next we hear, he was using his charisma to woo the loyalty of the Israelites for himself. Absalom was not only a consummate politician; he was also good-looking. "In all Israel there was not a man so highly praised for his handsome appearance as Absalom. From the top of his head to the sole of his foot there was no blemish in him." Every year when he got his annual haircut, he lost five pounds (14:25–26).

After four years of stealing the hearts of Israel with carefully orchestrated public relations techniques, Absalom excused himself to go to another city, where he began to conspire for the throne in earnest. Quickly he won followers, including one of David's wisest advisers, a man named Ahithophel.

Word reached David that Israel now supported Absalom. Swiftly David vacated Jerusalem with his followers, leaving behind 10 concubines to take care of the palace, and two priests—Abiathar and Zadok— to take care of the Ark of the Covenant and pass along information to David.

Snapshots

Fans of "The Andy Griffith Show" will want to read about the rock-chucking Shimei, possibly the patron saint of Ernest T. Bass (2 Samuel 16:5–14; 19:16–23).

David also sent back Hushai, one of his loyal advisers, who would pretend to defect to Absalom. Once installed at the palace, Hushai was to counteract the advice of Ahithophel, David's former adviser. He would also act as an informant, passing information to the priests, who would tell their sons, who would pass the news along to David.

As you can tell, this was a confusing and tumultuous time. It was hard to know who was supporting whom. As David left the city, several prominent people made it clear they would not be supporting him.

Plants, Plots, and Perverse Pleasures (2 Sam. 16:15–17:29)

Back at the palace, Ahithophel was already advising Absalom on how to establish himself as king. Absalom's first order of business was to sleep with the king's concubines in the sight of all the city, thereby establishing his supremacy. Without knowing that he was fulfilling Nathan's prophecy (12:11–12), Absalom had a tent set up on the roof of the palace, where he carried out Ahithophel's advice.

What Saith Thou?

Is suicide ever an acceptable way to die?

The Bible records only five people who killed themselves (six, if you count Samson, though most consider his death akin to dying on a battlefield). None were exactly models of righteousness. (So far, King Saul, his armor bearer, and now Ahithophel have killed themselves. Later victims will be an evil king of Israel and Judas Iscariot.) Nowhere does the Bible directly address suicide.

However, Jews and Christians traditionally view the commandment against murder (Exodus 20:13) as applying to suicide as well.

Next Ahithophel counseled Absalom to pursue David and strike him while he was tired, bringing the war to a swift end. With David slain, his whole contingent would likely return to Jerusalem and accept Absalom's rule. It was good advice, but Absalom decided to get a second opinion—from Hushai, the mole David had planted in the palace.

Hushai's advice, not surprisingly, directly contradicted Ahithophel's. He reminded Absalom of David's experience as a fighter and warned of rushing into conflict. He suggested that David would be in hiding, so it would be better to assemble all the troops available and attempt to wipe out all of David's followers in a full-scale attack. Absalom liked what he heard from Hushai because "the Lord had determined to frustrate the good advice of Ahithophel in order to bring disaster on Absalom" (17:14).

Hushai had bought David precious time in which to deploy his expert warriors. He passed the word to the priests, who told their respective sons, who got the word to David—and barely escaped capture in doing so. When Ahithophel saw that his advice would not be heeded, he realized that David had as good as won already. He went home where "he put his house in order and then hanged himself" (17:23).

A Really, *Really* Bad Hair Day (2 Sam. 18)

David had been king for a while, but he hadn't forgotten how to be a soldier on the run. He formed his followers into companies and assigned commanders to oversee them.

Before sending them off, David instructed his officers to "be gentle" with Absalom if they came upon him. The battle was severe. David's forces were victorious, but 20,000 men were killed that day. The battle had spread from the countryside into a neighboring forest, where "the forest claimed more lives that day than the sword" (18:8).

Absalom was riding his mule through a wooded area when his bushy hair got caught in the branches of a large oak tree. His mule kept going, leaving him dangling there, unable to get down. One of David's men found him and reported to Joab, who knew what needed to be done. It would have been a simple enough matter to capture and imprison the rebel son, but Joab didn't take any chances. He personally thrust three javelins into Absalom's heart, after which ten of his armor-bearers surrounded Absalom and finished him off. They threw his body in a big pit and heaped a large pile of rocks over him. The ironic comment is made that, prior to this event, Absalom had erected a stone monument to himself. However, he would now be remembered more for the second pile of rocks than the one he had constructed. The additional irony was that his thick hair, a source of pride in his society and perhaps even more so for someone as arrogant as he, was the cause of his downfall. David was once again a victorious king, but a heartbroken father. He returned to Jerusalem, but could not be consoled over Absalom's death. In fact, his expressed desire was that he might have died rather than his son (18:33).

Back in Business (2 Sam. 19:9–21)

The rest of 2 Samuel tells of the aftermath of Absalom's rebellion and a few other events from the life of David. His worst crisis is over, but so are his "glory days."

Snapshots

Several frequently overlooked stories are tucked into the closing pages of 2 Samuel:

David makes a wreck of a requiem (18:33–19:8).

After his victory, David settles matters with his adversaries and allies (19:9–39).

Joab settles some scores of his own (20:1–13).

A rebel's head is returned—special delivery—over a city wall (20:14–22).

Saul's family continues to suffer for his past offenses (21:1–14).

Tales of David's mighty men (21:15–22; 23:8–23).

David takes a census against God's wishes (2 Samuel 24: 1 Chronicles 21).

The Bible faithfully records David's flaws as well as his virtues. While we aren't always given as much information as we'd like in order to understand all the hows and whys, we can say simply that the life of David was one of extreme ups and downs. He is known as "a man after [God's] own heart" (1 Samuel 13:14), but we have seen that he was far from perfect. When we get to the writings of David (Chapter 13), we will see that he was as contrite after committing a sin as he was courageous standing up to Goliath or merciful when standing over a sleeping Saul. It is perhaps the genuineness of his repentance that made him stand out in God's eyes.

David was a passionate person with a wide range of emotions. He did most of the legwork to pull the tribes of Israel together into a great nation. And even though his sin with Bathsheba stands as the darkest mark on David's record, their son Solomon would be chosen by God to reign over the golden age of Israel.

The Least You Need to Know

➤ After Saul's death, David united the tribes of Israel into a great nation.

➤ David's adultery with Bathsheba was a turning point in his reign, leading to family struggle and national rebellion.

➤ In spite of the internal and external rebellions against David, he persevered and kept the nation united, setting up an era of peace and prosperity for his son, Solomon.

Chapter 11

The Riches-to-Rags Story of Israel and Judah

In This Chapter

➤ Solomon succeeds David as king

➤ The glory days of Israel

➤ Israel and Judah go their separate ways

➤ The death of David, the building of the temple, Solomon's wisdom, the Queen of Sheba, Elijah and Elisha, a lot of wicked kings, Israel and Judah both are taken into captivity

Many seemingly sudden tragedies are actually the result of a history of poor choices. Ignore dental hygiene, and your teeth eventually rot. Downplay your children's grievances long enough, and some day they may rebel against you. Similarly, this chapter will show how God allowed His people to be taken into captivity and experience great suffering. But it will be clear that these tragedies took place only after a long period of spiritual neglect and moral decay.

Solomon's Successful Succession (1 Kings 1)

David was still king, but was getting old. He became unable to get warm even when covered up, so his servants found another prescription for his problem. They secured a beautiful young virgin girl named Abishag to take care of David. It was also her job to lie with him to keep him warm, though it is clearly stated that "the king had no intimate relations with her"(1 Kings 1:4).

David's oldest living son, Adonijah, thought this would be an ideal time to position himself to be the next king. He followed Absalom's strategy of riding in a chariot preceded by 50 men. Like Absalom, Adonijah was an attractive guy. He had just about everything going for him—except his father's endorsement. He probably knew David was expecting Solomon to be the next king, because he threw a party that included all his brothers *except* Solomon. He also got the support of Joab and one of the priests named Abiathar. However, he didn't include Nathan the prophet or several other key officials in his plans.

What Saith Thou?

With all the resources of Israel at his disposal why wouldn't David be "driving" a classier animal than a mule?

We tend to associate mules with dirt farmers in overalls, but during this time they were the conveyance of choice for royalty.

Nathan heard of Adonijah's plans to become king and warned Bathsheba, Solomon's mother, that Adonijah's ambitions could put Solomon's life in danger. The two went to see the king. When David heard what was taking place, he commanded that Solomon be placed upon David's own mule, escorted to a public place, and anointed king over Israel. So it happened that while Adonijah and the other brothers were feasting together, celebrating Adonijah's accession to the throne, Solomon became king, to the blast of trumpets and the shouts of the crowd.

The people made so much noise shouting "Long live King Solomon!" that they disturbed Adonijah's party. When his guests learned what was happening, they panicked and left. Adonijah went to the public altar and clung to it, seeking God's protection from what the new king might do to him. Solomon agreed not to harm him as long as he behaved himself.

Wisdom? In Your Dreams! (1 Kings 2–4)

The Bible recounts that when David realized he was close to death, he called Solomon to him and gave him some advice. A lot of this advice, we are told, had to do with taking care of political enemies. David had overlooked a lot of personal offenses, yet those people were still around and were potential threats to Solomon. Adonijah's actions clearly indicated he still had his eye on the throne, so he was put to death, as were Joab and Shimei. Abiathar, the priest who had supported Adonijah, was forced to resign.

A more widespread problem at this time was that Israel had no centralized system of worship and had resorted to the habits of the surrounding peoples. With no established place of worship, there was a kind of "do it yourself" mentality where people would erect shrines in the hills. With no legitimate priests involved, what resulted was less than pure worship of God—frequently becoming outright idolatry. Even after Solomon built the temple, such shrine worship continued.

Yet while Solomon was worshiping at one of these places, God spoke to him in a dream. Solomon had just offered a thousand burnt offerings, and God responded by telling Solomon to "ask for whatever you want me to give you" (1 Kings 3:5). Think of the possibilities! All Solomon asked for, however, was "a discerning heart to govern your people and to distinguish between right and wrong" (v. 9). God was very pleased with this answer. Because Solomon hadn't wished for wealth or long life, God promised him wisdom *and* riches *and* honor *and* a long life—provided the king remained obedient to God's commands.

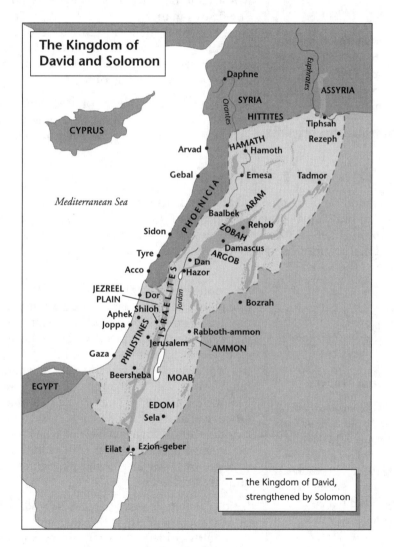

The Kingdom of David and Solomon

It didn't take long for Solomon to demonstrate his exceptional wisdom. Two prostitutes came before him to rule on their case (much like "People's Court"). The two women, who lived in the same house, had both given birth around the same time.

Manna from Heaven

As the wisest man on earth, Solomon became the consummate "answer man." He composed 3,000 proverbs and 1,005 songs. He was a careful observer of nature and could speak about trees, plants, and animals with authority. As his reputation grew, people came from all over the world to learn from him.

One of the infants had died in the night, and its mother, according to the other woman, had gotten up and quietly switched the babies, taking the living child and substituting the one who had died. Each claimed to be the mother of the remaining baby.

Solomon called for a sword and told his servant to cut the child in two and give each woman half. The woman whose child had died actually agreed to this settlement. The first woman, however, pleaded for Solomon to spare the child. She was willing to revoke her claim on the child if its life would be spared. Therefore, Solomon wisely discerned that this was the child's real mother, and he gave her custody of her baby.

Solomon's reign was a time of peace and prosperity. The people were safe and happy. Everyone "lived in safety, each man under his own vine and fig tree" (1 Kings 4:25).

Temple Temps (1 Kings 5–9)

With Solomon on his throne and all right with the world, he decided to turn his attention to building a permanent temple for the worship of God. He found a ready contractor in Hiram of Tyre, in Phoenicia, who was only too pleased to supply wood for the construction. (His source was the famous cedars of Lebanon—the best lumber available in the Middle East.)

Manna from Heaven

God had said that David's son would be the person to "build a house for my Name" (2 Samuel 7:13). The name of God symbolizes all that he is. In dedicating the temple to the name of God, Solomon acknowledged that God could not be confined to the temple or to any other building (1 Kings 8:27).

Solomon drafted 30,000 men to work rotating shifts: one month of forced labor in Lebanon and then two months at home. Some worked as stonecutters, others as carriers, transporting pieces of cut stone as much as 12 to 15 feet long—quite a task! All the cutting and shaping of the stonework was done at the quarry. At the temple site itself, "no hammer, chisel or any other iron tool was heard" (6:7). The temple was much like the tabernacle in its design. Outside stood a bronze altar for sacrifices and a large reservoir of water for the ceremonial cleansing of the priests. Ten mobile stands held smaller bowls of water, used by the priests during animal sacrifices.

Inside the temple was the Most Holy Place which housed the Ark of the Covenant, and the Holy Place, containing golden tables for bread dedicated to God (the "bread of the presence"), 10 gold lampstands, and a gold altar for burning incense).

Solomon's temple was of modest size—about 90 feet long, 30 feet wide, and 45 feet high. After all, only the priests would ever go inside. But it was a masterpiece of workmanship and design, intricately and beautifully carved, and covered inside with pure gold. When the temple was finished, Solomon filled it with objects of silver and gold that David had collected and dedicated to God. The Ark of the Covenant was placed in the Most Holy Place, still containing the stone tablets Moses had put there. As the priests withdrew, the glory of the Lord filled the temple in a cloud so thick the priests couldn't see what they were doing.

The dedication of the temple was accompanied by lengthy offerings and sacrifices, followed by a festival lasting 14 days.

Queen for a Stay (1 Kings 10)

Solomon's next project was a palace for himself, also made of cedar. This was a larger and more multipurpose edifice, and it took 13 years to construct.

Snapshots

A gold and ivory throne. Monkeys. Imported horses and chariots. Silver so plentiful it wasn't even worth keeping. A stroll around Solomon's compound must have been breathtaking. Get the full description in 1 Kings 10:14–29.

Soon Solomon's wealth was as legendary as his wisdom. The Bible says he was richer and wiser than anyone else on earth. One day Solomon received a visit from the Queen of Sheba, who had come a great distance—probably from what is now southwest Arabia or Yemen. She gave him a pop quiz to test his wisdom, and nothing she asked was too hard for him to explain. She had been impressed by what she had heard about Solomon, but she realized that wasn't even half the story. From her camel caravan she gave him gifts of gold, precious stones, and more spices than had ever been seen at one time. Solomon gave her gifts in return.

The Odds Against Success Are About a Thousand to One (1 Kings 11)

With everything Solomon had going for him, you'd think nothing would ever cause him serious problems. But the last we hear of him, we discover that he strayed from his loyalty to God in order to practice the religions of his wives. And by the way, he had 700 wives and 300 concubines. His harem included women from essentially every tribe around. By Hebrew law he was forbidden to marry such women for this very reason. Because his love for his female companions became greater than his love for God, he was told by God that his kingdom would be torn away from him. Yet for the sake of David who had been so close to God, the entire kingdom would not be lost, and the split would not come until after Solomon's lifetime.

Solomon began to have military enemies. To make matters worse, one of his own officers, a man named Jeroboam, rebelled after a prophet told him that he was to be the new king of Israel. Solomon tried to have Jeroboam killed, but he escaped.

Split Decision (1 Kings 12)

After 40 years of rule, Solomon died and was succeeded by his son, Rehoboam. Rehoboam did not inherit his father's wisdom. When Jeroboam showed up with a big crowd and requested tax cuts now that the kingdom was running smoothly, Solomon's counselors advised Rehoboam to agree and so win the people's favor. Instead, Rehoboam asked a younger crowd of advisers what *they* thought. They told him to crack down: Tell the rabble that Solomon had been tough but he was going to be tougher. Show them who was boss.

Rehoboam took his friends' advice. Bad move! Most of the tribes of Israel immediately rejected him as king and put their support behind Jeroboam. The first time Rehoboam tried to send his minister of forced labor into Israel, the people stoned the guy to death.

The nation of Israel—so briefly united under David and Solomon—now split and became two nations: Israel, made up of the 10 northernmost tribes; and Judah, comprising the tribe of Judah and part of the tribe of Benjamin. Though civil war was temporarily averted, from that point on there would never be much of a friendship between north and south.

With a few crucial exceptions, David and Solomon had modeled faithfulness to God, and the people had witnessed magnificent results of such faithfulness. Israel had become a legitimate world power. But from this point on, Israel and Judah each have a series of about 20 kings—few of whom will prove themselves to be faithful spiritual leaders. The people had seen the best that could happen from steadfast faith; now they're about to see the fruits of idolatry—and it won't be pretty.

Some kings are remembered for their political or social accomplishments, but far too few were concerned with what *God* wanted. The recurring comment made about most of the kings who follow is, "He did evil in the eyes of the Lord." The end result, as you will see, is conquest by their enemies followed by captivity. (Israel was destroyed by the Assyrians in 722 B.C.E. and sold into slavery, becoming the "lost tribes." Judah lasted until 605 B.C.E. when the Babylonians stormed Jerusalem and carried off all the people and possessions they felt would be of value to them.)

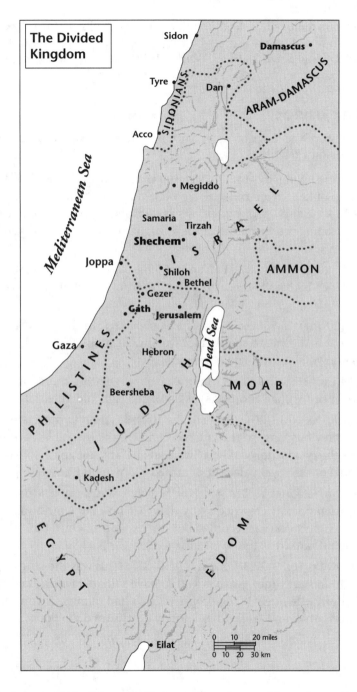

The Divided Kingdom

Sidon

Damascus

Tyre

Dan

ARAM-DAMASCUS

SIDONIANS

Acco

Mediterranean Sea

Megiddo

Samaria

Tirzah

Shechem

I S R A E L

Joppa

Shiloh

Bethel

AMMON

Gezer

Gath

Jerusalem

Gaza

Hebron

Dead Sea

PHILISTINES

Beersheba

J U D A H

M O A B

Kadesh

E G Y P T

E D O M

Eilat

0   10   20 miles
0 10 20 30 km

Although the temple had been built for authentic worship and was attended by Levitical priests who knew God's law, many shrines (referred to as "high places") remained throughout the land. In most cases, even the "good" kings failed to have

123

these pagan altars removed. Indeed, the first king on the list personally erected two golden calves in remote areas—surely hoping to keep his people out of Jerusalem, the capital of Judah (now a rival nation). While his intent seems to be primarily political, later kings will become full-fledged followers of Canaanite gods.

The Kings of Israel

Following is a list of the kings of Israel, with a thumbnail sketch of what happened during each person's reign.

➤ **Jeroboam I** (1 Kings 12–14:20)   Fearing that his people would endorse the leadership of Rehoboam of Judah, Jeroboam I set up two golden calves for them to worship. He also appointed priests at random. Warned by God through several signs (including the withering of his arm), he refused to repent and lost a son as a result.

➤ **Nadab** (1 Kings 15:25–32)   This son of Jeroboam followed his father's example. He was killed by Baasha (perhaps an officer in his army), who succeeded him as king.

➤ **Baasha** (1 Kings 15:33–16:7)   Baasha also walked "in the ways of Jeroboam," a phrase that had come to signify idol worship. A prophet named Jehu predicted the sure downfall of his whole family.

➤ **Elah** (1 Kings 16:8–14)   This son of Baasha was getting drunk one day when Zimri (one of his chariot officers) assassinated him and killed off his entire family.

➤ **Zimri** (1 Kings 16:15–20)   Some of the Israelites didn't appreciate Zimri knocking off their previous king, so they placed Omri on the throne. A battle ensued between the two factions. When Zimri saw he was not going to win, he entered the citadel of the royal palace and burned it down on himself.

➤ **Omri/Tibni** (1 Kings 16:21–28)   Not everyone was pleased with Omri as king; some simultaneously crowned a guy named Tibni. But Omri's followers were stronger. Tibni's death is recorded but not explained. Omri built the city of Samaria, but ranked as the worst king to date.

➤ **Ahab** (1 Kings 16:29–22:40; 2 Kings 9:30–37)   This was the king of evil kings. Among his other crimes, Ahab is said to have initiated the Baal worship of his foreign-born wife Jezebel. The prophet Elijah had numerous confrontations with Ahab. Both Ahab and Jezebel had bloody deaths involving dogs.

Snapshots

If reading through the list of kings gets a bit monotonous, take a few moments to check out some of the gory details of the reign of Ahab and Jezebel:

A guy rebuilds the city of Jericho—and triggers a centuries-old curse (Joshua 6:26; 1 Kings 16:34).

How far will an evil couple go to acquire one little vineyard? (1 Kings 21)

When God has an arrow with your name on it, there's not much you can do (1 Kings 22:1–40).

A most undignified way for a queen to die (2 Kings 9:30–37).

➤ **Ahaziah** (1 Kings 22:51–2 Kings 1:18)   A son of Ahab, Ahaziah also worshipped Baal. He fell through the lattice of his upper room and died later of his injuries because he sought help from Baal rather than God.

➤ **Joram** (2 Kings 3; 6:24–7:20)   Joram allied with Judah's king, Jehoshaphat, to defeat the Moabites. During his reign, Samaria is besieged by the Arameans.

➤ **Jehu** (2 Kings 9–10)   Jehu was singled out by God and anointed by an emissary of the prophet Elisha. Assigned to bring judgment on the house of Ahab, Jehu murdered more than 70 of Ahab's sons and relations, along with the priests of Baal, piling their heads at the city gates.

➤ **Jehoahaz** (2 Kings 13:1–9)   This son of Jehu had trouble with the Arameans, complicated by a severe reduction in military strength. He sought God's help only after his return to idolatry proved to be disastrous for Israel.

➤ **Jehoash** (2 Kings 13:10–14:16)   Jehoash did better against the Arameans. He also scored a victory against King Amaziah of Judah. But as a spiritual leader he was no better than his predecessors.

➤ **Jeroboam II** (2 Kings 14:23–29)   This second Jeroboam was able to gain back some of the territory Israel had previously lost, fulfilling a prophecy of Jonah.

➤ **Zechariah** (2 Kings 15:8–12)   Not to be confused with Zechariah the prophet, this son of Jeroboam II lasted all of six months before he was publicly assassinated.

➤ **Shallum** (2 Kings 15:13–15)   Shallum was assassinated a month later.

➤ **Menahem** (2 Kings 15:16–22)   Assyria was beginning to pose a serious threat. A violent and evil man, Menahem taxed the wealthy people of Israel to pay indemnity and save his country from destruction.

➤ **Pekahiah** (2 Kings 15:23–26)   Pekahiah was assassinated by one of his chief officers, Pekah.

➤ **Pekah** (2 Kings 15:27–31)   The Assyrians continued to close in on Israel during Pekah's lengthy reign. Eventually he was assassinated by Hoshea.

➤ **Hoshea** (2 Kings 17)   The last of the kings of Israel, Hoshea continued paying tribute to Assyria while secretly negotiating with Egypt for help against their common enemy. When the Assyrian king discovered Hoshea's double dealings, he had him imprisoned. Within three years Israel was completely defeated, and most of its citizens were deported. Assyria repopulated the land with outsiders.

Snapshots

Here are a few more little-known stories from the era of the kings:

It's not a good idea to try to fool one of God's prophets (1 Kings 14:1–18).

"If you would quit raining fire on my men, I'd like to ask you something" (2 Kings 1).

When Samaria is beseiged, food is so short that a donkey head sells for two pounds of silver and desperate mothers resort to cannibalism. But four lepers save the day (2 Kings 6:24–7:20).

If graveyards aren't scary enough, try witnessing an unexpected resurrection while hiding in one (2 Kings 13:20–21).

The Kings of Judah

While the kings of Israel were making one bad decision after another until they lost their kingdom, the kings of Judah were a little better—but not much.

➤ **Rehoboam** (1 Kings 14:21–31) As king, Rehoboam allowed worship of other gods and permitted the addition of male shrine prostitutes. Five years into his reign, an Egyptian king invaded and carried off the treasures in the temple and palace.

➤ **Abijah** (1 Kings 15:1–8)   "He committed all the sins his father had done before him."

➤ **Asa** (1 Kings 15:9–24; 2 Chronicles 14–16)   Asa got rid of the male shrine prostitutes and idols and restored silver and gold articles to the temple. His "heart was fully committed to the Lord all his life," and he even deposed his own grandmother for idol worship. Late in life, however, he suffered foot problems and refused to turn to God for help.

➤ **Jehoshaphat** (1 Kings 22:41–50; 2 Chronicles 17–21:3)   Son of Asa, Jehoshaphat again rid the land of male shrine prostitutes, appointed godly judges, and lived in peace with the kings of Israel.

➤ **Jehoram** (2 Kings 8:16–24)   Jehoram married one of Ahab's daughters (not a good sign). The Edomites, who had been subject to Judah, rebelled during his reign and established their own king.

➤ **Ahaziah** (2 Kings 8:25–29; 9:14–29)   Ahaziah visited Israel's king Joram, his ally, after Joram was wounded in battle. While he was there, he was put to death by Jehu, who had replaced Joram.

➤ **Athaliah** (2 Kings 11)   Athaliah was the mother of Ahaziah. On hearing about her son's death, she attempted to destroy the rest of the royal family. Only Joash, a baby son of Ahaziah, escaped. After seven years, Athaliah was put to death as part of a program of spiritual renewal.

Potent Quotables

"Do not be afraid or discouraged because of this vast army. For the battle is not yours, but God's.... You will not have to fight this battle." *(2 Chronicles 20:15, 17)*

This promise of God to King Jehoshaphat is a favorite among many believers as they face opposition and attempt to count on God's power rather than their own.

➤ **Joash** (2 Kings 12; 2 Chronicles 24:1–27)   Joash was only 7 years old when his reign began. He took up a collection to repair the temple but later turned to idolatry. His reign ended when his own officials assassinated him in retaliation for having a priest killed.

➤ **Amaziah** (2 Kings 14:1–22)   Success in battle allowed this son of Joash to regain some land previously lost to the Edomites, but he later lost people and property during a war with Israel.

➤ **Azariah** (also known as Uzziah) (2 Kings 15:1–7; 2 Chronicles 26)   This son of Amaziah implemented numerous social improvements (towers, cisterns, crops, and so on). But after proudly and defiantly assuming the role of priest, God afflicted him with leprosy, forcing him to spend the rest of his life in isolation.

➤ **Jotham** (2 Kings 15: 32–38) A reasonably good king, Jotham's chief accomplishment was rebuilding the Upper Gate of the temple.

Manna from Heaven

The prophet Isaiah was sent to tell Hezekiah that he was about to die. When Hezekiah prayed, God added 15 years to his life. As a sign that Isaiah was telling him the truth about his extended life expectancy, God caused a shadow to reverse itself 10 steps on a nearby stairway (2 Kings 20:1–11).

Manna from heaven

In Canaanite mythology, Asherah was the female counterpart of their primary god, El. The son of El was Baal, whose female companion was Ashtoreth—the equivalent of Ishtar in Babylon, Aphrodite in Greece, or Venus in Rome. The Israelites had dabbled in worship of these deities since the exodus, since much of the "worship" was of a sexual nature. But few were as devoted to these gods as King Manasseh. God had long ago instructed Israel to destroy Asherah poles (Exodus 34:13)—not set them up in his temple!

➤ **Ahaz** (2 Kings 16) This king's reign was dominated by trouble with the Assyrians. Ahaz paid indemnity, for which he is not fondly remembered. Devoid of any sensitivity to God, he sacrificed his own son "in the fire" to other gods—a detestable practice.

➤ **Hezekiah** (2 Kings 18–20) Hezekiah rid Judah of idols and shrines—even the bronze serpent Moses had erected in the wilderness, which had become a source of idolatry. During his reign, Israel fell to Assyria, but Judah was miraculously spared.

➤ **Manasseh** (2 Kings 21:1–18) Hezekiah's son rebuilt the idols his father had destroyed and even placed an Asherah pole in the temple. He consulted psychics and spiritualists, practiced sorcery, and sacrificed his own son to other gods. In addition, he "shed so much innocent blood that he filled Jerusalem from end to end." His wickedness was such that God determined to "wipe out Jerusalem as one wipes a dish, wiping it and turning it upside down."

➤ **Amon** (2 Kings 21:19–26) Amon was a lot like his father, Manasseh. After two years, his officials killed him in his palace.

➤ **Josiah** (2 Kings 22:1–23:30) Beginning his rule at 8 years old, Josiah was steadfastly faithful to God. His discovery of a copy of God's Law in the temple led to sweeping religious reforms—both in the physical restoration of the temple and the spiritual recommitment of the people. He eliminated every known idol and reinstituted the observance of the Passover (after Israel neglected it for about 300 years).

➤ **Jehoahaz** (2 Kings 23:31–35) During a three-month reign, he reverted to the evil practices that had gone on before. He was captured and carried off to Egypt, where he died.

➤ **Jehoiakim** (2 Kings 23:34–24:7)   Babylon was now becoming a serious threat. At first Jehoiakim paid tribute, but eventually he rebelled. The Babylonians sent reinforcements to subdue Judah.

➤ **Jehoiachin** (2 Kings 24:8–17; 25:27–30)   Jehoiakim's son, Jehoiachin, reigned for three months before he was forced to surrender Jerusalem to the Babylonians and was transported to Babylon along with 10,000 officers, soldiers, craftsmen, and artists in the first exile.

➤ **Zedekiah** (2 Kings 24:18–25:26)   Installed by Babylon as a puppet king, Zedekiah rebelled. Jerusalem was besieged, taken, and utterly destroyed. After his sons were killed before his eyes, he was blinded. All but the poorest people of Judah were marched into exile.

Snapshots

The kings of Judah had some interesting stories of their own:

Who do you want on the front lines as you march into battle? The singers, of course! (2 Chronicles 20)

One angel of God versus 185,000 vicious Assyrians: it's no contest! (2 Kings 18:17–19:37)

Reading Scripture, smashing idols, and burning bones (2 Kings 23).

The book of 1 Kings begins with the glory of Solomon, and 2 Kings ends with everyone in captivity: Israel at the hands of Assyria and Judah subservient to Babylon. More about the captivity comes to light in Chapter 14, "Tell-a-Vision Personalities," when we look at the prophets and their writings. It is a sad story to see the rapid spiritual and political decline of a once-great nation. Few, if any, stories about the kings (after Solomon) are familiar. But in this dark time, the two spotlights are the prophets Elijah and Elisha. These men were mentioned in the profiles of some of the kings, but their life stories are by far the most impressive in this portion of the Bible. Let's look briefly at what made them so memorable.

Down Come the Ravens, Up Goes the Chariot (1 Kings 17–19; 2 Kings 1–2)

Elijah appears in the Bible at the depth of the first spiritual slide in Israel: the rule of King Ahab and Queen Jezebel. He told Ahab that God was withdrawing rain from the kingdom for "the next few years" (1 Kings 17:1). As drought struck the land, Elijah drank from a brook, and God supplied him with food carried by ravens.

When the brook dried up, Elijah found lodging with a widow in a town called Zarephath. He miraculously extended the woman's food supply until the famine had ended. He also brought her son back to life after a serious illness.

After three years without rain, God again sent Elijah to Ahab. Elijah suggested a showdown on Mount Carmel. Because the people were being drawn into Baal worship, Elijah invited 450 prophets of Baal and 400 prophets of Asherah to join him. The prophets of Baal built an altar and spent an entire day calling on their god to send fire from the sky to light the altar, shouting and slashing themselves until blood flowed, to no avail. Elijah then had valuable water poured on his altar, drenching it not once, but three times. When he prayed, fire immediately fell from heaven, consuming the sacrifice, the water, the wood, and even the stones and the soil.

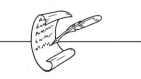

Manna from Heaven

This story of Elijah and the town of Zarephath is later mentioned by Jesus to emphasize his statement that "no prophet is accepted in his hometown" (Luke 4:24–27). During this time when Israel and Judah were so unfaithful, God found good people in other places to help his messengers.

The people immediately believed in the God of Elijah. The prophets of Baal were seized and killed. Elijah told Ahab to hurry home because it was about to rain, then outran the king's chariot down the mountain.

Elijah was then forced to hide from Jezebel. God encouraged and strengthened him, speaking to the prophet not in the fury of a powerful wind or a nearby earthquake or fire, but with a gentle whisper.

After training Elisha—his protégé—to take his place, Elijah was carried to heaven in a whirlwind. On the way to his point of departure, he parted the Jordan River with his cloak, as Moses had parted the Red Sea. There Elisha begged to let him inherit "a double portion of your spirit" (2 Kings 2:9) before a chariot of fire and horses of fire appeared and carried Elijah off.

Miracles In All Shapes and Sizes (1 Kings 19:19–21; 2 Kings 2–8:15)

Elisha carried on the work that Elijah had begun—using Elijah's very cloak to part the water on his return that Elijah had previously parted. He used a pinch of salt to purify a town's polluted water supply. He perpetuated a widow's supply of oil to get her out of debt. He "unpoisoned" a pot of stew with a bit of flour. He fed a hundred men with a small amount of bread. He caused a lost (and borrowed) axhead to float to the surface of the Jordan River to be retrieved. He brought a young boy back to life.

One of the stories about Elisha concerns his baldness. A group of youths taunted him about it, and he called down a curse on them. Two bears came out of the woods and mauled 42 of the jeering youths. (It must have been quite a crowd.)

Elisha was a frequent consultant to kings because of the accuracy of his prophecies. God's revelations to Elisha were so precise that opposing leaders thought their people must be leaking information. Not so, they protested. "Elisha, the prophet who is in Israel, tells the king of Israel the very words you speak in your bedroom" (2 Kings 6:12). Elisha helped King Jehoshaphat defeat the Moabites simply by digging ditches and filling them with water. He single-handedly captured an army of hostile Arameans after God temporarily blinded them. He was even consulted by the king of Aram (an enemy) about an illness. Elisha told the king's messenger that the king would recover from the illness, yet would die anyway. Sure enough, the messenger returned with the news, smothered the king to death, and took over as king.

Another Aramean, a commander named Naaman, had leprosy. He learned of Elisha's reputation from an Israelite servant girl. Naaman sent to the prophet for help, and Elisha replied through a messenger telling Naaman to wash himself seven times in the Jordan River. Naaman was incensed, first because Elisha hadn't come in person, and second because the Jordan was not the most scenic of rivers. But his servants convinced him he had nothing to lose. When he obeyed Elisha's instructions, he was immediately healed.

The power of God demonstrated through Elijah and Elisha stands in stark contrast to the spiritual apathy of most of the kings. God was still at work. Even though the nations of "his" people were declining and crumbling, God would continue to work through individuals who devoted themselves to him. The next chapter takes a look at four individuals who are noted for exceptional faithfulness during difficult times.

What Saith Thou?

Why would Elisha help the enemies of Israel and Judah?

Elijah and Elisha did only what God told them to do. The power of God had not ended simply because God's people had turned their backs on him. Instead, it was used to help people who were willing to receive it.

Snapshots

After Naaman's healing, a "behind the scenes" story about Elisha's servant provides a powerful lesson of how it isn't wise to try to "skim" for personal profit where the work of God is concerned (2 Kings 5:15–27).

The Least You Need to Know

➤ The rule of Solomon was unmatched in glory and wealth as Israel got a glimpse of the benefits of obedience to God.

➤ In spite of all Solomon's wisdom, he turned out to be not very smart. He committed idolatry—the one thing God warned him not to do, initiating the beginning of the end for Israel and Judah.

➤ With only a few exceptions, the kings of Israel and Judah were rotten, wicked, selfish, and idolatrous.

➤ Elijah and Elisha were primary spokesmen for God during this era of spiritual darkness. God's power became evident through their numerous miracles.

Chapter 12

Making the Best of a Bad Situation

In This Chapter

➤ Hebrew captives are released to return to Jerusalem and rebuild the temple, leading to a reformation by Ezra

➤ Nehemiah and others are released from captivity to rebuild the walls of Jerusalem

➤ A Jewish captive named Esther becomes queen and saves her people at risk of her own life

➤ Job suffers...and suffers...and suffers...yet perseveres

People tend to have one of two reactions when they see a person dedicated to his or her religious beliefs at a higher-than-average level. Some assume that the person is so religious because things are going well for her: "But if she had the problems *I* have to face, she would crack like a pecan under a steamroller." Others assume the opposite: "What a miserable life he has had. No wonder he's so religious. Nobody but God wants to keep hearing about his problems!"

We're going to look at four people in this chapter who break the stereotypes. They are all in lousy, undesirable positions, yet their faith takes their lives to new heights—and in doing so, also elevates the lives of those around them.

The Long Walk Home (Ezra 1–2)

When we left the Israelites, they were going into captivity—most being marched off to Babylon. The portion of biblical history that follows is referred to as the Postexilic Period.

About 70 years have passed. The Babylonians have been conquered by the Medes and the Persians. The people of Judah are still captives in a foreign country, but their contract had been traded, so to speak. (However, certain Persian leaders retained the title, "King of Babylon.")

Cyrus, the king of Persia, had a different philosophy concerning his POWs. While the Assyrians and Babylonians tried to destroy the religions of their captives and assimilate the people, Cyrus tended to show respect for those religions. When dealing with gods (or God) he didn't know, Cyrus didn't want to risk angering any of them. One of his first moves was to issue a decree that paroled everyone who wanted to go back to Jerusalem and rebuild their temple. This would be the first of several groups who returned to their homeland.

A collection was taken to accumulate silver, gold, livestock, and other goods that would be needed during the journey and after they got there. Cyrus's contribution was locating and returning the temple artifacts Nebuchadnezzar had absconded with years before.

In charge of the expedition was a man named Zerubbabel. Among the group were a number of people who would minister at the temple: priests, singers, gatekeepers, and other servants. The trip would be no weekend retreat, though. More than 40,000 people would travel about four months before reaching their destination (Ezra 7:8–9).

Manna from Heaven

The Feast of Tabernacles (also called Succoth or Sukkot) is one of the celebrations prescribed in the Law of Moses (Leviticus 23:33–43). Also known as the Feast of Booths, it commemorates the Israelites' journey from Egypt to Canaan, as well as the harvest of the Promised Land. During this week-long event, the people lived in temporary booths, made numerous offerings to God, and ate well. Some Jews continue to celebrate this festival.

Got No Church; Got No Steeple; All We've Got is a Bunch of People (Ezra 3)

As soon as everyone had settled in their towns, they assembled in Jerusalem to reconstruct the altar, offer sacrifices, and celebrate the Feast of Tabernacles—all before the foundation of the temple was even laid.

Masons and carpenters were hired, and trade arrangements were made to acquire new cedar logs from Phoenicia. When the work began, the priests and Levites blew trumpets and clanged cymbals, the people shouted and sang praises to God, while the older people wept in remembrance of what had once been. We are told that, "The sound was heard far away" (3:13).

A Temple of Doom? (Ezra 4–6)

However, not everyone was overjoyed to see the temple being rebuilt. Israel's former enemies were disturbed by the return of their old neighbors and employed various strategies to defeat the reconstruction project, including physical threats and legal roadblocks. Work on the temple was temporarily halted.

Some time later God sent the prophets Zechariah and Haggai to encourage the people, and the work resumed, though by that time no one could prove that the Persians had authorized this project. A formal inquiry was sent to King Darius, who not only confirmed the edict of Cyrus but ordered that the workmen's pay come from the royal treasury.

At last the new temple was completed and dedicated. The people also celebrated Passover with rejoicing. Once again God had led them out of foreign slavery to freedom in their own land.

Manna from Heaven

This temple is frequently referred to as Zerubbabel's temple to differentiate it from Solomon's temple, which had been destroyed, and Herod's temple, which was yet to be built.

And Then Along Came Ezra (Ezra 7–8)

Later, during the reign of the Persian King Artaxerxes, Ezra traveled to Jerusalem with another large group of Jewish exiles. Ezra, a descendant of the family of Aaron the high priest, was "a teacher well versed in the Law of Moses."

Artaxerxes liked Ezra and was generous in his offers of help. He donated tons of silver, gold, and artifacts to supply the new building, and he granted a tax-free status to anyone connected with the temple. It was a dangerous trip to Jerusalem, yet Ezra "was ashamed to ask the king for soldiers and horsemen to protect [them] from enemies on the road." Instead, he fasted and prayed, asking God for safety. God answered Ezra's prayer, and the group of about 1,500 men (plus women and children) arrived safely.

Next on Jeremiah Springer: Idol Worshipers and the Priests Who Marry Them! (Ezra 9–10)

Ezra had been in town about four months when people started revealing to him how bad their spiritual condition had become. Many of the men from the first batch of returning exiles had intermarried with neighboring women who were regularly involved with "detestable" religious practices in violation of Hebrew law. The people couldn't complain to the priests about the problem, because the priests and Levites were guilty along with the rest. Indeed, they had "led the way" for involvement in these idolatrous practices (Ezra 9:2).

135

What Saith Thou?

Was it perhaps a bit racist for the Jews to be so exclusive in whom they married?

Actually, many of the people who remained in Judah had the same ancestors as those who were carried away. The problem posed by intermarriage was religious, not ethnic. However, the people who stayed and intermarried would become the Samaritans, who did indeed feel the brunt of prejudice during New Testament times.

Ezra was genuinely "appalled" at this disclosure. He tore his clothes, pulled his hair, and sat there for most of the day. During the evening sacrifice, he prayed and poured out his feelings to God. He realized how much God had done to release the people from captivity, yet as soon as they were free, they rushed right back into the habits that had gotten them in trouble in the first place.

Ezra's heartfelt repentance didn't go unnoticed by others. In response to his weeping and praying, a large crowd soon joined him, also weeping bitterly. Then and there they determined to honor their original covenant with God, undoing the improper marriage covenants they had made. About 110 men were found who had taken foreign wives. Even though some of them had already had children, the wives and children were sent away.

So first Zerubbabel returned to Jerusalem to rebuild the temple. About eighty years later, Ezra returned and instituted religious reform. But the problems of Jerusalem are far from over.

Sayonara, Nehemiah (Nehemiah 1–2:10)

A dozen or so years after Ezra's return, we are introduced to another key figure named Nehemiah. Nehemiah's profession under King Artaxerxes was to serve as his cupbearer, the person who tasted the king's food and wine to make sure it was not poisoned. Nehemiah was trustworthy as well as cheerful, and the king liked him.

But one day some travelers came through, and Nehemiah asked how things were going in his homeland of Judah. They told him, "Those who survived the exile and are back in the province are in great trouble and disgrace. The wall of Jerusalem is broken down, and its gates have been burned with fire" (Nehemiah 1:3).

Nehemiah was crushed at the news. He mourned and fasted for several days, confessing Israel's sins and asking God for help. He was in no shape to entertain the king. He had never been morose in the presence of Artaxerxes before, and the king immediately recognized his state as "sadness of heart" rather than illness.

Nehemiah explained the reason for his depressed mood and even dared to ask for a leave of absence so he himself could see to the rebuilding of the walls. As he had done with Ezra, Artaxerxes threw his full support behind Nehemiah, granting safe passage, lumber, and military protection.

Stalling the Walling (Nehemiah 2:11–6:14)

Sure enough, when Nehemiah and his group arrived, they found considerable damage. The gates had been burned, the walls toppled. Despite the threat of opposition from neighboring enemies, word quickly spread and the walls soon started tumblin' *up*.

Rebuilding the city walls was conducted much like current Adopt-a-Highway plans. People started at an assigned place (usually one of the gates) and worked outward from there. When the wall was rebuilt to half its height, Nehemiah discovered a plot against Jerusalem, but he averted trouble by praying *and* posting a guard (Nehemiah 4:9).

The workers, however, began to get disheartened. Work continued, with Nehemiah's encouragement, but the people had to be on constant guard against attack. To make matters worse, a famine befell them. The wealthy took advantage of the poor, and things grew desperate. Once again Nehemiah intervened, ordering a stop to usury—the charging of exorbitant interest on loans—and forbidding the Israelites from enslaving one another (Leviticus 25:35–43).

Snapshots

Nehemiah faced persistent resistance from three stooges named Sanballat, Tobiah, and Geshem (2:19–20). If you have personal enemies of your own, perhaps you can pick up some tips from Nehemiah's handling of everything from verbal sarcasm to serious threats and dangerous ambushes (Nehemiah 4:7).

Wall-to-Wall Carpentry (Nehemiah 6:15–13)

Meanwhile, Nehemiah's enemies tried every trick they could think of to halt construction, but to no avail. Because Nehemiah stayed focused on the job before him rather than the mob around him, the walls were completed in only 52 days. Since the population of Jerusalem had been greatly reduced, Nehemiah's walls didn't need to enclose as much area as the original ones had. But the enemies of those in Jerusalem "were afraid and lost their self-confidence." They knew this motley group of people couldn't have made such progress without God's help.

A short while later, Ezra brought out the Law of Moses at a public assembly and read it aloud "from daybreak to noon" (Nehemiah 8:3). Levites stood around to make sure people understood what was being read. The words made the people weep. There they

Potent Quotables

"The joy of the Lord is your strength." (Nehemiah 8:10)

These much-loved words were first used by Nehemiah to challenge his people not to grieve.

were, starting from scratch after so many centuries. But Nehemiah insisted this was a day for rejoicing. He sent everyone out to eat and drink, instructing them to share with people who might not have anything.

Again, it was time for the people to celebrate the Feast of Tabernacles, and this time they did so with great vigor. They were overjoyed to be safely back home, and their celebration was at an intensity that had not been felt "from the days of Joshua…until that day" (8:17).

Israel's spiritual renewal also included assembling to hear the Law read, to confess sins, and to renew the covenant. A lottery was conducted to designate one out of every 10 people to live within the city of Jerusalem, while the others remained in the surrounding towns. And the wall was dedicated to God amid great rejoicing. The dedication was another joyful occasion. Two large groups of singers and musicians were formed. One started walking around the top of the wall clockwise, the other counterclockwise. When they met, the rejoicing was so loud that it could be heard for miles.

The reforms continued. To ensure the purity of the priesthood, Nehemiah saw to it that priests received supplies and food so that they would not seek other means of earning a living. He closed the city on Sabbaths to prevent trade and addressed problems with intermarriage. After decades of exile, Nehemiah's leadership was badly needed.

If You Knew Susa Like Esther Knew Susa (Esther 1–2:18)

Between the rule of Persian King Cyrus (who endorsed the return of Zerubbabel) and Artaxerxes (who gave the go-ahead for Ezra and Nehemiah to return) came the reign of King Xerxes, (also known as Ahasuerus). Xerxes is a key figure in the Book of Esther, a story of a near-disastrous clash between the Persian and Jewish cultures. It also offers an interesting perspective on the time of exile.

While the name of God is prevalent throughout Nehemiah and Ezra, you won't find it mentioned a single time in the Book of Esther. However, due to the situation and the results, it is clear that God was using Esther to accomplish big things. The drama in the Book of Esther holds up against the best of Shakespeare or John Grisham.

As the story opens, Xerxes is at his winter palace in Susa, just north of what is now the Persian Gulf, having a huge party (7 days, all you can drink) to show off his possessions. Apparently, he put his wife Vashti in this category, because he sent for her in order to put her on display as well. But Vashti refused, after which Xerxes became furious. One of his counselors suggested that this independent thinking was by no means a good model for women. If Queen Vashti got away with it, other females might try something just as ludicrous. So Vashti was immediately deposed as queen, never again to enter the presence of King Xerxes.

To replace her, a contest was held to see who would become the new queen. Women were cameled in from all over the kingdom, placed in the care of the king's eunuch (a castrated male servant), and given beauty treatments. It was like "Star Search: 479 B.C.E." Esther was a beautiful young Jewish woman who joined the competition at the urging of her cousin Mordecai, who had been raising her as a daughter since the death of her parents. The young women debuting for Xerxes' favor weren't simply getting quickie makeovers. Their beauty treatments lasted an entire year—six months of receiving oil of myrrh and another six months of perfumes and cosmetics. And there was no doubt as to what the "talent" of this contest was to be. Each contestant went to see Xerxes in the evening and wouldn't leave until the next morning, when she was placed in a harem for concubines. Most of the women weren't likely to ever see the king again. He was looking for one outstanding woman whom he could make queen. The rest would be relegated to concubine status.

Esther pleased the king and won his favor. He put a royal crown on her head and named her queen; then he threw a banquet in her honor and declared a national holiday to celebrate. Esther went to live in the palace, but on Mordecai's instruction, told no one that she was Jewish.

The Plot Thickens (Esther 2:19–4)

Mordecai kept in touch with Esther by hanging around the palace courtyard. One day he happened to overhear a couple of officers conspiring to assassinate Xerxes. Mordecai told Esther, who told Xerxes, who hanged the conspirators. The story of Mordecai's service was recorded in the official records.

Sometime later Xerxes promoted one of his officers named Haman. All bowed down to Haman as he rode past the king's gate to the city—all except Mordecai, who, as a Jew, would bow down only to God. As one person standing in a crowd of prostrate people, Mordecai stood out in a way that grated on Haman's nerves day after day. Haman became enraged. When he discovered that Mordecai was one of the Jewish exiles, his hatred extended to all Jewish people.

Haman went to Xerxes and complained of "a certain people…whose customs are different from those of all other people and who do not obey the king's laws" (Esther 3:8). Haman asked for permission to destroy them, and even volunteered to finance the mass execution himself. Xerxes agreed, but refused Haman's money. Word was sent

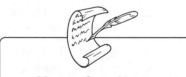

Manna from Heaven

A "hanging" in the Persian Empire was not like in the old American West. The Persians impaled the prisoner on a large pointy stake, then hung up the corpse to warn others.

throughout the kingdom that on a day that Haman had chosen by lot, almost a year in the future, all the Jews were to be annihilated, "young and old, women and little children" (v. 13).

Across the land, the Jewish people fasted, wept, and wore sackcloth and ashes (a sign of mourning)—including Mordecai, who wandered around the city wailing. He and Esther began to correspond by messenger. When she learned what had happened—and that Mordecai wanted her to intervene—she consented. She told him to ask all the Jews in Susa to fast for three days and nights. She had a plan, but it might cost her life if it didn't work.

Queen Saves the Godly (Esther 5–7)

After three days of fasting, Esther approached Xerxes. It seems that a queen ought to have the right to see the king anytime she so pleased, yet contact was always the king's prerogative. Anyone who dared visit the king in his inner court without being invited could be put to death. However, the king could sanction any such intrusion by extending his gold scepter.

It had been a month since Esther had spent time with Xerxes, but he was thrilled to see her. He was in a benevolent mood, offering to grant anything she wished up to half his kingdom. Her only request (for now) was to be allowed to host a banquet for Xerxes and Haman.

From this point onward, the most fascinating sequence of events takes place. Xerxes invites Haman to dinner, and Haman leaves beaming in pride that he is the only one Queen Esther invited to her banquet. While leaving, however, he sees Mordecai who again ignores him, so his wife and friends suggest he build a gallows and take care of Mordecai right away. He has a huge death machine built immediately.

That night a wave of insomnia hits Xerxes, so he has someone come in and read to him from the historical record of his reign. During the night he discovers the account of how Mordecai had saved his life, and realizes that nothing was ever done to reward such a hero. The next morning Haman arrives to ask permission to put Mordecai to death. But before he can even make his request, Xerxes wants his advice on how to reward someone the king wants to honor.

Haman, never one to be humble, assumes the king is talking about him and rattles off a list: (1) a royal robe the king has worn; (2) a horse the king has ridden with a royal crest on its head; and (3) a parade through the streets with a person in front telling

Potent Quotables

"Do not think that because you are in the king's house you alone of all the Jews will escape. For if you remain silent at this time, relief and deliverance for the Jews will rise from another place, but you and your father's family will perish. And who knows but that you have come to royal position for such a time as this?" (Esther 4:13–14)

Mordecai's words to Esther urge solidarity with all who suffer—and recognize the invisible hand of God.

everyone this person is a favorite of the king. Xerxes heartily approved and told Haman to go do all that stuff for Mordecai. Haman even had to lead Mordecai's horse through the streets, shouting, "This is what is done for the man the king delights to honor!"

When the parade is over, Haman rushes home, hiding his head in shame. Almost as soon as he gets there, he is escorted to his special dinner with Xerxes and Esther. At the dinner, Xerxes again asks what favor he can bestow on Esther. She tells him it would be nice if he spared her life and the lives of her people because "I and my people have been sold for destruction and slaughter and annihilation" (7:4). Xerxes is shocked that anyone would even suggest such a thing and wants to know the name of the person. We can't be sure that she pointed, but we know what Esther said: "This vile Haman."

The king storms out of the room in a rage. Haman realizes he is doomed, and throws himself on the couch where Esther is reclined to eat, begging for his life. At that moment Xerxes walks back in and assumes he is "molesting the queen."

One of the king's eunuchs (who had gone to fetch Haman for the party) speaks up and tells Xerxes something to the effect of, "You know what? There's a real big gallows next to Haman's house that he was planning to use on Mordecai." The king's reply is immediate: "Hang him on it!" Persian justice was swift.

An edict was immediately issued allowing the Jews to defend themselves against their enemies, Haman's property was given to Esther, and Mordecai took Haman's place in service to the king. The deliverance of the Jewish people came to be known as the days of Purim, an annual holiday. And they all lived happily (for a while) thereafter.

Manna from Heaven

The lot Haman cast to determine the day for the massacre of the Jews was called a **pur**. The name **Purim** is the plural of pur.

A Good Job Description (Job 1:1–4)

A story that's not quite so happy is the account of Job. Though the Book of Job (pronounced Jōbe) is next in the Bible, it does not take place in the same historical period. So far we have been more or less on a timeline straight through from Creation to the captivity and release of Israel and Judah. We've gone just about as far as we can before we get into New Testament times, so the rest of the Old Testament will backtrack over some of the history we've already covered.

Take This Job and Shove Him (Job 1:5–2:10)

Job was a wealthy and righteous man with 10 children, numerous flocks and herds, and many servants—in fact, he was "the greatest man among all the people of the

East" (Job 1:4). Job was so scrupulous about his religious observances that he used to offer sacrifices for each of his children, just in case they had done something wrong.

Manna from Heaven

The name **Satan** means "accuser," which becomes painfully apparent in the book of Job. Common images of Satan portray him as tempter or ruler of hell, but here he functions as a public prosecutor of God's people.

Potent Quotables

"Naked came I from my mother's womb, and naked I will depart. The Lord gave and the Lord has taken away; may the name of the Lord be praised." (Job 1:21)

Job's response to calamity stands out as one of the most remarkable statements of faith in the Bible.

In fact, Job was such a righteous man that God held him up as an example of how devoted a human being could be. The Bible describes a confrontation between God and Satan, where God singles out Job as the utmost model of someone who was "blameless and upright, a man who fears God and shuns evil" (v. 8).

Satan wasn't impressed by God's praise of Job. *Of course* Job was on good terms with God: God blessed everything Job did. Satan suspected that if Job's good life suddenly came to an end, Job's loyalty to God would, too. So God gave Satan permission to perform the experiment. Satan could do whatever he wanted, so long as he didn't harm Job's actual person.

The next scene would be comic if it weren't so devastating. One after another, messengers arrive at Job's house. While one is still telling him of a horrible catastrophe, another messenger starts in on yet another tragic event. His donkeys and oxen have been stolen, his servants killed, his sheep and shepherds destroyed by fire, his camels carried off by raiding parties—and all his children were feasting when a mighty wind hit, bringing the house down on them and killing them all.

Job went into mourning, tearing his robe and shaving his head. Yet even in his despair he worshipped God.

During the next confrontation between God and Satan, God pointed out the steadfastness Job had shown under such dreadful conditions. Still, Satan insisted that a personal attack on Job's health would quickly turn him away from God. With the prohibition that Satan not actually kill Job, God allowed Satan to test Job under such conditions.

So Satan afflicted Job with a terrible disease that caused painful sores to break out "from the soles of his feet to the top of his head." Job sat in a heap of ashes and scraped his wounds with a piece of broken pottery. As the disease progressed, he had terrifying dreams (7:14), weight loss (17:7), halitosis (19:17), peeling black skin (30:30), and other symptoms. Job's wife wasn't exactly Florence Nightingale during this painful time. The most tender advice we hear from her is, "Curse God and die!" Yet Job still refused to blame God. His response was, "Shall we accept good from God, and not trouble?" And in spite of everything that happened, Job did not sin in what he said.

With Friends Like These... (Job 3–37)

Soon word got around, and three friends of Job's came to comfort him. When they got there, they hardly recognized him. They wept, tore their clothing, put dust on their heads, and sat on the ground with him for a week without saying a word.

So far so good. It was when they started talking that the confusion started. The reader of Job sees the behind-the-scenes story. God is not at all displeased with Job. In fact, God is so impressed with Job that he was singled out for this experiment. *But Job doesn't know that*—nor do his friends. Most of the Book of Job recounts the friends' attempts to make sense of what has happened to Job, and Job's replies. As the dialog continues, traditional ways of looking at suffering are called into question—beginning with the assumption that suffering is our punishment for sin. When he can take no more of his friends' "counsel," Job calls upon God to show himself, to explain why all this evil has come upon him.

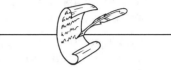

Manna from Heaven

Job's three friends were named Eliphaz, Bildad, and Zophar. Later they were joined by a fourth, Elihu. The lengthy debate of these five men is found in Job 3–37, and contains a reference to "the skin of my teeth" (19:20), Job's frustration with his friends (6:14–15; 13:3–5), magnificent expressions of faith (19:25–26), and numerous other nuggets of interest.

Another Voice Heard (Job 38–41)

Then God spoke. Out of a storm, God confronted Job and began asking him question after question—(more than 70!)—about creation, the marvels of nature, the constellations, and animals never seen that live high on mountains or under the sea. In response, Job was speechless. Job's questions to God were no match for God's inquiries to Job.

Job realized that if he could not comprehend God's perspective in regard to the basics of nature, it wasn't likely he would discern the mind of God in other situations—including his own. His inability to comprehend God did not excuse him from obedience and faithfulness.

Potent Quotables

"My ears had heard of you but now my eyes have seen you. Therefore I despise myself and repent in dust and ashes." (Job 42:5-6)

Even as he grappled with hard questions, Job maintained an attitude of humility and willing obedience.

Another Happy Ending (Job 42)

Having reprimanded Job, God turned to Job's friends who had naively tried to "straighten him out." God told them, "You have not spoken of me what is right, as my servant Job has" (42:8). Job prayed for his friends and offered sacrifices on their behalf, and everyone got off to a fresh start.

God made Job twice as prosperous as before. His friends and relatives started visiting again. He had 10 more children, and he lived long enough to see his great-great-grandchildren. He was more blessed in his later life than he had been previously.

Ezra, Nehemiah, Esther, and Job came faithfully through great trials. As we move to the writings section of the Bible, we will encounter numerous other expressions of faith—as well as other, less positive, emotions.

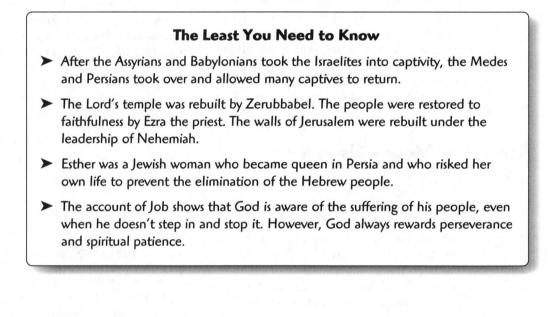

The Least You Need to Know

➤ After the Assyrians and Babylonians took the Israelites into captivity, the Medes and Persians took over and allowed many captives to return.

➤ The Lord's temple was rebuilt by Zerubbabel. The people were restored to faithfulness by Ezra the priest. The walls of Jerusalem were rebuilt under the leadership of Nehemiah.

➤ Esther was a Jewish woman who became queen in Persia and who risked her own life to prevent the elimination of the Hebrew people.

➤ The account of Job shows that God is aware of the suffering of his people, even when he doesn't step in and stop it. However, God always rewards perseverance and spiritual patience.

Chapter 13

Old Testament Lit. 101

In This Chapter

➤ The "honest to God" expressions of the Psalms

➤ The Book of Proverbs' bite-size chunks of wisdom

➤ Ecclesiastes: Wisdom for the person who's got it all

➤ Song of Songs: the fullness and splendor of love

So far in this guide we've been concentrating on biblical history. Now we're about to move down the hall from history class to literature. Until now we've heard a lot of what God has had to say about people. As we move into the Book of Psalms, we're going to reverse the trend and see what people have to say about God.

Psing Us a Psong, You're the Psalmist

The Book of Psalms is the largest known collection of ancient lyric poetry. The psalms vary in style, content, author, length, and musical purpose, but all are either about God or are addressed to God. Most, but not all, have notations that help determine who wrote it and/or how it was to be used.

Many psalms are attributed to David. For instance, Psalm 3 was a psalm about David "when he fled from his son Absalom." Psalm 51 is a stark confession written to reflect how David felt after the prophet Nathan confronted him about his adultery with Bathsheba. However, interpretation of certain notations makes it unclear whether David wrote all the psalms to which his name is attached. Some may have been merely *about* David—or the era of the kings in general.

Others credited with composing psalms were Asaph, Solomon, and even Moses.

Simile When You Say That

As a book of poetry, Psalms is intensely personal. It contains individual and group prayers, hymns and songs, and various other forms of praise. Some of the writers are so direct with God that their honesty might seem unsettling. Many use images (metaphors and similes) to represent God.

One of the most familiar images of God comes from what is probably the best known of the psalms—Psalm 23:

The Lord is my shepherd, I shall not be in want.

He makes me lie down in green pastures, he leads me beside quiet waters, he restores my soul. He guides me in paths of righteousness for his name's sake.

Even though I walk through the valley of the shadow of death, I will fear no evil, for you are with me; your rod and your staff, they comfort me.

You prepare a table before me in the presence of my enemies. You anoint my head with oil; my cup overflows.

Surely goodness and love will follow me all the days of my life, and I will dwell in the house of the Lord forever.

This psalm speaks of the protection, provision, and guidance of God, all in the context of a conscientious shepherd. If even those of us who work in high-rise cubicles can relate to a caring, sharing shepherd, how much more would people for whom flocks of sheep were a daily sight?

Here are some more images of God from the Psalms:

➤ **Shield** "You are a shield around me, O Lord; you bestow glory on me and lift up my head" (3:3).

➤ **Judge** "God is a righteous judge, a God who expresses his wrath every day" (7:11).

➤ **Creator** "When I consider your heavens, the work of your fingers, the moon and the stars which you have set in place, what is man that you are mindful of him...?" (8:3–4).

➤ **Rock/Fortress** "The Lord is my rock, my fortress, and my deliverer; my God is my rock, in whom I take refuge" (18:2).

➤ **Savior** "He reached down from on high and took hold of me; he drew me out of deep waters" (18:16).

➤ **Avenger** "He is the God who avenges me, who subdues nations under me, who saves me from my enemies" (18:47).

➤ **Landlord** "The earth is the Lord's, and everything in it, the world, and all who live in it" (24:1).

➤ **Teacher** "Good and upright is the Lord; therefore he instructs sinners in his ways. He guides the humble in what is right and teaches them his way" (25:8–9).

➤ **Warrior** "Contend, O Lord, with those who contend with me; fight against those who fight against me. Take up shield and buckler; arise and come to my aid. Brandish spear and javelin against those who pursue me" (35:1–3).

➤ **Refuge** "God is our refuge and strength, an ever-present help in trouble" (46:1).

➤ **Redeemer** "God will redeem my life from the grave; he will surely take me to himself" (49:15).

➤ **Father** "A father to the fatherless, a defender of widows, is God in his holy dwelling. God sets the lonely in families…" (68:5–6).

➤ **Mother bird** "Surely he will save you from the fowler's snare and from the deadly pestilence. He will cover you with his feathers, and under his wings you will find refuge" (91:3–4).

➤ **King** "The Lord reigns, he is robed in majesty…. Your throne was established long ago; you are from all eternity" (93:1–2).

Manna from Heaven

Asaph led one of David's three choirs (1 Chronicles 25:1). Some psalms also contain a heading referring to the Sons of Korah, who were members of another Old Testament choir. However, these people were more likely the presenters of the psalm rather than the authors.

Manna from Heaven

A **buckler** was a special, extra-large, full-body shield. Soldiers also carried a traditional smaller shield, so the buckler was usually the responsibility of the armor-bearer.

Be Honest

When people think of God as a creator, king, and judge, they are correct to a certain extent. Yet this is only a *part* of who God is. As the psalm writers meditated and got a better picture of the totality of God, the other aspects of shield, shepherd, and savior became evident. As a result, they were better able to open up and be honest about their feelings. Because the psalms contain people's heartfelt prayers to God—whether joyful, angry, sad, desperate, or full of longing— they tend to be unflinchingly honest. Psalm

73, for example, does not hesitate to express to God things that many of us hardly dare to think. The first 14 verses of the psalm are filled with the author's observations of how dirty, rotten, despicable people prosper and breeze their way through life while pure and godly people suffer and get jealous. Yet the second half of the psalm describes the psalmist's visit to the temple to seek understanding about the problem. Clearly, if the psalmist had not been so honest with God to begin with, he might not have found the answers he was seeking.

Top of the Charts

With 150 psalms to sing, there's no way we can cover them all. Here are a few psalms you might want to begin with. When you get time, read more and add your personal favorites to the list.

Psalm 1 is a concise, poetic contrast of godliness and wickedness.

Psalm 10 asks where God is when times get tough.

Psalm 19 discovers God in nature. It then brings the God of creation into a personal relationship with sinful human beings.

Psalm 22 begins with "My God, my God, why have you forsaken me?" Jesus recites portions of this song from the cross, and New Testament authors refer to it frequently.

Psalm 46 attests that God is there for us—no matter what!

Psalm 55 expresses David's dependence on God when close friends have betrayed him.

Psalm 90 is attributed to Moses, who asks for compassion from an all-powerful God.

Psalm 100 is popular at Thanksgiving, connecting the giving of thanks with praise, worship, and joy.

Psalm 117 is the shortest psalm (and biblical chapter). Yet in two verses it manages to extol God's great love, faithfulness, and endurance.

Psalm 119, in contrast, is the longest. Written in eight-verse stanzas, the psalm is an alphabetic acrostic, with each verse in a stanza beginning with the next successive letter of the Hebrew alphabet (the equivalent of A to Z). And essentially every one of the 176 verses makes a reference to the word of God (commands, precepts, statutes, law, and so on).

Psalms 120–134 are known as "songs of ascents." The name probably refers to their use: They were sung as people ascended to Jerusalem (which was at a high altitude) to worship there. Note the references to lifting up one's eyes: to the hills (121:1), to God (123:1), and so forth.

Psalm 137 is a mournful remembrance of time spent in exile.

Psalm 139 is an intensely personal account of the intimate knowledge God has of his people.

Psalms is a favorite book among many Bible readers. Whatever the mood or the immediate need, one or more psalms will probably reflect the feeling or address the problem. As we meditate on these honest expressions of biblical psinger-psongwriters, we may learn to become more honest with God ourselves.

Solomon Says

Where the psalms tend to evoke poetic praise and feelings, the Book of Proverbs stresses a more no-nonsense, practical form of wisdom. Indeed, imparting wisdom was the reason for writing the book (Proverbs 1:1–7). Solomon is identified as the author in the opening verse, yet later portions make it clear that other writers are involved as well.

What Saith Thou?

While flipping through Psalms, you see a lot of the word *Selah*. Who or what is a "Selah"?

The best guess is that *Selah* was a musical direction at one time, perhaps meaning "Strike up the band." Some people interpret it like an *Amen* ("so be it"). The truth is, no one's sure anymore.

Now Listen Up!

The first nine chapters of Proverbs are essays addressed to "my son" or "my sons." Today we would say "my children." In these discourses, we hear the voice of a respected father or elder of the community imparting wisdom to younger listeners on the benefits of wisdom and the pitfalls of "folly." Solomon is a writer who combines an eye for detail with clever wit. For example, when he sees a young man being seduced by a woman with "crafty intent," we read: "All at once he followed her like an ox going to the slaughter, like a deer stepping into a noose till an arrow pierces his liver, like a bird darting into a snare, little knowing it will cost him his life" (Proverbs 7:22–23).

Both wisdom and folly are personified as women. Wisdom "calls aloud in the street" (1:20), "is more precious than rubies" (3:15), "will set a garland of grace on your head and present you with a crown of splendor" (4:9), and promises, "Leave your simple ways and you will live; walk in the way of understanding" (9:6).

In contrast,

> "The woman Folly is loud; she is undisciplined and without knowledge.... 'Let all who are simple come in here!' she says to those who lack judgment.... But little do they know that the dead are there, that her guests are in the depths of the grave" (Proverbs 9:13, 16, 18).

The rest of the book consists of much shorter, more concise nuggets of wisdom. Some have the feel of fortune-cookie sayings. Indeed, they are reminiscent of the sayings of Confucius. These proverbs are, however, several centuries older.

Potent Quotables

The fear of the Lord is the beginning of wisdom, and knowledge of the Holy One is understanding.
(Proverbs 9:10)

It is important to *use* wisdom while reading *about* wisdom. These proverbs weren't written to be taken out of context and applied randomly as dogma. We need to use a little common sense as we go along. For example, Proverbs 26:4 makes a lot of sense when it says: "Do not answer a fool according to his folly, or you will be like him yourself." We've all gotten involved with people who liked to argue for the sake of argument. Or perhaps you've tried to reason with a drunk person, only to find yourself growing loud and incoherent. Sometimes it's best just to let it go.

However, the very next verse of Proverbs gives just the opposite advice: "Answer a fool according to his folly, or he will be wise in his own eyes" (26:5). This, too, can be good advice. When you hear someone speaking in an offensive or belittling manner, sometimes you need to speak up with a well-chosen word of your own.

So which piece of advice is correct? They both are. We just need to have the wisdom to know which option to take in any given situation.

Beautiful Women, Pig Snouts, and Other Words of Wisdom

Here is a sampling of some classic wisdom from the book of Proverbs—along with a few of the more obscure proverbs.

"When words are many, sin is not absent, but he who holds his tongue is wise" (10:19).

"Like a gold ring in a pig's snout is a beautiful woman who shows no discretion" (11:22).

"A gentle answer turns away wrath, but a harsh word stirs up anger" (15:1).

"Better a meal of vegetables where there is love than a fattened calf with hatred" (15:17). (Pull that one out at the next family gathering!)

"Pride goes before destruction, and a haughty spirit before a fall" (16:18).

"Many are the plans in a man's heart, but it is the Lord's purpose that prevails" (19:21).

"Wine is a mocker and beer a brawler; whoever is led astray by them is not wise" (20:1).

"A good name is more desirable than great riches; to be esteemed is better than silver or gold" (22:1).

"Train a child in the way he should go, and when he is old he will not turn from it" (22:6).

"Do not exploit the poor because they are poor, and do not crush the needy in court, for the Lord will take up their case and will plunder those who plunder them" (22:22–23).

"Who has woe? Who has sorrow? Who has strife? Who has complaints? Who has needless bruises? Who has bloodshot eyes? Those who linger over wine, who go to sample bowls of mixed wine. Do not gaze at wine when it is red, when it sparkles in the cup, when it goes down smoothly! In the end it bites like a snake and poisons like a viper. Your eyes will see strange sights and your mind imagine confusing things. You will be like one sleeping on the high seas, lying on top of the rigging. 'They hit me,' you will say, 'but I'm not hurt! They beat me, but I don't feel it! When will I wake up so I can find another drink?' " (23:29–35)

"An honest answer is like a kiss on the lips" (24:26).

"As a dog returns to its vomit, so a fool repeats his folly" (26:11).

"Without wood a fire goes out; without gossip a quarrel dies down" (26:20).

"As iron sharpens iron, so one man sharpens another" (27:17).

The book concludes with a discourse on "a wife of noble character" (31:10–31), a detailed tribute to a woman who not only takes care of her husband and children but

also oversees a successful business. She does her own buying, selling, and manufacturing. She is wise and "clothed with strength and dignity" (v. 25). As a result, "her children arise and call her blessed; her husband also, and he praises her…. Give her the reward she has earned, and let her works bring her praise at the city gate" (vv. 28, 31).

Potent Quotables

There are three things that are stately in their stride, four that move with stately bearing: a lion, mighty among beasts, who retreats before nothing; a strutting rooster; a he-goat; and a king with his army around him. (Proverbs 30:29–31)

For the writers of Proverbs, wisdom is no mere abstraction. It is the very bedrock of life—a foundation for stronger family ties, better business relationships, a respectable work ethic, addiction prevention, the development of positive characteristics, and an awareness that God sees every action we take. It exemplifies the Old Testament view that wisdom means living in, for, and to God.

Ecclesiastes: The Book of Meaning—and Meaninglessness

From Proverbs we move on to Ecclesiastes, a word roughly translated as "teacher." Though not all agree that the author was Solomon, he was clearly someone who had lived long and had a number of experiences—none of which he found particularly fulfilling.

From its opening sentence, Ecclesiastes contains a lot of statements you wouldn't expect to find in the Bible. "'Meaningless! Meaningless!' says the Teacher. 'Utterly meaningless! Everything is meaningless'" (Ecclesiastes 1:2). Another translation of "meaningless" is "utterly temporary." This prelude sets the tone of the whole book.

While Proverbs centered on the importance and positive attributes of wisdom, Ecclesiastes suggests that human wisdom has its limits. The teacher starts out with enthusiasm: "I devoted myself to study and to explore by wisdom all that is done under heaven" (1:13). But his conclusion was much less encouraging: "I learned that this, too, is a chasing after the wind. For with much wisdom comes much sorrow; the more knowledge, the more grief" (1:18).

When the accumulation of wisdom didn't satisfy him as he wished, the Teacher turned to various pleasures of life, including "cheering myself with wine, and embracing folly" (2:3). He got involved in building projects, gardening, the accumulation of wealth, and more. "I denied myself nothing my eyes desired; I refused my heart no pleasure" (2:10). Still, nothing rid him of the nagging feeling of meaninglessness. He even came to despise his life and his work because he realized that when he died, someone else would inherit all he had toiled to acquire. His only moderately positive observation was that "a man can do nothing better than to eat and drink and find satisfaction in his work. This, too, I see, is from the hand of God, for without him, who can eat or find enjoyment?" (2:24) At times he might complain about the life God had given him, but he knew from experience that nothing else would be better.

He realized, too, that much of life is a matter of timing. The oft-quoted passage from Ecclesiastes 3 makes the point well: Though we might want to love, laugh, build, and live in peace *all the time*, wisdom accepts with gratitude whatever we receive—and *when*ever. The joyful aspects of life can be appreciated only in the context of life's struggles.

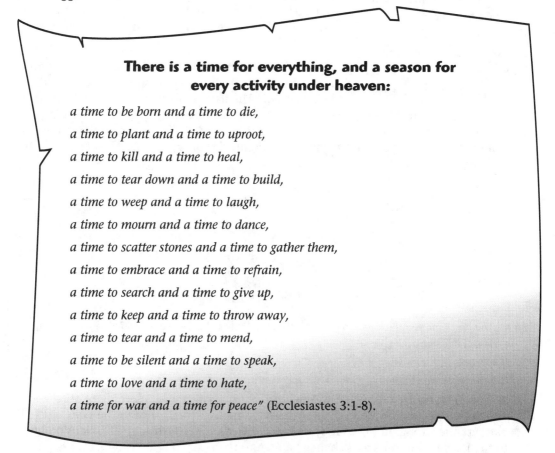

**There is a time for everything, and a season for
every activity under heaven:**

a time to be born and a time to die,

a time to plant and a time to uproot,

a time to kill and a time to heal,

a time to tear down and a time to build,

a time to weep and a time to laugh,

a time to mourn and a time to dance,

a time to scatter stones and a time to gather them,

a time to embrace and a time to refrain,

a time to search and a time to give up,

a time to keep and a time to throw away,

a time to tear and a time to mend,

a time to be silent and a time to speak,

a time to love and a time to hate,

a time for war and a time for peace" (Ecclesiastes 3:1-8).

In his search, the Teacher saw that death is the great equalizer of rich and poor, human and animal, hard worker and lazy lout, oppressors and oppressed. "All go to the same place; all come from dust, and to dust all return" (3:20). But he also noticed the effect of sharing the burdens of life: "Two are better than one, because they have a good return for their work: if one falls down, his friend can help him up.... Also, if two lie down together, they will keep warm. But how can one keep warm alone? Though one

Potent Quotables

Naked a man comes from his mother's womb, and as he comes, so he departs. He takes nothing from his labor that he can carry in his hand. (Ecclesiastes 5:15)

An early version of "You can't take it with you!"

may be overpowered, two can defend themselves. A cord of three strands is not quickly broken" (4:9–12).

He saw that people seldom think they have enough of whatever they desire. For example, lovers of money never have quite enough of it to make them happy. The more they acquire, the more they worry about what they have. Instead, the Teacher says, we should accept whatever wealth we might accumulate as a gift of God (5:19–20). His advice in all things was to "stand in awe of God" (5:7). We can mouth off to other people and get away with it, but we need to watch what we say when we're dealing with God (5:1–7).

The disappointment experienced in his search eventually colored the Teacher's basic outlook. He came to believe that: "The day of death [is] better than the day of birth" (7:1); "It is better to go to a house of mourning than to go to a house of feasting" (7:2); and "Sorrow is better than laughter" (7:3). But who can blame him? We still tend to reflect more on the meaning and brevity of life at funerals than we do at birthday celebrations.

Snapshots

The next time you think life isn't fair, try perusing Ecclesiastes 6–7 (or essentially anywhere else in this Bible book).

Although he realized that God was behind all things and was deserving of obedience and praise, the randomness of life bothered him: "The race is not to the swift or the battle to the strong, nor does food come to the wise or wealth to the brilliant or favor to the learned; but time and chance happen to them all" (Ecclesiastes 9:11).

And yet the Teacher ends with this advice: "Now all has been heard; here is the conclusion of the matter: Fear God and keep his commandments, for this is the whole duty of man. For God will bring every deed into judgment, including every hidden thing, whether it is good or evil" (Ecclesiastes 12:13–14).

In a way, it's encouraging to think of people in the tenth century B.C.E. sitting around asking themselves: Why am I here? What's life all about? Is there a purpose to all of this? People are still asking these questions today—and feeling at times the same frustration.

Aren't there times, after all, when even the best we can squeeze out of life seems meaningless? We try to fill the emptiness with whatever we can find—cash, possessions, relationships, power and position; yet some days none of that seems like enough. As we remember the writer of Ecclesiastes, perhaps we will also remember his secret: a stubborn devotion to wisdom and an acknowledgment that God is still living and active. (See especially 3:9–14.)

Ecclesiastes isn't the most upbeat portion of Scripture, yet it adds a perspective that's hard to find elsewhere. And as we move on, we go from the depths of confusion and despair to the heights that only love can bring.

The Song of Songs (Parental Warning: Explicit Lyrics)

Following Ecclesiastes is the Song of Songs (or Song of Solomon), another unusual and somewhat mystifying book. Perhaps the author was Solomon; or perhaps the song is *about* Solomon.

And what is the song about? Love, obviously—but is it about ordinary romantic love, or is it an allegory? Some say the song is about the relationship of love between God and the nation of Israel, or Christ and the church as his bride, or Christ and the individual.

The majority of the song is a dialog between the "Beloved" (a woman) and her "Lover" (the man). Other voices are heard, too: friends who are celebrating with the couple.

The song begins with kisses, love, perfumes, and a request to be taken to the king's chamber—and then it begins to heat up (1:1–4). The first portion of the song reads like an intimate romance conducted through the mail or a private Internet chat room. Lover and Beloved praise each other with enticing and flattering language.

At least, it was flattering to *them*. These days a woman might not be as happy to hear that her hair is like a flock of goats, her teeth are like a flock of sheep, her temples are like the halves of a pomegranate, her neck is like a tower, or her breasts are like two fawns (4:1–7). The description sounds like Picasso's kind of woman. Really, the Lover is praising the Beloved's flowing black hair, lovely white teeth, rosy face, majestic bearing, and soft, enticing body.

Potent Quotables

"Your stature is like that of the palm, and your breasts like clusters of fruit. I said, 'I will climb the palm tree; I will take hold of its fruit.'" (Song of Songs 7:7–8)

This line worked for the Lover on his honeymoon. However, it's not recommended for casual conversation.

The Lover, for his part, is described as an apple tree among the trees of the forest (unique and unexpected, but welcome). He comes leaping across the mountains like a gazelle or a young stag. He has a golden complexion, wavy black hair, bright sparkling eyes, and a body like a statue (5:10–16). After visiting with him, the Beloved needs food for strength because she is "faint with love" (2:3–9).

Next the wedding processional is described. In a cloud of dust and the aroma of exotic spices, Solomon's carriage approaches, escorted by 60 warriors. The cedar carriage is trimmed in silver and gold and is upholstered with purple. The groom is wearing a crown created just for the occasion (3:6–11).

The rest of the song continues the back-and-forth compliments between the Beloved and her Lover. There is no doubt that desire accompanies the description.

You might think that the Song of Songs has little widespread application, but it concludes with a theme that challenges us all. The depth of love that fueled the passion between the Beloved and her Lover is the secret of a happy life. Perhaps true, genuine love is the antidote to the chronic deep funk felt by the writer of Ecclesiastes. For here is what the Beloved says:

> *Place me like a seal over your heart, like a seal on your arm; for love is as strong as death, its jealousy unyielding as the grave. It burns like blazing fire, like a mighty flame. Many waters cannot quench love; rivers cannot wash it away. If one were to give all the wealth of his house for love, it would be utterly scorned* (Songs 8:6–7).

The song comes to a close as the Beloved and her Lover prepare to go away "and be like a gazelle or like a young stag on the spice-laden mountains" (8:14). The writings portion of the Bible ends there as well.

The rest of the Old Testament covers the lives of the prophets, which we will examine in the next chapter. In the meantime, may you be on the road to unquenchable love with a psalm in your heart, a proverb on your lips, and the wisdom to overcome any feelings of meaninglessness you may encounter along the way.

The Least You Need to Know

➤ The Book of Psalms contains 150 songs that focus on God, though they vary in style, tone, author, and purpose.

➤ The proverbs provide common-sense advice for a worthy—and worthwhile—life.

➤ Ecclesiastes takes a stark look at life and the underlying struggle for meaning.

➤ The Song of Songs is a sensual account of love between man and woman, as well as a tribute to the glory of love itself.

Chapter 14

Tell-a-Vision Personalities

In This Chapter

➤ The prophets: God's representatives to the people

➤ Prophecies for short-term and long-range future events

➤ What happens when you keep saying things other people don't want to hear

➤ Ezekiel's wheels and bones; Jeremiah in the pits; Daniel in the lions' den; Shadrach, Meshach, and Abednego; Jonah and the big fish; and a number of other prophets and their visions

---

Get a Bible and hold the pages from the beginning of Isaiah to the end of Malachi between your fingers. These are the Old Testament books of prophecy. As you can see, it's a lot of material to cover in a single chapter.

The prophets were messengers—go-betweens sent to Judah, Israel, and foreign nations. Some worked before God's people were taken into captivity; others worked during the exile, both in Israel and in Babylon and Assyria; and some received their call after the exile.

Isaiah: Hot Lips, Warm Heart

Isaiah lived during the turbulent time when Assyria was asserting itself against Israel and Judah. Israel fell to Assyria in 722 B.C.E., and Judah narrowly avoided being similarly swallowed up. Isaiah's message was that Judah's sinfulness would soon lead to its capture as well—in this case, by the Babylonians.

Manna from Heaven

The angels seen by Isaiah were **seraphs**, and this is the only biblical mention of them. They stood upright and had hands, feet, and voices—and they also had six wings: two to cover their faces, two to cover their feet, and two used to fly. The word *seraphs* is translated as "burning ones," which might refer to their passion for God as well as the method they used to purify Isaiah.

Isaiah's call to be a prophet is described in Isaiah 6. In a vision, he saw God enthroned in the temple and surrounded by angels. God was seeking a representative, but Isaiah was acutely aware of his sinfulness and that of his people. An angel took a live coal from an altar and touched it to Isaiah's lips, explaining that "your guilt is taken away and your sin atoned for." With that taken care of, all Isaiah could say is, "Here am I. Send me!"

Bad News, Good News

Isaiah worked as a prophet for no less than 58 years. He had a wife and a couple of children. He was also a very literate person and is perhaps the most-quoted and most comprehensive of the prophets. If your image of prophets is one of antisocial eccentrics, half-crazed from rejection and desert heat, Isaiah immediately breaks the stereotype.

Isaiah's message includes the certainty of God's judgment—on his generation and those to come who would be raised in captivity. Yet he tempers his words of judgment with equally powerful prophecies of God's comfort.

Isaiah had a great deal to say about the Messiah who would come to provide comfort on a more permanent basis. Here is a sampling of his prophecies, including the coming Messiah's virgin birth, his character, and his crucifixion:

➤ "Therefore the Lord himself will give you a sign: The virgin will be with child and will give birth to a son, and will call him Immanuel" (7:14).

➤ "For to us a child is born, to us a son is given, and the government will be on his shoulders. And he will be called Wonderful Counselor, Mighty God, Everlasting Father, Prince of Peace" (9:6).

➤ "He had no beauty or majesty to attract us to him, nothing in his appearance that we should desire him. He was despised and rejected by men, a man of sorrows, and familiar with suffering…. He was pierced for our transgressions, he was crushed for our iniquities; the punishment that brought us peace was upon him, and by his wounds we are healed" (53:2–3, 5).

Rebels, Rebels Everywhere

Isaiah's writings contain many prophecies against the enemies of Israel and Judah. Included in his address to Babylon is this passage: "How you have fallen from heaven, O morning star, son of the dawn! You have been cast down to the earth, you who once laid low the nations!" You said in your heart, 'I will ascend to heaven; I will raise my throne above the stars of God; I will sit enthroned on the mount of assembly, on the utmost heights of the sacred mountain. I will ascend above the tops of the clouds; I will make myself like the Most High.' But you are brought down to the grave, to the depths of the pit" (14:12-15).

Some think this passage refers to Satan; others to the ruthless Assyrian ruler Sennacherib, or to an unnamed Babylonian monarch. In any case, the passage portrays the destruction of those who arrogantly oppose God.

Isaiah was no less direct in addressing God's own people: "These are rebellious people, deceitful children, children unwilling to listen to the Lord's instruction. They say to the seers, 'See no more visions!' and to the prophets, 'Give us no more visions of what is right! Tell us pleasant things, prophesy illusions…stop confronting us with the Holy One of Israel'" (30:9–11). According to a legend dating back to the second century, Isaiah was eventually killed by King Manasseh for speaking out against the evil in Judah. It was later written (but not confirmed) that Isaiah was sawed in two.

Isaiah also passed along some wonderful promises, such as these from a favorite passage:

What Saith Thou?

How can we tell if a prophecy is immediate or long-range?

It's not always easy to differentiate. Sometimes it almost seems as though the prophets made vague predictions to fit a lot of circumstances, or prophesied so far into the future that no one could ever prove them wrong. However, some of the prophets' predictions included the fall of Israel and Judah, and even the length of time to be spent in captivity, so they were easily verified (also tending to verify their more long-term prophecies). Still, it isn't easy to go so far back in history and determine exactly what is meant in every case.

"Do you not know? Have you not heard? The Lord is the everlasting God, the Creator of the ends of the earth. He will not grow tired or weary, and his understanding no one can fathom. He gives strength to the weary, and increases the power of the weak. Even youths grow tired and weary, and young men stumble and fall; but those who hope in the Lord will renew their strength. They will soar on wings like eagles; they will run and not grow weary, they will walk and not be faint" (40:28–31).

Don't Cry for Me, Jeremiah

Ever since Three Dog Night recorded "Joy to the World," it has been difficult to initiate a serious discussion about Jeremiah. But this prophet was more bulldog than bullfrog— even though there wasn't a whole lot of joy in his world.

Jeremiah is frequently called "the weeping prophet" because of the anguish he suffered on behalf of his people, whose afflictions he strongly identified with. He also suffered on his own account. Jeremiah didn't have much positive news to pass along, and he was not widely liked for his messages.

Jeremiah received his prophetic call when he was quite young: "Now the word of the Lord came to me, saying, 'Before I formed you in the womb I knew you, before you

Manna from Heaven

In the geography and botany of Jeremiah's world, the almond tree was the first to bloom in spring, and was even named the "awake tree." Of course, everyone watched for the buds each year, so this concept of intent watchfulness is used to symbolize God's attention to his people.

were born I set you apart; I appointed you as a prophet to the nations'" (1:5). When Jeremiah protested that he was only a child, God touched his mouth to symbolize placing his words there. Almost immediately Jeremiah saw two visions: an almond tree, which symbolized that God was watching; and a boiling pot tilted away from the north, symbolizing the enemies (Babylon) who would pour from the north, bringing destruction upon Judah.

If You Can't Say Something Nice...

God's message through Jeremiah was that his once-devoted people were no longer faithful: "Go up and down the streets of Jerusalem, look around and consider, search through her squares. If you can find but one person who deals honestly and seeks the truth, I will forgive this city" (5:1). Because of the people's sinfulness, God would allow the enemies of Judah to overpower the nation. When the people asked why, Jeremiah's answer was straightforward: "As you have forsaken [God] and served foreign gods in your own land, so now you will serve foreigners in a land not your own" (5:19).

The people didn't particularly care for this message. In fact, they tried to kill the messenger—Jeremiah (11:18–20). But God protected him.

They're Clay in My Hands

Once God sent Jeremiah to observe a potter at work. When the craftsman messed up the clay pot he was making, he simply reworked the clay until he got it right. God told Jeremiah that Judah was like clay in a potter's hands (18:1–6). If the nation would not repent, God would "break down and destroy it" and begin again. When Jeremiah passed along this message, there was hope in his words—even if the hope lay beyond an unavoidable judgment. He told the people that God would initiate a period of exile for the people of Judah that would last 70 years (25:11). After this time, however, would come a time of reconciliation and restoration.

During the long siege of Jerusalem, Jeremiah advised King Zedekiah to surrender to Babylon. The king's life would be spared and the city kept from destruction. Zedekiah refused. When the Babylonians broke through the city wall, he fled and was captured. Zedekiah's sons were killed before his eyes; he himself was blinded and hauled off to Babylon, and Jerusalem was burned to the ground.

King Nebuchadnezzar had given explicit word that Jeremiah was not to be harmed. Although most of the people were taken into exile, Jeremiah remained in Judah, eventually being dragged off to Egypt by Jewish military officers (along with others still remaining in Jerusalem). There he remained active, prophesying to Jews and Egyptians alike.

Snapshots

Don't miss these other significant events in the life of Jeremiah:

A fashion statement makes a prophetic statement (13:1–11).

Smashing a piece of pottery gets Jeremiah beaten and placed in stocks (19–20:3).

Death threats for Jeremiah, and the actual death of a peer (26:7–11, 20–23).

Jeremiah wears a yoke; a false prophet destroys the yoke; God destroys the false prophet (Jeremiah 27–28).

Jeremiah invests in real estate—even with Babylonians at the gate (32).

Jeremiah has to rewrite his book due to a ruthless "editor" (36:19–32).

After a false accusation of desertion, it's the dungeon for Jeremiah (37).

The prophet gets a sinking feeling—and for good reason (38:1–13).

Egyptian stones predict Babylon's spreading influence (43:8–13).

As reassurance of God's forgiveness and God's promise, Jeremiah even wrote a letter to the exiles in Babylon, telling them to build houses and settle down, to marry and raise families, and to pray for their foreign city. As the city prospered, so would they (29:1–9).

How Deserted Lies the City

Back in Jerusalem, the scene was one of utter calamity. A record of the misery has come down to us in the Book of Lamentations, a collection of five dirges or funeral poems. Though it can't be proven, it has long been believed that Jeremiah was the author of this book as well as the one that bears his name. Its opening words give you a flavor of the rest:

Potent Quotables

"For I know the plans I have for you,' declares the Lord, 'plans to prosper you and not to harm you, plans to give you hope and a future." (Jeremiah 29:11).

This promise of deliverance would prove to be just as certain as the 70 years of captivity that Jeremiah had foretold.

> *How deserted lies the city*
> *once so full of people!*
> *How like a widow is she,*
> *who once was great among the nations!*
> *She who was queen among the provinces*
> *has now become a slave.*

Now that the city of Jerusalem lay desolate, burned and empty, it was tragic enough to dwell on the fall of what had been the glorious center of a prosperous world power. But just prior to its fall, the scene inside the city had turned ugly. When the Babylonians came, it wasn't a matter of dropping a couple of bombs and taking the city. The siege was conducted over a couple of years, and the final months were intense.

Trapped inside the city, the people were desperate for food and hope. They went so far as resorting to the cannibalism of their own children (2:20; 4:10). Jeremiah himself was still a target of conspiracies (3:61-63). And when the Babylonians finally broke through, the women were raped, the rulers hung up by their hands, and the able-bodied forced to work (5:11-13). Yet the writer of Lamentations has not utterly lost hope. Deep in the heart of his lament come these words of promise: "Because of the Lord's great love we are not consumed, for his compassions never fail…. They are new every morning; great is your faithfulness…. The Lord is good to those whose hope is in him, to the one who seeks him. It is good to wait quietly for the salvation of the Lord" (Lamentations 3:22–26).

Ezekiel: This Wheel's on Fire

We come now to Ezekiel. Born a bit later than Isaiah and Jeremiah, Ezekiel, a temple priest, was one of the 10,000 people carted off to Babylon during the first exile 10 years before the fall of Jerusalem (2 Kings 24:14). There he became a prophet to the exiles, predicting the fall of Jerusalem and then—after his prediction had been validated—preaching a message of hope and salvation.

A Face Like an Angel

Ezekiel had amazing visions. The book begins with an account of his first: a windstorm with flashing lightning in its midst and, at the center, a fire "like glowing metal" that surrounded four living creatures. Each creature had four faces: one like a man, one like a lion, one like an ox, and one like an eagle. The creatures had wings and could move "back and forth like flashes of lightning." Somehow they were connected to sparkling wheels, which allowed them to turn in any direction. Spread out over them was an awesome expanse of something that sparkled like ice. The sound of their wings was "like the roar of rushing waters, like the voice of the Almighty, like the tumult of an army" (Ezekiel 1:1–24).

These creatures show up again in Ezekiel 10, where they are called *cherubim*, another order of angels separate from the seraphim. Cherubim were stationed at the entrance of the Garden of Eden to prevent reentry, and two were carved on top of the Ark of the Covenant. Their primary function seems to be to attend to God. We will see these four-faced beings again when we get to the Book of Revelation.

Over all this noise came a voice. When Ezekiel looked up, he saw "the appearance of the likeness of the glory of the Lord" (1:28). On a throne of sapphire (or the semi-precious blue stone lapis lazuli) sat a figure of what looked to be glowing metal, like fire, surrounded by a radiance of brilliant light like a rainbow.

God said he was sending Ezekiel to "the Israelites, to a rebellious nation that has rebelled against me" (2:3). Ezekiel was handed a scroll on which were written "words of lament and mourning and woe," and God told him to eat it. He did as instructed, and it tasted sweet like honey.

After this Ezekiel sat for seven days, overwhelmed 3:15).

What Saith Thou?

Why would a scroll of bitter words taste sweet?

Other biblical writers spoke of digesting the words of God, including David (Psalm 19:9–10), Jeremiah (Jeremiah 15:16), and John (Revelation 10:9–11). The sweetness must come from the source (God) rather than the content (which for Ezekiel's people was judgment).

God and Ezekiel Down by the Boneyard

Ezekiel was called upon to engage in unusual, sometimes bizarre, symbolic actions as a way of getting the people's attention. One such assignment was to make a model of Jerusalem, complete with siege ramps and battering rams around it, and then lie on his left side for 390 days, followed by 40 days on his right side. This was to symbolize periods of atonement for the sins of Israel and Judah. An iron pan was placed between Ezekiel and his model city, perhaps to signify the barrier the sinful Israelites had erected between themselves and God. During this time, as he symbolically bore the sins of the Israelites upon himself, he was to eat rations of water with bread cooked over human excrement, symbolizing the defilement of his people. When Ezekiel objected to the violation of ceremonial cleanliness, God allowed him to use dried cow manure as fuel instead (Ezekiel 4).

Manna from Heaven

The use of **animal manure** as a fuel, dried and mixed with straw, was not unusual in a land where wood supplies were limited.

In Ezekiel's best-known vision, the prophet saw himself standing before a vast expanse of very dry bones. The Lord instructed him to prophesy to them. Ezekiel obeyed, and a rattling sound was heard as the bones began to clatter back together, becoming full skeletons, then growing tendons, flesh, and skin. Ezekiel prophesied again, and breath entered the bodies. They came to life as "a vast army" (Ezekiel 37:1–14). God wanted the people to know that he was able to bring them back to life—no matter how long they had been separated from him or how crushed they were by misfortune.

Ezekiel concludes his book with a detailed vision of the temple. Earlier he had seen a vision of God's glory leaving the temple, which had deteriorated spiritually before being destroyed physically (Ezekiel 10–11). Now he beholds another similar temple. As an angelic being takes measurements, Ezekiel records the exact specifications for this new temple. When he is finished, Ezekiel sees the glory of the Lord return and fill the temple as before (Ezekiel 40–48).

Snapshots

The life of Ezekiel contains other noteworthy events:

In days prior to hard-hats, Ezekiel gets a hard head instead (3:7–9).

Why his unofficial job description was "watchman" (3:16–17, 33:1–9).

The strangest things happen to Ezekiel's hair (Ezekiel 5).

The prophet is forbidden from mourning his wife's death (24:15–27).

An offensive proverb is retired (18:1–4).

A prophecy against a wicked leader is applied by some to Satan (28:11–19).

Staying Cool Under Pressure

Another visionary among the exiles was the prophet Daniel. According to the book that bears his name, Daniel was a youth when he was led away to exile in Babylon, where he and three friends were trained to serve King Nebuchadnezzar, who wasn't the easiest man to work for. One night the king had a troubling dream. He assembled his staff of "magicians, enchanters, sorcerers, and astrologers" (2:2) and commanded them to tell him what he had dreamed and what it meant. If they couldn't, he would have them "cut into pieces and [their] houses turned into piles of rubble" 2:5).

Before he could carry out this threat, Daniel intervened and asked the king to wait. That night, God, "the revealer of mysteries," revealed Nebuchadnezzar's dream to Daniel.

The king had dreamed of an enormous statue with a head of gold, a chest and arms of silver, a belly and thighs of bronze, and feet of iron mixed with baked clay. A rock had been supernaturally cut out of a mountain and rolled at the statue, smashing its feet and bringing the whole thing down in pieces.

Daniel explained that each section of the statue represented a kingdom. Nebuchadnezzar (Babylon) was the head of gold. Three others would follow (the Persians, the Greeks, and the Romans, respectively). The rock symbolized that "in the time of those kings, the God of heaven will set up a kingdom that will never be destroyed, nor will it be left to another people. It will crush all those kingdoms and bring them to an end, but it will itself endure forever" (2:44).

Nebuchadnezzar was overwhelmed at Daniel's ability to recall and interpret with such precision. Daniel received an immediate promotion, and so did his three friends.

Some time later, Nebuchadnezzar constructed a 90-foot statue of gold and set it up on the plain outside the city, commanding that everyone in his kingdom bow down to it whenever a musical cue was sounded. Apparently Daniel wasn't around that day, but Shadrach, Meshach, and Abednego refused to bow and were sentenced to be thrown into a fiery furnace. When they were tied up and tossed in, the flames were so hot that the men throwing them into the furnace were instantly killed. The Israelites, however, were unharmed. Before the king called them to come out, they could be seen walking around in the furnace, talking with a fourth figure

Manna from Heaven

Daniel and his friends had all received Babylonian names, to better absorb them into their new culture. In the Bible, Daniel is called by his Hebrew name rather than the Babylonian name of Belteshazzar, but his friends are remembered by their Babylonian monikers: Shadrach, Meshach, and Abednego.

What Saith Thou?

So who was the fourth person in the furnace?

Perhaps Nebuchadnezzar was almost correct. One explanation from a Judeo-Christian perspective is that the furnace visitor was a *theophany* —an appearance of God in human guise. Some Christians speculate this was an appearance of Jesus before his human incarnation. Or perhaps it was an angel, because angels show up later in the Book of Daniel.

whom Nebuchadnezzar described as looking "like a son of the gods" (3:25). When they came out, their clothes and hair didn't even smell like smoke! Once again, Nebuchadnezzar was impressed. He decreed that nothing bad should ever be said about the God of Shadrach, Meshach, and Abednego. Then he gave them another promotion.

A Beastly King...Or the King of Beasts

A couple of rulers later, Daniel ran into a similar situation. This time, at the urging of Daniel's enemies in court, King Darius passed a law forbidding his subjects to pray to any god (or any man) other than himself for the next 30 days. Daniel paid no attention. He continued to pray to God three times a day as he always had. The king was fond of Daniel, but rules are rules. The Israelite was arrested and tossed into a lions' den. A stone was placed over the entrance. Meanwhile, the king passed a sleepless night without food or entertainment, thinking about Daniel being devoured by lions.

At the first light of dawn, Darius rushed to the den and called out to Daniel. "O king, live forever!" came Daniel's reply. "My God sent his angel, and he shut the mouths of the lions. They have not hurt me because I was found innocent in his sight. Nor have I ever done any wrong before you, O king" (Daniel 6:22). The king had Daniel extracted from the den, and a new law was passed decreeing that "in every part of my kingdom people must fear and reverence the God of Daniel" (6:26).

The last six chapters of Daniel are mostly prophecies and visions. He dreamed of four beasts, representing the same four kingdoms as in Nebuchadnezzar's dream, and he foresaw the intense suffering his people would endure at the hands of a person most believe to be Antiochus IV Epiphanes, who ruled during the period of the Maccabees between the Old and New Testaments. Several other visions seem to refer to a point still in the future. They are helpful in providing a context for other prophecies in the Book of Revelation.

What Saith Thou?

Was Daniel's deliverance in the lions' den really an act of God? Couldn't the lions just have been full, lethargic, or domestic?

One might think Daniel caught a lucky break except for the rest of the story. When the men who had schemed against Daniel were tossed into the same den (along with their wives and children), "before they reached the floor of the den, the lions overpowered them and crushed all their bones" (6:24).

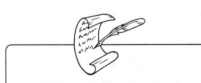

Manna from Heaven

The Book of Daniel makes reference to Gabriel (8:17) and Michael (10:13, 21; 12:1), the only two angels mentioned by name in the Bible.

Snapshots

The Book of Daniel is filled with thrilling stories, including these:

The "Daniel diet" has remarkable results (1:8–20).

King Nebuchadnezzar becomes a beast for seven years—complete with grazing, claws, and body hair (Daniel 4).

King Belshazzar sees the writing on the wall (Daniel 5).

A response to Daniel's prayer is delayed three weeks due to a little celestial warfare (10:1–14).

Spending Some Time in the Minors

With four prophets down and 12 to go, it doesn't seem we're making good progress. However, the final dozen are known collectively as the Minor Prophets, not because they are of less importance but because their writings are considerably shorter. Hosea and Amos were sent to Israel. Obadiah, Jonah, and Nahum prophesied regarding the enemies of Israel and Judah. The rest spent their time in Judah: four before the exile and three afterward. So if these "minor" prophets are seen as a team, they made a major impact on their world. Following is a brief summary about each person and his ministry.

Hosea

Like Ezekiel, Hosea's life became an object lesson for his message. He was told (some say "allowed") to marry a prostitute named Gomer, who proved unfaithful to him. She left him and their three kids (who may or may not have been Hosea's) to chase other guys. He eventually redeemed her financially, and they were reconciled. Not surprisingly, Hosea's message to Israel was that "There is no faithfulness, no love, no acknowledgment of God in the land.... A spirit of prostitution leads them astray; they are unfaithful to their God" (4:1, 12). Yet if the Israelites were willing to repent, they would find God to be loving and forgiving.

Joel

Focusing on the judgment of God's people, Joel prophesies that "the great and dreadful day of the Lord" (2:31) will be preceded by an invasion of locusts (either literal or symbolizing foreign invasion). Also, "the sun will be turned to darkness and the moon to blood" (2:31).

Amos

Amos worked as a shepherd and as caretaker of a grove of figs. He prophesied during a relatively prosperous time, warning the "complacent" that social injustice was a symptom of spiritual sin, and that judgment would follow.

Obadiah

The Israelites (descendants of Jacob) and the Edomites (descendants of Esau) had been at odds ever since the original twins were in the womb (Genesis 25:21–26). In this shortest book of the Old Testament, Obadiah addresses Edom's superior attitude after Israel has been crushed by outsiders. He knows that a similar end is coming to Edom, while Israel will eventually be restored to God.

Jonah

The best known of the minor prophets, Jonah was also the most reluctant to speak for God. Of course, he *was* sent to Nineveh—soon to become the capital city of the Assyrian Empire. Because this was about the last place he wanted to spend time, Jonah fled from God, boarding a ship headed in the opposite direction from Nineveh. He didn't get far. A storm rose up and Jonah was reluctantly thrown overboard by the ships crew, where he was swallowed by "a great fish." After three days inside the belly of the beast, during which he had time to pray and restore his courage, Jonah was vomited onto dry land. When he got out, he did proceed to Nineveh to deliver God's message of warning. But when the Ninevites actually repented and were spared, Jonah became indignant. He apparently wanted to witness a firestorm on the city. While watching from a distant hill, God caused a vine to grow and provide him with shade. The next day, however, a worm killed the vine, causing the heat to bear down on Jonah. When the prophet again became irate, God pointed out that he had more concern about himself and one little vine than he did for a city of 120,000 people.

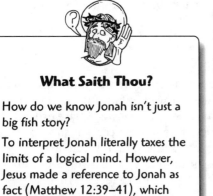

What Saith Thou?

How do we know Jonah isn't just a big fish story?

To interpret Jonah literally taxes the limits of a logical mind. However, Jesus made a reference to Jonah as fact (Matthew 12:39–41), which adds credibility to the account.

Micah

The prophet Micah foresaw the fall of the northern kingdom of Israel, but his message was that the people of Judah were just as guilty. Amid the message of coming judgment and the need for repentance is a significant prophecy that the coming Messiah would be born in Bethlehem (5:2).

Nahum

The Book of Nahum is something of a sequel to Jonah. After the Ninevites repented and were spared (thanks to the work of Jonah) they soon reverted to their old, sinful ways. Nahum predicted the ultimate fall of Ninevah, which took place not long afterward.

Habakkuk

The Book of Habakkuk is a transcript of a conversation between God and the prophet. Habakkuk wanted to know why God was planning to allow the violent Babylonians to overpower Judah. After their dialogue, Habakkuk consented to "wait patiently for the day of calamity" (3:16).

Zephaniah

Zephaniah was descended from kings, which may be why his writing reflects an insight into political matters. He foretold the coming judgment on Judah, which he refers to as "the day of the Lord."

Haggai

When the Jews returned to Jerusalem to rebuild their temple, they faced opposition and allowed the work to be postponed. Haggai's call was to encourage them to get back to work.

Zechariah

A contemporary of Haggai's, Zechariah had essentially the same calling. He also preached on the coming Messiah, including the price of his betrayal (11:12–13). His writing is filled with interesting imagery and symbolism: gold lampstands, flying scrolls, chariots, a woman in a basket, bad shepherds, and more.

Potent Quotables

Though the fig tree does not bud and there are no grapes on the vines, though the olive crop fails and the fields produce no food, though there are no sheep in the pen and no cattle in the stalls, yet I will rejoice in the Lord, I will be joyful in God my Savior. (Habakkuk 3:17-18)

During a time when so much was going wrong, Habakkuk shows a remarkable level of faith and optimism.

Malachi

The book of Malachi, a prophet in Israel after the exile, closes the canon of the Old Testament. It explores themes of faithfulness and tithing (given a tenth of your possessions/income) to God, and it predicts a return of "the prophet Elijah" to precede the coming of the Messiah (4:5–6).

One chapter of concise summaries can't do justice to all those pages of prophecy that you held between your fingers as the chapter began. But perhaps you now know enough to spend time on your own and start to make sense out of the unique and fascinating lives of the Old Testament prophets.

The Least You Need to Know

➤ The prophets weren't always popular, but they were always right about what was going to happen.

➤ While all the prophets had essentially the same job, they had a wide variety of experiences and responses.

➤ Many prophecies remain unfulfilled, providing much speculation about events yet to occur.

Part 3
The New Testament

Just when people thought they had God figured out, along came Jesus to shatter their preconceptions. His teachings were new in every sense of the word. People were amazed because "he taught as one who had authority, and not as their teachers of the law" (Matthew 7:29).

He didn't teach, "Out with the old and in with the new." Rather, he began to show how the old way of doing things was a precursor to a new and better way. Jesus confirmed that, indeed, God should be revered as creator, lord, king, judge, and good shepherd—just as the Old Testament had instructed. He also brought to light the less familiar Old Testament images of God as a loving father, a sacrificial savior, a divine counselor/comforter, and even a friend. As Jesus modeled what God was like, he hugged little children, touched "unclean" lepers, and patiently trained dense disciples. His examples of love and forgiveness were unprecedented and extended to adulteresses caught in the act, greedy tax collectors, pretentious religious leaders, helpless victims of illness, disloyal friends, and even the very people who eventually put him to death. The New Testament provides a more comprehensive insight into the nature and character of God.

Sensitive readers will certainly find significance in the gospel stories of Jesus and his followers. For those with a more detached, cognitive approach to all things religious, the epistles provide logical arguments to explain the importance of Jesus' life, death, and resurrection. And, of course, Revelation—an apocalyptic book—is a challenge for all of us.

Even if the New Testament is somewhat familiar to you, perhaps you can find new insight this time through. And if it's all new territory to you, may your spiritual awareness increase from chapter to chapter.

Chapter 15

God's Baby Gift

In This Chapter

➤ What happened between the Old and New Testaments

➤ The births of John the Baptist and Jesus

➤ A look at the guest list at the first Christmas party

➤ The early life of Jesus, and a few of his relationships

With this chapter we begin the New Testament. Going from the Old to the New Testament is something like getting a cool new teacher as a midyear replacement for an older, more traditional one. You know the new person has to abide by many of the same rules and regulations, yet the mood picks up with a more relaxed and creative teaching style.

Where Are We Going?

The next four chapters look at the biblical account of the life of Jesus from the gospels of Matthew, Mark, Luke, and John. Rather than go straight through each book, we will attempt to observe them as a whole. The author's goal in each case was to present the story of Jesus, so we will try to do the same thing by combining the content of the four books. This chapter focuses on the birth and early life of Jesus; the next chapter, "We're Going to Need to See Some I.D.," covers the miracles of Jesus; Chapter 17, "Did I Hear That Right?" looks at an assortment of Jesus' teachings; and Chapter 18, "Arose by Any Other Name…" examines the death and resurrection accounts. In a few cases, the gospel writers provide slight variations of the same accounts. We will draw from whichever account provides the clearest picture for the topic being discussed, and will examine instances in which discrepancies seem significant.

Manna from Heaven

The word **gospel** means "good tidings" or "good news." Matthew, Mark, and Luke are known as *synoptic* gospels (from a Greek word meaning *seeing together*) because of their similarity in language and content. The Book of John is quite different from the other three and provides much additional insight into Jesus' life.

It may seem a bit out of proportion to spend four chapters covering four New Testament books and then five chapters to cover the other 23. However, the gospels are filled with gripping stories, unusual relationships, hard-to-understand teachings, contrasts with Old Testament practices, and a vast panorama of insight into what's really important in life. To rush through this body of work might not provide the depth of understanding needed to interpret the rest of the New Testament adequately.

In addition, people's opinions about the person of Jesus Christ are vastly different. Various passages are cited to support different views. For the full picture, we need to examine a wide range of biblical insight into the person of Jesus. As we compile information and see how Jesus responded in a variety of situations, we can come to a more enlightened conclusion.

What Have We Missed?

It may look as if the New Testament picks up just a couple of pages after the Old Testament ends, but approximately 400 years of history have gone by in that space. The Israelites have returned to their homeland after 70 years in captivity, but they haven't ceased to be the "possession" of some larger empire. The Persians ruled until about 330 B.C.E., when Alexander the Great began to conquer much of the known world in the name of Greece. While the Persians had been content to let individual territories maintain their languages and religions, Alexander's goal was to unify the nations under a single culture and language, a process known as *Hellenization*. However, Alexander gave the Jews leeway to practice their religion, and he made a few other exceptions for them. Under successive Greek rulers, even these rights would be taken away.

Eventually the Jews fought for and won their independence—but not for long. One particularly cruel leader named Antiochus IV Epiphanes began to impose his standards on the Jews—like it or not. He destroyed all written copies of the Jewish Scriptures he could find. He refused to allow the people to circumcise their sons or observe the Sabbath. He even had an image of Zeus set up in the temple and sacrificed a pig to him on the altar—perhaps the event Daniel foresaw and called "the abomination that causes desolation" (Daniel 8:13; 12:11).

The Empire of Alexander the Great and His Successors

Empires of Alexander
Seleucid empire
Ptolemid empire
Cilicia Province

But the actions of Antiochus were too much for a devoted Jewish family which was given the name *Maccabees* (Maccabee means "the Hammerer.") The resulting Maccabean revolt restored a certain amount of order to Jewish life. The temple was purified and a celebration was held, which became an annual festival. By 63 B.C.E. the Romans came rolling in, taking Jerusalem by force, slaughtering priests, and defiling the temple. The Romans imposed their own leaders on the Jews, allowing them a degree of tolerance but keeping them on a rather short leash. It was not a happy arrangement for the Jewish people.

Unplanned Parenthood (Luke 1)

It was into this setting that two important babies were born. The first baby's parents had already given up on having kids. Zechariah (some Bible versions use "Zacharias") was a priest in the temple; his wife Elizabeth was also a descendant of Aaron. They were old and childless. But one day in the temple, the angel Gabriel popped up in front of Zechariah, promising him a son and instructing him to name the child John. The child would grow to fulfill a specific mission: "to turn the hearts of the fathers to their children and the disobedient to the wisdom of the righteous—to make ready a people prepared for the Lord" (Luke 1:16–17).

Snapshots

Gabriel's visit left Zechariah speechless—literally. Read about it in Luke 1:18–22, 57–66.

Manna from Heaven

The name **Jesus** was the Greek equivalent of the Old Testament name Joshua, meaning, "The Lord saves."

Gabriel had another stop to make as well: in Nazareth, at the house of a young virgin girl named Mary, who was engaged to be married. His salutation troubled her: "Greetings, you who are highly favored! The Lord is with you" (Luke 1:28). Gabriel assured Mary that everything would be all right. She had been chosen to give birth to a son to be named Jesus. And by the way, this would be no ordinary child. Gabriel told her, "He will be great and will be called the Son of the Most High. The Lord God will give him the throne of his father David, and he will reign over the house of Jacob forever; his kingdom will never end" (vv. 32–33).

If You Don't Mind My Asking

Mary did point out one problem in her likelihood of having a child: her virginity. The angel's reply? "Nothing is impossible with God" (v. 37). The mechanics of the conception remain a mystery, other than Gabriel's explanation that "The Holy Spirit will come upon you, and the power of the Most High will overshadow you. So the holy one to be born will be called the Son of God" (v. 35).

Gabriel passed along the news that Mary's relative, Elizabeth, was also miraculously pregnant. Elizabeth had gone into seclusion until her delivery, but after Mary became pregnant she went to join her. As soon as the two mothers-to-be got near each other, Elizabeth's baby "leaped in her womb" and Elizabeth was filled with the Holy Spirit and exclaimed: "Blessed are you among women, and blessed is the child you will bear!" (1:39–42) Mary stayed with Elizabeth for about three months before returning home. About that time, Elizabeth gave birth to her baby and named him John.

"You're WHAT?"

In the thrill and anticipation of all the unexpected pregnancies, one person was not so excited. Joseph was Mary's fiancé, and all he knew was that his betrothed was pregnant and that he wasn't the father. While this situation isn't particularly rare these days, we must remember that in Joseph's time it would have been a scandal of enormous proportions. (A legal engagement was as binding as a marriage—just without the sex.) We get some insight into his character when we read that he didn't make a public spectacle or bring charges against Mary. Rather, "because he was a righteous man and did not want to expose her to public disgrace, he had in mind to divorce her quietly" (Matthew 1:19).

But an angel appeared to Joseph in a dream and reassured him. "Do not be afraid to take Mary as your wife, for the child conceived in her is from the Holy Spirit" (1:20). Joseph went ahead and married Mary as God had commanded, though it is clearly stated that they didn't sleep together until after the birth of Jesus (Matthew 1:24–25).

It's Beginning to Look a Lot Like Christmas (Matthew 2; Luke 2)

When it comes to Bible knowledge, the one thing most people know is the Christmas story. We know what the Bible says about the heartwarming account of Mary riding her donkey to Bethlehem and then going into labor but being told by the innkeeper that there was no room. We know about the skies filled with singing angels, and the baby in the stable being visited by three wise men, among others.

Actually, most of that information is traditional rather than biblical. The Bible doesn't tell us how Mary got to Bethlehem. No innkeeper is mentioned. As far as we can tell, one angel speaks directly to the shepherds and others show up, but we can't be for sure they were singing. We know of a manger, but not a stable. The account of the visiting Magi never tells us how many made the trip. You search the Bible in vain to prove that "Away in a manger the baby awakes, but little Lord Jesus, no crying he makes." And while we're at it, the Bible never suggests that Jesus Christ was given the middle initial H. So let's see what we *do* know.

You might remember from the Book of Micah the prophecy that Jesus would be born in Bethlehem. But nothing mystical happened to get Joseph and Mary out of their home town of Nazareth (in Galilee, west of the Galilean sea) and into Bethlehem (south of Jerusalem). A governmental decree required them to make the trip to participate in a Roman census. Because Joseph was descended from David, he had to check in at David's hometown of Bethlehem—about a three-day trip from Nazareth traveling due south.

While in Bethlehem, Mary went into labor. The inns were booked, but she found someplace that had a manger (a food trough for farm animals). Though just about every nativity scene you'll see shows a free-standing stable, it is just as likely that Jesus was born in a cave, which was a common place to shelter animals.

The birth might have gone unnoticed except for some very unusual events. To begin with, nearby shepherds were directed to the Christ child by an angel, backed up by a "great company of the heavenly host, praising God" (Luke 2:13). The shepherds left their flocks, found the baby with his parents, and came back glorifying God and telling everyone what they had seen.

"We've Been Expecting You"

When Jesus was eight days old, he was taken to the temple to be circumcised. A man there named Simeon had been told he would live to see "the Lord's Christ" (or Messiah; both mean "anointed one") (Luke 2:25–26). Upon realizing Jesus was the one he had been waiting for, Simeon praised God and blessed Mary and Joseph. Another who recognized the child was an old widowed woman named Anna. She had spent years in the temple fasting and praying; now she spoke out and told all who would listen that the redemption of Jerusalem had come.

Meanwhile, a group of travelers, called Magi in the Bible, was headed toward Bethlehem from somewhere in the east. Astrologers, most likely, they had seen a special star and were bringing gifts for "the one who has been born king of the Jews" (Matthew 2:1–2). On the way, they stopped at the palace of King Herod to see what he knew. Alerted to a potential rival, Herod asked them to "go and make a careful search" and let him know what they found out. The Magi soon found the child and offered him their gifts: gold, incense, and myrrh.

Potent Quotables

'Fear not; for, behold I bring you good tidings of great joy, which shall be to all people. For unto you is born this day in the city of David a Savior, who is Christ the Lord. And this shall be a sign unto you: Ye shall find the babe wrapped in swaddling clothes, lying in a manger.' And suddenly there was with the angel a multitude of the heavenly host, praising God, and saying, 'Glory to God in the highest, and on earth peace, good will toward men.' (Luke 2:10–14, KJV)

We've reverted to the *King James Version* for this more familiar translation of the popular Christmas recitation.

Some Kid!

Note that, by this time, Jesus is called a "child" rather than "baby;" the Magi also found him in a "house." The nativity scenes that show the wise men and shepherds together are misleading. The Magi probably arrived months or years later than the shepherds.

Warned by God in a dream not to return to Herod, the Magi went home by another route. Herod was furious when the Magi failed to report back. He gave orders that all male children under the age of 2 from Bethlehem and the surrounding area be killed. Joseph and Mary, who had been warned in advance, skipped town and headed for Egypt, where they remained until Herod's death. Then they returned to Nazareth and settled there.

The Bible doesn't say much about Jesus' childhood. The only story we have is of an annual family trip to Jerusalem to celebrate Passover when Jesus was 12. On the way home, Jesus' parents discovered that he wasn't in their group. Returning, they searched the city for three days before finding him in the temple, listening to the teachers and asking searching questions.

Mary scolded him for the worry he had caused them. But Jesus responded, "Why were you searching for me? Didn't you know I had to be in my Father's house?" (Luke 2:49) Mary didn't understand exactly what he was talking about, yet she "treasured all these things in her heart." And even though Jesus was obviously a special child, the Bible tells us he was obedient to his parents and that he "grew in wisdom and stature, and in favor with God and men" (Luke 2:51–52).

And the Word Became Flesh (John 1:1–18)

Here we should pause and point out that the Book of John offers a different look at the significance of the birth of Jesus. While Matthew and Luke show us the frailty of a tiny baby, John proclaims that the event was no less than the power of the Word of God becoming flesh. God had sent Moses with the written Word, but the people hadn't responded very well. God sent prophets to speak the Word boldly, but the prophets were rejected. Now the Word had been born into our world as flesh and bone.

Jesus would not only quote words off a page; he would also model them. The words would come alive in the context of emotions: love, pain, anger, dread, sadness, joy. The concepts could no longer be dismissed as theoretical standards handed down from on high, but would become realities proven out in the best and worst situations of life.

How John Became "the Baptist" (Matthew 3; Luke 3; John 1:29–34)

Meanwhile, Elizabeth and Zechariah's son John was also becoming a mature and impressive personality. He "grew and became strong in spirit; and he lived in the desert until he appeared publicly to Israel" (Luke 1:80). When next we see him, he has become a preacher working in the area of the Jordan River, "preaching a baptism of repentance for the forgiveness of sins" (Luke 3:3).

John lived a simple lifestyle, wearing camel's-hair clothing and eating locusts and wild honey. (Some believe these "locusts" were the fruit of the locust tree.) His message was blunt: People should repent of their sins, share what they had, be honest, act decently toward one another, and otherwise straighten out their lives to "prepare the way for the Lord." Some suspected he might be the Messiah. But John explained that his baptism was only "with water"; someone was coming who would baptize "with the Holy Spirit and with fire" (3:16).

Manna from Heaven

The **Pharisees** were a devout subgroup within Judaism, with a reputation as experts in Jewish law. Their traditions and way of life set them apart and may have made them easy to recognize.

Manna from Heaven

The **Sadducees** were another Jewish subgroup. It is known that they differed from the Pharisees on certain theological points; evidence also suggests that they were a somewhat elitist group, connected with wealth and power.

John was equally outspoken in his criticism of religious leaders like the Pharisees and Sadducees. He eventually landed in prison after rebuking Herod for immorality.

Yet another religious division were the *Essenes*, mostly unmarried men who maintained a simple, communal lifestyle.

As John was preaching, Jesus came to be baptized. John protested: Jesus should baptize *him,* not the other way around. Jesus insisted. Throughout his ministry he was to identify completely with those he had come to save. Moreover, though he had no sins to repent of, baptism was nevertheless the start of a new life for Jesus. When Jesus came up out of the water, "he saw the heavens opened" and "the Spirit descended like a dove on him."

At the same time a voice came from heaven: "This is my Son, whom I love; with him I am well pleased" (Matthew 3:16–17). It was at that point that Jesus began his ministry.

Some people like to point to Jesus' baptism as an ideal example of the distinctions of the Holy Trinity. God the Father spoke from heaven, God the Son was being baptized, and God the Holy Spirit descended like a dove. As explained in the Westminster Shorter Catechism, "There are three persons in the Godhead, the Father, the Son, and the Holy Ghost; and these three are one God, the same in substance, equal in power and glory."

The Devil Couldn't Make Him Do It (Matthew 4:1–11)

While Jesus, as God, was wearing human skin, he was allowed to be tempted by the devil. Like his baptism, this was a way to model godly behavior to human beings. Otherwise, we would tend to think Jesus had it too easy and wouldn't appreciate the fact that he became human. Jesus passed his test without resorting to supernatural means, taking away any inclination we might have to justify sin with the excuse that "The devil made me do it!"

But after three attempts, the devil gave up. He left, and angels came to minister to Jesus. Yet the reprieve was not a permanent one. Luke tells us that the devil left him until an opportune time (Luke 4:13). Jesus would regularly face temptation, just as we do.

Snapshots

Read about the devil's three temptations—and Jesus' method of dealing with them—in Matthew 4:1–13.

The Dusty Dozen (Matthew 4:18–22; 9:9; Luke 10:2–4; John 1:35–51)

After his baptism and temptation, Jesus began his public ministry. His first two disciples were sent by John. One of them, Andrew, fetched his brother Simon soon after, saying, "We have found the Messiah." When Jesus saw Simon, he told him, "You are Simon, son of John. You will be called Cephas" (which translates into Greek as "Peter").

Another story says that Jesus recruited Andrew and Peter while they were casting their nets on the shore of the Sea of Galilee. Jesus said, "Come, follow me and I will make you fishers of men"—and they left their nets at once and followed him. Down the shore a bit he saw two more brothers, James and John, fishing from a boat with their father. They, too, listened to him and followed.

Another time Jesus passed a man named Philip and again said, "Follow me." Philip, in turn, told his friend Nathanael that he had found the one Moses wrote about in the Law, and about whom the prophets also wrote—Jesus of Nazareth, the son of Joseph. Nathanael (also known as Bartholomew) was skeptical. Nazareth was a podunk town not even mentioned in the Old Testament. How could anything significant come from there? When he met Jesus face-to-face, however, his doubts evaporated. Here are the names of the rest of the Twelve:

➤ Matthew (Levi), who left his job as a tax collector to go with Jesus

➤ Simon, who was called the Zealot

➤ Thomas

➤ James, son of Alphaeus (the other James was the son of Zebedee)

➤ Thaddaeus (also known as Judas, the son of James)

➤ Judas Iscariot

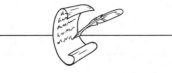

Manna from Heaven

The **Zealots** were a patriotic Jewish faction organized to resist the intrusion of the Romans. They weren't opposed to violence and assassination to accomplish their mission.

What Saith Thou?

Why was worship being conducted in synagogues rather than the temple?

From the time of the exile—and perhaps earlier—the Jews began to gather in synagogues for religious enrichment. A synagogue could be established in any town with 10 married Jewish men and was less for public worship than for studying the Holy Scriptures. Participation in the synagogues was one main way that the Pharisees kept themselves before the public. However, people still made an effort to get to the temple in Jerusalem when they could.

The disciples came from a broad spectrum of jobs, personalities, and backgrounds. In most respects, they were like us: pretty ordinary. Yet they became Jesus' inner circle, chosen after a night of prayer (Luke 6:12) and later given authority to drive out evil spirits and to heal every disease and sickness. With the exception of occasional onsets of fear or doubt, all but one stood by Jesus in the best and worst days of his public ministry. Jesus had many other followers and disciples, but none so close as the original Twelve.

One Reason *Why* You Can't Go Home Again (Luke 4:14–30)

Jesus was a popular preacher and healer, and before long he had quite a following. Early in his ministry he went back to his hometown of Nazareth, where he visited the synagogue. When he was handed a scroll of sacred scripture to read aloud, it turned out to be the scroll of the prophet Isaiah: "The Spirit of the Lord is upon me, because he has anointed me to preach good news to the poor. He has sent me to proclaim freedom for the prisoners and recovery of sight for the blind, to release the oppressed, to proclaim the year of the Lord's favor" (Luke 4:18–19; Isaiah 61:1–2).

All eyes were on Jesus as he prepared to speak about the reading. Jesus told them, "Today this scripture is fulfilled in your hearing." He spoke so well that at first people were impressed with this son of Joseph. But he went on to preach about Elijah and Elisha being sent to live with the Gentiles because the Jews were unbelieving, adding that no prophet is accepted in his hometown, the people realized he was talking about them. They got so irate that they ran Jesus out of the synagogue, planning to throw him over a cliff; but he walked right through the crowd and went on his way. Perhaps his escape was miraculous, or maybe he was able to simply walk away from trouble without escalating the situation.

Jesus' encounters with people one-on-one provide some of the best illustrations we have of who he was. Let's look at a few examples.

Nic at Night (John 3:1–21)

One night Jesus received a visit from a Pharisee named Nicodemus, who sincerely desired to understand what Jesus was teaching. Nicodemus got to the point. Jesus couldn't perform the miracles he was doing, he said, unless God was behind them. Jesus replied, "I tell you the truth, no one can see the kingdom of God unless he is born again" (or "born from above").

Nicodemus didn't know what to make of this apparent non sequitur, and Jesus' next remarks—all about water and the Spirit and the wind—didn't help any. Of course, Jesus was talking about a spiritual rebirth. Nicodemus still didn't understand. The poor guy was sitting there with strange images in his mind as he asked his next question: Surely he cannot enter a second time into his mother's womb to be born! Jesus then went on to explain that the second birth was a spiritual one. Nicodemus was still struggling, but could only ask, "How could this be?" Jesus went on to explain that he was going to have the same effect on people as the bronze snake in the wilderness that Moses had lifted up: People who looked to him for salvation would be saved from death and find new life. (The story he referred to is in Numbers 21:4-9.) Then Jesus spoke what has become the most quoted verse in the Bible (John 3:16).

> *"For God so loved the world that he gave his one and only Son, that whoever believes in him shall not perish but have eternal life. For God did not send his Son into the world to condemn the world, but to save the world through him* (John 3:16–17).

It's significant to note that if Nicodemus had tried to fake a level of spiritual depth he didn't actually have, he wouldn't have been willing to ask a few foolish-sounding questions, and we might not have received such a succinct summary of God's plan. In spite of Nicodemus's initial struggling, he apparently went on to believe in Jesus. He stepped forward after Jesus' crucifixion to help take care of the body, and he was a minority voice among those Pharisees whose majority regularly resisted the credence of Jesus' teachings.

A Chat Around the Water Cooler (John 4:1–42)

Another unusual relationship with Jesus sprang up one day at about noon while he and his disciples were traveling through Samaria. Jesus was tired and decided to rest beside a well while the disciples went to get some food. While he was sitting there, a Samaritan woman came for water.

To the woman's shock, Jesus asked her for a drink. It was unusual for a man to approach a woman so boldly, and even more unusual for Jews to associate with Samaritans. She asked him why he was talking to her. He answered, "If you knew the gift of God and who it is that asks you for a drink, you would have asked him and he would have given you living water."

Manna from Heaven

The conflict between the Jews and **Samaritans** dated back to the exile, when many of the Jews who were not deported intermarried with foreigners. Their descendants became the Samaritans. Over time they had developed their own religion—an offshoot of Judaism, with some differences. Since that time the prejudice had become both religious and racial.

Caught off-guard, like Nicodemus, the woman didn't comprehend what Jesus was trying to tell her. He continued, "Everyone who drinks this water will be thirsty again, but whoever drinks the water I give him will never thirst. Indeed, the water I give him will become in him a spring of water welling up to eternal life."

She asked for some of that special water, so Jesus told her to go get her husband and come back. She said she wasn't married. Jesus told her she had been married five times, and was currently living with a man who wasn't her husband. Now he had her attention! Jesus hadn't made a big deal about the fact that she was a woman and a Samaritan, but even knowing what he did about her private life, he had initiated a conversation with her.

As the dialog continued, she quickly realized that she was speaking not simply to a prophet but to the promised Messiah. She went to bring back a crowd of her friends, and many of them believed in Jesus because of her testimony.

Can Someone Get This Lady a Robe? (John 8:1–11)

Another encounter with Jesus took place apparently against the wishes of both parties. A woman was caught in the act of adultery and paraded (perhaps naked) in front of the Pharisees, who made her stand before Jesus. By this time the Pharisees had begun to look for ways to trip Jesus up and diminish his popularity. They decided to see whether they could make him uphold the death sentence in the Jewish law, which would greatly tarnish his nice-guy image. If he refused, they could accuse him of not following the law (Leviticus 20:10). So they asked: "Teacher, this woman was caught in the act of adultery. In the Law Moses commanded us to stone such women. Now what do you say?"

The act of adultery usually requires two people, both of whom, according to the law, should have been sentenced to death. Since the woman had been caught in the act, there should have been a man standing next to her, but it seems that the male involved had conveniently escaped.

It was quite a set-up. Jesus, however, was not one to be entrapped. He began writing in the dust with his finger, saying nothing. There has been much speculation about what he wrote, but no one really knows. Still they pressed him for a response. So Jesus said, "If any one of you is without sin, let him be the first to throw a stone at her." Then he resumed his writing on the ground.

One by one, the scribes and Pharisees began to depart, until only the woman was left with Jesus. He stood up and asked her: "Woman, where are they? Has no one condemned you?" She said no. Jesus continued: "Then neither do I condemn you. Go now, and leave your life of sin."

We don't know whether she took Jesus' advice. However, this story, like the other two, sheds light on the interpersonal skills of Jesus. He showed no prejudice—not for a member of his opponents the Pharisees; not for a Samaritan whom other Jews equated with dogs; and not for this woman whose sin was completely exposed. He didn't condone sinful actions, but neither did he resort to using guilt or shame. Jesus' ministry reflected Jesus' birth. The people involved weren't limited to any particular race, religion, or economic level. Jewish shepherds, Gentile Magi, the angels of heaven, and faithful temple attendants were all invited to celebrate the birth. Likewise, Jesus continued to invite skeptics, Samaritans, Pharisees, and sinners of all kinds to believe in him. Some would take him up on his offer, and others would walk away.

So far, the claim that Jesus was God has been made by the angel Gabriel (Luke 1:35), the voice of God the Father (Matthew 3:17), John the Baptist (John 1:32-34), and Jesus himself (John 4:25-26). But for his peers who needed a little additional evidence, the next chapter focuses on the miracles Jesus performed.

The Least You Need to Know

➤ The 400 years between the Old and New Testaments were a somewhat turbulent time for the Jewish people, leading up to their conquest by the Roman Empire.

➤ According to the Bible, the births of Jesus and John the Baptist were both accompanied by supernatural events.

➤ Jesus was baptized and tempted, and he endured everything ordinary human beings do. Yet even as a pre-teen, he showed signs of being special.

➤ Jesus was a popular teacher, and lots of people followed him around, but he chose 12 to be his closest disciples.

➤ In his relationships with other people, Jesus frequently came across as intriguing, likable, and forgiving.

Chapter 16

We're Going to Need to See Some I.D.

In This Chapter

➤ Jesus' miracles give credence to his teachings

➤ Jesus demonstrates control over nature, disease, and even death

➤ Jesus turns water to wine, walks on water, feeds multitudes, casts out evil spirits, raises people from the dead, and more

---

It's not uncommon for individuals to make bold claims to be spiritual guides, gurus, or even gods. They talk a big game, and they may have some success. Frequently, though, when the dust settles, the leader is gone and his followers have taken poisoned Kool-Aid, burned their compound down around them, or are found dead in purple shrouds and black Nikes.

As Jesus' ministry continued, he made some statements that were considered by many to be outrageous—if not outright blasphemous. We'll take a closer look at some of those statements in the next chapter. But first let's examine some of Jesus' miracles. Jesus used logic and reason to defend his claims, but it was the power of his miracles that truly punctuated the power of his words.

Demons, Diseases, and Disabilities

Jesus performed all kinds of miracles, but the kind for which he was most known were those he worked in one-on-one encounters with people in need of healing. Sometimes people came to him on behalf of loved ones, sometimes for themselves. Those who were sick or unable to walk were often brought by friends or relatives. In each case, the Bible stresses that faith was necessary for healing to take place—even if it was the faith of a parent or a friend.

Jesus Heals a Ceiling Fan (Mark 2:1–2)

Jesus' authority became an issue early in his ministry. He already had a large following, and crowds would gather wherever he went. One day when he was teaching, the crowd not only filled the house but flowed into the yard as well.

Jesus had developed a reputation as a healer, and in one instance a paralyzed man wanted to be able to walk. Four friends literally carried him to see Jesus, but the crowd was so thick they couldn't get anywhere close. They decided the only way Jesus would be accessible was from above, so they crawled up on the roof and dug a hole. Then they lowered their friend, lying on his mat, down to where Jesus was.

Manna from Heaven

The spaces between the wooden beams of a Palestinian roof were usually filled with grass, clay, and tree branches, sometimes covered with clay tiles.

Jesus' response was unexpected. He said to the paralyzed man, "Son, your sins are forgiven." Teachers of the law were offended. Only God had the authority to forgive sins; Jesus had spoken blasphemy! But before they said a word, Jesus posed them a question. Which would be easier: to tell the guy his sins were forgiven, or to tell him to get up and walk? Obviously it would be easier to say his sins were forgiven, because it couldn't be proven. A command to walk, on the other hand, could be easily confirmed or disproved.

Then to prove that his words weren't simply hot air, Jesus turned to the man: "I tell you, get up, take your mat, and go home." And that's exactly what the man did. The miracle of healing only served to verify the even greater miracle of forgiveness.

Nothing Up His Sleeve...

No doubt the skeptics in the crowd tried to figure out whether Jesus was using some kind of magician's trick to do his miracles—as would most of us if we saw him at work today. But his methods were rarely the same.

To the crippled man in the previous story and another man with the same problem (John 5:1–15), he had only to speak. To heal a woman with a similar condition, he laid his hands on her as he spoke. Another time a Roman centurion begged help for his servant, who lay paralyzed in the man's house. Jesus offered to go heal him. But the centurion was familiar with giving orders and knew how authority worked. He asked that Jesus simply "say the word" and get the job done. Amazed at the faith of this non-Jewish man, Jesus did what he asked. He spoke and the servant was healed long-distance "at that very hour" (Matthew 8:5–13).

In another case Jesus touched a leper to purify him—which, to an "unclean" and untouchable person, surely must have been appreciated (Mark 1:40–45). Another time ten lepers stood at a distance and asked for help (Luke 17:11–19). Jesus told them to present themselves to the priests, and along the way they were healed.

When dealing with people who were possessed by evil spirits, Jesus frequently "drove out the spirits with a word" (Matthew 8:16; Luke 4:31–37). But one day he encountered a man whose demonic possession had made him a wild man. He lived in the tombs and had frequently been chained for his own good, yet he had superhuman strength to break out of his chains. Jesus commanded the spirit to leave the man, but the spirit answered back, pleading not to be tortured. Jesus asked for a name and the spirit replied, "My name is Legion, for we are many." The demons asked to be released into a herd of about 2,000 pigs feeding nearby. Jesus "gave them permission," and the whole herd ran down the hill and into the lake, drowning. The man was restored to his right mind, but the villagers begged Jesus to leave (Mark 5:1–17).

What Saith Thou?

Weren't a lot of symptoms of diseases attributed to demon possession before science discovered how to treat them?

This is certainly true in a historic sense, yet the Bible validates the reality of demons. Common sense tells us that Jesus would have no credibility as a healer if he were supposedly casting out demons that didn't actually exist. The prominent opinion is that demons are (usually) unseen, bodyless, supernatural beings. Many believe they are angels who supported Satan in his rebellion against God, and continue to work against God's purposes. In some cases, after Jesus removed an evil spirit from a person, the person's physical malady (blindness, muteness, etc.) was eliminated as well.

Here's Mud in Your Eye

Blind people also came to Jesus for healing. In some cases, Jesus healed them by touching their eyes (Matthew 9:27–31; 20:29–34). In another instance he spat on the ground to create a mud poultice to apply to a blind man's eyes, and then sent the man to wash in a particular pool. When the man did, his sight was restored. Another time Jesus spat directly on a blind man's eyes before touching them (Mark 8:22–26). In this case, the man's vision was still a little hazy; he said people looked like "trees walking around." When Jesus touched his eyes a second time, the man's sight was fully restored.

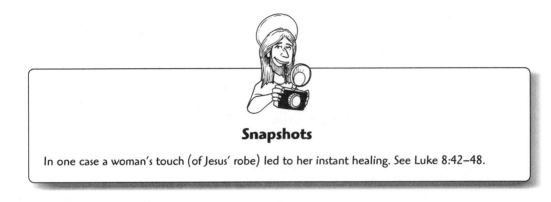

Snapshots

In one case a woman's touch (of Jesus' robe) led to her instant healing. See Luke 8:42–48.

It's Not Hard to Rule Mother Nature

Some of the more dramatic miracles of Jesus recorded by the gospel writers were performed away from the public eye. These miracles showed his authority over nature—yet in every case it is clear that Jesus' intent was not to intimidate or impress people, but to teach them the meaning of faith.

Manna from Heaven

Planning a wedding was no less challenging in Jesus' day than it is today. The bride and groom both dressed elaborately. The groom was escorted by friends and musicians through town to the bride's house, returning with her and her family to his house. Along the way all their friends joined the procession for music and dancing. The bridegroom fed the lot of them at a feast held before the consummation of the wedding that night. And it wasn't unusual for the partying to continue for a week or two. No wonder the wine ran out!

Six Huge Bottles of Wine on the Floor (John 2:1–11)

Jesus' first miracle was a case in point. He, his mother, and his disciples had been invited to a wedding. Apparently the guest list had exceeded what the wedding couple had planned for, because Jesus' mother slipped over to him and told him they were out of wine. She seemed to expect him to do something about it. He told her, rather sharply, "My time has not yet come."

Yet Mary persisted, instructing the servants to do whatever Jesus told them. He told the servants to fill six stone jars with water. Each of the jars held from 20 to 30 gallons. When the jars were filled to the brim, Jesus told them to take a sample to the "master of the banquet" (something akin to the emcee at a modern wedding reception). The water had become wine. The master of the banquet deemed it superior to what they had been drinking—though normally, people would start with their best wine to impress their guests and pull out the cheap stuff after people's taste buds had become less discerning!

The Ones That Didn't Quite Get Away (Luke 5:1–11)

Jesus and his disciples spent a lot of time around the water, so it's not surprising to discover that's where several of his miracles took place. Early in his ministry, for example, he showed up at the Sea of Galilee after some of his soon-to-be disciples had been fishing all night. Jesus got into Peter's boat and taught a crowd of people on the shore. When he finished, he told Peter to go out into the deep water and cast his nets.

Peter protested. Jesus was a skilled teacher, but Peter was the experienced fisherman. He had spent all night in that area and hadn't caught a thing; he knew the waters were temporarily fished out. Still, he obeyed—and, wouldn't you know it—as soon as his nets hit the water, they were filled with so many fish that they began to break. Peter quickly called for help from his partners, James and John, who came out in a second boat. The fish were so plentiful that both boats were in danger of sinking, but they made it back to shore with their catch.

After returning to land, Peter fell at Jesus' feet and said, "Go away from me, Lord; I am a sinful man." That's when Jesus told Peter that from then on his job would be to catch people rather than fish. So the fishermen left their boats and followed Jesus.

Snapshots

An uncannily similar (and therefore noteworthy) miracle took place at the end of Jesus' time with his disciples. The events are recorded in John 21:1–14.

When Nature Calls, Call Back (Matthew 8:23–27; 14:22–33)

At least two more significant miracles took place out on the water. The first was while Jesus and the disciples were traveling from one place to another. During the journey, a sudden storm arose—so strong that the waves were coming into the boat. Jesus didn't notice. He had gotten so tired out from healing people that he was asleep.

The frantic disciples finally woke him to report that they were about to drown. Jesus' reply was short: "You of little faith, why are you so afraid?" (Matthew 8:26) Then he stood up and rebuked the winds and waves. Immediately the sea became calm.

A somewhat similar miracle took place later when the disciples crossed the sea on their own. Jesus wanted to pray for a while and then meet up with them. They just didn't know it would be in the middle of the Sea of Galilee!

During the wee hours of the morning (sometime between 3:00 and 6:00 A.M.) the boat was nowhere close to land, and the disciples were fighting a strong wind. That was bad enough, but when they looked up, they spotted what they thought was a ghost walking toward them across the water.

It turned out to be Jesus. "Take heart, it is I; do not be afraid," came his voice across the water. Peter, ever the impulsive one of the Twelve, challenged Jesus: "Lord, if it's you, tell me to come to you on the water." Jesus said, "Come."

Potent Quotables

They were amazed, saying, 'What sort of man is this, that even the winds and the sea obey him?' (Matthew 8:27)

As terrified as the disciples had been by the storm, Jesus' solution must have been pretty disconcerting. It was an insight into their teacher they hadn't yet discovered.

Peter stepped onto the water and began walking toward Jesus. But after he had taken a few steps, the surreality of the situation was too much for him. He gave in to his fear and began to sink, crying out to Jesus for help. Jesus reached out and caught him. "Why did you doubt?" he asked. The two of them stepped into the boat, and the wind abruptly stopped. The disciples all worshipped Jesus and said, "Truly you are the Son of God."

We're Trying to Divide This Food, but It Keeps Multiplying (Matthew 14:13–21)

A few of Jesus' miracles involved fish but not fishing. One day he spent the day in a remote area teaching and healing the sick. He had gone there to be alone, but large crowds had followed him. As evening came on, there were several thousand people in need of a square meal—and there was no food to give them.

The disciples knew just what to do: send the people home to scrounge up their own dinner. Jesus didn't think much of this advice. He told them, "They do not need to go away. You give them something to eat."

Manna from Heaven

When we think of a loaf of bread, we think of something that lasts a couple of people a week or so. These loaves were probably the size of large biscuits or circles of pita bread. In fact, the same account in John suggests that the "five small barley loaves and two small fish" were a young boy's sack lunch (John 6:1–15).

Yeah, right. They had exactly five tiny loaves of bread and two dried fish. But Jesus took the food, gave thanks, and began to break it, handing the pieces to the disciples to distribute to the people. "All ate and were satisfied." When the disciples cleaned up, they collected 12 baskets of leftovers. The five loaves and two fish had served 5,000 men and who knows how many women and children.

Snapshots

What do you think the disciples would do if given a second chance to feed a multitude with more food and fewer people? Find out in Matthew 15:29–38.

Straight from the Fish's Mouth (Matthew 17:24–27)

Yet another fish-related miracle involved, of all things, the temple equivalent of the IRS. Two collectors of the temple tax approached Peter, wanting to know whether Jesus paid his taxes. Peter said he did.

Later Jesus asked Peter, "From whom do the kings of the earth collect duty and taxes: from their own sons or from others?" Apparently he knew about the tax collectors, even though he hadn't been there. Peter answered, "From others." Jesus seemed to think it amusing that he, of all people, should pay a temple tax—a case of the Son paying the Father. But to avoid upsetting the authorities, Jesus told Peter to go fishing and look in the mouth of the first fish he caught. In it he would find a coin—enough to pay both their taxes.

The Tree That Didn't Give a Fig (Mark 11:12–14, 19–25)

Toward the end of his ministry, Jesus and the disciples were traveling to spend the day in Jerusalem. Jesus was hungry, so when he saw a fig tree in the distance with its leaves already out, he went to see whether there were figs on it, although it wasn't yet fig season. (Fig trees often put out fruit before leaves.) When Jesus got closer, he saw the tree had no figs. He said to it, "May no one ever eat fruit from you again."

The next morning the group passed the tree again. Peter pointed out to Jesus that the tree had withered from the roots, and Jesus reminded his disciples of the power of prayer. "I tell you, whatever you ask for in prayer, believe that you have received it, and it will be yours." Perhaps he also wanted them to remember that appearances are worthless if we do not also bear good fruit.

Jesus performed numerous miracles to prove his authority over sickness and disease, and others to demonstrate his power over nature. He didn't wander around with rampant disregard for the natural order of the world, but he showed that even the laws of nature could be altered when God determined to do so. And in a few instances— three that we know of—Jesus also displayed power over death itself.

193

I Was Dead for a While, but I'm Much Better Now (Mark 5:21–43)

One day a synagogue official named Jairus went to Jesus with an urgent request to return to his home and heal his 12-year-old daughter, who was near death. It was one of those days when Jesus could hardly move for the crowd pressing in on him, but he began to make his way toward Jairus' house.

On the way a group of men met them and told them not to bother—the girl had already died. At once Jesus told the distraught Jairus, "Don't be afraid; just believe." Continuing to the house, they found it filled with mourners. Everyone was wailing and crying, but they paused to laugh incredulously when Jesus declared that the child was only sleeping. Unperturbed, Jesus sent everyone from the room but Peter, James, John, and the girl's parents. Then he walked over to the girl, took her by the hand, and told her to get up. Immediately she stood up and began to walk around. Jesus told the astonished witnesses to fix the girl something to eat, and gave them strict orders not to let the story get around.

What Saith Thou?

Why did Jesus wait two days before setting off for Bethany?

If Lazarus died on the day the messenger left Bethany to find Jesus, and if he was placed in the tomb the same day in accordance with Jewish custom, then he would indeed have been dead for four days when Jesus arrived. Tradition also held that the soul lingered near the body for three days, and some speculate that Jesus deliberately timed his arrival for the day on which Lazarus' death would be "final." At any rate, Jesus' timing demonstrated beyond any question his absolute power over the grave.

Another time Jesus was visiting a village called Nain, where he passed a funeral procession. The dead youth was the only son of a widowed woman. Jesus felt compassion for the woman and told her not to cry. He approached the coffin, touched it, and said, "Young man, I say to you, get up." The former corpse sat up and started to talk. We have no idea what he said, but it must have been interesting.

Another Stinking Resurrection (John 11)

The third (and best-known) resurrection we know about was more personal for Jesus. He had made friends with a brother and two sisters named Lazarus, Mary, and Martha, who lived in Bethany, not far from Jerusalem. Toward the end of his ministry, when Jesus was residing across the Jordan to keep away from his enemies in Judea, word reached him that Lazarus was seriously ill. Bethany was a day's journey away; there was no time to lose. Yet Jesus waited two days before starting the journey. When he got there, Lazarus had been dead and in the tomb for four days.

Martha went out to meet him on the road. She can't be blamed, perhaps, for pointing out that "if you had been here, my brother would not have died." When Jesus promised that her brother would rise again, she assumed he was talking about the afterlife. Jesus' next words were bold and hope-inspiring: "I am the resurrection and the life. He who believes in me will live, even though he dies; and whoever lives and believes in me will never die" (John 11:25–26).

At the house, everyone was crying, and Jesus, deeply moved, also wept. People often ask why Jesus wept for Lazarus, even though he knew what he was about to do. Was he moved to tears by the sadness of others? Or because he knew that what he was about to do would lead to his own death? Was he about to bring Lazarus back from a much better place? We just don't know.

Accompanying the mourners to Lazarus' tomb—a cave with a large stone across the entrance—Jesus commanded, "Take away the stone." Martha protested. After four days in the heat of their climate, the odor would be unbearable. Or as the King James Version puts it, "Lord, by this time he stinketh" (11:39, KJV). Jesus insisted, and the stone was removed.

Jesus prayed and thanked God for what was about to happen. Then he called in a loud voice, "Lazarus, come out!" In what must have looked like a scene from *The Mummy*, Lazarus came out with his hands and feet still wrapped in linen strips and a cloth around his face. As the assembled people stared in total disbelief, Jesus spoke up and told them to remove the grave clothes and set the poor guy loose.

In light of such a miracle, many people immediately put their faith in Jesus. And from that day on, the religious leaders plotted to take Jesus' life. In addition, Lazarus had become a living testimony to what had happened, so the chief priests started looking for opportunities to kill him as well (John 12:10).

Some Relationships Require a Miracle

We looked at three one-on-one relationships of Jesus at the end of the last chapter. In this (and the next two) chapters, we'll examine a few other relationships.

Some of the people healed by Jesus felt especially close to him. Take the man out of whom "Legion" the demon had been cast, leading to the Great Pig Suicide Stampede. This man had been the village weirdo, an all-too-real reminder of the dark side of the spiritual world. Now, mercifully free, he wanted to stay with Jesus and become a disciple. Instead, Jesus sent him home to his family. "Tell them how much the Lord has done for you, and how he has had mercy on you." Jesus' command reminds us that there are many ways to serve God.

Others faced new problems after being healed. The man who received his sight after the application of a mud poultice came home so changed that his neighbors weren't even sure he was the same person. They carted him off to the Pharisees, who didn't know what to do. When someone violates the Sabbath by doing good, is it a sin, or not?

Potent Quotables

"Whether he is a sinner or not, I don't know. One thing I do know. I was blind but now I see." (John 9:25)

This blunt retort from the man who had been blind is often quoted for its metaphorical power, as in the words of the well-known hymn:

Amazing grace, how sweet the sound/That saved a wretch like me!/ I once was lost but now am found;/ was blind but now I see.

The Pharisees kept questioning the man, but he had seen nothing. Until he washed in the pool of Siloam, he had been blind; he had no idea what Jesus looked like. But as the Pharisees kept pressuring him, he finally said, "If this man were not from God, he could do nothing" (John 9:33). It was not what the Pharisees wanted to hear. In frustration, they banned him from the temple.

The story might have ended there, but we are told that Jesus heard what had happened and went to find the man. Jesus asked, "Do you believe in the Son of Man?" The man replied that he would if he knew who he was. Jesus said, "You have now seen him; in fact, he is the one speaking with you" (John 9:37). When the blind man realized that Jesus was the one who had healed him, he worshipped him. The man could no longer enter the temple, but he believed he had seen the promised Christ. (Read the whole story in more detail in John 9.)

A Drop in the Miracle Bucket

The Bible mentions only about 35 miracles that Jesus performed. Yet it seems clear that he did many, many more. He would spend days at a time healing people who were brought to him. In fact, as John wrapped up his gospel, he seemed to realize he had left out more than he had included. The last verse reads: "Jesus did many other things as well. If every one of them were written down, I suppose that even the whole world would not have room for the books that would be written."

One person who found consolation in Jesus' miracles was John the Baptist. From his prison cell, John heard about some of the things Jesus was doing, and he sent some of his disciples to ask whether Jesus was indeed the Messiah. Jesus replied: "Go back and report to John what you hear and see: The blind receive sight, the lame walk, those who have leprosy are cured, the deaf hear, the dead are raised, and the good news is preached to the poor" (Matthew 11:4–5). Jesus' words must have been a comforting assurance to John, who was put to death not long afterward.

The miracles of Jesus were his I.D. that he was someone special. Any number of people could have made the claims he did, but the miracles force the issue of his authority. Looking back across history, the miracles of Jesus (as well as the other supernatural biblical phenomena) require processing. Some people believe they actually, literally took place, and the stories provide fuel for their faith. Others who dispute the deity of Jesus must also view his miracles as more mythology than truth. But either way you look at them, the miracles make some pretty good stories.

Snapshots

The death of John the Baptist is a fascinating, if tragic, story found in Matthew 14:1–12.

The next chapter takes a closer look at some of the things Jesus said that comforted and offended people. You're likely to be surprised by some of the statements the Bible says came from Jesus' mouth.

The Least You Need to Know

➤ Jesus performed numerous miracles which served to validate his bold and occasionally bewildering teachings.

➤ Jesus' miracles revealed his power over disease, nature, and death.

➤ Jesus' healing miracles were a compassionate response to hurting people.

➤ Although the recipients of Jesus' healing were usually quick to believe in him, many casual observers remained skeptical.

Chapter 17

Did I Hear That Right?

In This Chapter

➤ A sampling of Jesus' 40 recorded parables, including the Good Samaritan and the Prodigal Son

➤ The Sermon on the Mount

➤ What Jesus said about hell, the claims he made about himself, and other miscellaneous teachings

In the past couple of chapters we've taken a look at what Jesus did and how he acted. In this chapter we want to examine what he said (according to the Bible). The statements of Jesus are not always easy to understand, much less easy to implement. But it's important to struggle a bit to comprehend them, because what he says tends to affect us, even today.

C. S. Lewis, the Oxford professor of literature and noted children's author, has an often-cited quote applying to this issue:

> "I am trying here to prevent anyone saying the really foolish thing that people often say about Him: 'I'm ready to accept Jesus as a great moral teacher, but I don't accept His claims to be God.' That is the one thing we must not say. A man who was merely a man and said the sort of things Jesus said would not be a great moral teacher. He would either be a lunatic—on a level with the man who says he is a poached egg—or else he would be the Devil of Hell. You must make your choice. Either this man was, and is, the Son of God: or else a madman or something worse. You can shut Him up for a fool, you can spit at Him and kill Him as

a demon; or you can fall at His feet and call Him Lord and God. But let us not come with any patronising nonsense about His being a great human teacher. He has not left that open to us. He did not intend to" (*Mere Christianity*© 1943, 1945, 1952, by Macmillan Publishing Co., Inc.).

Was Jesus who he said he was? Was he a clever impostor? Or was he just a misguided simpleton? This chapter will attempt to draw attention to various quotations of Jesus scattered through the gospels. Look them over and come to your own conclusions.

Higher Education (Matthew 5–7)

One of the more familiar and significant blocks of Jesus' teaching was what is known as his "Sermon on the Mount." It is debated whether this was a collection of his teachings or one extended discourse, but either way it was probably not a sermon as we think of preaching. It was a teaching session for his disciples and anyone else who wanted to listen (Matthew 5:1–2), and more than likely it was broken up with questions, debates, and tangents that varied from the topic at hand.

One thing we know for sure: Jesus had some ideas and ideals that were fresh, unexpected, and quite unorthodox. From the opening statements of the Sermon on the Mount, popularly known as the *Beatitudes* (declarations of blessedness), it was quite clear that Jesus had some different opinions about life.

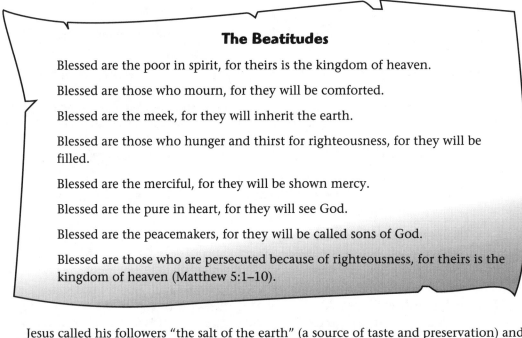

The Beatitudes

Blessed are the poor in spirit, for theirs is the kingdom of heaven.

Blessed are those who mourn, for they will be comforted.

Blessed are the meek, for they will inherit the earth.

Blessed are those who hunger and thirst for righteousness, for they will be filled.

Blessed are the merciful, for they will be shown mercy.

Blessed are the pure in heart, for they will see God.

Blessed are the peacemakers, for they will be called sons of God.

Blessed are those who are persecuted because of righteousness, for theirs is the kingdom of heaven (Matthew 5:1–10).

Jesus called his followers "the salt of the earth" (a source of taste and preservation) and "the light of the world" (an object of everyone's attention). Clearly, Jesus was expecting to see some changes made in the lives of those who believed in him.

Yet Jesus made it clear that his was no new theology. He said, "I have not come to abolish them [the Law and the Prophets] but to fulfill them" (Matthew 5:17). He also told his listeners, "Unless your righteousness surpasses that of the Pharisees and the teachers of the law, you will certainly not enter the kingdom of heaven" (5:20).

The Spirit of the Law

To explain what he meant in practical ways, Jesus redefined murder as unresolved anger or name-calling for the sake of putting down others. He redefined adultery as mental lust. By his revised definitions, righteous living was not simply a matter of going as far as possible just as long as you didn't cross the ultimate line. Rather, it involved not even allowing situations to lend themselves to violence or inappropriate sex.

Manna from Heaven

Exceeding the righteousness of the Pharisees must have seemed like a hopeless challenge. The Pharisees had broken down the Old Testament laws into 248 commandments and 365 prohibitions—and they were adamant about upholding every single one. But Jesus wasn't speaking about a holiness contest. His intent was to help his listeners internalize righteousness so that it permeated their actions.

At a time when a husband could divorce his wife for any reason (a wife could not divorce at all), Jesus said divorce was wrong with the possible exception of marital unfaithfulness. He taught that the way to avoid making unnecessary oaths was to always keep one's word. He told his followers to "love your enemies and pray for those who persecute you." He said that if someone hits you, you should turn the other cheek—to minimize the conflict. If you are sued, give the other person more than he's demanding.

Do all this, Jesus says, and "your Father, who sees what is done in secret, will reward you" (Matthew 6:4, 6, 14, 18). In other words, don't make a show about praying, giving to the needy, fasting, and so on. Just do the right thing, simply and humbly. You might not get as many pats on the back, but God will notice and reward accordingly.

Don't Worry, Be Holy

Jesus knew that to follow such teachings would require a conscious choice. His listeners would have to decide what was most important to them because "where your treasure is, there your heart will be also" (Matthew 6:21). He taught, "No one can serve two masters. Either he will hate the one and love the other, or he will be devoted to the one and despise the other. You cannot serve both God and Money" (Matthew 6:24).

Jesus also told his followers not to worry about things like food and clothing, but to pray and trust in God. God created and cares for birds, grass, flowers, and things that are temporary; he will care much more for people, whom he created to be eternal:

"Seek first [God's] kingdom and his righteousness, and all these things will be given to you as well." Jesus also told listeners not to be so concerned about the future that they neglect the present: "Do not worry about tomorrow, for tomorrow will worry about itself. Each day has enough trouble of its own" (Matthew 6:33–34).

Stop judging one another, Jesus said. One person judging another is like a person with a plank of wood jammed in his eye trying to take a speck of sawdust out of someone else's (7:1–5). (Perhaps Jesus had a twinkle in his own eye as he said this.) He encouraged people to ask, seek, and knock, believing that God will not only answer, but also meet needs.

Jesus spoke of a broad road with a wide gate that leads to destruction. The road to eternal life, in contrast, is narrow and has a small gate. It's there, but few people go to the trouble to look for it. Meanwhile, others are deceived by false prophets who "come to you in sheep's clothing, but inwardly they are ferocious wolves" (7:15). You can evaluate people the same way you do trees: Good ones will have good fruit, and bad ones will have rotten fruit.

Jesus also said a lot of people would speak in his name—maybe even do great and miraculous things. Yet, in the final judgment it would come out that they had never actually known him (7:21–23). Invoking the name of Jesus is not automatically a sign of genuine Christian faith. Throughout history, people have committed all kinds of atrocities in the name of Jesus. But as we are seeing, Jesus would never endorse such actions.

Potent Quotables

In everything, do to others what you would have them do to you, for this sums up the Law and the Prophets. (Matthew 7:12)

The Sermon on the Mount contains this well-known expression of the "Golden Rule."

As a final challenge, Jesus explained that whoever applied what he was telling them would be like a wise man who built his house on a rock. Such people would prevail over the storms of life because of their strong foundations. Otherwise, they would be like the man who built his house on sand. The same storms are certain to come, but without a solid base the house will fall "with a great crash" (7:24–27).

The people had never heard a teacher like Jesus. They were amazed, because "he taught as one who had authority, and not as their teachers of the law."

Coming Down with a Code

Challenging as its principles are, at least the Sermon on the Mount is clear and straightforward. Jesus' teachings weren't always so easy to understand, though, because he liked to teach with parables—vivid stories that illustrated his meaning in deep and memorable ways. Some were mysterious at first hearing, such as the one about a person sowing seeds (Matthew 13:1–9). Some of the seed fell on the hard path, where the birds came and ate it. Some fell in rocky places, where it sprang up quickly but wilted and died when the sun came up because its roots didn't go deep enough to draw water. Some seed landed in thorns, which eventually choked the growing plants. And some fell on good soil, where it produced a crop of 100, 60, or 30 times what was sown.

Even the disciples were left scratching their heads after this one. But when they asked Jesus what it meant, his explanation made sense. The seed represented the message Jesus was teaching. The soils were like various human hearts. When some-one was too hard-hearted (like the hard path) for the seed to take root, the Evil One could snatch away what had been sown, like a crow on a kernel of corn. Others might hear and begin to grow, but wilt at the first signs of trouble or persecution. Still others might try to mix the message in with other priorities (such as money) and fail to grow in faith. But those who allowed the message to take root and grow to fullness might be surprised at the size of the "crop" (Matthew 13:18–23).

What Saith Thou?

Why did Jesus teach in parables rather than just saying what he meant?

Parables were a kind of code that could be cracked only with a degree of spiritual discernment. People who were following Jesus and thinking about his teachings could figure out what the parables meant; others had to start from scratch. The better people got at understanding the parables, the more sense they could make of everything else Jesus said.

Parables of the Kingdom

Not all the parables required rocket scientists to solve them. Some were short and to the point, such as the parables about the "kingdom of heaven." For example, the kingdom of heaven is compared to these:

➤ A mustard seed, because a tiny seed is planted that soon becomes a large and protective plant (Matthew 13:31–32)

➤ Yeast, because a little bit mixed into a large batch of bread affects the whole loaf (Matthew 13:33)

➤ Hidden treasure, because once you find it, you will want to let go of everything else to secure it (Matthew 13:44)

➤ A pearl of great value, which a wise merchant will acquire by trading everything else he has (Matthew 13:45)

➤ A fisherman's net, because it will catch both good and worthless fish, which will be separated later (Matthew 13:47–50)

➤ A seed that grows continually and mysteriously, produces grain, and is harvested (Mark 4:26–29)

A Parable for Every Occasion

Jesus used parables to teach about the importance of prayer. A praying person, he said, is like someone pounding on a friend's door at midnight, in need of something. Because of the relationship between the two, the person will get out of bed, open the door, and help his friend (Luke 11:5–8). In another instance, the praying person is seen as a widow before an unjust judge, coming back again and again to plead her case against those who had mistreated her (Luke 18:1–8). Even though the judge is selfish and possibly crooked, he agrees to do as the widow asks so he can get some peace. (The point of this parable is to show the benefit of persistence, not to imply that God is unjust!)

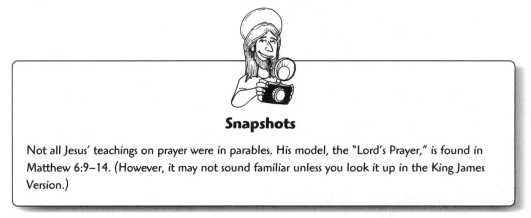

Snapshots

Not all Jesus' teachings on prayer were in parables. His model, the "Lord's Prayer," is found in Matthew 6:9–14. (However, it may not sound familiar unless you look it up in the King James Version.)

The importance of devoting oneself to God's work is another frequent topic of parables. Through parables we discover that the use of our talents tends to multiply them (Matthew 25:14–30). Servants (even God's servants) have their place—and it's not at the head of the table (Luke 17:7–10). And sometimes the boss seems terribly unfair, even when the boss is God. Otherwise, why would someone who worked only an hour get the same pay as someone who had worked all the livelong day? (Matthew 20:1–16)

Other parables contrast hypocrisy with humility. The story of a Pharisee and a tax collector is an indictment against religious self-righteousness. It says that God will accept the prayer of one who struggles to confess his sins much more readily than a prayer "offered" in a spirit of self-congratulation (Luke 18:9–14).

Jesus told stories about the absurd complacency of a rich man who decided to raze all his barns to build bigger ones—and who died that very night (Luke 12:16–21); of a great banquet where the guests made excuses not to attend, so the host recruited "the poor, the crippled, the blind, and the lame" (Luke 14:16–24); of a servant who was forgiven a multimillion-dollar debt to the king, yet who wouldn't cancel a peer's debt of a few dollars—and lived to regret it (Matthew 18:23–35).

Much of what Jesus had to say about the end times was accompanied by parables. The most familiar is about 10 virgins waiting to see the bridegroom at a wedding party. All of them had lamps, but only five had brought along extra oil. When the first five ran out of fuel and went to buy more, the bridegroom came and they missed the big event (Matthew 25:1–13).

And there were other parables. But two have become classic literature, so let's take a closer look at them.

The Good Samaritan (Luke 10:25–37)

One day, while teaching, Jesus fielded a question by an expert in the law who wanted to know his views on how to inherit eternal life. Jesus tossed the question back to him: "What does the law say?" The expert quoted two Old Testament passages: "Love the Lord your God with all your heart and with all your soul and with all your strength and with all your mind" (Deuteronomy 6:5), and "love your neighbor as yourself" (Leviticus 19:18). Jesus gave him an 'A' and told him to follow his own advice. But then the expert asked a follow-up question. "Who is my neighbor?"

In answer, Jesus told a story of an unfortunate man on his way from Jerusalem to Jericho, who was robbed, beaten, stripped, and left for dead. A priest came along, and later a Levite; both passed by on the other side of the street when they saw the man lying at the side of the road.

One can only hope the poor guy was unconscious. Otherwise, he would have laid there in the road, bleeding and incapacitated, as he watched two people ignore his immediate physical needs—people who were responsible for attending to his spiritual needs. Fortunately, a third man came along—a compassionate Samaritan who overcame the prejudice between the Jews and Samaritans and saw not an enemy, but a fellow human being in need.

First, he anointed the man's wounds with oil and wine, and bandaged them. Then he placed him on his own donkey and escorted him to an inn for overnight care. Before leaving the inn the next morning, he paid the innkeeper a sum of money and told him to watch out for the guy until the Samaritan could return, promising to reimburse any additional expenses that might be incurred.

Jesus concluded the parable with a question—one very similar to what the law expert had asked: "Which of these three do you think was a neighbor to the man who fell into the hands of the robbers?" The answer, of course, was the one who had shown him mercy. Jesus responded, "Go and do likewise."

Manna from Heaven

All priests were Levites, but not all Levites were priests. Both groups were involved in taking care of worship responsibilities and therefore had to be extremely careful not to come into contact with the dead—a form of ritual pollution that would render them unfit for service (Leviticus 21:11–12).

The Prodigal Son and Other Lost Things (Luke 15)

To set the scene for the next parable, imagine Jesus in a teaching setting with religious authorities and other skeptics lurking in the background. Jesus' detractors were muttering to themselves because Jesus was spending so much time with "sinners," even going so far as to share meals with them.

Suddenly Jesus started telling stories about different things, but with a running theme. First he told of a shepherd with 100 sheep in his care. If he takes them out to feed and returns with only 99, what does he do? The sheep are *all* his responsibility, so he leaves the 99 in a safe place and goes in search of his single lost sheep. When he finds it, the discovery is cause for a big celebration.

Or consider a woman who owns only 10 coins, one of which is lost. In her attempt to recover it, she'll turn on all the lights in the house, pull out the broom, and clean until it turns up. When she finally finds it, she, too, will celebrate.

Jesus used both of these stories to illustrate the mood in heaven when one person repents: "I tell you that in the same way there will be more rejoicing in heaven over one sinner who repents than over 99 righteous persons who do not need to repent." Then he launched into a story about a lost son.

It seems a man had two sons, the younger of whom grew restless on the old homestead and wanted to see the world. He asked if he could receive his share of the inheritance in advance, and the father granted his wish by dividing the property between the two sons.

The younger son hit the road and went to a distant country, where he "squandered his wealth in wild living." After his money was gone, a famine hit. He had to take a job feeding pigs—a particularly distasteful task for a Jewish person who was to have nothing to do with these animals (Leviticus 11:7–8). To make matters worse, the pigs were eating better than he was!

Manna from Heaven

The familiar word **prodigal** is not used in this story—at least, not in recent translations. Though it might be assumed that the word means "runaway" or perhaps "returning," the actual definition of *prodigal* is "wastefully or recklessly extravagant."

It dawned on him that his father's servants were also doing better than he was. He made up his mind to swallow his pride and go home—no longer as a son, but as one of the hired men. He even practiced the speech he would give to convince his dad to take him back.

But the father looked up and saw the son "while he was still a long way off." (Was he keeping an eye down the road, watching and hoping?) Filled with compassion, the father ran to meet his son. When he got there, he threw his arms around him and kissed him. The son started his speech but didn't get a chance to finish. The father sent for a robe, ring, and sandals, outfitting his son with all the entitlements of a valued member of the family. A feast was planned to celebrate the return of the son.

A lesser storyteller might have ended the story there with "and they all lived happily ever after." But Jesus wasn't finished.

The noise of the celebration eventually reached the older brother, who inquired what was going on. When the servants told him, he was irate. After all, he was out working in the field while back at the house there was music and dancing. He turned his back and refused to join the festivities.

The father came out to reason with his older son, but big brother had a big chip on his shoulder. He said, not unreasonably, that because he had stayed home and obeyed the father, he was being taken for granted. In contrast, "when this son of yours who has squandered your property with prostitutes comes home, you kill the fattened calf for him!" (An interesting insight into the older son's mindset—Who had said anything about prostitutes?)

Gently the father tried to reason with his older son, assuring him that "you are always with me, and everything I have is yours." But he also pointed out that the older son was missing the point. "We had to celebrate and be glad, because this brother of yours was dead and is alive again; he was lost and is found."

Jesus knew that many of his listeners—especially the Pharisees and experts in the law—would relate to the feelings of the older brother. It's not too hard to see the justification for celebrating when lost property is found, such as a sheep or a coin. Such occasions are always good reasons to throw a big party. But when people are involved, for some reason we have an inner desire to see them "get what they've got coming." God, represented by the father in Jesus' story, frequently has a different outlook on people. He celebrates the recovery of any "lost" person. When we are the prodigals, we tend to grasp for his mercy and hold on tight. When we see others receive God's mercy and forgiveness, however, we may not be so quick to understand.

Hellfire and Damnation

According to Mark, Luke, and especially Matthew, Jesus had much to say about the end times—including hell. The word is mentioned about a dozen times in the New Testament—all but once by Jesus himself.

The Jewish concept of eternal punishment and eternal bliss became more defined during the period between the Old and New Testaments. The Old Testament speaks of a place of afterlife called Sheol, a vague and unpleasant place where all the dead would go, but from which the godly expected to be delivered (Psalm 16:10).

The New Testament speaks of both Hades and Gehenna. Hades, a word borrowed from Greek mythology, was another general term for death, the grave, and the afterlife in general. Gehenna, on the other hand, was specific. In Hebrew it means "the valley of Hinnom"—Hinnom being a garbage pit where the filth of Jerusalem and the bodies of executed criminals were disposed of, and where a fire was kept burning perpetually to dispose of the remains of animal sacrifices. It was there that two infamous kings of

Judah killed their own sons in human sacrifices to foreign gods (2 Chronicles 28:1–3; 33:1–6). It was as unpleasant a place as people could imagine, and was thus an appropriate image for a place of everlasting torment.

Here are a few of Jesus' teachings concerning hell:

➤ "The subjects of the kingdom will be thrown outside, into the darkness, where there will be weeping and gnashing of teeth" (Matthew 8:12).

What Saith Thou?

Is Jesus serious about cutting off body parts?

Most people agree that Jesus did not mean for these statements to be taken literally. Jesus used the literary form of hyperbole (extreme exaggeration) to make a serious point: Hell is a place to be avoided. Though it isn't always easy to conform one's will to God's, it's better than the ultimate consequence of continued disobedience.

➤ "If your hand causes you to sin, cut it off. It is better for you to enter life maimed than with two hands to go into hell, where the fire never goes out. And if your foot causes you to sin, cut it off. It is better for you to enter life crippled than to have two feet and be thrown into hell. And if your eye causes you to sin, pluck it out. It is better for you to enter the kingdom of God with one eye than to have two eyes and be thrown into hell, where 'their worm does not die, and the fire is not quenched'" (Mark 9:42–48).

➤ "Do not be afraid of those who kill the body but cannot kill the soul. Rather, be afraid of the One who can destroy both soul and body in hell" (Matthew 10:28).

➤ "Then he will say to those on his left, 'Depart from me, you who are cursed, into the eternal fire prepared for the devil and his angels....' Then they will go away to eternal punishment, but the righteous to eternal life" (Matthew 25:41, 46).

Snapshots

We discover more about hell in Jesus' story of the rich man and Lazarus (not the same Lazarus who was raised from the dead). Found in Luke 16:19–31, some people think it's a parable. But because Jesus identifies a character by name, others suggest it's a factual account.

Based on Jesus' comments, hell is a place of perpetual darkness, yet eternal fire. It was created for the devil and his angels, yet it can become the destination of unrighteous humans. The only thing that will be taking place in hell is suffering. The image frequently portrayed of the devil as ruler of hell, inflicting pain on others, is by no means biblical. The devil is just another captive. (We'll get more insight into this topic in the Book of Revelation.)

New Wine and Hard Teachings

Jesus realized the things he was teaching were so new that people couldn't conveniently "tack them on" to their existing beliefs. He compared them to new wine, which could not be placed in an old wineskin, or a new piece of cloth, which could not be sewn onto clothing that had already shrunk.

Below is a selection of some of Jesus' miscellaneous statements. Included are several of his more difficult and/or controversial quotes. Be aware that they all need to be taken both in the context of the passages in which they appear, and in the context of Jesus' entire body of teachings.

Manna from Heaven

Goatskins were used as water bottles as well as to ferment grape juice into wine or milk into yogurt. The skin was sewn with the hair on the outside. During fermentation, the skin would expand. As it did, it would lose its elasticity and be of no further use. It would burst if a new batch of wine were stored in it. New wine required new wineskins.

➤ "I am sending you out like sheep among wolves. Therefore be as shrewd as snakes and as innocent as doves" (Matthew 10:16).

➤ "All men will hate you because of me, but he who stands firm to the end will be saved" (Matthew 10:22).

➤ "Whoever acknowledges me before men, I will also acknowledge him before my Father in heaven. But whoever disowns me before men, I will disown him before my Father in heaven" (Matthew 10:32-33).

➤ "Do not suppose that I have come to bring peace to the earth. I did not come to bring peace, but a sword. For I have come to turn 'a man against his father, a daughter against her mother, a daughter-in-law against her mother-in-law—a man's enemies will be the members of his own household'" (Matthew 10:34-36, partially quoting Micah 7:6).

➤ "Anyone who loves his father or mother more than me is not worthy of me; anyone who loves his son or daughter more than me is not worthy of me; and anyone who does not take his cross and follow me is not worthy of me. Whoever finds his life will lose it, and whoever loses his life will find it" (Matthew 10:37-39).

➤ "Every sin and blasphemy will be forgiven men, but the blasphemy against the Spirit will not be forgiven. Anyone who speaks a word against the Son of Man will be forgiven, but anyone who speaks against the Holy Spirit will not be forgiven, either in this age or in the age to come" (Matthew 12:31-32).

➤ "What good is it for a man to gain the whole world, yet forfeit his soul?" (Mark 8:36)

➤ "How hard it is to enter the kingdom of God! It is easier for a camel to go through the eye of a needle than for a rich man to enter the kingdom of God" (Mark 10:24–25).

➤ "I have come to bring fire on the earth, and how I wish it were already kindled! But I have a baptism to undergo, and how distressed I am until it is completed!" (Luke 12:49-50)

➤ "If your brother sins, rebuke him, and if he repents, forgive him. If he sins seven times in a day, and seven times comes back to you and says, 'I repent,' forgive him" (Luke 17:3-4).

Snapshots

The Gospels are filled with the teachings of Jesus, but here are a few more short, "don't miss" passages:

Matthew 11:28–29; 18:15–17; 19:14

Mark 10:29–31

Luke 6:39–40; 10:1–24

John 5:39–40; 8:28–29; 15:12–14

Jesus' Not-So-Secret Identity

Some of Jesus' peers refused to consider that he might be the Holy One. Even today, certain people deny that Jesus ever claimed to be God. Therefore, many of the more controversial teachings of Jesus were the claims he made about himself. Following are a few samples:

➤ "All things have been committed to me by my father. No one knows the Son except the Father, and no one knows the Father except the Son and those to whom the Son chooses to reveal him" (Matthew 11:27).

➤ "I am the bread of life. He who comes to me will never go hungry, and he who believes in me will never be thirsty" (John 6:35).

➤ "I am the light of the world. Whoever follows me will never walk in darkness, but will have the light of life" (John 8:12).

➤ "I tell you the truth, before Abraham was born, I am!" (John 8:58).

➤ "I am the good shepherd. The good shepherd lays down his life for the sheep. The hired hand is not the shepherd who owns the sheep. So when he sees the wolf coming, he abandons the sheep and runs away" (John 10:11–12).

➤ "I am the resurrection and the life. He who believes in me will live, even though he dies; and whoever lives and believes in me will never die" (John 11:25–26).

➤ "I am the way and the truth and the life. No one comes to the Father except through me. If you really knew me, you would know my Father as well. From now on, you do know him and have seen him" (John 14:6-7).

➤ "I am the true vine, and my Father is the gardener...I am the vine; you are the branches. If a man remains in me and I in him, he will bear much fruit; apart from me you can do nothing" (John 15:1, 5).

As the C. S. Lewis quote said at the beginning of this chapter, when people heard these claims and other teachings, they had to gravitate one way or the other. If they believed him, then they had to treat him as the person he claimed to be. But if they didn't believe him, they had to reject essentially everything he said, and therefore couldn't value him as a teacher.

We conclude this chapter with a look at one more of Jesus' personal relationships. Here we see that the choice of whether to believe is not always an easy one.

Snapshots

The story of Zacchaeus (Luke 19:1–10) shows what can happen when people *do* respond to what Jesus says.

The Loved One That Got Away (Mark 10:17–23)

A rich young man ran up to Jesus and asked him, "Rabbi, what must I do to inherit eternal life?" Jesus gave the standard answer: "You know the commandments: 'Do not murder, do not commit adultery, do not steal, do not give false testimony, do not defraud, honor your father and mother.'"

The young man said he had kept these commandments "since I was a boy." Something about him must have touched Jesus' heart. Mark records that "Jesus looked at him and loved him." Then Jesus said, "One thing you lack. Go, sell everything you have and give to the poor, and you will have treasure in heaven. Then come, follow me."

The man was crushed. His "face fell." He was very wealthy, and he couldn't imagine doing as Jesus had instructed. He went away sad. In theory he could affirm what Jesus was teaching, but in practice he had well-defined limits. In contrast, Peter, a poor fisherman, commented that "We have left everything to follow you!" Perhaps that is why Jesus declared it is easier for a camel to pass through the eye of a needle than for a rich person to enter the kingdom of heaven. Possessions do encumber people spiritually as well as materially.

Jesus' teachings changed lives. They still do. Those who respond to what he said may find their priorities rearranged, their hearts opened, their expectations overturned. Jesus and the gospel are and were a serious threat to the status quo. We'll see in the next chapter how this played out as the conflict between Jesus and the religious authorities escalated.

The Least You Need to Know

➤ Jesus' teachings were unlike anything the people had ever experienced—they were authoritative without being stuffy.

➤ Much of what Jesus taught was in parable form, with a hidden meaning only those with some degree of spiritual enlightenment could understand.

➤ Jesus made many bold claims in regard to his own divinity.

➤ Jesus extended invitations for people to follow him, but he never forced himself on anyone. He always provided the option to let the person walk away.

Chapter 18

Arose by Any Other Name...

In This Chapter

➤ Opposition to Jesus intensifies

➤ Jesus' crucifixion, death, burial, and resurrection

➤ Post-resurrection appearances of Jesus

➤ The transfiguration, the entry into Jerusalem, the Last Supper, the Garden of Gethsemane, the death of Jesus, reports of his resurrection

Scientists are currently seeking a "unified theory" of how things work in our universe. The laws that rule physical science (gravity and such) don't seem to match those governing quantum physics (atoms). Yet many scientists believe if they think and look hard enough, they will discover a single theory that makes sense in every instance.

Understanding God is like that. The Old Testament God sometimes appears to be one of wrath and judgment, at times wiping out whole civilizations or doling out harsh punishments for seemingly small acts of disobedience. The New Testament picture of God as seen in the person of Jesus is nothing like that. He hugs lepers, forgives disgraced women and men, and is much harder on the religious leaders than the "little people" who have a reputation for sinning and hard partying. This kind and compassionate Jesus affirms the whole of the Law, yet declares that "Anyone who has seen me has seen the Father" (John 14:9). We are told that God does not change (Malachi 3:6). So we, like scientists, can only continue to gather evidence and struggle to make sense out of what we find.

The Big Question

Everyone who knew Jesus realized he was someone special, but exactly who he was seemed less clear. One day Jesus asked his disciples what kind of rumors they were hearing about him. They reported that some people were speculating that he was the reincarnation of John the Baptist, Elijah, Jeremiah, or some other prophet. Jesus asked, "But what about you? Who do you say I am?"

Potent Quotables

"Get behind me, Satan!" (Matthew 16:23)

First spoken by Jesus during his temptation (Matthew 4:10), the saying is here addressed directly to Peter when the disciple begins to oppose the mission of Jesus.

Peter was quick with an answer: "You are the Christ, the Son of the living God" (Matthew 16:16). Jesus praised Peter's insight because it had to have come from God—yet he cautioned them against telling anyone that he was the Christ. He "began to explain to his disciples that he must go to Jerusalem and suffer many things at the hands of the elders, chief priests and teachers of the law, and that he must be killed and on the third day be raised to life" (Matthew 16:21).

Such teachings didn't sit well with the disciples. At one point Peter pulled Jesus aside to contradict him. Peter was devoted to Jesus, and was unwilling to listen to predictions of doom. But Jesus tried to explain that bigger things were in play than mere life and death. And then he made the statement that, "Some who are standing here will not taste death before they see the Son of Man coming in his kingdom" (Matthew 16:28).

Glow (but Don't Tell It) on the Mountain (Luke 9:28–36)

As a fulfillment of Jesus' statement, the next biblical account is that of the Transfiguration. Jesus took Peter, James, and John up a high mountain, and there he prayed. As he did so, he was "transfigured" (changed). His face began to glow like the sun, and his clothing became "as bright as a flash of lightning." Moses and Elijah appeared "in glorious splendor" and began to talk with him about his coming death.

Peter, James, and John had been feeling drowsy, but this got their attention. Peter was boldly offering to build shelters for Jesus and the two other figures when a cloud descended around them and they heard a voice from heaven, repeating the words spoken at Jesus' baptism: "This is my Son, whom I love; with him I am well pleased. Listen to him!" (Matthew 17:5) The disciples hit the ground in terror, but Jesus helped them up and told them not to be afraid. When they looked around, the prophets had departed; everything appeared to be back to normal. Jesus told his disciples not to tell anyone what they had seen until after his resurrection.

An Entrance Fit for a King (Luke 19:28–44)

As Passover approached, Jesus rode into Jerusalem on a (borrowed) donkey, a symbol of kingship. People were coming from all around to celebrate the festival, and there was a sizable crowd with him on the road. As word spread that he was coming, people covered his path with palm branches and cloaks, shouting praises. Jesus' popularity had never been higher than during this "triumphal entry" into the royal city. But within a week the shouts would change to "Crucify him," and Jesus would be dead.

Jesus the Bouncer (Mark 11:15–18)

These days people milk popularity for all it is worth—networking with other bigshots, inking endorsement deals, and so forth. Jesus took a slightly different tack: He went to church.

He and the disciples went to the temple, which was the one place every good Jewish person would visit while in Jerusalem. As such, it had become something of a "tourist trap." Currency exchanges, tax collecting, and animal sales were booming inside the temple precincts. Some of the transactions were no doubt legitimate, but what *wasn't* getting done, it seemed, was worship of God.

Jesus went through the temple overturning the tables of the merchants and running them out. His words have been long remembered: "Is it not written: 'My house will be called a house of prayer for all nations'? But you have made it 'a den of robbers'" (Mark 11:17).

Snapshots

Get a more detailed account on how Jesus felt about the religious hypocrisy of his day in Matthew 23. And Chapters 24 and 25 of Matthew are Jesus' "signs of the end of the age."

Final Countdown

Certainly the clearing of the temple did not help endear Jesus to the religious authorities who opposed him. Nor did his popularity with the people, which frankly frightened the Pharisees. They began to look in earnest for a way to get rid of him (Mark 11:18).

Jesus was not a helpless victim at the mercy of more powerful forces. Rather, he was a willing sacrifice for others who *were* helpless and hurting. He knew his arrest was coming, but he remained in Jerusalem, choosing not to flee. His powerful enemies he addressed publicly as hypocrites, blind guides, snakes, and a brood of vipers.

As the countdown continued, Jesus taught that in days to come his followers would be hated, persecuted, and killed. Many would turn away from their faith, yet during these "end times" the whole world would hear about the gospel of the kingdom of God (Matthew 24:9–14).

Just as certain people saw Jesus as a threat and a menace to society, others were starting to believe he was more than just a man—and perhaps more than just a prophet. While Jesus was attending a party at the home of Mary, Martha, and Lazarus (a short while after Jesus brought Lazarus back from the dead), Mary came into the room with a jar of expensive perfume. She poured it onto Jesus' feet, filling the air with its aroma, then wiped his feet with her hair.

Judas Iscariot, the treasurer for Jesus and the disciples, objected: The perfume could have been sold for a year's wages and given to the poor. (The depth of his concern is questionable, considering that he was a thief who skimmed from the disciples' money bag.) Jesus said, "Leave her alone. She bought it so that she might keep it for the day of my burial. You always have the poor with you, but you do not always have me" (John 12:1–8). At that point, Luke says, "Satan entered Judas" (Luke 22:3). Judas went to the chief priests and asked what he could get as a bounty on Jesus. They paid him 30 silver coins, and he began to look for an opportunity to turn Jesus in to them when there weren't a lot of people around (Matthew 26:14–16).

A Meal Worthy of a DaVinci Painting

When the time came to prepare the Passover meal, Jesus sent a couple of the disciples to find a certain man carrying a jar of water and give him the message that Jesus needed accommodations. The man provided them with an upper room (Mark 14:12–15).

Before eating, Jesus took off his outer garment, tied a towel around his waist, and began to wash his disciples' feet, drying them with the towel. Peter didn't want to let his teacher serve him like a slave. But when Jesus said, "Unless I wash you, you have no part with me" (John 13:8), Peter quickly changed his mind.

During the meal, Jesus announced that one of his disciples was about to betray him. All were greatly distressed, and each worried whether he would be the one. Judas, too, said, "Surely not I, Rabbi?" Jesus answered, "Yes, it is you." (Matthew 26:20–25). Then he added, "What you are about to do, do quickly" (John 13:27). Again we are told that "Satan entered into [Judas]." He left, and Jesus continued to prepare his other disciples for what was coming.

Manna from Heaven

In the dusty land of Palestine, water for washing feet was commonly offered to guests upon their arrival. Sometimes a household slave might do the washing; it was also not uncommon for a disciple to wash his teacher's feet. Here Jesus reverses the custom to demonstrate the meaning and significance of humility.

He took bread, gave thanks, broke it, and said, "Take and eat; this is my body" (Matthew 26:26). Then he took the cup of wine and said, "Drink from it, all of you. This is my blood of the covenant, which is poured out for many for the forgiveness of sins. I tell you, I will not drink of this fruit of the vine from now on until that day when I drink it anew with you in my Father's kingdom" (Matthew 26:27–29). This was Jesus' "Last Supper," which is still commemorated in churches under various names: communion, Mass, Eucharist, the Lord's Supper, and so forth.

Disciples Squabble, Then They All Fall Down

As the disciples' discussion returned to who might betray Jesus, they began to argue—not for the first time—about which one of them was the greatest. Again Jesus explained that they must not live by the world's standards. Rather, he said, "The greatest among you should be like the youngest, and the one who rules like the one who serves" (Luke 22:26).

Jesus addressed Peter directly, warning him that his faith was going to be tested. Peter swore he would stand by Jesus, even if it meant imprisonment and death. But Jesus said that by the time the rooster crowed the next morning, Peter would have denied him three times.

Potent Quotables

Do not let your hearts be troubled. Trust in God; trust also in me. In my Father's house are many rooms; if it were not so, I would have told you. I am going there to prepare a place for you. And if I go and prepare a place for you, I will come back and take you to be with me that you also may be where I am. (John 14:1-3)

For the last time Jesus comforted his disciples and promised to take care of them always. Soon he would return to his Father. But in his absence he promised to send the Holy Spirit, whom he referred to as a "Counselor" or "Comforter." (John 14:16, 26)

In these precious last hours, Jesus challenged them to love one another as he had loved them (John 15:12–15). Yes, there would be a time of grief, but their grief would turn to joy (John 16:17–24). Jesus prayed for himself, for his disciples, and for all future disciples who would eventually come to believe in him.

Then Jesus and his disciples went out to the Mount of Olives, to an olive grove called Gethsemane. Jesus wanted to pray by himself, and he wanted his disciples to pray as well, that they would not be tempted in the midst of what was to come. He was "overwhelmed with sorrow to the point of death" (Matthew 26:38) and prayed: "My Father, if it is possible, may this cup be taken from me. Yet not as I will," he told God, "but as you will." Three times he went to check on his disciples, and three times found them sleeping. Meanwhile, he was praying with such intensity that "his sweat was like drops of blood falling to the ground." As he prayed, an angel appeared to strengthen him (Luke 22:43–44).

What Saith Thou?

Who was the streaker in the garden?

When Jesus was arrested, one of his followers was grabbed by the crowd and left his linen garment behind, escaping in the buff (Mark 14:51–52). Because this incident is only mentioned in Mark, and because the guy was "a young man," many people speculate this might have been John Mark—not one of the 12 disciples, but a young seeker whom we will meet in the next chapter. According to tradition, the house where Jesus and the disciples ate the Last Supper was owned by John Mark's father.

When he went to wake his exhausted disciples the third time, a crowd came up to them, armed with swords and clubs. Judas stepped forward and gave Jesus a kiss. At this signal, several men approached Jesus to arrest him.

Peter jumped forward, swinging a sword. But he was a fisherman, not a soldier. All he hit was the ear of a servant of the high priest, a man named Malchus. Jesus stopped Peter, explaining that he could summon legions of angels if he wished. However, the arrest was something he was expecting. Jesus reattached Malchus' ear, and went with the arresting officers while his disciples ran. But he asked his captors, "Am I leading a rebellion, that you have to come out with swords and clubs to capture me? Every day I sat in the temple courts teaching, and you did not arrest me. But this has all taken place that the writings of the prophets might be fulfilled" (Matthew 26:55-56).

Trial, Trial Again

Jesus' enemies had him, but they didn't seem to know what to do with him. First he was taken to Annas, the father-in-law of Caiaphas, the high priest (John 18:12–14), then to Caiaphas himself, who questioned him about his teaching before a large assembly of "chief priests, elders, and teachers of the law" (Matthew 26:57–68). Jesus had little chance of a fair trial in any of the religious proceedings because we know Caiaphas had already prophesied (and plotted) that Jesus should die (John 11:49-53).

Caiaphas insisted he answer whether he was "the Christ, the Son of God." Jesus replied: "Yes, it is as you say. But I say to all of you: In the future you will see the Son of Man sitting at the right hand of the Mighty One and coming on the clouds of heaven" (Matthew 26:64). At once Caiaphas pronounced him guilty of blasphemy. Some of those present spat in his face, struck him with their fists, slapped him, taunted him, and pronounced him worthy of death. The next morning, the entire Sanhedrin—the highest court in Judaism—concurred.

Meanwhile, the disciples weren't faring much better. Judas finally realized what the consequences of his action were going to be. He tried to undo it by giving the money back, but the chief priests weren't about to let him off the hook. He threw the money he had received into the temple, went out, and hanged himself. The "blood money" was used to purchase a burial field for foreigners, which came to be known as the Field of Blood.

Manna from Heaven

The Sanhedrin was something like the Jewish Supreme Court. It was supposed to consist of 70 members plus the high priest who presided, but sometimes the membership was closer to 100.

Peter and John had been bold enough to sneak into the courtyard of the high priest, hoping to find out what was happening to Jesus without getting caught themselves. As Peter warmed himself at a fire, a servant girl recognized him and asked whether he wasn't one of Jesus' disciples; he promptly denied it. A little later the girl saw him again and started asking the people around her what they thought. Peter, who had a strong Galilean accent, again denied knowing Jesus. Finally a relative of the man whose ear Peter had cut off asked, "Didn't I see you with him in the olive grove?" This time Peter began to curse and swear that he knew nothing about what they were discussing.

At that moment a rooster began to crow, and "the Lord turned and looked straight at Peter" (Luke 22:61). Then Peter remembered what Jesus had said, that before the rooster crowed Peter would deny him three times, and he went outside and wept bitterly.

With Jesus pronounced guilty, the Jewish leaders took him to Pilate, the Roman governor of Judea, to ask for the death penalty. When they got there, however, Pilate didn't see how this Jewish quarrel had anything to do with him. Why didn't they sentence the prisoner themselves? The truth was that, under Roman law, the Jews had no power to put someone to death. For that they needed Pilate. Their charge of blasphemy wouldn't have meant much to Rome, so they told him Jesus claimed to be a king and opposed paying taxes to Caesar.

Pilate summoned Jesus inside for a one-on-one conversation. He asked if Jesus was a king, to which Jesus replied, "My kingdom is not of this world." (John 18:36) Pilate took Jesus back to his accusers and told them he found no reason to kill him. They were shouting out all sorts of charges, but Jesus didn't say a word in response, which amazed Pilate. But when someone let it slip that Jesus was a Galilean, Pilate thought he had discovered a loophole. Rather than sentencing Jesus, he sent him to Herod. Pontius Pilate was the governor over all of Judea, but Herod was the specific ruler over Galilee. (This Herod was a son of the Herod who had ruled when Jesus was born.)

Herod had long wanted to meet Jesus. He was hoping to see a miracle first-hand, but Jesus did not offer to oblige him. In response to Herod's questions he remained silent. At that point Herod and his soldiers began to ridicule Jesus. They dressed him in a kingly robe and sent him back to Pilate.

Now Pilate tried a new strategy. He suggested that Jesus be flogged and then released. After all, it was traditional at Passover for the governor to pardon a prisoner as a gesture of good will. But to Pilate's surprise, the crowd voted to release a convicted thief and murderer named Barabbas rather than release Jesus.

Pilate's wife had told him of a dream she had, warning him to have nothing to do with "that innocent man" (Matthew 27:19). Besides, Pilate seemed to like Jesus—and he was more than a little worried about the confidence and authority that Jesus seemed to display (John 19:7-12). He turned Jesus over to his soldiers, who flogged him, dressed him in a purple robe, twisted together a crown of thorns for his head, and placed a staff in his hand. Mockingly some bowed down as others struck him and spat in his face.

Pilate then tried one final time to convince the crowd to leave Jesus alone. But when they threatened to go over Pilate's head to Caesar, Pilate finally relented and turned Jesus over to be crucified. Before doing so, however, he washed his hands in front of the crowd and told them, "I am innocent of this man's blood. It is your responsibility!" (Matthew 27:24)

Cross Purposes

Jesus' robe was removed, his clothes were returned, and he was marched to a place outside the city called Golgotha, carrying the large wooden crossbar (cross) to which his hands would be nailed. When he could no longer manage the weight of his cross, a man named Simon of Cyrene (now Libya) was recruited to carry it.

When they reached Golgotha, Jesus was offered an anesthetic, which he tasted but refused to take. Then he and two criminals were crucified.

Crucifixion was a heinous way to die. Roman citizens were exempt from such treatment and only inflicted it on others. Nails were driven through the wrists, pinning the prisoner to the crossbar; the crossbar was then raised and attached to the upright beam, after which the feet would be nailed to the upright through the heels. Death would come fairly quickly if no other support was

Manna from Heaven

Crucifixions were carried out at Golgotha, Hebrew for "Place of the Skull" (Latin: *Calvary*), thought to be the name of a hill just outside the city wall.

provided for the feet. Unable to raise himself to take a breath, the victim would eventually die of asphyxiation. With support, death could take two or three days.

Pilate had a sign prepared for Jesus' cross which read, "Jesus of Nazareth, the King of the Jews" (John 19:19). The sign was written in Latin, Greek, and Aramaic. Many of the chief priests wanted to edit the sign to read that Jesus *said* he was the king of the Jews. But Pilate refused, saying, "What I have written, I have written" (John 19:22).

As Jesus hung there, the soldiers divided up his clothing, while onlookers stood around mocking him. One of the thieves with whom he had been crucified also mocked him. But the other was contrite, pointing out that Jesus' punishment, unlike theirs, was undeserved. He asked: "Jesus, remember me when you come into your kingdom" (Luke 23:42), and Jesus promised to do so.

It took Jesus about three hours to die. As he drew his final breath, Matthew records that a series of strange events took place throughout Jerusalem. The curtain of the temple that separated the Most Holy Place "was torn in two from top to bottom." The earth shook and rocks split. Tombs broke open, and the bodies of righteous people who had died came alive and were seen by many people (Matthew 27:50–53). Even the Roman soldiers who witnessed these events, including an experienced centurion, responded that Jesus must have been "the Son of God" (or "a son of God").

Jesus' crucifixion took place on Friday; the next day was the Sabbath. The Jewish authorities were eager to get the bodies off the crosses and attended to before the Sabbath fell. They asked the Romans to break the legs of the crucifixion victims to hasten their deaths. When the soldiers came to Jesus, they saw that he was already dead. So instead of breaking his legs, they thrust a spear into his side, releasing a sudden flow of blood and water (John 19:31–37).

Potent Quotables

The Bible records seven utterances made by Jesus on the cross:

1. "Father, forgive them, for they do not know what they are doing." (Luke 23:34)

2. (To the thief on the cross) "I tell you the truth, today you will be with me in paradise." (Luke 23:43)

3. (To his mother) "Dear woman, here is your son." (To the apostle John) "Here is your mother." (John 19:26–27)

4. "My God, my God, why have you forsaken me?" (Matthew 27:46)

5. "I am thirsty." (John 19:28)

6. "It is finished." (John 19:30)

7. "Father, into your hands I commit my spirit." (Luke 23:46)

Friends in High Places

The death of Jesus brought out the courage in some of his followers among the Jewish leaders. One was Joseph of Arimathea, a secret disciple on the Sanhedrin who had opposed their sentence of death for Jesus. Joseph "went boldly to Pilate and asked for Jesus' body" (Mark 15:43). Pilate was surprised that Jesus had died so quickly, but granted Joseph's request. Joseph bought some linen cloth, wrapped the body, and placed it in his own tomb. He was helped by Nicodemus, the Pharisee who had visited Jesus at night. Nicodemus brought about 75 pounds of myrrh and aloes, which the two men placed in strips of clean linen cloth and wrapped around the body. When they finished, a large stone was rolled across the entrance to the tomb.

Further plans were made to tend to the body when the Sabbath had ended. But remembering how Jesus had said he would rise after three days, the religious authorities went to Pilate to ask that a guard be posted at the tomb to prevent the disciples from stealing the body. Pilate agreed (Matthew 27:65). They put a seal on the stone and posted a guard.

Alive Again

It must have been an incredibly depressing Passover for the friends and followers of Jesus. Not only had their leader been suddenly arrested and executed, but they had not been able to say good-bye. They had scattered and run, and by the time they returned, he was dead.

The next morning, even before daylight, a group of women took additional spices to anoint Jesus' body and headed for the tomb. On the way, they worried about who would move the stone for them when they got to the tomb.

But upon arriving, they saw the stone had already been moved. The gospel of Matthew tells what happened: "There was a violent earthquake, for an angel of the Lord came down from heaven and, going to the tomb, rolled back the stone and sat on it. His appearance was like lightning, and his clothes were white as snow. The guards were so afraid of him that they shook and became like dead men" (Matthew 28:2–4). Now the women entered the tomb and found it empty, but two brilliant angels told them Jesus had risen!

Potent Quotables

Good news from two angels:

"Do not be afraid, for I know that you are looking for Jesus, who was crucified. He is not here; he has risen, just as he said. Come and see the place where he lay." (Matthew 28:5–7)

The women hurried back to tell the disciples, who were somewhat skeptical. But Peter and John took off running toward the tomb. John was faster, but he stopped at the entrance of the tomb while Peter barged right in. Sure enough, it was empty. Only the linen grave clothes lay where the body had been.

The disciples went back home, but Mary Magdalene stood outside the tomb, crying. When the two angels asked why she was crying, she said that someone had taken Jesus away, and she didn't know where he was.

Then she turned and saw a figure she took to be the gardener. Distractedly she asked him if he knew where Jesus was. He answered her, "Mary!" She looked again. It was Jesus! He told her not to hold on to him "because "I have not yet returned to the Father" (John 20:17), but he sent her to spread the word that he was returning to "my Father and your Father, to my God and your God."

After this initial sighting of Jesus were numerous others, and in many varied places:

➤ To the other women (Matthew 28:8-10);

➤ To two disciples (not of the Twelve) on the road to Emmaus (Luke 24:13-35);

➤ To Peter (Luke 24:34);

➤ To the apostles while Thomas was absent (John 20:19-23);

➤ To the apostles including Thomas a week later (John 20:24-29);

➤ To a group of apostles who had gone fishing (John 21:1-14);

➤ To more than 500 disciples at once (1 Corinthians 15:6);

➤ To James (most likely Jesus' half-brother) (1 Corinthians 15:7);

➤ To a group of disciples who saw him ascend into heaven (Acts 1:3-11).

Apparently the post-resurrection form of Jesus was unique. He appeared in rooms where the doors were locked (John 20:19–20), yet he also ate food to show that his body had substance (Luke 24:42–43). Though he had forbidden Mary to touch him at first, he later encouraged Thomas to feel the marks in his hands and side (John 20:27). Jesus was around for 40 days between his crucifixion and his ascension into heaven (Acts 1:3).

Getting the Story Straight

With no body, the Roman soldiers were in trouble. The Jewish religious leaders didn't look good, either. They had made a special effort to guard the tomb, so now the absence of Jesus' body was particularly embarrassing. The Roman guards met with the Jewish leaders and agreed to say they had fallen asleep and the disciples had stolen the body (Matthew 28:11-15). The guards got a lot of money to promote this story. After all, the penalty for snoozing on guard duty could be death. In addition to the bribe, the Jewish leaders promised to cover for the guards with their superiors.

It has been pointed out that this story is ludicrous. In the first place, the disciples hadn't exactly shown themselves to be courageous enough to carry out the covert operation necessary to pluck a cadaver from under the noses of a group of trained Roman guards. In addition, tradition says that ten of the apostles were killed for their faith. (Judas killed himself and John was exiled on an island.) If they knew Jesus' body was stashed somewhere, surely they would not *all* have been willing to die for a lie. And if the Jewish leaders or Romans had possession of the body, why didn't they pull it out and quash the Christian movement before it could get started?

For Pete's (and Thom's) Sake

We've been concluding each of these chapters about Jesus by examining some of his relationships. In this chapter, let's not overlook some of the people he was closest to—his disciples. One example is Thomas. He had previously been willing to boldly die for Jesus (John 11:16), yet we are quick to brand him as "Doubting Thomas." Because he wasn't around when Jesus appeared to the apostles the first time, he wouldn't take the others' word for it even though he was outnumbered ten to one. It seems that Jesus made another special appearance just to allow Thomas to see for himself. The confidence of his followers was important to Jesus.

Another example was Peter. He really believed he had the moxie to stand up for Jesus, but when the going got tough all it took was a servant girl to cause him to deny his Lord. Think how Peter must have felt to see Jesus die and be buried. He would have been expecting to live with his guilt and shame for the rest of his sorry life. But as soon as the news began to spread that Jesus was alive again, a special angelic dispatch was sent with the message to "Go, tell his disciples *and Peter*." (Mark 16:7; emphasis added).

At one of Jesus' post-resurrection appearances (John 21), he called Peter aside. Three times Jesus asked, "Do you love me?" The third time, Peter was hurt. Why did Jesus keep asking that? Perhaps the three affirmations of faith were to counteract in Peter's mind those three denials on the night of Jesus' arrest. Jesus also told Peter three times to "Feed my sheep." And Jesus predicted Peter's death as well: "When you are old you will stretch out your hands, and someone else will dress you and lead you where you do not want to go" (John 21:18).

Manna from Heaven

Tradition says Peter was martyred for his faith—crucified upside down because he didn't feel worthy to die in the same manner as Jesus.

Jesus encouraged all his disciples during his final days on earth. Even though he was leaving, he promised to be with them always—part of his "Great Commission" found in Matthew 28:18–20. The next chapter explains how that was possible.

The Least You Need to Know

➤ The opposition to Jesus came to a climax as the Jewish leaders convicted Jesus of blasphemy and crucified him.

➤ In his last days Jesus made it clear to those close to him that they should expect trouble, but that their grief would turn to joy.

➤ Jesus rose from the dead on Sunday after he was buried on Friday.

➤ Many remarkable events accompanied Jesus' crucifixion and resurrection.

➤ Jesus told his followers to carry on in his absence.

Chapter 19

The Church Hits the Road

In This Chapter

➤ Conflict about Jesus continues

➤ Peter and others carry on Jesus' ministry

➤ Paul becomes an apostle

➤ Christianity spreads among the Gentiles

➤ The ascension of Jesus, the Day of Pentecost, Paul's three "road trips"

Rumors of Jesus' resurrection spread quickly through the known world. Jerusalem was the political and religious center of Jewish culture, as well as a crossroads for merchants and travelers. Soon, the good news proclaimed by Jesus' followers was racing down the well-built, well-traveled Roman roads to all kinds of remote locales.

Onward and Upward (Acts 1)

That Luke was the author of Acts, as well as the gospel that bears his name, has been widely accepted. He wasn't one of the 12 apostles, but he knew and traveled with the Apostle Paul. His book of Acts is the earliest history of the church that we have. It picks up where the gospels leave off and propels the reader through many of the events experienced by the first-century Christians.

The book of Acts begins with Jesus' farewell address to his followers, instructing them to wait in Jerusalem, where they would soon "be baptized with the Holy Spirit" (Acts 1:5). After challenging them to be his witnesses, Jesus was taken into heaven "before their very eyes." Two angelic beings appeared to tell them he would some day return in the same manner that he left (Acts 1:11).

Jesus' followers numbered about 120 persons, including Mary his mother, the apostles, and other disciples, both women and men. They lived a communal life, we are told, "constantly devoting themselves to prayer" (Acts 1:12–14).

What Saith Thou?

We have been told that Judas "went away and hanged himself" (Matthew 27:5). But here we read that "he fell headlong, his body burst open and all his intestines spilled out" (Acts 1:18). Two prevalent theories to reconcile these divergent accounts are: (1) The body hung so long that it burst when it was cut down; or (2) The concept of "hanging" conformed to the Old Testament definition, which was what we would consider *impaling*.

Manna from Heaven

In the Jewish calendar, the day of Pentecost is an annual celebration, also called the Feast of Weeks because it fell 50 days (a week of weeks) after Passover (Leviticus 23:15–22). For Christians, the festival commemorates the events described in this section.

Not long after Jesus' ascension, Peter proposed that a longtime follower of Jesus be elected to take Judas' place as the 12th apostle. After prayer, and the casting of lots, a man named Matthias was chosen. However, nothing more is said of him, and this is the Bible's final mention of casting lots.

On a Wind and a Prayer (Acts 2:1–41)

On the day of Pentecost, the whole group was assembled when a sudden sound came from heaven like the rush of a violent wind. "Tongues of fire" appeared, resting on each disciple, and they began to speak in other languages. We aren't told where they were at the time, but it must have been a public place, because people who were visiting Jerusalem from all over the world heard with amazement this group of unschooled Galileans speaking fluently in various languages. There is little question that this was the "baptism of the Holy Spirit" Jesus had told his followers to expect.

The biblical concept of speaking in tongues arouses much controversy. In the account described in Acts 2, the reference was to the ability to speak an existing, but unlearned, language. Some people feel this is the only valid definition. Others expand the definition to include the ability to speak in "ecstatic utterances" in a language unlike any known to exist. Some people feel the spiritual gift of speaking in tongues was only temporary and provided to bolster the faith of the early church; others are convinced it continues to this day. The next chapter will provide additional insight from the viewpoint of the Apostle Paul.

Some observers accused the believers of drunkenness. But Peter spoke out. No, they weren't drunk, he said; after all, it was only 9:00 A.M. Rather, this was a fulfillment of Joel's prophecy that "[God] will pour out [his] spirit on all people. Your sons and daughters will prophesy, your young men will see visions, your old men will dream dreams" (Acts 2:17–18). Peter went on to testify about Jesus, how he had lived, died, and been raised from death by God. At his passionate words, his listeners were "cut to the heart" and asked what they should do. Peter replied, "Repent and be baptized, every one of you, in the name of Jesus Christ for the forgiveness of your sins" (Acts 2:38). In response, 3,000 people became Christians that day.

Peter Principal (Acts 2:42–5)

During this time, Peter stepped into the leadership role to keep things organized and moving ahead. At first there were few problems. The close-knit community shared meals, prayer, study, and even possessions. Each day new believers joined their ranks.

Peter spoke and acted with authority. When asked for money by a crippled beggar, Peter healed him instead. The two went to the temple together, the man leaping for joy and praising God. As people stared at the former beggar in amazement, Peter testified again about Jesus, challenging the people to repent. For this he and John were tossed into jail overnight, to be released the next day with a warning. Yet the number of believers had already risen to more than 5,000.

Snapshots

Don't miss the account described in Acts 4:32–5:11. It contrasts the consequences of genuine giving and sharing with those of selfish, secret hoarding. We'll hear more about Barnabas, who is introduced here. Ananias and Sapphira, however, are another story.

Word of Peter's gifts as a healer and an evangelist began to spread. Sick people lined up in the hope that his shadow would fall on them and heal them. Crowds began to form wherever the apostles were, seeking health and healing. The religious authorities didn't like it, of course, and the apostles were soon arrested and imprisoned, only to be freed by an angel during the night. The next morning at daybreak they were back at the temple, teaching as before.

Eventually the Sanhedrin, the Jewish tribunal, got involved, ordering the apostles to stop teaching about Jesus, and even threatening them with death when they refused. However, a wise leader named Gamaliel suggested they back off. If the apostles were teaching lies, they would eventually fail. On the other hand, if they really represented God, they would succeed in spite of anything the Sanhedrin might do to impede them.

The members of the Sanhedrin went along with this advice, sending the apostles home with nothing but a flogging and a stern warning not to speak in the name of Jesus. Rejoicing "that they were considered worthy to suffer dishonor for the sake of the name," the apostles went right back to doing as they had before.

The Subordinate Seven (Acts 6–8)

As the church grew, the apostles began to think about getting some administrative help so that they could concentrate on preaching and teaching. They appointed seven men to see to the day-to-day running of the church while they continued with the other crucial aspects of ministry.

One of the seven was Stephen, "a man full of God's grace and power" who "did great wonders and miraculous signs among the people" (Acts 6:8). Stephen's eloquence made him more than a match for his non-Christian opponents. To silence him, they concocted a charge of blasphemy, and Stephen was seized and dragged before a local council. Asked whether the charges against him were true, Stephen boldly began to recount a long history of Israelite faithlessness, eventually charging his accusers of murdering "the Righteous One" whom God had sent. Then Stephen lifted his eyes and said, "Look, I see heaven open and the Son of Man standing at the right hand of God" (Acts 7:56). It was the last straw. With cries of "Blasphemy!" the crowd dragged Stephen outside the city and stoned him. Stephen prayed for Jesus to receive his spirit, saying, "Lord, do not hold this sin against them" (Acts 7:59–60). Then "he fell asleep."

Manna from Heaven

The Bible doesn't refer to these men as **deacons**, but later job descriptions of deacons seem to describe the role these seven filled. The Greek word for *deacon* can be translated as "minister" or "servant." Some deacons in the early church were women.

Meanwhile, a young man named Saul stood by watching and condoning the mob action. He would become a zealous opponent of the Jewish believers in Jesus, even going so far as to conduct house-to-house searches for them. Believers who had been gathering in Jerusalem began to scatter. The apostles remained centered in Jerusalem, while those who left "preached the word wherever they went."

Philip was another of the seven "deacons." He went to Samaria and made quite a name for himself casting out evil spirits and healing the sick. He was even followed by a local sorcerer who tried to purchase the "secret" of his power (8:9–24).

Directed by an angel to go into the desert, Philip came across an Ethiopian eunuch, a high-ranking government official who had come to worship in Jerusalem. Instructed by the Holy Spirit, Philip approached the man's chariot, where he heard the eunuch reading from Isaiah. (People usually read aloud in ancient times.) Philip asked, "Do you understand what you are reading?"

The man was doing no better than most of us do when we pick up a Bible and try to read Isaiah. But he happened to be at a passage describing the future Messiah. Philip explained that Jesus was the one who had recently fulfilled that very passage. The eunuch became a believer, and Philip baptized him on the spot. The Bible then says that, "when they came up out of the water, the Spirit of the Lord suddenly took Philip away, and the eunuch did not see him again, but went on his way rejoicing" (Acts 8:40). We don't hear anything else about the eunuch, but some people like to believe he was among the first (if not *the* first) to carry the gospel of Jesus to Africa. Philip next shows up in Azotus, about 19 miles from Gaza.

What Saith Thou?

What does it mean to "receive the Holy Spirit"?

It is generally accepted that from the day of Pentecost onward, when people put their faith in Jesus they are filled and empowered with the Holy Spirit at that moment. A personal relationship with Jesus carries with it the association with the other members of the Godhead as well—God the Father and God the Holy Spirit.

Blinded by the Light (Acts 9:1–31)

Meanwhile, back in Jerusalem, Saul was preparing to go to Damascus, a four-day journey away. The book of Acts says that he had obtained written authorization from the high priest to look for believers there, bring them back to Jerusalem, and put them in jail.

Before he got there, however, he made an unexpected stop. A light from heaven flashed, throwing him off his horse, and a voice asked him, "Saul, Saul, why do you persecute me?" Saul asked, "Who are you, Lord?" He was told, "I am Jesus, whom you are persecuting. Now get up and go into the city, and you will be told what you must do."

Saul got up, but he couldn't see a thing. His companions had to lead him the rest of the way to Damascus. For three days he was completely blind. He waited, refusing to eat or drink anything.

Meanwhile, God told a disciple named Ananias living in Damascus to meet Saul and take care of him. Ananias was taken aback. He knew all about Saul and what he'd been up to. Nevertheless, Ananias obeyed. God told him, "This man is my chosen instrument to carry my name before the Gentiles and their kings and before the people of Israel" (Acts 9:15).

When Ananias placed his hands on Saul, something like scales fell from Saul's eyes, his sight returned, and he got up and was baptized. Immediately he began speaking in the synagogue and telling people that Jesus was the Son of God—to the immense surprise of his listeners. Non-believers conspired to kill him, but his new friends put him in a basket and lowered him down the wall to safety. He returned to Jerusalem, where Barnabas (another brave disciple) helped persuade the church that Saul had genuinely converted. Meanwhile, the church continued to grow.

Peter, Peter, Reptile Eater (Acts 9:21–12)

Peter, meanwhile, was traveling the country doing things such as healing the sick and raising the dead. One day he fell into a trance, during which he saw heaven open and something like a large sheet being lowered. A heavenly voice told Peter to "kill and eat." Inside the sheet were all kinds of animals, reptiles, and birds—many of which were not on the "clean" list of permissible food for Jews. (See Leviticus 11.) Peter protested, but the invitation was made a second and third time. The voice said, "Do not call anything impure that God has made clean" (Acts 10:15). Then the sheet was taken back into heaven.

Peter wondered about the meaning of the vision, but he didn't have to wait long. God had sent Gentile messengers to the house where Peter was staying to invite him to spend time with a God-fearing centurion named Cornelius. The vision was to reassure Peter that God had removed barriers between the Jews and the Gentiles. Previously, they were not to intermingle, but a new rule would be in effect from now on. As Peter preached about Jesus, the Gentiles who were there began to praise God and speak in tongues. When Peter saw that they had been filled with the Holy Spirit, he gave permission for them to be baptized.

Manna from Heaven

It was in Antioch that the term **Christian** originated. It may have begun as a mocking or derogatory term but was soon appropriated as a name of honor by Christ's followers.

Soon news came from Antioch that Gentiles there were also converting in large numbers. Barnabas went to check on them and confirmed "the evidence of the grace of God" (Acts 11:23). He sent for Saul, and the two of them spent a year instructing the Gentiles in their new faith.

Opposition to the believers continued to intensify. King Herod arrested many church leaders and even had James put to death. Sensing that persecuting Christians was good politics, he imprisoned Peter and planned a sensational trial after Passover. Sixteen Roman soldiers were assigned to guard Peter, and two of them were literally chained to him in an inner cell. However, on the night before his trial, as Peter was sleeping soundly, he had a visitor. He was "touched by an angel" as his visitor gave him a swift kick in the side. He told Peter to get up, and the chains fell off his wrists. The angel escorted Peter through two sets of guards and right out the gate leading to the city. The gate opened by itself. When they got to the next block, the angel disappeared, but Peter was free.

Snapshots

Peter's miraculous prison escape makes good reading. So does King Herod's wormy end. The stories are found in Acts 12.

Road Trip #1 (Acts 13–15:35)

When Saul and Barnabas had completed their work in Antioch, the Holy Spirit directed them to a new ministry—a "road trip" of sorts. They first sailed to Cyprus, taking with them the young John Mark, a relative of Barnabas (Colossians 4:10).

From Cyprus they sailed north to the mainland where John Mark bailed out on them to return to Jerusalem. Paul and Barnabas continued to a city called Pisidian Antioch (not the same Antioch previously mentioned).

When visiting a new city, Paul usually went first to the local synagogue, which had regular teaching times and frequently invited visitors to speak. The people of Pisidian Antioch responded to Paul's message and even invited him back, but the local Jewish leaders managed to make life unpleasant for Paul and Barnabas until the two missionaries moved on. At Iconium they left after discovering a plot to stone them. In Lystra, the next stop, Paul healed a crippled man. The people weren't used to this kind of thing, and they began to spread the word that Barnabas was Zeus and that Paul was Hermes. The citizens wanted to offer sacrifices to Paul and Barnabas, who quickly set the record straight. But by this time some of their opponents from cities they had already visited caught up with them. They stoned Paul and dragged him out of the city, thinking he was dead. He left the next day with Barnabas, and they continued their trip.

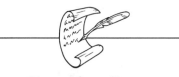

Manna from Heaven

Paul's Roman citizenship frequently proved to be of value during his travels. Roman citizens were exempted from demeaning public spectacles such as flogging and crucifixion, and had certain rights to appeal sentences they felt were unfair. The emperor could grant citizenship to an individual or entire city. Citizenships were occasionally purchased or inherited. Paul, however, was born a Roman citizen (Acts 22:28).

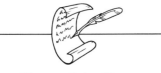

Manna from Heaven

At this point in the narrative, the mentions of Saul begin to refer to him as Paul. The name change isn't explained. Many people think it was a simple matter of shifting from the traditional Hebrew name to a similar Greco-Roman variation, since Paul would be ministering primarily to Gentiles rather than Jews.

They retraced their itinerary, going back to the cities where they had already been and encouraging the believers in each place, eventually ending up in Antioch, the city where they had begun their mission together. There they learned that certain Jewish believers in Antioch were teaching that circumcision was a requirement for salvation. Paul and Barnabas strongly disagreed. Returning to Jerusalem with a delegation, they took the matter up with the apostles and elders. Much discussion ensued, but it was hard to argue with Peter's experience with his vision of the sheet, and with Paul's reports of how God was working among the Gentiles. After a difficult struggle, the Council in Jerusalem elected that they should "not make it difficult for the Gentiles, who are turning to God" (Acts 15:19), emphasizing instead the more essential issues of sexual purity and separation from idolatrous practices. It was James, the half-brother of Jesus and the head of the Jerusalem church, who proposed a compromise requiring Gentile Christians to observe portions of the Mosaic law but not to undergo circumcision.

Road Trip #2 (Acts 15:36–21:36)

After a period of time, Paul wanted to return to the places where he had gone before to see how people were doing. Barnabas wanted to take John Mark again, but Paul wouldn't hear of it. In fact, the disagreement was so strong that they went their separate ways. Barnabas took John Mark and returned to Cyprus. Paul recruited another man named Silas to accompany him.

What Saith Thou?

Since Paul was reporting that circumcision wasn't required for salvation, why have Timothy circumcised?

Paul knew the Jewish people in the area might be a bit suspicious of Timothy because of his Gentile father. While circumcision wasn't essential, it certainly wasn't improper. In this case it seemed to be a concession made for the expediency of ministry.

This road trip was a bit longer than the previous one so we have space only for a few highlights.

Derbe/Lystra (Acts 16:1–5)

Paul met a young disciple named Timothy, the son of a Jewish mother and Greek father. Paul wanted to take Timothy along on his journey, and had him circumcised.

Philippi (Acts 16:6–40)

After being directed to this area by a vision, Paul met Lydia, a seller of purple cloth, who worshiped God. She responded to Paul's message and was baptized.

Thessalonica/Berea (Acts 17:1–15)

Most places Paul visited, he received a lot of opposition, but he got a different response from the Bereans. They "received the message with great eagerness and examined the Scriptures every day to see if what Paul said was true." Many people believed as a result.

Athens (Acts 17:16–34)

While wandering around Athens, Paul was distressed by the number of statues to the various Greek gods. Athenians loved debate and discussion, however, and Paul had an intelligent encounter with Epicurean and Stoic philosophers. Having seen an altar dedicated "TO AN UNKNOWN GOD," he used it as an opportunity to introduce them to his God, whom they didn't know. Some of the people scoffed at him, but others were quite interested and requested further discussion.

Corinth (Acts 18)

In Corinth Paul hooked up with a Christian couple named Aquila and Priscilla, who shared his original trade of tentmaking. He stayed and worked with them for a while, teaching in the synagogue on the Sabbaths. When Silas and Timothy caught up with him there, Paul went back to preaching full-time, and stayed a year and a half.

Ephesus (Acts 19)

Paul then spent more than two years in Ephesus, and God performed great miracles through him. People would carry handkerchiefs or aprons that had touched Paul to sick people, and illnesses were cured and evil spirits were cast out. Again the power of the Holy Spirit was coveted by people who didn't understand it. When the seven sons of a priest named Sceva tried an exorcism in Jesus' name, the spirit talked back to them saying, "Jesus I know, and I know about Paul, but who are you?" Then the possessed man "jumped on them and overpowered them all" (Acts 19:16). He beat them so severely that they ran away naked and bleeding. As a result, many of the local sorcerers renounced their practices and burned their scrolls publicly.

Opposition to Paul arose from another front as well. A silversmith named Demetrius made a living by selling silver statues of Artemis, the Greek goddess of the hunt who had somehow become a fertility

Manna from Heaven

The **Stoics** advocated suppressing personal desires. The **Epicureans** were at the other end of the scale. Their movement had begun with high standards of devotion to happiness based on intellectual pursuits, but this had degenerated into a philosophy of seeking happiness through sensual gratification. These two philosophies had many adherents throughout the Roman empire.

233

goddess in Ephesus. A huge temple to her stood in the city, and the people believed a statue of her had fallen from heaven. Fearing that Paul's message would put him out of business, Demetrius rallied other tradesmen, who went through Ephesus shouting, "Great is Artemis of the Ephesians!" until the city was in an uproar and the lives of Paul and his friends were in danger from the mob. The city clerk finally got the people settled down and told them they had no valid complaint. Paul had done nothing overtly threatening. It was ruled that Demetrius could file a civil complaint if he wished, but otherwise Paul was innocent and the crowd should disperse.

Potent Quotables

It is more blessed to give than to receive (Acts 20:35).

Paul gives Jesus credit for this quote. Surprisingly, however, it is not found in any of the gospels.

Troas (Acts 20:1–12)

Paul had planned to stop at Troas only for a night, but he had a lot to tell the people. As he kept talking until midnight, a young person named Eutychus nodded off on a third-story window ledge and fell to his death. Paul wrapped his arms around the young man and restored him to life.

Miletus (Acts 20:13–38)

Paul was hoping to arrive in Jerusalem by Passover, so rather than return to Ephesus, he met the Ephesian elders in Miletus. There he said a fond farewell, challenging them to watch over the church and protect it from "savage wolves" who were sure to follow. Then they prayed together, and the elders saw him off.

Home to Jerusalem (Acts 21:1–36)

On the way home, Paul greeted believers wherever he went. One stop was at the home of Philip (the deacon), whom we learn had four unmarried prophetess daughters. While there, a prophet from Judea took Paul's belt, tied his hands and feet with it, and predicted, "In this way the Jews of Jerusalem will bind the owner of this belt and will hand him over to the Gentiles" (Acts 21:11). Paul's friends begged him not to return, but he said he was willing not only to be bound but also to die for Jesus if necessary.

When he arrived in Jerusalem, he and the apostles traded stories of what had been happening. A false rumor had begun to spread in Jerusalem that Paul was telling people to turn away from Moses' law and to not circumcise their children. To discredit the rumor, Paul went through a Jewish purification ceremony with a number of other men. Some of the Jews of Jerusalem were still alarmed by Paul's association with the Gentiles, however, viewing Paul as a traitor to his people. Things were turning ugly when a Roman commander showed up and arrested Paul, saving him from the hostile crowd.

Road Trip #3 (Acts 21:37–28)

The Romans were really confused. In a terrible case of mistaken identity, they at first thought Paul was an Egyptian terrorist who had previously led 4,000 people in a revolt. But Paul told them exactly who he was—complete with the story of what had happened to him on the road to Damascus. The crowd was still making loud accusations, and the Roman commander was about to have Paul flogged to get to the truth. But when Paul mentioned his Roman citizenship, he was placed in chains instead. Paul was later moved to Caesarea.

During this time Paul survived a number of trials—both legal and physical—that climaxed in a catastrophic shipwreck on the island of Malta. The islanders were kind to the castaways, preparing a fire to shelter them from the rain and cold. As Paul was putting wood on the fire, a poisonous viper fastened onto his hand. The natives thought he must be a murderer receiving his due punishment, and expected Paul to drop dead right there, but they changed their minds and decided he was a god when he shook the deadly serpent into the fire and went on with what he was doing. Later Paul healed the chief official of the island and other people from various illnesses.

The group wintered on the island and left for Rome three months later. There Paul was placed under guard but was provided with his own residence, where he was permitted to meet with other believers. We are told that he lived in this way for two years. There the Book of Acts comes to a screeching halt. We never find out what became of Paul. Some hold that he was eventually released and resumed his travels, even getting as far as Spain. Others believe that Peter and Paul both died in Rome during the first major persecution of Christians, which was ordered by the Emperor Nero in the year 66. It's unlikely we will ever know the specifics for sure.

Snapshots

If you read through Paul's travels in more detail, you'll find a lot of fascinating stories. For example:

How do you deal with a disruptive sorcerer? (13:6–12)

An arrest, an imprisonment, an earthquake—and a happy ending (16:16–40).

A contract on Paul's life motivates 40 assassins (23:12–24).

A series of trials, some crooked officials, and some pompous royalty (24–26).

A magnificently detailed account of a storm and shipwreck (Acts 27).

Acts provides a historical framework for the growth of the church. As we turn to the letters of Paul, we will find numerous references to his road trips, as well as the deepening spiritual insight he developed along the way.

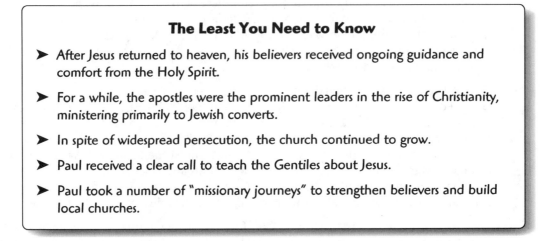

The Least You Need to Know

➤ After Jesus returned to heaven, his believers received ongoing guidance and comfort from the Holy Spirit.

➤ For a while, the apostles were the prominent leaders in the rise of Christianity, ministering primarily to Jewish converts.

➤ In spite of widespread persecution, the church continued to grow.

➤ Paul received a clear call to teach the Gentiles about Jesus.

➤ Paul took a number of "missionary journeys" to strengthen believers and build local churches.

You've Got Mail!

In This Chapter

➤ A letter to the Romans, and two to the Corinthians

➤ Some basic doctrines of Christianity

➤ Paul addresses problems in the growing church

➤ Paul's personal struggles; his opinions of his fellow preachers; and his teachings about love and marriage, spiritual gifts, women in the church, lawsuits, and more

In these days of voice mail, e-mail, pagers, fax machines, and other kinds of instant communication, one form of personal correspondence is on a sharp decline: the personal letter. Yet if the sender is someone special to you, nothing compares to the texture of a letter in your hands as you read two-day-old news. It's still hard to electronically dot *i*'s with hearts. You can't perfume a faxed message. And cold, exact fonts have removed the individuality of personal handwriting styles.

We've seen the eyewitness accounts of Jesus in the Gospels, and we've had a quickie history lesson in Acts. Now we move into the Epistles (letters) of the New Testament. Most, you will notice, were written by the Apostle Paul. Paul's extensive traveling took him to many places, and he tried to keep up with what was going on in the churches by letter when he couldn't be there in person.

Buón Giorno, Roma (Romans 1–3)

The order of the letters that appears in the Bible is not based on chronology. Dates are difficult to determine in any case, so we will simply follow the traditional order, beginning with the book of Romans, a crucial early Christian document in which Paul sets forth and clarifies many of the basic doctrines of his faith.

As the letter opens, Paul is eagerly awaiting the opportunity to preach in Rome, the capital of the civilized world. Despite all that he had already suffered for his faith, he declares, "I am not ashamed of the gospel, because it is the power of God for the salvation of everyone who believes: first for the Jew, then for the Gentile. For in the gospel a righteousness from God is revealed, a righteousness that is by faith from first to last, just as it is written: 'The righteous will live by faith'" (Romans 1:16–17). Characteristically, Paul begins with a summary of what is to follow. The remainder of the letter will be devoted to exploring and defending these claims.

Paul contrasts "the righteousness of God" with "the godlessness and wickedness of men" (Romans 1:18). When God's truth is suppressed by wickedness, the quality of life suffers. Although people claimed to be wise, "they became fools and exchanged the glory of the immortal God for images made to look like mortal man and birds and animals and reptiles. Therefore, "the wrath of God is being revealed from heaven" (Romans 1:18–23).

Paul isn't talking about people who make an innocent or thoughtless mistake, only to have God immediately start slinging thunderbolts. The description of these wicked people is graphic and precise: "They have become filled with every kind of wickedness, evil, greed, and depravity. They are full of envy, murder, strife, deceit, and malice. They are gossips, slanderers, God-haters, insolent, arrogant, and boastful; they invent ways of doing evil; they disobey their parents; they are senseless, faithless, heartless, ruthless. Although they know God's righteous decree that those who do such things deserve death, they not only continue to do these very things but also approve of those who practice them" (Romans 1:29–32). Because of such wickedness, Paul says, "God gave them over" to their sins (Romans 1:24, 26, 28).

One case was the issue of sexual preference. Paul says, "God gave them over to shameful lusts. Even their women exchanged natural relations for unnatural ones. In the same way the men also abandoned natural relations with women and were inflamed with lust for one another. Men committed indecent acts with other men, and received in themselves the due penalty for their perversion" (Romans 1:26-27).

Manna from Heaven

Paul does not intend to liken the wrath of God to human wrath. People quickly get out of control and do things they don't mean to do. God, however, never acts irrationally. Divine wrath is reserved for those who defy his will or callously misuse others.

Yet Paul isn't picking on any particular segment of society. His concern is for wickedness in general—including the wickedness of "you who pass judgment on someone else" (Romans 2:1), "those who are self-seeking and who reject the truth and follow evil" (2:8), and fellow Jews who believed themselves to be righteous because they followed Mosaic law (2:17–29). By the time Paul is finished, he has reached a chilling conclusion: "There is no one righteous, not even one; there is no one who understands, not one who seeks God" (Romans 3:10).

Abraham, Adam, and Jesus (Romans 4–5)

Paul next considers Abraham, who, before the giving of the law, "believed God, and it was credited to him as righteousness" (4:3). In Christ, a faith-based relationship with God has again been made possible. Abraham, Paul writes, is a model for all believers, both Gentiles (the uncircumcised) and Jews (circumcised). In all cases, faith is the crucial ingredient, though Jews remain bound to the Mosaic law.

Speaking of the sin of Adam, Paul writes that "just as the result of one trespass was condemnation for all men, so also the result of one act of righteousness was justification that brings life for all men" (5:18–19). Jesus not only atoned for the sins of the world; he also became the source of righteousness for anyone who believes.

Rather than striving for righteousness and worrying about what's going to happen to us, we can have peace and joy because of Christ—even during times of suffering. It's like a ladder from suffering to hope: "We know that suffering produces perseverance; perseverance, character; and character, hope. And hope does not disappoint us, because God has poured out his love into our hearts by the Holy Spirit, whom he has given us" (5:3–5).

But if Abraham was doing fine without the law, why go to all the trouble of creating and having Moses record all those Old Testament rules? Because the law pointed out the shortcomings of human beings. Without any written standard, we all tend to think we're pretty good people. But the exacting instructions of the law force people to come face-to-face with the extent of their sinful condition. "But where sin increased, grace increased all the more" (5:20), says Paul. The law didn't bring salvation; it only highlighted the need for God to step in and deal with the issue of sin.

Potent Quotables

"You see, at just the right time, when we were still powerless, Christ died for the ungodly. Very rarely will anyone die for a righteous man, though for a good man someone might possibly dare to die. But God demonstrates his own love for us in this: While we were still sinners, Christ died for us." (Romans 5:6–8)

Everything Old Is New Again (Romans 6–7)

Paul was way ahead of his readers. He knew some people would suggest that since increased sin seemed to bring out the depths of God's grace, why not sin all we can? Belief in Christ brings salvation and righteousness, but it also requires a commitment to change. Paul calls this being "baptized into his death" (6:3). Just as Jesus rose into a glorious new life, so must we. When someone lives in Christ, the "old self" is crucified with Jesus, enabling the person to break free of the bondage of sin and become "alive to God in Christ Jesus" (6:11).

Paul revealed that he, too, struggled with his sinful nature: "I know that nothing good lives in me, that is, in my sinful nature. For I have the desire to do what is good, but I cannot carry it out. For what I do is not the good I want to do; no, the evil I do not want to do—this I keep on doing…. What a wretched man I am! Who will rescue me from this body of death? Thanks be to God—through Jesus Christ our Lord!" (7: 18-19, 24–25)

The Benefit Plan (Romans 8)

Paul goes on to list what it means to be "in Christ":

➤ We no longer fear God's condemnation (8:1).

➤ We break free from the hold of sin and death (8:2).

➤ Our minds become focused on higher things (8:5).

➤ We are adopted into God's family with full rights of children, including the right to call God "Abba" and share in Jesus' inheritance (8:15–17).

➤ We await a future that will blow away any suffering we experience during this lifetime (8:18).

➤ The Holy Spirit begins to intercede with God on our behalf (8:26–27).

➤ We become "more than conquerors" (8:37).

Manna from Heaven

The word **Abba** (Romans 8:15) comes from an Aramaic (not Swedish) word that is an intimate term for *father*. Because of a believer's new relationship with God, the former fear and trembling can be replaced with confident love and trust in God as a heavenly dad.

These transformations among believers are part of a lifelong process known as *sanctification*. The root word is the same from which we get the word "saint," and the concept is that of being "set apart" (*from* the sinfulness of the world and *for* service to God).

Snapshots

Acting like a "saint" is no simple matter. Romans 6–8 describes the process of sanctification as well as other related doctrines, including adoption (8:12–17, 23), predestination (8:28–30), and glorification (attaining a new, perfect status after death and resurrection) (8:30).

The Choice of a New Generation (Romans 9–11)

Romans was written to a predominantly Gentile audience. The Jews, who had basked in the light of being God's chosen people for so long, were fast becoming a minority in the formation of the church. The Gentiles were jumping on this bandwagon in droves.

Paul felt deep sadness for his fellow Jews who refused to believe in Jesus. He had the hindsight of having been one of them, but had since had a stunning conversion. Yet as he saw others who would not believe, he wrote: "I have great sorrow and unceasing anguish in my heart. For I could wish that I myself were cursed and cut off from Christ for the sake of my brothers, those of my own race, the people of Israel" (9:2–3). He explained that the Jews should not think it odd that God might choose to bless people whom they didn't expect. He recalled stories of Abraham, Jacob and Esau, Moses and Pharaoh, and others to remind them that God's sovereign will in the past had not always been predictable. Yet Paul spoke from personal experience and attested that God had not forgotten the Jews (11:1–2). The bottom line of this section is that, "There is no difference between Jew and Gentile—the same Lord is Lord of all and richly blesses all who call on him, for, 'Everyone who calls on the name of the Lord will be saved'" (10:12-13).

Potent Quotables

"If God is for us, who can be against us? . . . Who shall separate us from the love of Christ? . . . For I am convinced that neither death nor life, neither angels nor demons, neither the present nor the future, nor any powers, neither height nor depth, nor anything else in all creation, will be able to separate us from the love of God that is in Christ Jesus our Lord" (Romans 8:31, 35, 38-39).

Then Paul makes an extraordinary claim. The "stumbling" of the Jewish people had a hidden purpose: to bring about the salvation of the Gentiles, who had been "grafted" into the promise of Abraham like "wild olive shoots" by the advent of Christ (11:11–21). In fact, he tells his Gentile readers that if they can be grafted into God's family, so can the cultivated branches that were broken off (that is, the Jews). God's covenant with Israel was unconditional.

Altar Egos (Romans 12–16)

In the final chapters of Romans, Paul challenges his readers to be "living sacrifices" (12:1), no longer conforming to worldly behavior. Someone has said that the problem with living sacrifices is that they can crawl off the altar. It is up to believers to go on *choosing* to obey God. In doing so, Paul reminds them to put their spiritual gifts to use (12:3–8), develop a deeper level of love for one another (12:9–21), submit to those in authority (13:1–7), leave behind sinful practices (13:8–14), and avoid doing anything that might damage a "weaker brother" in the church (14:1–15:13).

1,000 Prostitutes—No Waiting (1 Cor. 1:1–8)

Following Paul's letter to the Romans are two epistles to the Corinthian church. Corinth was one of the most important cities in Greece, and Corinthian Christians had a lot of competition from a large temple to Aphrodite that had a thousand temple prostitutes. As one might expect, some of the "religious" sexual misconduct was beginning to creep into the Christian church. But that was only one of many problems faced by the Corinthian believers.

While Romans seemed to be in large part a doctrinal study, the letters to the Corinthians are generally more direct and practical. Paul wrote 1 Corinthians in response to a message he received about quarrels and problems in the church. As soon as Paul got his salutations out of the way, he went right to work in clarifying how a church ought to function.

Whom Do You Love? (1 Cor. 1:10–4)

First came the problem of divisions in the church. Leadership was becoming a popularity contest. Paul had his supporters, but so did Peter, Apollos, and others (1 Corinthians 1:11–12). Church members had begun to quarrel about who was the best leader. Paul reminded his readers that they had only one leader: Jesus. Only he had been crucified on behalf of the church, and it was in his name that the members had been baptized. Indeed, the very fact that a religious movement had been built on the crucifixion of one person was "foolishness" to those who didn't understand the significance. However, "to us who are being saved it is the power of God" (1:18). Consequently, no one had the right to brag about any specific minister. Rather, "Let him who boasts boast in the Lord" (1:31).

As Paul reminds his readers, "I came to you in weakness and fear, and with much trembling" (2:3). Whatever had been accomplished was the work of the Holy Spirit, not Paul. "I planted the seed, Apollos watered it, but God made it grow. So neither he who plants nor he who waters is anything, but only God, who makes things grow" (3:6–7).

The Corinthian Christians were immature and still needed spiritual "milk, not solid food" (3:1-3). Many had become arrogant (4:8-13, 18). Paul warned that each person's work will be "revealed with fire" (3:13), which will burn works of wood, hay, or straw. But those that are of gold or costly stones will survive the fire and be of great value.

Potent Quotables

"The foolishness of God is wiser than man's wisdom, and the weakness of God is stronger than man's strength." (1 Corinthians 1:25)

Incest and Outplacement (1 Cor. 5–6:11)

Word had reached Paul that some of the Corinthians had apparently interpreted his doctrine on grace as a license to do anything and everything. One of the church members, he had heard, "[had] his father's wife" (5:1). The woman was probably a stepmother rather than the man's birth mother, but a sexual relationship was still forbidden between them (Leviticus 18:8). Yet the church sat by while this guy kept attending services. Paul told the church members to stop being so tolerant and to "expel the wicked man from among you" (1 Corinthians 5:12). An excommunicated member could always be reinstated when he repented and got his life back in order. In the meantime, he was in danger of corrupting the entire congregation.

Paul reminded his readers that the outside world was watching the goings-on in the church. He suggested it was a bad idea for one Christian to sue another and go to court before a nonbelieving judge. It was far better, he said, for someone in the church to be chosen to mediate disputes. "Why not rather be wronged? Why not rather be cheated?" (6:7). Life is never completely fair, so it is better for Christians to willingly let someone else have the upper hand in certain circumstances than to always insist on one's rights.

Manna from Heaven

Homosexuality is again listed as a sin (1 Corinthians 6:9–11), but so are greed, drunkenness, adultery, stealing, and swindling. Those who crusade against homosexuals with cruel and vicious statements don't seem to realize that *slanderers* is on the same list.

Paul reminded the Christians of what they used to be: sexually immoral, idolaters, adulterers, male prostitutes, homosexual offenders, thieves, misers, drunkards, slanderers, and swindlers (6:9–10). Such people don't get into the kingdom of heaven unless they repent and commit to change, yet some of the Corinthians were slipping back into their old ways.

The Wonderful World of Sex (1 Cor. 6:12–7)

But lest people begin to connect sex with sin, Paul clarifies the matter by launching into the topic of marriage. Sex was God-invented for the purpose of maximum physical intimacy. The original purpose was to bring a "oneness" to marriage.

Potent Quotables

Do you not know that your body is a temple of the Holy Spirit, who is in you, whom you have received from God? You are not your own; you were bought at a price. Therefore honor God with your body.
(1 Corinthians 6:19-20)

Sex is about as close as people can get to "becoming one flesh" (6:17). And that's exactly why sexual sins get so much attention in the Bible. Indiscriminate sexual intercourse is a matter of "becoming one" with no long-term commitment. For Christians who supposedly belong to Jesus, Paul compares sex outside of marriage to "taking the members of Christ and uniting them with a prostitute" (6:15). Therefore, believers are instructed to "flee sexual immorality" (6:18).

Paul was single and celibate, and he considered marriage a major distraction. However, he told his readers, "It is better to marry than to burn with passion" (7:9). Marriage was not to be taken lightly. After a separation, marriage partners were expected to either remain unmarried or to reconcile (7:10–11).

Snapshots

Avoid the wedding bell blues! More detailed instructions concerning marriage can be found in 1 Corinthians 7.

Taking the Heat for the Meat That You Eat (1 Cor. 8)

Another problem the church faced had to do with the principle of Christian freedom. Most of the meat sold in the marketplace or served at parties had been previously offered to pagan gods. Some Christians felt that because those gods weren't real, it didn't matter if they ate it. Other Christians were horrified at the practice. Paul established a common-sense rule: "Be careful…that the exercise of your freedom does not become a stumbling block to the weak" (8:9). In other words, don't offend people, even if you think you know better. Paul's own rule was to do without rather than continue something that might make a fellow Christian stumble in his faith (8:13). Though he felt entitled to certain rights for the work he did (payment, support, and so on), he never demanded them. "On the contrary, we put up with anything rather than hinder the gospel of Christ" (9:12). And minor things like food should never interfere with a person's testimony to believers. Paul later advised people to accept invitations to dine with unbelievers and "eat whatever is put before you without raising questions of conscience" (10:27).

Spreading the gospel was Paul's highest goal (9:16). He considered himself a servant to everyone to whom he spoke—Jew or Gentile, weak or strong: "I have become all things to all men so that by all possible means I might save some" (9:22). He compared himself to a long-distance runner who was competing with many others for the prize. He was determined to finish the race and get "a crown that will last forever" (9:25).

Order in the Church! (1 Cor. 10–11)

Chapter 10 contains guidelines for corporate church worship. For the sake of order, his rules were fairly straightforward. Men were not to have their heads covered; women were. Men were to have short hair; women were to have long hair. The Lord's Supper was a sacred meal to be partaken of worthily; it did not exist so people could pig out or get drunk.

Contemporary denominations and individual churches within denominations vary as to the extent of formality in worship services. Some still try to do everything exactly as prescribed by Paul in this passage. Others believe the cultural practices of the day dictated some of the specific instructions, and have updated them or dismissed them as outdated.

As for spiritual gifts, their purpose was to *unify* believers, not divide them. Even though there were numerous gifts, there was only one body. Paul compared the church to a human body, which is a single entity even though it is made up of many different parts. Jesus, he says, is the head of the body. It's up to the other parts to work together to

Manna From Heaven

Most churches still have some form of the **Lord's Supper** as a sacrament, but vary as to its frequency and meaning. For instance, most Protestant churches teach that the bread and wine (or grape juice) are *symbols* of Jesus' broken body and blood (11:23–26). The Roman Catholic and Eastern Orthodox churches, however, believe in the transubstantiation of the elements into the *literal* body and blood of Christ while maintaining the appearance of bread and wine. Whatever the method, the purpose of this sacrament is to "proclaim the Lord's death until he comes" (11:26).

walk, talk, speak, see, and so forth. And the only way for a body to operate effectively is for each part to perform its own function without being jealous of others or seeking to be self-sufficient.

It sounds like a simple concept, yet it takes only a few people to bring dysfunction to the body instead of unity. Paul implored people to work together, both in times of suffering and in times of success (12:26). And leading into what is probably the best known chapter of the New Testament, Paul asks the Corinthians to "eagerly desire the greater gifts" (12:31).

The Gift of Love
(1 Corinthians 13)

If I speak in the tongues of men and of angels, but have not love, I am only a resounding gong or a clanging cymbal. If I have the gift of prophecy and can fathom all mysteries and all knowledge, and if I have a faith that can move mountains, but have not love, I am nothing. If I give all I possess to the poor and surrender my body to the flames, but have not love, I gain nothing.

Love is patient, love is kind. It does not envy, it does not boast, it is not proud. It is not rude, it is not self-seeking, it is not easily angered, it keeps no record of wrongs. Love does not delight in evil but rejoices with the truth. It always protects, always trusts, always hopes, always perseveres.

Love never fails. But where there are prophecies, they will cease; where there are tongues, they will be stilled; where there is knowledge, it will pass away. For we know in part and we prophesy in part, but when perfection comes, the imperfect disappears. When I was a child, I talked like a child, I thought like a child, I reasoned like a child. When I became a man, I put childish ways behind me. Now we see but a poor reflection as in a mirror; then we shall see face to face. Now I know in part; then I shall know fully, even as I am fully known.

And now these three remain: faith, hope and love. But the greatest of these is love.

Snapshots

With love guiding the thoughts and actions of believers, they are to identify and begin to use their spiritual gifts for the good of others. Lists of spiritual gifts can be found in Romans 12:6–8; 1 Corinthians 12:4–11, 28–30; and Ephesians 4:11–12.

Five Intelligible Words (1 Cor. 14)

In Corinth, spiritual gifts were being pursued without regard for the common bond of love. Speaking in tongues was gratifying, but it didn't do the group a lot of good unless someone could interpret what was being said. Paul had the gift of speaking in tongues, yet he said, "I would rather speak five intelligible words to instruct others than 10,000 words in a tongue" (14:18). He challenged his readers to "try to excel in gifts that build up the church" (14:12).

Even while using spiritual gifts, order was essential in the church (14:26–33). He instructed: "Women should remain silent in the churches. They are not allowed to speak, but must be in submission, as the Law says. If they want to inquire about something, they should ask their own husbands at home; for it is a disgrace for a woman to speak in the church" (14:34–35). Not surprisingly, these statements have not made Paul a popular hero among feminists. In Paul's defense, many people suggest he was addressing married women in this passage, allowing single women or those with unbelieving husbands to participate (11:5). Others feel there were a few particularly disruptive women to whom Paul was directing his comments. But however one feels about literal interpretation or cultural adaptation, the primary emphasis remains that order should be established and maintained for group worship settings.

Manna from Heaven

During times of harvest, **firstfruits** referred to the first sheaf of grain, which was dedicated to God. It was a symbol of the entire harvest, as well as for God's ownership of the crop. Paul's use of the word in regard to resurrection illustrates that Jesus would be the first to rise and return to God, but he would be followed by many others.

All Rise (1 Cor. 15–16)

Paul goes on to speak of his faith in Jesus' resurrection, without which the Christian faith is "futile" (15:17). Paul wanted people to realize that Jesus was only the first to rise—the "firstfruits" (15:20), to use a term his readers would be familiar with.

People who expect to awake from the dead and enter God's presence should have a different outlook on life than those who don't. Paul himself had risked his life repeatedly to tell people about Jesus and train them to live as Christians. If he weren't convinced of a literal resurrection, he might as well eat, drink, and die without going to so much trouble. He was persuaded, however, that the human (perishable) body would be replaced with a spiritual (imperishable) body (15:35–49). Not even death can put an end to the lives of those who believe in God. Paul also said that the day would come when certain believers would be changed "in a flash, in the twinkling of an eye," and would not experience death (15:51–52). This event is frequently referred to as the Rapture, which will be discussed in Chapter 23.

Same Church, Different Problems (2 Cor. 1–5)

The Book of 2 Corinthians is a follow-up letter by Paul—the most personal of any of his writings. The focus is a defense of his ministry. Although he affirms his commitment to the Corinthians, we learn that he is canceling a planned visit. Paul speaks of the fragility of Christians as "jars of clay" within which lie great treasure, and he reminds his readers that, "We are hard pressed on every side, but not crushed; perplexed, but not in despair; persecuted, but not abandoned; struck down, but not destroyed" (4:7–9).

Snapshots

Judgment's a'comin'—even for believers. If you're looking for insight, assurance, or tips for preparing, they're all in 2 Corinthians 5.

Tidings of Contusions and Joy (2 Cor. 6–9)

Paul begins to describe some of the hardships he has faced on behalf of his work: "troubles, hardships, and distresses; beatings, imprisonments, and riots; hard work, sleepless nights, and hunger" (6:4–5). He speaks of "having nothing, and yet possessing everything" (6:10). He is beginning to defend his credibility, because soon he will address some specific claims being made against him.

He also gave the Corinthians a warning: "Do not be yoked together with unbelievers" (6:14). If two combative animals are strapped together in the same yoke, not much productive work gets done. Similarly, Christians who bond too closely with nonbelievers eventually find themselves in conflict situations. This admonition is frequently applied to marriages, but is just as valid in business and other relationships where a different moral standard between two partners can lead to disputes. And in this specific reference, it might be that Paul is referring to false teachers who are impugning his reputation. If the church were to "yoke" itself to such impostors, much harm could be done.

Paul had a great deal of love for the Corinthian believers, but he found himself in a delicate situation. Being truthful might sound as if he were scolding them, when all he wanted was what was best for them. So he told them again how much he truly cared for them (7:2–16). He also challenged them in response to their giving to needy churches (8:1–9:15). He explained that the principle for giving was similar to planting crops: "Whoever sows sparingly will also reap sparingly, and whoever sows generously will also reap generously" (9:6).

Paul versus the Super-Apostles: A Grudge Match (2 Cor. 10–13)

Now Paul got down to business. Apparently a number of false teachers had been encroaching on the Corinthian believers, setting themselves up against Paul and making accusations to arouse suspicion toward him. Paul was placed in the uncomfortable position of "boasting" about himself and what he had done for God and for the church. He sarcastically refers to his adversaries as "super-apostles" (11:5; 12:11).

Paul felt strongly that his accusers were "false apostles, deceitful workmen, masquerading as apostles of Christ. And no wonder, for Satan himself masquerades as an angel of light" (11:13-14). Paul, for his part, had all the same credentials (11:21–23), and much more experience—not all of it pleasant. "I have worked much harder, been in prison more frequently, been flogged more severely, and been exposed to death again and again. Five times I received from the Jews the forty lashes minus one. Three times I was beaten with rods,

What Saith Thou?

What was Paul's "thorn in the flesh"? Some people speculate it might have been epilepsy, an eyesight problem, migraine headaches, some other physical ailment, or even his human adversaries. It seems to be something that threatened to impair his ministry, yet one he could count on God to overcome.

once I was stoned, three times I was shipwrecked, I spent a night and a day in the open sea, I have been constantly on the move. I have been in danger from rivers, in danger from bandits, in danger from my own countrymen, in danger from Gentiles; in danger in the city, in danger in the country, in danger at sea; and in danger from false brothers. I have labored and toiled and have often gone without sleep; I have known hunger and thirst and have often gone without food; I have been cold and naked. Besides everything else, I face daily the pressure of my concern for all the churches" (11:23–28).

He goes on with tantalizing hints about being "caught up to the third heaven" 14 years earlier, witnessing things he was not even permitted to talk about (2 Corinthians 12:1–6). It would be easy for someone to become proud at such knowledge; so, Paul added, "There was given me a thorn in my flesh, a messenger of Satan, to torment me. Three times I pleaded with the Lord to take it away from me. But he said to me, 'My grace is sufficient for you, for my power is made perfect in weakness.' Therefore I will boast all the more gladly about my weaknesses, so that Christ's power may rest on me. That is why, for Christ's sake, I delight in weaknesses, in insults, in hardships, in persecutions, in difficulties. For when I am weak, I am strong" (2 Corinthians 12:7–10).

Paul asserted that he considered himself "nothing," yet was not in the least inferior to any of the so-called "super-apostles" (12:11); indeed, he was willing to "speak in the sight of God" (12:19) about his own behavior. The Corinthian church, however, needed to do the same. Paul told them, "I am afraid that when I come I may not find you as I want you to be, and you may not find me as you want me to be. I fear that there may be quarreling, jealousy, outbursts of anger, factions, slander, gossip, arrogance, and disorder. I am afraid...I will be grieved over many who have sinned earlier and have not repented of the impurity, sexual sin, and debauchery in which they have indulged" (12:20–21).

Paul closed his letter with a challenge to the church to shape up, hoping that the firm tone of his letter would prevent a personal conflict when he arrived in person (13:10).

Same As It Ever Was

The problems in Corinth were not so different from those in many churches today: sexual problems, arrogance, cliques and factions among members, and a propensity to hear what they wanted to hear, even if the words came from false prophets. Could such a church really change?

Happily, the answer seems to have been yes. Paul did follow up his second letter with a personal visit. He had said he would spend as much time in Corinth as needed before going elsewhere in the area (10:15–16). He wrote the Book of Romans during this visit to Corinth, where he said, "There is no more place for me to work in these regions" (Romans 15:23). So it seems the Corinthians actually listened to Paul. What a surprise!

The next chapter continues the epistles of Paul. From here on, his letters are more "bite-sized." Yet, they contain numerous encouragements, exhortations, promises, and warnings that still apply to believers today.

The Least You Need to Know

➤ Paul's letters came to be accepted as Scripture and are included in the Bible.

➤ Paul's letter to the Romans focuses on the basics of the gospel message, explains essential concepts, and addresses questions about the rules governing Jews and Gentiles.

➤ The Books of 1 and 2 Corinthians were letters to a church with major problems, yet they are filled with encouragement, hope, and optimism.

Chapter 21

More of the Apostle's Epistles

> ### In This Chapter
>
> ➤ Paul's letter writing continues
>
> ➤ False teachers begin to infiltrate the church
>
> ➤ Paul serves as a spiritual mentor for younger church leaders
>
> ➤ Paul's views on salvation, the armor of God, Christian freedom, obedience and submission, the second coming of Jesus, and more

Suppose you're the CEO of a business that has just opened franchises throughout the world. It probably wouldn't be long before you were hearing from the managers about a variety of problems. Some complaints would very likely be similar—perhaps customers feel you're charging too much for licorice pudding. Others would apply specifically to a particular location (which is why McDonald's restaurants in India don't sell a lot of beef).

Paul found himself in a similar position. His extensive travels had resulted in the formation or growth of a number of different churches. As he wrote follow-up letters to them, much of what he says is similar because the churches were going through the same "growing pains." Other comments were specific to that community.

Galatian Salutations

Paul's letter to the Galatians was actually addressed to several churches. It was to be read and then copied and/or passed along to the next church. A specific problem faced by the people in this area was a group known as the Judaizers, who were trying to enforce certain Jewish traditions as requirements for Christianity. Especially at issue was circumcision. Jewish Christians who were a bit uncomfortable associating with Gentiles all of a sudden found themselves attracted to the arguments of the Judaizers. Paul felt that the message he had preached was under attack, and warned, "If anybody is preaching to you a gospel other than what you accepted, let him be eternally condemned!" (Galatians 1:9).

You might remember from Paul's travels in Acts that he had Timothy circumcised, which might suggest he agreed with the Judaizers. Yet in this instance he tells of traveling with another young Gentile Christian named Titus who was not circumcised because, "God does not judge by external appearance" (Galatians 2:1–6).

Paul also told of a confrontation he had with Peter, of all people. Peter had begun a ministry to Gentiles and had started eating and associating with them. Yet when other Jews visited who weren't quite so comfortable mixing with Gentiles, Peter also started separating himself from them. Even Barnabas was drawn into this practice of segregation. Paul called it "hypocrisy" and "opposed [Peter] to his face, because he was clearly in the wrong" (2:11–21).

Paul called his readers "you foolish Galatians!" (3:1) for trying to convert something that came freely from God's Spirit (salvation) into something that required "human effort" (circumcision). As far as God is concerned, Paul declared, "There is neither Jew nor Greek, slave nor free, male nor female, for you are all one in Christ Jesus" (3:28).

Potent Quotables

"I have been crucified with Christ and I no longer live, but Christ lives in me." (Galatians 2:20)

Paul saw his conversion as no less than the death of who he used to be and a new birth into whom God wanted him to be.

Since the Jews were the ones being drawn into the Judaizers' faulty doctrine, Paul gave a short lesson in Jewish history using Abraham, Sarah, Hagar, and Isaac to show that it was preferable to be "children of promise" who were free rather than remain slaves to the law (3–4). For Paul, the choice was between Jesus and freedom, or the law and slavery (5:1). This was no small decision. As for the Judaizers who insisted on circumcision, Paul wrote: "As for those agitators, I wish they would go the whole way and emasculate themselves!" (5:12) He sarcastically reasoned that if a little bit off the top was such a good thing, they could please God even more by lopping off the whole thing.

Finally, Paul challenged the Galatians to care for their own needs as well as those of others. "Each one should carry his own load," he writes, and also "carry each other's burdens" (6:2, 5). He reminded them, "Let us not become weary in doing good, for at the proper time we will reap a harvest if we do not give up" (6:9). Paul's desire was for Christians to grow in maturity, mutual responsibility, devotion to God, and love for one another.

Snapshots

Like a "Before " and "After" ad, Paul describes (in great detail) the difference an encounter with Jesus can make in a person's character. He contrasts the "acts of the sinful nature" with the "fruit of the Spirit" in Galatians 5:19–23.

An Emphasis on Ephesus

You may remember from Acts that Paul once spent more than two years in Ephesus—his longest recorded time in a single location (Acts 19:8–10). Ephesus was also where Paul got in trouble when his message threatened the income of the idol makers, who were dependent on the city's temple of Artemis. (Kids' tunics in the surrounding areas probably read, "Grandma went to Ephesus and all I got was this T-shirt and a lousy statue of Artemis.")

The letter to the Ephesians begins with a dense summary of a number of classic Christian themes, such as God's adoption of believers, redemption, forgiveness of sins, God's hidden purposes, and believers' inheritance in Christ.

And Paul makes it clear that such benefits to believers are bestowed by God rather than earned: "For it is by grace you have been saved, through faith—and this not from yourselves, it is the gift of God—not by works, so that no one can boast. For we are God's workmanship, created in Christ Jesus to do good works, which God prepared in advance for us to do" (Ephesians 2:8-10).

The letter speaks of Jesus as "the chief cornerstone" (2:20), the foundation upon which the rest of the building (the church) rests. With the Corinthians, Paul had used the human body as a symbol of many members comprising a unified whole. Here the same concept is illustrated by a holy temple made of many stones (2:19–22). Paul speaks of the "mystery" of the gospel—the fact that Gentiles were being united with Jews into the same body of believers (3:1–13). He goes on to pray that the Ephesians would come "to grasp how wide and long and high and deep is the love of Christ" because God "is able to do immeasurably more than all we ask or imagine" (3:18–20). Therefore he urged the Ephesians to "live a life worthy of the calling you have received" (4:1) by using their spiritual gifts, becoming spiritually mature, and "attaining to the whole measure of the fullness of Christ" (4:13).

According to Paul, faith should permeate daily living. He told the Ephesians to be humble, gentle, and patient with each other (4:2). Quit lying and start telling the truth (4:25). Learn to get angry without sinning and to settle disputes before the sun sets (4:26–27). Work for a living instead of stealing (4:28). Watch your language (4:29). Replace bitterness, wrath, brawling, slander, and all malice with kindness and compassion (4:31–32). Don't even hint or joke around about sexual immorality (5:3–5). Wise up and don't let anyone mislead you (5:6). Don't get drunk; be filled with the Holy Spirit instead (5:18). Submit to one another and encourage each other with thanksgiving and spiritually uplifting music (5:19–21).

As far as daily living within the home, Paul instructed women to submit to their husbands. Husbands, on the other hand, were commanded to love their wives "just as Christ loved the church and gave himself up for her" (5:25). It's too bad that with all the discussion about what the Bible says about the submission of women, many people never hear the second half of Paul's instructions. If husbands treated their wives like Jesus treated people, most wives would never have any complaints.

Continuing the theme of order in the households, the letter states that children are to obey their parents (6:1–3) and slaves their masters (6:5–9). Again, however, the relationship is viewed as a reciprocal one. Fathers should not exasperate their children. Masters should treat slaves with respect, without threatening them. Some people have

Potent Quotables

"For our struggle is not against flesh and blood, but against the rulers, against the authorities, against the powers of this dark world and against the spiritual forces of evil in the heavenly realms" (Ephesians 6:12).

used passages such as this one from Ephesians to defend slavery as "biblical." Slavery was a fact of life in the Roman empire, and Paul dealt with the situation he faced. He didn't dictate the circumstances. In addition, slavery had nothing to do with race in ancient times. Anyone could become a slave. Misfortunes ranging from military defeat to debt could force a person into slavery for months, years, or even a lifetime.

Paul's letter to the Ephesians ends with the image of a Christian as a warrior standing against "the devil's schemes," wearing the belt of truth, the breastplate of righteousness, the readiness that comes from the gospel of peace, the shield of faith, the helmet of salvation, and the sword of the Spirit (which is the word of God) (6:10–18).

Philippians: Don't Worry, Be Joyful

Paul's letter to the Philippians was written from prison, but you'd never know it. This is one of the most optimistic books of the Bible, with a repeated emphasis on joy. Paul was speaking from experience when he told his readers that, "he who began a good work in you will carry it on to completion until the day of Christ Jesus" (Philippians 1:6).

Paul was "in chains for Christ" (1:13), but his work had been helped by his imprisonment, not hindered. The imperial guard was hearing his message, and other people were stepping up to speak where Paul couldn't. Paul realized some such preachers were motivated by selfish ambition, but he wasn't bothered as long as what they said was true and other people got to hear the message.

At this point in his life, Paul said he could have been equally happy with life or death. Either way he would have it good: "For to me, to live is Christ and to die is gain. If I am to go on living in the body, this will mean fruitful labor for me. Yet what shall I choose? I do not know! I am torn between the two: I desire to depart and be with Christ, which is better by far; but it is more necessary for you that I remain in the body" (1:21–24).

Paul told the Philippians that they, too, could expect suffering for Christ's sake (1:29–30), and he challenged them to remain humble. Jesus was their example. Jesus had left heaven (where he was God) so he could be a servant to human beings. The result had been his humiliating crucifixion. But as a result, "God exalted him to the highest place and gave him the name that is above every name, that at the name of Jesus every knee should bow, in heaven and on earth and under the earth, and every tongue confess that Jesus Christ is Lord, to the glory of God the Father" (2:9–11).

Potent Quotables

"Do not be anxious about anything, but in everything, by prayer and petition, with thanksgiving, present your requests to God. And the peace of God, which transcends all understanding, will guard your hearts and your minds in Christ Jesus." (Philippians 4:6–7)

Paul warned the Philippians to watch out for people who didn't have their best interests in mind—especially those who promoted the necessity of circumcision. While acknowledging how much he had in common with these people, Paul felt he had moved on. "Whatever was to my profit I now consider loss for the sake of Christ" (3:7).

Roman citizenship was a big deal to the people of Philippi, a Roman colony. So Paul used citizenship as a metaphor for those who believed in Jesus: "Our citizenship is in heaven. And we eagerly await a Savior from there, the Lord Jesus Christ" (3:20).

Two women in the Philippian church had apparently been feuding. Paul pleaded with them to work out their problems. To the whole church he exhorted: "Rejoice in the Lord always. I will say it again: Rejoice!" (4:4)

The Philippians had collected a monetary gift for Paul, for which he thanked them. However, he said he had learned to be content in all circumstances; indeed, he was able to attest that, "I can do everything through him who gives me strength" (Philippians 4:13). Recalling that the Philippians had graciously shared what they had with him, Paul promised, "My God will meet all your needs according to his glorious riches in Christ Jesus" (4:20).

Snapshots

What's been on your mind lately? See if it meets Paul's criteria in Philippians 4:8.

Colossians: Who's Number One?

The Galatians and the Ephesians had the Judaizers to contend with; the Colossians had not only Judaizers but another group, one with a philosophy that came to be known as Gnosticism (based on the Greek for "knowledge"). Many Gnostics considered themselves orthodox Christians, yet preached a version of the gospel very different from Paul's. Most of their teachings are only hinted at in the Bible. However, it seems they too were a legalistic bunch who endorsed angel worship, the attainment of knowledge unknown to most people, and a life of self-imposed restrictions. They also downplayed the importance of Jesus.

Paul encouraged the Colossians not to be taken in by the teachers of falsehood. After all, God had already "rescued us from the dominion of darkness and brought us into the kingdom of the Son he loves" (1:13). He was the source of "the word of truth" (1:5–6). As for secret knowledge, Christians were privy to "the knowledge of [God's] will through all spiritual wisdom and understanding" (1:9). Paul wanted this church to know the Gnostics had nothing on them, and gave them a rousing defense of the supremacy of Christ:

➤ He is the image of the invisible God (1:15).

➤ He is the firstborn over all creation (including angels) (1:15).

➤ By him all things were created (1:16).

➤ He is before all things, and in him all things hold together (1:17).

➤ He is the head of the church (1:18).

➤ He is the firstborn from among the dead (1:18).

➤ The fullness of God dwells in him (1:19).

➤ He has the power to reconcile all things to God (1:20).

Paul's argument seeks to beat the Gnostics at their own game. As pagans, the Colossians had once been outsiders, estranged from God, but Christ had changed their status to that of insiders—provided they did not abandon the true gospel, "the mystery that has been kept hidden for ages and generations, but is now disclosed to the saints. To them God has chosen to make known among the Gentiles the glorious riches of this mystery, which is Christ in you, the hope of glory" (1:26–27). While the Gnostics kept searching for (and even paying to acquire) "secret" knowledge, God was readily revealing spiritual mysteries to those who turned to him.

Potent Quotables

Whatever you do, work at it with all your heart, as working for the Lord, not for men, since you know that you will receive an inheritance from the Lord as a reward. It is the Lord Christ you are serving. (Col. 3:23–24)

Rather than getting caught up in needless rules and regulations (2:16–23), Paul said it was far better to "set your hearts on things above, not earthly things" (3:2). Then Paul closes with a lengthy list of personal greetings (4:7-18).

One and Two Thessalonians: Guess Who's Coming (Back) to See Us?

Paul's first letter to the Thessalonians was among the earliest of his recorded epistles. Paul and Silas had preached in Thessalonica but, before long, had been run out of town by an angry mob (Acts 17:1–9). Still, Paul says, he didn't consider his time with the Thessalonians a failure (1 Thessalonians 2:1). The faith of those who had become believers was now famous in Macedonia and Achaia (1:4–10). Paul remembers them with great tenderness: "We loved you so much that we were delighted to share with you not only the gospel of God but our lives as well" (2:8).

When Paul and Silas had been unable to return to Thessalonica as they had hoped, they sent Timothy to spend some time with the believers. Paul was worried that they didn't have enough spiritual depth to sustain hard times, but to his great joy, Timothy had brought back a glowing report (2:17–3:10).

Paul's admonition to live a godly life was consequently brief. He gave them a vivid picture of the reward they could expect: "The Lord himself will come down from heaven, with a loud command, with the voice of the archangel and with the trumpet call of God, and the dead in Christ will rise first. After that, we who are still alive and are left will be caught up together with them in the clouds to meet the Lord in the air. And so we will be with the Lord forever" (4:16–17).

This event would occur suddenly—"like a thief in the night" (1 Thessalonians 5:2). Paul wasn't trying to scare the Thessalonian church into obedience. Quite the contrary! He wanted them to "encourage each other with these words" (4:18). The expectation of Jesus' return is supposed to be a source of joy and hope for believers.

What Saith Thou?

How can a person be expected to "pray continually" (1 Thessalonians 5:17)?

Paul's definition of prayer may be broader than what we're used to. Rather than being an occasional obligation, he saw prayer as the privilege and opportunity of staying in touch with God throughout each day, as much as possible. (The Greek word for "continually" was also used to describe a hacking cough.) Paul seemed to view prayer more as an inner attitude than an external expression.

Lest any attempt to use that expectation as an excuse for idleness, however, Paul's next words uphold the value of hard work (5:12, 14). Then he concludes: "Be joyful always; pray continually; give thanks in all circumstances, for this is God's will for you in Christ Jesus. Do not put out the Spirit's fire" (5:16–19).

Paul's follow-up letter to the church (2 Thessalonians) was similar to the first. He again implores the people to remain faithful, to give thanks to God, and to look forward to the second coming of Jesus. He told them, "The secret power of lawlessness is already at work; but the one who now holds it back will continue to do so till he is taken out of the way. And then the lawless one will be revealed, whom the Lord Jesus will overthrow with the breath of his mouth and destroy by the splendor of his coming" (2 Thessalonians 2:7–8). For a while, however, "The coming of the lawless one will be in accordance with the work of Satan displayed in all kinds of counterfeit miracles, signs and wonders, and in every sort of evil that deceives those who are perishing" (2:9–10).

Their future was not in doubt, according to Paul. He promised them, "The Lord is faithful, and he will strengthen and protect you from the evil one" (3:3).

Paul as Mentor (1 and 2 Timothy; Titus)

Unlike the other letters we've studied, 1 and 2 Timothy and the letter to Titus are addressed to individuals. All three have a teaching purpose: They describe the characteristics of an effective church leader.

Timothy was the person who had joined Paul on his travels—the one Paul had circumcised on account of his Gentile father. But Timothy's mother and grandmother are noted for their faith (2 Timothy 1:5), so Timothy probably received the basic teachings of Judaism and then Christianity from them.

Paul begins by warning Timothy about teachers of false doctrines (1 Timothy 1:3–11), contrasting such teachings with the grace and mercy of God (1:12–20). Paul spoke of his own old life in contrast with his new life as a Christian, challenging Timothy to "fight the good fight, holding on to faith and a good conscience" (1 Timothy 1:18–19).

It wasn't always easy, as indicated by Paul's mention of Hymenaeus and Alexander, two men he had "handed over to Satan"—put out of church fellowship until they could learn not to blaspheme (1 Timothy 1:20).

Paul refers to himself as "the worst" among sinners (1 Timothy 1:15). Aren't such self-deprecating statements to be avoided by people who believe they were created in God's image and are among His children?

Paul's expectations for church leaders were quite specific: "The overseer must be above reproach, the husband of but one wife, temperate, self-controlled, respectable, hospitable, able to teach, not given to drunkenness, not violent but gentle, not quarrelsome, not a lover of money. He must manage his own family well and see that his children obey him with proper respect.... He must not be a recent convert.... He must also have a good reputation with outsiders, so that he will not fall into disgrace and into the devil's trap" (1 Timothy 3:2–7). A similar list is provided for deacons (3:8–13).

A lengthy section addresses how the leader should behave toward young and old; another looks at how to care for widows (5:1–21), a numerous segment of in the early church. All elderly, he charges, should be treated with special respect. Additional advice for church leaders follows: be direct with listeners (4:4–6), forget myths and legends and stick to the truth (4:7), train spiritually as intently as some people train physically (4:8), be diligent and don't neglect your pastoral gift (4:14–16).

Paul's views were conservative by today's standards, but they weren't legalistic. He tells Timothy to "stop drinking only water, and use a little wine because of your stomach and your frequent illnesses" (5:23). Speaking about evil people who would rather get rich than seek God, Paul said that

What Saith Thou?

While there is certainly no value in *false* modesty, it can also be argued that the better someone comes to know God, the clearer the person sees his or her sinfulness. It's interesting to note Paul's comments across time. In 1 Corinthians (believed to be written in 55 A.D.) Paul refers to himself as "the least of the apostles" (1 Corinthians 15:9). In Ephesians (A.D. 60), he calls himself "less than the least of all God's people" (Ephesians 3:8). To Timothy he writes (probably between 63 and 66 A.D.) that, "Christ Jesus came into the world to save sinners of whom I am the worst." It's not that Paul was feeling worse about himself. Rather, his awareness of God was expanding, and he saw himself smaller in contrast.

Potent Quotables

"Don't let anyone look down on you because you are young, but set an example for the believers in speech, in life, in love, in faith and in purity." (1 Timothy 4:12)

"the love of money is a root of all kinds of evil" (6:10). It's not the money itself but the attitude toward it that creates problems. This is borne out in Paul's later instruction: "Command those who are rich in this present world not to be arrogant nor to put their hope in wealth, which is so uncertain, but to put their hope in God" (6:17).

2 Timothy

By the time Paul wrote his second letter to Timothy, his conditions had changed. He was in a dungeon expecting to die. According to one tradition, Paul was beheaded not long after writing this letter. A close reading seems to reveal a sense of urgency in his instructions to Timothy.

Paul encouraged Timothy to be bold in representing Jesus (2 Timothy 1:5–10). He explained that "God did not give us a spirit of timidity, but a spirit of power, of love, and of self-discipline" (1:7). Many of Paul's other associates had deserted him (1:15), so Timothy's continued friendship was much valued. In considering the hardships of Christian life, Paul compared Christians to soldiers (who live to please their commanding officer), athletes (who must obey the rules if they expect to win the prize), and farmers (who work hard, have patience, and eventually receive the payoff of the harvest).

Paul told Timothy, "Flee the evil desires of youth, and pursue righteousness, faith, love, and peace along with those who call on God out of a pure heart. Don't have anything to do with foolish and stupid arguments, because you know they produce quarrels" (2 Timothy 2:22–23).

The last days are coming, warned Paul, and there will be signs to look for: "People will be lovers of themselves, lovers of money, boastful, proud, abusive, disobedient to their parents, ungrateful, unholy, without love, unforgiving, slanderous, without self-control, brutal, not lovers of the good, treacherous, rash, conceited, lovers of pleasure rather than lovers of God—having a form of godliness but denying its power" (2 Timothy 3:2–5). Sounds like the nightly news.

The best defense is a good spiritual offense: "Continue in what you have learned and have become convinced of, because you know those from whom you have learned it, and how from infancy you have known the holy Scriptures, which are able to make you wise for salvation through faith in Christ Jesus" (3:14–15). Paul had absolute confidence in the accuracy and authenticity of scripture (3:16).

Finally, Paul tells Timothy to preach and be prepared for any opportunity, demonstrating great patience and careful instruction (4:1). Before long, he said, many people would be receptive only to teachers who "say what their itching ears want to hear" (4:3).

Potent Quotables

"I have fought the good fight, I have finished the race, I have kept the faith. Now there is in store for me the crown of righteousness, which the Lord, the righteous Judge, will award to me on that day." (2 Timothy 4:7–8) After a lifetime of faithful service, Paul could face death with complete confidence.

This time as Paul sent his greetings, he implored Timothy to visit him as soon as possible. He also asked for John Mark, which is an encouraging biblical note (4:11). You might remember that before Paul's second journey, he and Barnabas argued so strongly about taking Mark (Paul was opposed) that they split up (Acts 15:36–41). But now, years later, Paul says of Mark: "He is helpful to me in my ministry."

Titus

Like Timothy, Titus had traveled with Paul on occasion, and the two were close. Apparently, Paul and Titus were responsible for taking the Christian gospel to Crete, and Titus had remained there to get the church up and running (Titus 1:5).

Paul gave Titus similar criteria for appointing leaders as he had given Timothy (Titus 1:6–9; 2:1–15). Faithfulness to the gospel was especially important in Crete because the people there had a widespread reputation for lying, laziness, and generally being up to no good (1:10–14). Paul asserted that the Christian believers needed to establish and uphold a much higher standard by being subject to their rulers, peaceable and considerate to one another, and generally humble toward everyone. Paul warned Titus to "avoid foolish controversies and genealogies and arguments and quarrels about the law, because these are unprofitable and useless" (3:9). He also recommended a "third strike" rule for dealing with troublemakers. Belligerent people were to get two warnings. If they refused to change, they were to be avoided by believers from that point onward (3:10–11).

Philemon: A Runaway Slave Makes A Round Trip

Philemon is Paul's last and shortest letter—and his most personal. It seems that Philemon, a Christian, had a slave named Onesimus, who had stolen some of Philemon's property and fled. While on the lam, Onesimus bumped into Paul (a prisoner at the time) and became a Christian. Having persuaded him to return to his owner, Paul gave Onesimus a letter in which he entreated Philemon's forgiveness for the converted slave.

Paul's strategy is masterful. He had the authority to command Philemon to take back his slave, he says, but he'd rather ask nicely (vv. 8–9). Actually, he had found Onesimus useful and would have liked to keep him around, but he was trying to do the right thing to restore the broken relationship. Then Paul springs the punch line. He asks Philemon to receive Onesimus as a fellow Christian, no longer as a piece of property. Paul even offered to pay for anything Onesimus might owe (v. 18).

Manna from Heaven

Onesimus means "useful," and Paul enjoys playing on the name. "Mr. Useful" hadn't lived up to his name at first. Yet eventually Paul could write: *"Formerly he was useless to you, but [since his conversion] he has become useful both to you and to me"* (v. 11).

This short story points out some of the strange goings-on in the early church as both slaves and masters became Christians.

Paul's letters show him to be a caring and insightful leader. He could be direct and say hard things when he needed to, but he seemed to prefer to encourage. Just as he had "died" to his old self and had been raised with Christ, he wanted everyone else to know the joy and hope of the Christian path toward God.

> ### The Least You Need to Know
>
> ➤ Not all of Paul's letters survived, but those that did offer a window into his life and ministry.
>
> ➤ Paul's epistles were written from a variety of places to a variety of churches and people, addressing concerns both general and specific.
>
> ➤ Although Paul isn't reluctant to challenge and correct, he was clearly motivated by his love for the churches and his desire to do everything possible to strengthen growing Christians.

Chapter 22

Still More People Doing the Write Thing

In This Chapter

➤ The Book of Hebrews connects Old Testament traditions with New Testament doctrines

➤ Letters from James, Peter, John, and Jude

➤ False teachings compete with the gospel message

Some people choose their reading material on the basis of the author alone. They find someone they like and read everything he or she ever wrote. Others enjoy more variety and appreciate the nuances and stylistic differences of diverse authors.

The past two chapters focused on the writings of the Apostle Paul. Now we're moving into the writings of some of Paul's associates. While some of the content of these letters will be familiar, we will also encounter some new ideas and perspectives.

Hebrews: Everything Old Is New Again

The author of the Book of the Hebrews remains a mystery. People speculate it might have been Paul, Barnabas, Apollos, Luke, Philip, or even Priscilla. But barring a major archaeological discovery, we will probably never know for sure.

The theme of Hebrews is that the life, death, and resurrection of Jesus fulfill and build upon the groundwork established in the Old Testament. To establish this argument, the author sets about to demonstrate the uniqueness (and superiority) of Jesus. First, he says Jesus is superior to the angels (Hebrews 1–2). God never claimed any of the angels as a son (1:5). The angels are servants as Jesus was, yet Jesus has a throne "that will last for ever and ever" (1:8). Besides, the angels worship Jesus (1:6). While Jesus was a human being, he was "made a little lower than the angels," like other human beings (2:6–7), but this "demotion" was only temporary. After his resurrection, Jesus was "crowned with glory and honor" (2:9).

Second, the author says that Jesus is greater than Moses (3–4:13). Moses built God's house, but Jesus was the architect (3:2–6). In addition, Jesus did away with the need for the curtain that shielded the Most Holy Place—the very presence of God. Both were surrounded by unbelievers, but Moses finally cracked under the pressure (Numbers 20:2–13), whereas Jesus saw his mission through to its painful and humiliating conclusion on the cross.

Potent Quotables

The word of God is living and active. Sharper than any double-edged sword, it penetrates even to dividing soul and spirit, joints and marrow; it judges the thoughts and attitudes of the heart. Nothing in creation is hidden from God's sight. Everything is uncovered and laid bare before the eyes of him to whom we must give account. (Hebrews 4:12–13)

Third, the author writes that Jesus is superior to Aaron (Moses' brother and Israel's first high priest) or any Old Testament high priest (4:14–10). The high priests had to meet certain qualifications and then be chosen by God to serve. Jesus was more than qualified to represent his people before God, and he was certainly chosen by God to save the world from its sins (5:8–9).

The writer calls Jesus "a high priest forever, in the order of Melchizedek" (5:10; 6:20). Melchizedek served as the priest to whom Abraham paid tribute (Genesis 14). Before the law was established, Melchizedek was a priest for God. Under the law, priests had to come from the tribe of Levi, but Melchizedek predated the tribes. So although Jesus was not a Levite (he came from the tribe of Judah) he had nevertheless fulfilled the role of high priest, "not on the basis of a regulation as to his ancestry but on the basis of the power of an indestructible life" (Hebrews 7:16).

Potent Quotables

For we do not have a high priest who is unable to sympathize with our weaknesses, but we have one who has been tempted in every way, just as we are—yet was without sin. Let us then approach the throne of grace with confidence, so that we may receive mercy and find grace to help us in our time of need. (Hebrews 4:15–16)

The priesthood of Jesus is also exceptional in its effectiveness. "Unlike the other high priests, he does not need to offer sacrifices day after day, first for his own sins, and then for the sins of the people. He sacrificed for their sins once for all when he offered himself" (7:27).

God has established a new covenant with his people, one based on the mediation of Jesus between people and God. This new covenant makes the previous one obsolete (8:6-13). Under the old covenant, only the high priest could enter the Most Holy Place, and then only once a year after making a blood sacrifice for his own sins and the sins of the people. The author of Hebrews didn't downplay the importance of the Law. Rather, it was described as "only a shadow of the good things that are coming" (10:1). The offering of animal sacrifices was "an annual reminder of sins" (10:3), but "it is impossible for the blood of bulls and goats to take away sins" (10:4). The blood of Jesus, however, got the job done "once for all" (9:12, 26), making him a far superior high priest.

For Christians, the difference between the former covenant and the new one has to do with accessibility to God. If the sins of believers no longer separate them from a holy God, the relationship between people and God can become much stronger. So the author of Hebrews sets forth a number of challenges (10:22–25):

Manna from Heaven

In Hebrews 9:4 we get an inventory of what was kept in the Ark of the Covenant in the tabernacle: a gold jar of manna (Exodus 16:33), Aaron's staff that budded (Numbers 17:1–11), and the stone tablets of the covenant—the Ten Commandments (Exodus 25:16, 21).

➤ "Let us draw near to God with a sincere heart in full assurance of faith."

➤ "Let us hold unswervingly to the hope we profess, for he who promised is faithful."

➤ "Let us consider how we may spur one another on toward love and good deeds."

➤ "Let us not give up meeting together, as some are in the habit of doing, but let us encourage one another—and all the more as you see the day approaching."

Along with the challenges are some warnings. In effect, the author says "This is it." If people reject this sacrifice for their sins, there are no other options. God remains a judge, and "it is a dreadful thing to fall into the hands of the living God" (10:30–31).

Because faith makes belief possible, the next section of Hebrews looks at the Bible's "Faith Hall of Fame," citing patriarchs, prophets, judges, and even Rahab the prostitute as examples of faithful persons. It was faith, the author asserts, that made Abel's sacrifice acceptable when Cain's wasn't. Faith allowed Enoch to escape death. Noah's faith kept him afloat when others were sinking. The list continues through Abraham, Joseph, Moses, Samson, David, Samuel, and the prophets. Moreover, faith allowed God's people to endure numerous trials that otherwise would have been too severe: lions, flames, imprisonment, torture, humiliation, stonings, poverty, and more.

Potent Quotables

Now faith is being sure of what we hope for and certain of what we do not see.... And without faith it is impossible to please God, because anyone who comes to him must believe that he exists and that he rewards those who earnestly seek him. (Hebrews 11:1, 6)

Yet all these faithful people, the author declares, died without receiving what God had promised—a Messiah. Now that the Christ has come, everyone

Potent Quotables

Do not forget to entertain strangers, for by so doing some people have entertained angels without knowing it. (Hebrews 13:2)

Abraham and others in the Bible encountered angels, and the producers of certain television programs would like us to think it still happens frequently.

What Saith Thou?

Is James kidding or what? How are we supposed to be giddy about the lousy experiences of life?

In a spiritual sense, joy is not a synonym for happiness. Rather, the deep sorrows of life can reveal a spiritual joy based on Jesus' promise that "great is your reward in heaven" (Matthew 5:12) when such things occur. It's a more optimistic outlook, but along the same lines of Nietzsche's philosophy that, "Whatever doesn't kill me makes me stronger." Joy is spiritual fruit (Galatians 5:22) and evidence that God is active in the life of a believer.

who believes verifies the faith of those who came before. "God had planned something better for us so that only together with us would they be made perfect" (11:40). And he describes these ancestors as "a great cloud of witnesses" watching and waiting for us to act. Therefore, "Let us throw off everything that hinders and the sin that so easily entangles, and let us run with perseverance the race marked out for us. Let us fix our eyes on Jesus, the author and perfecter of our faith, who for the joy set before him endured the cross, scorning its shame, and sat down at the right hand of God" (12:1–2).

Faith requires discipline and persistence. Believers must learn to endure hardship (12:7) and to live in peace with each other (12:14). They must "see to it...that no bitter root grows up to cause trouble and defile many" (12:15). They are to keep treating one another as brothers and sisters (13:1). Remember those in prison (13:3). Keep the marriage bed pure (13:4). Don't love money (13:5). Obey those in authority (13:17). And continually offer God a "sacrifice of praise" (13:15).

James: Uncommonly Common Sense

The Book of Hebrews begins with a theological approach and ends up with some practical advice. Immediately afterward comes the Book of James, a common sense guide for living a better Christian life.

No Wonder Mom Liked Big Brother Better

Of the four men named James in the New Testament, most people believe the author of this book was Jesus' brother (probably the next oldest child of Mary). Although he didn't believe in Jesus as the son of God to begin with, he did so later and became a leader of the church in Jerusalem.

Jesus had told his listeners to rejoice and be glad "when people insult you, persecute you, and falsely say all kinds of evil against you" (Matthew 5:11–12). James' letter begins, "Consider it pure joy, my brothers, whenever you face trials of many kinds, because you know that the testing of your faith develops perseverance" (1:2–3).

God doesn't want us to have any holes in our spiritual arsenal, James explains. If believers are missing something, they are to ask God in faith, without doubting. God will provide for those who trust him (James 1:5–8).

James also echoes Jesus' teachings that humility will be rewarded. Rich people can prosper spiritually as long as they realize that power and position are only temporary. Perseverance under trial is more important than being able to buy one's way out of a tight spot (1:9–12).

James refuted the common perception that evil and misfortune come from God. God never tempts anyone to do evil, he said; God sends us only the best. "Don't be deceived, my dear brothers. Every good and perfect gift is from above, coming down from the Father of the heavenly lights, who does not change like shifting shadows" (1:16–17). As a result, we should pursue righteousness. In doing so: "Everyone should be quick to listen, slow to speak and slow to become angry" (James 1:19-20).

Bible, Bible on the Wall

James compares the Bible to a mirror. Suppose a person gets up in the morning, looks in a mirror, and discovers he or she is afflicted with bed head, spinach between the teeth, and an assortment of crusty substances around the eyes, nose, and mouth. Would the person shrug and go to work? Not likely! Having seen his or her physical shortcomings in the mirror, the person would want to take care of whatever was amiss. Similarly when someone looks into the Bible and sees places where he or she comes up short, that person should take action. Or as James says, "Do not merely listen to the word, and so deceive yourselves. Do what it says" (1:22–25).

James warned against church members showing favoritism based on wealth. He had observed certain people playing up to the richer members. Love for one another does not discriminate, he reminded his audience (2:1–13). He had especially harsh words for wealthy people who abused others simply because they were able to do so (5:1–6).

What Saith Thou?

Doesn't James contradict Paul in his outlook on faith?

Paul had written, "It is by grace you have been saved, through faith...not by works, so that no one can boast" (Ephesians 2:8–9). James says, "What good is it...if a man claims to have faith but has not deeds?... Faith by itself, if it is not accompanied by action, is dead" (James 2:14, 17). Paul downplays "works," while James emphasizes them. The difference is that Paul is speaking to a predominantly Gentile audience about *salvation*, whereas James is talking to (mostly) Jewish believers about appropriate Christian behavior.

Hebrews emphasizes the importance of faith; James emphasizes the importance of actions as *proof* of faith. How else can you model something so intangible? James insists that "deeds" make the difference. *Active* faith is what changes lives (2:14–26).

Snapshots

A riddle from James: What do Abraham, Rahab the Jericho prostitute, and demons have in common? (Answer: James 2:18–26)

It's Hard to Lick Your Own Tongue

James's next observations apply to the power of our tongues. If we could only control them, he suggests, we would be a lot closer to perfection. It takes only a small bit to control a large horse, or a small rudder to control a large ship. But the tongue is like a spark that can take down an entire forest. One minute we use it to praise God, and the next we're swearing at a neighbor. "My brothers, this should not be" (3:1–12).

Truly wise people learn to control their tongues, which includes not boasting about such an accomplishment! Wisdom that is accompanied by "bitter envy and selfish ambition" is not genuine wisdom. True wisdom is accompanied by humility and good deeds, and results in peace, mercy, sincerity, and other virtues (3:13–18).

Then, as now, greed was a major source of conflict, tempting people to quarrel, fight, covet, or kill. Instead, James says, we should ask God for what we need. "Humble yourselves before the Lord, and he will lift you up" (4:10). Humility before God also requires acknowledging that God may have plans for us that we haven't made for ourselves. When telling one another our plans for the future, it's a good idea to add the phrase, "If it is the Lord's will" (4:15). James' readers should have been familiar with the Old Testament proverb: "Many are the plans in a man's heart, but it is the Lord's purpose that prevails" (Proverbs 19:21).

Often God's will is difficult to determine. Christians must learn to wait for it as a farmer waits for crops to grow. Patience and perseverance are much better ways to pass the time than grumbling. James reminds his readers of the patience of the prophets who spoke for God with little reward, and of Job who was eventually rewarded for the great perseverance he displayed in the face of difficulties. James also urges people not to use oaths. Rather, it is better to "let your 'Yes' be yes, and your 'No,' no" (James 5:7–12).

Finally, James reminds us of the importance of prayer. Active prayer might involve songs of praise, calling in the elders of the church for healing of sicknesses, or confessing sins to one another and to God. It is also important to minister to Christians who have strayed from a godly lifestyle. Because "Whoever turns a sinner from the error of his way will save him from death and cover over a multitude of sins" (James 5:20).

Peter's Priority Mail

Like the letter of James, Peter's letters are also practical in their approach. They set forth guidelines for living a holy life in the midst of a pagan society, including patiently, enduring of the suffering that will inevitably result—and indeed, that Peter's audience had probably already experienced.

An Invitation to Join the Priesthood

Peter begins his first letter by reminding his audience of their "new birth" and the "inheritance that can never perish, spoil or fade—kept in heaven for you" (1 Peter 1: 3–4). Christians should not be surprised when they have to suffer. "Now for a little while you may have had to suffer grief in all kinds of trials. These have come so that your faith—of greater worth than gold, which perishes even though refined by fire—may be proved genuine and may result in praise, glory and honor when Jesus Christ is revealed" (1:6–7).

Lest believers become indifferent or begin to take the gospel for granted, Peter reminds his readers that prophets and angels longed to witness the salvation of God before it arrived (1:10–12). Christians should therefore be motivated to be holy because God is holy (1:13–16).

Referring to the experience of salvation, Peter uses the term "born again" (1:23) because new Christians, like newborn infants, have a lot of growing and learning to do. They must rid themselves of "all malice and all deceit, hypocrisy, envy, and slander of every kind. Like newborn babies, crave pure spiritual milk, so that by it you may grow up in your salvation now that you have tasted that the Lord is good" (2:1–3).

To some people's surprise, "born again" isn't a frequent phrase in the Bible. Jesus used it with Nicodemus (John 3:3, 7) and Peter uses it a couple of times, but that's about it.

Echoing Paul (Ephesians 2:20), Peter speaks of Jesus as the chief cornerstone with believers as other "living stones" that "are being built into a spiritual

Manna from Heaven

Holiness entails "separation from sin," and is one of the characteristics of God. Believers remove themselves from previous sinful influences or practices and set themselves apart for (holy) service to God. In doing so, they become more like him.

house to be a holy priesthood" (1 Peter 2:5). Christians become "aliens and strangers in the world" (2:11), and Peter advises them to lead such good lives that even unbelievers who accuse them of doing wrong will be impressed by their good deeds (2:12).

Imitating the Savior's Behavior

Christian behavior includes submission and respect for "every authority," including kings, governors, masters, and those who are kind and gentle as well as those who are harsh (2:13–18.) The example of submission was Jesus, who "suffered for you, leaving you an example, that you should follow in his steps" (2:21–25).

Peter agreed with Paul that wives should be submissive to their husbands, but he had more respect for women than merely relegating them to "trophy wife" status. Peter went on to explain that the real beauty of a woman didn't come from "outward adornment" of hairstyles, jewelry, or clothes. Rather, women should be aware of "the unfading beauty of a gentle and quiet spirit, which is of great worth in God's sight" (3:4). In addition, Peter commanded husbands to treat their wives with respect (3:7). These were cutting-edge teachings in a society where women were given little more respect than servants.

Peter advised, "Always be prepared to give an answer to everyone who asks you to give the reason for the hope that you have. But do this with gentleness and respect, keeping a clear conscience" (3:15–16). Because everyone can expect a degree of suffering in life, Peter says it's better to suffer for doing good than for doing evil (3:17). The end of all things is near (4:7), he says, so Christians must clean up their behavior and set positive examples for the rest of the world (4:3-11). Above all, they should "love each other deeply, because love covers over a multitude of sins" (4:8).

Potent Quotables

Be self-controlled and alert. Your enemy the devil prowls around like a roaring lion looking for someone to devour. (1 Peter 5:8)

Rather than bickering with each other, hoarding money, and abusing power, Christians should model submission and humility (5:1–5). As they learn to humble themselves before God, they discover grace to get through any situation, as well as release from all their anxiety (5:5–6). Peter's final promise in this first letter is that after a short period of suffering, "The God of all grace…will himself restore you and make you strong, firm, and steadfast" (5:10).

Peter signs off from "Babylon," a nickname for Rome that came into use after Rome destroyed Jerusalem in the year 70. The Book of Revelation similarly identifies the city of Rome as "Babylon."

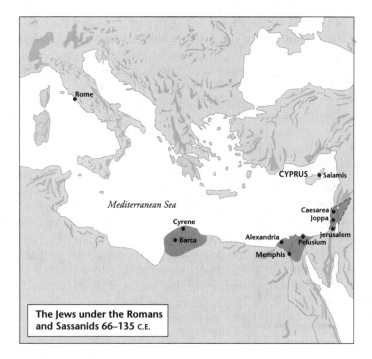

The Jews under the Romans and Sassanids 66–135 C.E.

Just a Second Peter

Peter's second letter addresses heresy and division in the churches. Reminding his readers of the abundant gifts of God that would sustain them (2 Peter 1:2–5), he urges them to "make every effort to add to your faith goodness; and to goodness, knowledge; and to knowledge, self-control; and to self-control, perseverance; and to perseverance, godliness; and to godliness, brotherly kindness; and to brotherly kindness, love" (1: 5–7). Becoming Christ-like was not a one-time event, but a lifelong process.

"We did not follow cleverly invented stories when we told you about the power and coming of our Lord Jesus Christ," Peter writes, "but we were eyewitnesses of his majesty" (1:16). He warns that false teachers would prove bolder than angels when it came to perverting the message of God. And if God had not spared the sinning angels, he would certainly deal with defiant human beings. Yet God was capable of protecting the faithful people among the corrupt. He had taken care of Noah while the rest of the world drowned, and he had rescued Lot from the destruction of Sodom and Gomorrah. Peter could say with certainty that, "The Lord knows how to rescue godly men from trials and to hold the unrighteous for the day of judgment, while continuing their punishment" (2:9). God had rebuked the false prophet Balaam with a talking donkey (Numbers 22), and he would also confront the false prophets who were threatening the first-century Christians (2 Peter 2:13–22).

The skeptics of the first century were not unlike those of our time. While believers taught that Jesus would return, the skeptics were already "scoffing" because he hadn't yet done so. Peter explained that God's timetable is not like our own. If Jesus seems slow in returning, it's for the benefit of the people who are slow to believe in him. When he does return, "the day of the Lord will come like a thief. The heavens will disappear with a roar; the elements will be destroyed by fire, and the earth and everything in it will be laid bare" (3:10).

Peter advises the faithful to keep from getting too caught up in what the false teachers were saying, or become overly distressed by their taunts. God would deal with them—as well as believers—in due time. As long as Christians maintained holy and godly lives, they need not worry about the jeers or threats of scoffers. Rather, "we are looking forward to a new heaven and a new earth, the home of righteousness" (3:13). Believers are to be on guard to keep from being deceived, and in the meantime should "grow in the grace and knowledge of our Lord and Savior Jesus Christ" (3:17–18).

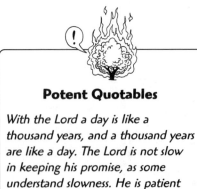

Potent Quotables

With the Lord a day is like a thousand years, and a thousand years are like a day. The Lord is not slow in keeping his promise, as some understand slowness. He is patient with you, not wanting anyone to perish, but everyone to come to repentance. (2 Peter 3:8–9)

Dear John Letters

The next epistles (1 John, 2 John, and 3 John) are accepted by tradition as the writings of John, the disciple of Jesus—the same John who wrote the fourth gospel and the Book of Revelation. Unlike most of the other writers, he doesn't identify himself. It's not unusual, however, because even in his gospel he always identified himself in the third person as "the disciple whom Jesus loved."

John, like most of the other epistle writers, was faced with false teachers and young, immature believers. He attests that, "God is light; in him there is no darkness at all" (1 John 1:5). So-called believers who claim a relationship with God but continue to walk in darkness expose themselves as liars. John declares that those who hate fellow Christians don't really love God (2:9–10). Moreover, we need not try to hide our sins, because it is clear that everyone sins. It is far better to confess them, because when we do, "we have one who speaks to the Father in our defense—Jesus Christ, the Righteous One" (1:8–9; 2:1).

It is impossible, says John, to love the things of God and the things of the world at the same time (2:15). The standards are diametrically opposed and mutually exclusive. In this context he introduces the term *antichrists* (2:18, 22), defined as anyone "who denies the Father and the Son." In Revelation he will write about *the* antichrist, a single figure who epitomizes this attitude.

John invites Christians to dwell on the great love of God that has been "lavished on us" (3:1). Because of God's love, we can be called his children, and indeed we shall be like him someday (3:2). Consequently, we need to show deeper levels of love to each other: "This is how we know what love is: Jesus Christ laid down his life for us. And we ought to lay down our lives for our brothers. If anyone has material possessions and sees his brother in need but has no pity on him, how can the love of God be in him?" (3:16–17)

John instructs believers to "test the spirits to see whether they are from God" (4:2). The spirit of the antichrist does not acknowledge "that Jesus Christ has come in the flesh" (4:2–3). But the promise to believers is that "the one who is in you is greater than the one who is in the world" (4:4).

Christianity doesn't work because we love God. On the contrary, it works because God "loved us and sent his son as an atoning sacrifice for our sins" (4:10). Love isn't just a nice thing Christians are supposed to do. It is the very basis of our faith. Therefore, "since God loved us, we also ought to love one another. No one has ever seen God; but if we love one another, God lives in us and his love is made complete in us" (4:11–12).

John defines God as love (4:7–9, 16) and says, "There is no fear in love. But perfect love drives out fear, because fear has to do with punishment. The one who fears is not made perfect in love" (4:18). John also asks: If believers don't love each other when we can see, hear, and touch one another, how do we dare claim to love God (4:19–21)?

Therefore, obedience to God and love for one another are intertwined and are the things that allow believers to "overcome the world" (5:1–12). We can have confidence to approach God with our needs, knowing that "if we ask anything according to his will, he hears us. And if we know that he hears us—whatever we ask—we know that we have what we asked of him" (5:14–15).

The second letter of John, addressed to "the elect lady and her children" (a Christian congregation) is written specifically to warn its audience of false teachers, a growing menace (2 John 7–8).

John advocates separation from false teachers: "If anyone comes to you and does not bring this teaching [that Jesus was truly God], do not take him into your house or welcome him. Anyone who welcomes him shares in his wicked work" (2 John 9–11).

The third epistle of John was addressed to someone named Gaius. John had received word of Gaius' faithfulness and wrote to encourage him, saying that, "I have no greater joy than to hear that my children are walking in the truth" (3 John 4). He commended Gaius for showing hospitality and respect for some teachers he had sent to preach the gospel.

What Saith Thou?

Why does John say that no one has seen God? Lots of people saw him, right?

God appeared in various forms to Moses, Abraham, Jacob, Isaiah, Ezekiel, and others. Jesus was a form of God (John 14:9). Yet no one has experienced God's full glory: "You cannot see my face, for no one may see me and live." (Exodus 33:20)

Jude Says Hey

The last of the epistles in the New Testament is written by someone identifying himself as Jude (a variation of Judas). Scholars have speculated as to which of several men this might be, but one common belief is that this was another half-brother of Jesus (because Jude says he is "a brother of James" [Jude 1:1]).

It appears that Jude wanted to sit down and write his friends a perky and enthusiastic letter (v. 3), but he found it necessary to warn them of false teachers instead. (You probably see a trend developing by now.) Like other epistle writers, Jude wasn't very tolerant of such people: "Certain men whose condemnation was written about long ago have secretly slipped in among you. They are godless men, who change the grace of our God into a license for immorality and deny Jesus Christ our only Sovereign and Lord" (v. 4).

In a mini-history lesson, Jude reminds his readers that God always comes through for his people, even while destroying those who oppose him. This was true for the Israelites in Egypt and for Lot in Sodom and Gomorrah. The false teachers even slandered celestial beings—yet not even the archangel Michael would directly rebuke the devil without God's authority (vv. 8–10). According to Jude, "These men speak abusively against whatever they do not understand" (v. 10).

Jude continues the history lesson by mentioning three corrupt figures: Cain (Genesis 4:1–16), Balaam (Numbers 22–24), and Korah (Numbers 16). These false teachers would receive God's harsh judgment, as would their modern counterparts whom Jude called "blemishes at your love feasts, eating with you without the slightest qualm—shepherds who feed only themselves. They are clouds without rain, blown along by the wind; autumn trees, without fruit and uprooted—twice dead. They are wild waves of the sea, foaming up their shame; wandering stars, for whom blackest darkness has been reserved forever…grumblers and faultfinders; they follow their own evil desires; they boast about themselves and flatter others for their own advantage" (vv. 12–13, 16). You get the feeling Jude didn't think too highly of these guys.

Jude called for Christians to "keep yourselves in God's love as you wait for the mercy of our Lord Jesus Christ to bring you to eternal life" (v. 21).

Yours Truly

Jude is last in the list of New Testament letters. Sixty-five Bible books down; one to go. Our final chapter deals with the Bible's final book: Revelation. Prepare yourself. It's going to be a bumpy ride.

The Least You Need to Know

➤ Various spiritual leaders wrote letters (epistles) to encourage and instruct others.

➤ More than just news and greetings, the New Testament letters dealt with problems in the church.

➤ Many recipients of the letters shared similar problems, such as the intrusion of false teachers into Christian communities.

➤ Each epistle speaks of God's ability to provide for those who remain faithful.

Chapter 23

It's the End of the World As We Know It

In This Chapter

➤ John sees a remarkable vision

➤ Jesus catches up on some correspondence

➤ A peek into heaven

➤ Judgments, the four horsemen of the apocalypse, the beast and the antichrist, 666, Armageddon, the end of Satan

If you've read all the way through this book to this point, you are to be commended. But then, if you went straight to this chapter as a starting point, who can blame you? Revelation is a remarkable Bible book. For some Christians it's a vision of the end of the world; for others, it's a snapshot of a time when the church of Jesus Christ first came into collision with the mighty Roman empire. Some see a complicated roadmap of the last days, replete with hidden messages; others an allegory of spiritual struggle. Either way, it's a lot of fireworks.

However, let it be said up front that of all the books in the Bible, this one is by far the hardest to understand. You can collect a roomful of people who have studied biblical prophecy all their lives, yet probably no two people will agree on every aspect of Revelation. The language is symbolic, leading to numerous possibilities for interpretation. People can't even agree if John's vision describes events that have already taken place, or things yet to come. They debate whether the descriptions are literal or allegorical. And don't get them started about how the sequence of events is going to lay out when the time comes. Understanding Revelation requires tying its content to many other Bible books—both Old and New Testament. So it's very difficult for someone with a sketchy Bible knowledge to approach Revelation and get much out of it on the first reading.

Club Med Meets Century One (Rev. 1)

Authorship is attributed to John—Jesus' disciple who also wrote a gospel and three epistles. The book was written from the island of Patmos where many people believe John had been exiled by Rome.

While he was there, John received a revelation of "what must soon take place" (1:1). As Revelation begins John was given the task of describing what he had seen to seven churches in the province of Asia—Ephesus, Smyrna, Pergamum, Thyatira, Sardis, Philadelphia, and Laodicea. The figure giving the instructions was someone "like a son of man" wearing a robe and golden sash. "His head and hair were white like wool, as white as snow, and his eyes were like blazing fire" (1:15). His feet were glowing like bronze in a furnace. His voice sounded like rushing water. His face was like the sun. In his right hand he held seven stars, representing the seven churches. John writes, "When I saw him, I fell at his feet as though dead" (1:17). The man told him not to be afraid and then identified himself: "I am the First and the Last. I am the Living One; I was dead, and behold I am alive for ever and ever! And I hold the keys of death and Hades" (1:17–18). Through this description, John identifies the speaker as Jesus.

Manna from Heaven

The island of **Patmos** was west of Asia Minor (now Turkey) in the Aegean Sea. It was about 30 square miles and may have served as an "Alcatraz" for prisoners of the Roman Empire.

John had spent three years with Jesus, but seeing this image of his Lord was far different than being around Jesus as a human teacher and companion. Yet John faithfully acted as scribe and began to record what Jesus dictated.

Rate-a-Church (Rev. 2–3)

Jesus began an evaluation of each of the seven churches, following a formula:

1. A description of himself
2. Good things about the church
3. Things wrong with the church
4. A challenge
5. A promise

Each of the churches had a unique profile. Ephesus received a lot of praise for doing good things, yet Jesus had the criticism that, "You have forsaken your first love" (2:4). They were challenged to "repent and do the things you did at first" (2:5).

Smyrna received a glowing review, even though church conditions weren't ideal. They were in poverty and were being slandered, yet as far as spiritual things were concerned they were rich (2:9).

The church in Pergamum was encountering a lot of hostility and resentment. One of its members named Antipas had even been martyred for his faith. Jesus noted their faithfulness, yet also pointed out that various groups of false teachers were beginning to seduce the church (2:12–17). He told them, too, to repent.

Thyatira, he said, was making progress, yet there, too, members were beginning to get caught up in sexual immorality and idolatry. ("That woman Jezebel" probably refers to a female church member who was seducing others—either spiritually or literally.) Jesus explained that he was giving the church time to take care of the problem, but if they didn't do so soon, *he* would (2:18–29).

Sardis was a facade of a church. The people had a reputation for being alive and active, but Jesus saw them as dead. They were in need of an immediate spiritual jump start to wake them up. Yet Jesus also singled out the "few people" who were still faithful and promised to reward their persistent faith (3:1–6).

Philadelphia, like Smyrna, received high praise. Jewish rivals (the "Synagogue of Satan") were making life rough for the church. As a reward for their patient endurance, Jesus promised that, "I will also keep you from the hour of trial that is going to come upon the whole world to test those who live on the earth." They would also receive rewards that would never be taken away (3:7–13).

In this case, the last *was* the least. Jesus had nothing good to say about the church at Laodicea. They didn't appear to be a terrible church, but neither were they excited about what they were doing. As Jesus put it, "I know your deeds, that you are neither cold nor hot. I wish you were either one or the other! So, because you are lukewarm—neither hot nor cold—I am about to spit you out of my mouth." The word for *spit* actually means "vomit." This church made Jesus want to puke! The people were self-satisfied and took pride in their ability to care for themselves. Still, Jesus offered acceptance if they were willing to "be earnest, and repent" (3:14–22).

Manna from Heaven

The **teaching of Balaam** (2:14) was the use of physical (sexual) seduction to weaken spiritual integrity (Numbers 25:1-3; 31:16). The Bible doesn't say much about the **Nicolaitans** (Revelation 2:6, 15), but it is assumed they were another sect that attempted to water down God's standards by compromising with secular society.

Potent Quotables

Here I am! I stand at the door and knock. If anyone hears my voice and opens the door, I will come in and eat with him, and he with me. (Revelation 3:20)

This saying is often cited as an enduring offer of Jesus. It has even more impact in this context of being directed to an apathetic and misdirected church.

Each of the seven churches received a promise directed to the one "who overcomes," a theme that continues throughout the book. The people who were tolerating false teachers were shown what would eventually happen to the deceivers. Those who were becoming apathetic and lukewarm about the Jesus who had lived among them would discover the authority he commands on high. Those who were suffering and hurting were given a glimpse of how things would be when God finally announced it was time to balance the scales of justice.

Indeed, John's visions would be perceived quite differently by Christians than by nonbelievers who might hear of them. Believers who were the underdogs in Roman society could take great comfort in what was to come. For those who continued to resist God, however, John's peek into the future could be horrifying.

Up, Up, and Away (Rev. 4–5)

Next John saw a door standing open in heaven and heard a voice inviting him to "Come up here, and I will show you what must take place after this" (4:1). A radiant figure seated on a throne was surrounded by "24 elders, also enthroned," dressed in white and wearing gold crowns. Around him thunder pealed and lightning flashed. There were four living creatures covered with eyes in front and back, one like a lion, one like an ox, one like a man, and one like an eagle. Each had six wings. Day and night they never stopped saying, "Holy, holy, holy is the Lord God Almighty, who was, and is, and is to come." As the four creatures spoke, the elders fell before the figure on the throne, laying their crowns before the throne and praising God.

The figure on the throne held a scroll in his right hand. It had writing on both sides and was sealed with seven seals. "A mighty angel" asked for volunteers who might be worthy to open the scroll, but there were no responses. John, who was witnessing this, was so heartbroken that he started to cry. But one of the elders comforted him: "The Lion of the tribe of Judah, the Root of David, has triumphed. He is able to open the scroll and its seven seals" (5:1–5).

Manna from Heaven

The number **7**, which occurs so frequently in Revelation, was highly significant in Jewish tradition. From the time that God rested on the seventh day, the number had signified completeness and/or perfection.

Then John saw a lamb in the center of everything, looking as if it had been killed. It had seven horns (symbols of power) and seven eyes (thought to represent the Holy Spirit). As the Lamb took the scroll, the four living creatures and 24 elders all fell before him and sang a new song: "You are worthy to take the scroll and to open its seals, because you were slain, and with your blood you purchased men for God from every tribe and language and people and nation. You have made them to be a kingdom and priests to serve our God, and they will reign on the earth" (5:6–10). Immediately "thousands upon thousands" of angels took up the song and sang praises to the lamb. Also singing were "every creature in heaven and on earth and under the earth and on the sea, and all that is in them" (5:11–14).

Scroll with the Punches (Rev. 6–7)

When the lamb opened the first seal, John saw a white horse with a rider holding a bow, who was given a crown. He rode out "as a conqueror bent on conquest." The second seal summoned a fiery red horse. Its rider was given a large sword and the power to take peace from the earth. The third seal brought a black horse, with a rider holding a pair of scales. It represented greed and deceit. The fourth seal brought a pale horse bearing Death, with Hades following close behind. They were given power over a fourth of the earth to kill by sword, famine, and plague, and by the wild beasts of the earth." This is the biblical presentation of the four horsemen of the apocalypse, although the term as such never appears.

At the opening of the fifth seal, John saw the souls of all who had been killed for expressing their faith in God. In a loud voice they asked how much longer it would be before God avenged them and judged the earth. They were told to "wait a little longer," because still others would be martyred; in the meantime they were given white robes (6:9–11).

The sixth seal triggered an earthquake. The sun turned black, the moon turned blood red, and stars began to fall from the sky "as late figs drop from a fig tree when shaken by a strong wind." Mountains and islands were moved, and the "mighty" people of the earth cried out for the mountains to fall on them to hide them from the wrath of God (6:12–17).

Between the opening of the sixth and seventh seals, John saw four angels "who had been given power to harm the land and the sea." But first, another angel arrived to place a seal of protection on 144,000 people "from all the tribes of Israel."

John then saw another group of people so large it could not be counted. They were standing before God's throne, wearing white robes, holding palm branches, and praising God. An elder identified them: "These are they who have come out of the great tribulation; they have washed their robes and made them white in the blood of the Lamb." Consequently, "never again will they hunger; never again will they thirst. The sun will not beat

Manna from Heaven

The **soul** is the term frequently used to describe the part of a person that is not material, in contrast to the body. Other terms used to refer to the inner person are *mind, will, heart,* and *spirit.* Some people are content to make two distinctions, distinguishing body from soul. Others prefer three: body, soul, and spirit. While the body is temporary and will decay, the soul is eternal.

What Saith Thou?

Has the great tribulation happened yet?

Some assume that the great tribulation refers to the Roman persecutions experienced by first-century Christians. Others believe it anticipates an event yet to come: a final extended period of hostility toward God's people before the second coming of Jesus.

upon them, nor any scorching heat. For the Lamb at the center of the throne will be their shepherd; he will lead them to springs of living water. And God will wipe away every tear from their eyes" (7:9–17).

The Trumpet Septet You Never Want to Hear (Rev. 8–9)

When the seventh seal was opened, "there was silence in heaven for about half an hour" (8:1)—a somber pause in preparation for the gravity of what was about to happen. Then John saw seven angels with trumpets. Another angel stood at the heavenly altar with a golden censer (a ceremonial firepan). He was given "much incense to offer, with the prayers of all the saints, on the golden altar before the throne" (8:3). Smoke arose and went up before God. Then the angel took the censer, filled it with fire from the altar, and hurled it to earth, setting off thunder, lightning, and an earthquake.

The angels began to sound their trumpets in sequence. The first brought "hail and fire mixed with blood" upon the earth, burning a third of the trees and green grass. At the second, "something like a huge mountain, all ablaze, was thrown into the sea," turning a third of it to blood, killing a third of the sea creatures, and destroying a third of the ships. The third trumpet heralded a great blazing star falling from the sky to the rivers and springs of the earth, polluting a third of the fresh water and causing people to die because of the bitterness of the water. The star was called Wormwood (named after a bitter plant). The fourth angel blew his trumpet and the sun, moon, and a third of the stars turned dark. Then an eagle flew by and called out, "Woe! Woe! Woe to the inhabitants of the earth, because of the trumpet blasts about to be sounded by the other three angels" (8:12–13).

When the fifth angel sounded his trumpet, John saw a star that had fallen from the sky to the earth. But apparently the star represents something or someone, because "the star was given the key to the shaft of the Abyss" (9:1). He opened it, releasing dark smoke and locusts that "came down upon the earth and were given power like that of scorpions of the earth" (9:3). They were commanded not to harm the plant life but to attack people lacking the seal of God on their foreheads, causing five months of painful agony.

Manna from Heaven

The Abyss is sometimes referred to as "the bottomless pit." It is the prison of rebellious spirits (the place the evil spirits had wished to avoid when they begged Jesus to be cast into the herd of pigs instead [Luke 8:31]).

When reading descriptions such as those of the locusts (9:7–11), it should be noted that John is writing with a first-century mentality and vocabulary. Try to imagine transporting anyone from the Roman Empire into our culture where it's his job to describe television, fax machines, airplanes, and other wonders for his peers 2,000 years back in time. Some people suggest John might have been describing things unknown to him, but familiar to us—tanks, helicopters, etc.

At the sixth trumpet, 200 million mounted troops assembled, wiping out "a third of mankind with fire, smoke, and sulfur." Yet the people on earth still did not repent (9:13–21).

God's Witness Protection Program (Rev. 10–11:14)

Between the sixth and seventh trumpets, John describes a mighty angel, holding an open scroll and "robed in a cloud, with a rainbow above his head; his face was like the sun, and his legs were like fiery pillars" (10:1). He stood with one foot on the sea and one foot on the land and shouted with what sounded like a lion's roar. "When he shouted, the voices of the seven thunders spoke" (10:3).

John began to record what the seven thunders had said, but a voice from heaven stopped him from doing so. With all that was being revealed to John, it's amazing that *anything* would have remained a secret. But John did record the angel's announcement: "There will be no more delay! But in the days when the seventh angel is about to sound his trumpet, the mystery of God will be accomplished, just as he announced to his servants the prophets" (10:6-7).

And John also recorded an account of two witnesses for God who wear sackcloth and are given power to prophesy for 1,260 days (11:3). They will have extraordinary power: "If anyone tries to harm them, fire comes from their mouths and devours their enemies.... These men have power to shut up the sky so that it will not rain during the time they are prophesying; and they have power to turn the waters into blood and to strike the earth with every kind of plague as often as they want" (11:5-6).

Their powers are reminiscent of Moses and Elijah, but when they finish their testimony, these two witnesses will be killed by "the beast that comes up from the Abyss." Their bodies will lie in the street in public view for three and a half days. The wicked people of the world will gloat and throw parties to celebrate their deaths. But at the end of the three and a half days, God again gives them breath and they stand up. A loud voice from heaven says, "Come up here," and they ascend in a cloud as their enemies watch. Terror strikes those who observe this event, and the fear intensifies as at that very hour a severe earthquake strikes, destroying a tenth of Jerusalem and killing 7,000 people. The survivors are so shaken they give glory to God (11: 1-14).

Manna from Heaven

Revelation 11:7 is the first reference to **the beast**, who is also called the **Antichrist** (though the word isn't used in Revelation). He will become the primary source of hostility toward God's people during the last days.

What Saith Thou?

Who is John talking about in Rev. 13:18?

The number 666 has been frequently interpreted to be a numerical code for Nero Caesar, the first Roman emperor to persecute Christians (though numbers can be manipulated to fit other names as well). Another suggestion is simply to consider 666 to be as imperfect a number as possible. Since seven was considered "perfect," six is the number that comes up short. Therefore, one six is provided for the dragon (Satan), one for the first beast (the Antichrist), and one for the second beast (the false prophet). Other than such speculation, we have no way to know whom John is writing about.

The Seventh Trumpet (Rev. 11:15–14)

At the sounding of the seventh trumpet there was loud praise from heaven. The elders fell on their faces to worship God because "the time has come for judging the dead, and for rewarding your servants the prophets and your saints and those who reverence your name" (11:18). The heavenly temple was opened, revealing the Ark of the Covenant. Again, there was lightning, thunder, an earthquake, and a hailstorm.

If you've been putting your basic math skills to use, you may have come to the conclusion that *three and a half years* is a significant amount of time. So far, references have been made to "42 months" (11:2), "1,260 days" (11:3), and "a time, times and half a time" (12:14). The 1,260 days equal forty-two months of thirty days each. And if a "time" equals a year, the equation works out to a time (1 year) + times (2 years) + half a time (1/2 year), totaling three and a half years. According to many scenarios, this will be the length of the Great Tribulation. Daniel wrote of seventy "sevens" which seemed to indicate periods of time. Trouble occurs at the middle of one "seven." If he is speaking of a seven-year period, then the middle would be, again, the beginning of a three-and-a-half-year tribulation (Daniel 9:20–27).

John saw a dragon (identified as Satan) cast out of heaven (12:9). As the dragon stood on the shore, John saw a beast coming out of the sea with 7 heads and 10 horns—each horn bearing a crown with a blasphemous name. One of its heads appeared to have had a fatal wound that healed. The beast "resembled a leopard, but had feet like those of a bear and a mouth like that of a lion" (13:2). The beast was given power by the dragon, and the two began to make war against God's people. Then another beast appeared, with two horns like a lamb but speaking like a dragon. In function, he served as the personal assistant to the first beast, causing the world to worship the first beast. But the second beast had great power of his own, even causing fire to fall from heaven. This second beast is frequently referred to as the false prophet.

The second beast set up an image of the first beast and made the image seem to breathe and speak. All who refused to worship the image were put to death. The second beast "forced everyone, small and great, rich and poor, free and slave, to receive a mark on his right hand or on his forehead, so that no one could buy or sell unless he had the mark, which is the name of the beast or the number of his name." Added to this observation was a comment: "This calls for wisdom. If anyone has insight, let him calculate the number of the beast, for it is man's number. His number is 666" (13:16–18).

Just when things seem to be hopelessly grim for God's people, John sees other visions that are much more encouraging. John saw the lamb with the 144,000 sealed believers, who "sang a new song" that no one else could learn. They faithfully wore God's seal rather than the beast's mark, and they "kept themselves pure" (14:1–5). Three angels proclaimed God's judgment to every nation, predicted the fall of Babylon the Great, and warned of the fate of anyone who worshipped the beast or received his image. Such people "will drink of the wine of God's fury, which has been poured full strength into the cup of his wrath. He will be tormented with burning sulfur in the presence of the holy angels and of the Lamb. And the smoke of their torment rises for ever and ever" (14:9–12).

Then a voice from heaven said, "Blessed are the dead who die in the Lord from now on" (14:13). But it wasn't God's people who were dying in the next vision. John saw "one 'like a son of man' with a crown of gold on his head and a sharp sickle in his hand." He was told, "Take your sickle and reap, because the time to reap has come, for the harvest of the earth is ripe." The figure swung his sickle "and the earth was harvested." Two more angels came out of the temple, one who had charge of the fire (a symbol of judgment) and the other with a sickle of his own. The angel with the sickle "gathered grapes [representing the wicked] and threw them into the great winepress of God's wrath."

As a result of this harvest, "blood flowed out of the press, rising as high as the horses' bridles" for a distance of about 180 miles.

While the wicked people of earth were being slaughtered as God's judgment came to pass, those who had been victorious over the beast (by not receiving his mark or worshiping his image) were being rewarded by God. They held harps given them by God and used them to sing his praises (15:2-4).

Bowled Over (Revelation 16–18)

Afterward John saw seven angels with seven plagues. Each angel was handed a golden bowl "filled with the wrath of God" to be poured out on the earth. When the first angel poured out his bowl, painful sores broke out on all the people who had the mark of the beast. The second angel's bowl turned the sea to blood, and every living sea creature died. The third angel did the same to the fresh rivers and springs.

The fourth angel poured his bowl onto the sun, giving the sun power to scorch people with fire; the wicked cursed God but refused to repent. The fifth angel poured his bowl "on the throne of the beast," plunging the earth into darkness; people still refused to repent. The sixth angel poured his bowl onto the Euphrates River, drying it up "to prepare the way for the kings from the East." Three froglike evil spirits came from the mouths of the dragon, beast, and false prophet, summoning "the kings of the whole world" for a major battle. They met at a place called Armageddon.

The seventh angel's bowl was poured into the air and was followed by a voice shouting, "It is done!" As the earth shook, islands and mountains disappeared and 100-pound hailstones pelted people from the sky. Again, people cursed God.

Manna from Heaven

Revelation 16:16 is the Bible's only mention of Armageddon, although many of Israel's big battles had taken place at that location on the plain at the base of Mount Megiddo.

Another angel came down from heaven to announce the fall of "Babylon the Great," stating that, "When the kings who had committed adultery with her and shared her luxury see the smoke of her burning, they will weep and mourn over her" (18:2, 9). The merchants will mourn as well because they no longer have an outlet for their merchandise. There would be no hope for the city's future. A mighty angel hurled an enormous boulder into the sea and said, "With such violence the great city of Babylon will be thrown down, never to be found again" (18:21).

Rider on the Storm (Rev. 19–20)

While John was listening to this elegy for the fall of Babylon, he heard "what sounded like the roar of a great multitude in heaven shouting" (19:1). Heaven was opened and John saw a white horse whose rider is called Faithful and True. His eyes were like blazing fire. He had numerous crowns on his head and led the armies of heaven, also riding white horses and dressed in clean, white linen. He was dressed in a robe dipped in blood, and his name was "the Word of God." On his robe and thigh was another of his names: "King of Kings and Lord of Lords" (19:11–16).

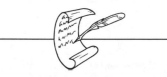

Manna from Heaven

This thousand-year period of time is frequently referred to as the **millennium** (Latin for "a thousand years").

The beast had assembled "the kings of the earth and their armies" to battle against the rider and his army. But the beast and the false prophet were captured and "the two of them were thrown alive into the fiery lake of burning sulfur." The rest of the opponents "were killed with the sword that came out of the mouth of the rider on the horse, and all the birds gorged themselves on their flesh" (19:19–21).

Then an angel descended from heaven holding the key to the Abyss. He seized the dragon (Satan), threw him into the Abyss, and sealed him in for a thousand years.

Then John saw "the souls of those who had been beheaded because of their testimony for Jesus and because of the word of God." The people who hadn't worshipped the image of the beast or received his mark all came back to life and "reigned with Christ a thousand years" (20:1–4).

At the end of the thousand years, Satan is released from the Abyss and immediately returns to deceiving people. He gathers an army as numerous "as the sand on the seashore" and surrounds "the camp of God's people, the city he loves." But fire falls from heaven to destroy them. At that point, the devil himself will be thrown into the lake of burning sulfur to join the beast and the false prophet. "They will be tormented day and night for ever and ever" (20:7–10).

With Satan out of the way, the rest of the dead are judged at "a great white throne" (20:11). "The sea gave up the dead that were in it, and death and Hades gave up the dead that were in them, and each person was judged according to what he had done…. If anyone's name was not found written in the book of life, he was thrown into the lake of fire" (20:13, 15). Death and Hades were also thrown into the lake of fire, which is called "the second death."

Trying to Make Sense of It All

Just about the only thing clear about Revelation is that it is confusing. Because it incorporates so many symbols into the description of events, there are too many different interpretations to attempt to explain them all. And, as was previously mentioned, there is disagreement as to the order of those events. For example, does the rapture occur before, after, or in the middle of the great tribulation? At what point does the millennium take place? In what order are the judgments? (If Christians are raptured early on, and if those who die during the great tribulation arise to rule with Christ, then the only people left at the great white throne of judgment are those who have rejected him and are doomed to hell.)

However, there are three basic interpretations of the events that probably should be included here:

➤ *Amillennialism* interprets the thousand years as more figurative than literal. The reign of Jesus is perceived as an internal rule in the lives of believers—those on earth who have put their faith in him and those in heaven as

Manna from Heaven

One of the terms frequently associated with the last days is the **rapture**, a word not used in the Bible. This is the event referred to by Paul when, "The Lord himself will come down from heaven, …and the dead in Christ will rise first. After that, we who are still alive and are left will be caught up together with them to meet the Lord in the air. And so we will be with the Lord forever" (1 Thessalonians 4:16-17). Some people feel that those who are raptured will be among the army of Christ in the final battle described in Revelation.

well. But even amillennialists are quite varied as to their specific interpretations of the other events in Revelation.

➤ Another view is *postmillennialism*, which purports that Jesus returns *after* the millennium. The theory is that due to the preaching of the gospel, the world will become an increasingly better place, devoted to Christian teachings and principles. The thousand-year reign and the eventual return of Christ would be the culmination of this period of spiritual enlightenment. Postmillennialism now has fewer proponents than it once did.

➤ *Premillennialism* requires taking the events of Revelation as literally as possible. Since the return of Jesus (19:11-21) occurs before the thousand-year reign (20: 1-6), it is *pre*-millennial. But again, premillennialists don't agree as to when the rapture of believers takes place with regard to the great tribulation.

Snapshots

Here are a few Revelation snapshots that you might want to check out in more depth:

The "locusts" that your local pest control company will have nothing to do with (9:3–11)

An equally bizarre "breed" of horses (9:17–19)

In heaven, John has a strange snack and is given a job (10:9–11:2)

A dragon and an archangel do battle over a pregnant woman and her child (Revelation 12)

A prostitute and a scarlet beast party for a while, but then break up (Revelation 17)

Heaven: New and Improved (Rev. 21–22)

But one thing most people agree on is that faithful believers are eventually rewarded eternally. The Book of Revelation (and the Bible) concludes with a magnificent vision of the future home of God's people.

John describes a new heaven and earth because "the first heaven and the first earth had passed away, and there was no longer any sea" (21:1). The Holy City, also called the new Jerusalem, came down out of heaven as a loud voice said, "Now the dwelling of God is with men, and he will live with them. They will be his people, and God himself will be with them and be their God. He will wipe every tear from their eyes.

There will be no more death or mourning or crying or pain, for the old order of things has passed away" (21:3–4).

The city was clear as crystal, and shone with a brilliant light. It had a high wall with 12 gates, on which were written the names of the 12 tribes of Israel. The wall was built on 12 foundations, upon which were the names of "the 12 apostles of the Lamb" (21:9–14).

John witnessed the measuring of the city. It was about 1,400 miles wide, long, and high (providing the possibility for either a cube or a pyramid). The wall around it was about 200 feet thick and made of jasper. The city itself was gold, as pure as glass. The foundations of the walls were different kinds of precious stones. The gates were pearls (pearly gates are true to Scripture), with "each gate made of a single pearl." The main street of the city was of pure gold "like transparent glass" (21:15–21).

This city needed no temple, sun, or moon. The presence of "the Lord God Almighty and the Lamb" gave abundant light. Night would no longer exist, nor would impurity (21:22–27).

A river flowed from God's throne down the middle of the main street. On each side of the river stood the tree of life, which had 12 different kinds of fruit, yielding fruit every month. In this setting, God and his people "will reign for ever and ever" (22:1–6).

In his epilogue, John quotes Jesus three times in saying, "Behold, I am coming soon" (22:7, 12, 20). John is told, "Do not seal up the words of the prophecy of this book, because the time is near." And Jesus says, "Blessed are those who wash their robes, that they may have the right to the tree of life and may go through the gates into the city."

John closes with a dire warning: "If anyone adds anything [to the words of this book], God will add to him the plagues described in this book. And if anyone takes words away from this book of prophecy, God will take away from him his share in the tree of life and in the holy city, which are described in this book" (22:7–21).

While this chapter has been little more than a read-through to introduce you to the events, characters,

What Saith Thou?

Hasn't the tree of life popped up somewhere before?

If you can remember all the way back to Genesis, the tree was in the Garden of Eden. In their sinful condition, Adam and Eve were not permitted to eat of it. In the new Jerusalem, however, the tree bears fruit for all to enjoy.

Potent Quotables

The one who testifies to these things says, "Surely I am coming soon."

Amen. Come, Lord Jesus!

The grace of the Lord Jesus Christ be with all the saints. Amen. (Revelation 22.20–21)

Even in the turbulent context of Revelation, these final statements of the Bible are words of hope and grace.

and symbols, there are numerous other commentaries you can read if you wish to go deeper into this intriguing Bible book. As you start examining the events in depth, you'll probably be referred to Daniel, Zechariah, 1 Thessalonians, and numerous other Old and New Testament references. If you begin a pursuit of deeper knowledge, may God reward your search.

The End? Or Just the Beginning?

Congratulations! You've completed an overview of the entire Bible. You're ready to begin again. No, not with this book, though we hope it will continue to be a helpful reference. Rather, it's time to take out your own Bible. If we've done our job, it will seem a bit less mysterious than before, but no less intriguing.

However you approach it, we pray that your search may be fruitful. May you continue reading, struggling, and pondering for yourself the tremendous truths you find between its covers.

The Least You Need to Know

➤ While in exile, John saw and recorded some awesome visions of future events.

➤ The Book of Revelation was originally written to motivate first-century churches to remain true to their faith.

➤ A few of the characters and objects are clearly defined, but many of the symbols in Revelation are open to interpretation.

➤ In the end, the bad guys lose and the good guys win.

The Books of the Bible

THE OLD TESTAMENT

Law

Genesis
Exodus
Leviticus

Numbers
Deuteronomy

Histories

Joshua
Judges
Ruth
1 Samuel
2 Samuel
1 Kings

2 Kings
1 Chronicles
2 Chronicles
Ezra
Nehemiah

Writings

Esther
Job
Psalms

Proverbs
Ecclesiastes
Song of Songs

Prophets

Isaiah
Jeremiah
Lamentations
Ezekiel
Daniel
Hosea
Joel
Amos
Obadiah

Jonah
Micah
Habakkuk
Nahum
Zephaniah
Haggai
Zechariah
Malachi

THE NEW TESTAMENT

Gospels

Matthew

Mark

Luke

John

History

Acts

Epistles

Romans

1 Corinthians

2 Corinthians

Galatians

Ephesians

Philippians

Colossians

1 Thessalonians

2 Thessalonians

1 Timothy

2 Timothy

Titus

Philemon

Hebrews

James

1 Peter

2 Peter

1 John

2 John

3 John

Jude

Apocalypse

Revelation

The Three Divisions of the Historical Books

BOOK	DATE	COVENANT RELATIONSHIP	SECULAR RELATIONSHIP
PRIOR TO THE KINGDOM—1405–1075 B.C.E.			
JOSHUA	1405–1375	The promised land occupied by faith and courage.	Egypt had withdrawn from Palestine (internal problems). Seven nations of Canaan ripe for promised judgement.

BOOK	DATE	COVENANT RELATIONSHIP	SECULAR RELATIONSHIP
JUDGES	1375–1075	Demonstrations of blessing for obedience and judgement for apostasy as promised.	Small local kingdoms harass the various tribes. The Philistines immigrate from Crete to challenge Israel.
RUTH	c. 1330	True faith attracts a woman of neighboring Moab.	The Davidic line is traced to Moab through Ruth. Israel's peaceful relations with Moab.

THE RISE AND FALL OF THE KINGDOM—1070–586 B.C.E.

BOOK	DATE	COVENANT RELATIONSHIP	SECULAR RELATIONSHIP
SAMUELS	1100–970	The establishing of a faith-king to rule the kingdom for God.	The powerful Philistine invaders nearly take over the land of Canaan.
KINGS	970–586	The kingdom is challenged by Canaanite idolatry and is divided and finally taken to a land of idolatry.	Israel is harassed by Egypt and Syria and is finally exiled by Assyria and Babylon.
CHRONICLES Creation of Adam 586		The Davidic line of kings traced, and the rise and fall of Solomon's temple.	Surrounding kingdoms and empires are seen rising and falling to serve God's design for the Davidic kingdom.

THE REMNANT'S CARE IN THE TIMES OF THE GENTILES—537–432 B.C.E.

BOOK	DATE	COVENANT RELATIONSHIP	SECULAR RELATIONSHIP
EZRA	537–458	The return form exile to rebuild the temple and to restore proper worship.	The new Persian Empire begins policy of returning captured people and their gods to their native countries.
NEHEMIAH	445–430	They return from exile to rebuild Jerusalem's wall and establish a limited governorship in the land.	The Persian rulers' continued goodwill allows the remnant to rebuild for protection against local adversaries.
ESTHER	483–473	The divine care of the covenant people while out of the covenant land.	Persia rules from India to the Hellespont. The Jewish people seek to remain faithful to their heritage while living under foreign rule.

Where Can You Go from Here?

The following tools serve different purposes in helping you come to grips with the contents of the Bible. Bible translations range from a word-for-word literal translation to paraphrases. Some of these Bibles include study, devotional, and life application helps for individuals and small groups. Parallel Bibles contain multiple columns on the same page of various translations of the same text.

Daily readings and excerpts help with reading plans. Chain references provide cross-references of words and concepts throughout the Bible. Some authors paraphrase their own modern versions. Other Bibles appeal to specialized market niches, although this category is too large to include here.

Concordances are single-word references to every occurrence of that word found in the Bible. Commentaries are often multi-volume explanations of the text; a single-volume commentary gives you the basics. Atlases explain the topography and geography in historical context. Manners and customs books give you the cultural background. Dictionaries and encyclopedias give topical information. Handbooks cover even more facts on individual books of the Bible.

The best places to find an extensive selection of Bibles and Bible resources is in a large chain bookstore or a religious or Christian bookstore. Ask the salesperson for help based on your needs and goals. Here is a variety of popular examples from a diverse spectrum.

Bibles:

The Daily Bible: In Chronological Order. NIV. Eugene, OR: Harvest House Publishers, 1984.

The Disciple's Study Bible. NIV. Nashville: Holman Bible Publishers, 1988.

Holy Bible. KJV. Grand Rapids: Zondervan Publishing House, 1983.

Kohlenberger, John R., III, Ed. *The One-Minute Bible: The Heart of the Bible Arranged into 366 One-Minute Readings*. NIV. Bloomington, MN: Garborg's, 1992.

Ryrie Study Bible, Expanded Edition. NAS. Chicago: Moody Press, 1994.

The Layman's Parallel Bible. KJV, NIV, LB, NRSV. 1991.

Life Application Study Bible. NLT. Wheaton, IL: Tyndale House Publishers, 1988.

New American Bible. Grand Rapids: Catholic World Press, 1987.

The New Jerusalem Bible, Reader's Edition. NY: Doubleday, 1990.

The New Oxford Annotated Bible with the Apocrypha: Revised and Expanded. NRSV. NY: Oxford University Press, 1994.

The NIV Quiet Time Bible. Downer's Grove, IL: InterVarsity Press, 1994.

The NIV Serendipity Bible: For Personal and Small Group Study, Revised and Expanded. Grand Rapids, MI and Littleton, CO: Zondervan Publishing House and Serendipity House, 1988.

The NIV Study Bible. Grand Rapids, MI: Zondervan Publishing House, 1995.

The One Year Bible, NLT in 365 Daily Readings. Wheaton, IL: Tyndale House Publishers, 1996.

Plaut, W. Gunther, Ed. *The Torah, a Modern Commentary.* NY: Union of American Hebrew Congregations, 1981.

The Thompson Chain-Reference Study Bible. NKJV. Nashville: Thomas Nelson Publishers, 1983.

Vaughan, Curtis, Gen. Ed. *The Bible from 26 Translations.* Grand Rapids: Baker Book House, 1988.

Bible Translation Abbreviations:

NIV—New International Version

NRSV—New Revised Standard Version

NKJV—New King James Version

LB—Living Bible

NAS—New American Standard

NLT—New Living Translation

Resources:

Achtemeier, Paul J., Gen. Ed. *HarperCollins Bible Dictionary.* San Francisco: HarperCollins Publishers, 1985.

Anderson, Ken. *Where to Find It in the Bible, the Ultimate A to Z Resource.* Nashville: Thomas Nelson Publishers, 1996.

Barker, Kenneth L., and John R. Kohlenberger, Consulting Eds. *NIV Bible Commentary*. Grand Rapids, MI: Zondervan Publishing House, 1994.

Beitzel, Barry J. *The Moody Atlas of Bible Lands*. Chicago: Moody Press, 1985.

Day, A. Colin. *Roget's Thesaurus of the Bible*. NY: HarperCollins, 1992.

Gardner, Paul D., Ed. *The Complete Who's Who in the Bible*. Grand Rapids: Zondervan Publishing House, 1995.

Guthrie, D., and J. A. Motyer, Eds. *The New Bible Commentary*. Grand Rapids: Wm. B. Eerdmans Publishing Co., 1970.

Hendricks, Howard G., and William D. Hendricks. *Living by the Book*. Chicago: Moody Press, 1991. (inductive Bible study method)

Mears, Henrietta C. *What the Bible is All About*. Rev. Ed. Ventura, CA: Regal Books, 1983.

Packer, J. I., and M. C. Tenney, Eds. *Manners and Customs of the Bible*. Nashville: Thomas Nelson Publishers, 1980.

Peterson, Eugene H. *The Message: New Testament*. Colorado Springs: NavPress, 1992.

Pfeiffer, Charles F., and Everett F. Harrison. *The Wycliffe Bible Commentary*. Chicago: Moody Press, 1990.

Pritchard, James G., Ed. *The Harper Atlas of the Bible*. Harper & Row, 1987.

Strong, James. *The New Strong's Exhaustive Concordance of the Bible*. Thomas Nelson Publishers, 1995.

Unger, Merrill F. *The New Unger's Bible Dictionary*. Chicago: Moody Press, 1957.

———. *Unger's Bible Handbook: An Essential Guide to Understanding the Bible*. Chicago: Moody Press, 1967.

Wangerin, Walter, Jr. *The Book of God: The Bible as a Novel*. Grand Rapids: HarperCollins and Zondervan, 1996.

Reading the Bible in One Year

It is quite possible to read the Bible in its entirety over the course of one year without having to become a perpetual hermit or live on four hours sleep. If you find about a half hour each day and a quiet spot, you'll succeed. If you miss a day you'll have to do double duty the following day. Chapters in the Bible are short so it's not like reading four chapters of a novel. In the morning you begin (on New Year's Day) with the first books of the Old and New Testaments—Genesis and Matthew. In the evening you start with approximately the second halves of each—a minor prophet in the Old Testament and the first book after the Gospels in the New Testament.

This way you get a good variety of readings each day and stay on four parallel tracks. Or you can decide that you will only be able to get away once per day to read and so you'll read all four at some point during your waking hours. It is probably better, if you're reading this much to save some in-depth study or research time for a day when you have more free time. The point is to read it through, perhaps making notes related to questions, and go back when you have an inclination to approach the text in a more serious manner. Once you get into this habit it might be hard to stop!

JANUARY

		Morning					Evening			
GENESIS	1	MATTHEW	1	1	EZRA	1	ACTS	1
"	2	"	2	2	"	2	"	2
"	3	"	3	3	"	3	"	3
"	4	"	4	4	"	4	"	4
"	5	"	5	5	"	5	"	5
"	6	"	6	6	"	6	"	6
"	7	"	7	7	"	7	"	7
"	8	"	8	8	"	8	"	8
"	9–10	"	9	9	"	9	"	9
"	11	"	10	10	"	10	"	10
"	12	"	11	11	NEHEMIAH	1	"	11
"	13	"	12	12	"	2	"	12
"	14	"	13	13	"	3	"	13
"	15	"	14	14	"	4	"	14
"	16	"	15	15	"	5	"	15
"	17	"	16	16	"	6	"	16
"	18	"	17	17	"	7	"	17
"	19	"	18	18	"	8	"	18
"	20	"	19	19	"	9	"	19
"	21	"	20	20	"	10	"	20
"	22	"	21	21	"	11	"	21
"	23	"	22	22	"	12	"	22
"	24	"	23	23	"	13	"	23
"	25	"	24	24	ESTHER	1	"	24
"	26	"	25	25	"	2	"	25
"	27	"	26	26	"	3	"	26
"	28	"	27	27	"	4	"	27
"	29	"	28	28	"	5	"	28
"	30	MARK	1	29	"	6	ROM.	1
"	31	"	2	30	"	7	"	2
"	32	"	3	31	"	8	"	3

FEBRUARY

Morning					Evening			
GENESIS	33	MARK	4	1	ESTHER	9–10	ROM.	4
"	34	"	5	2	"	1	"	5
"	35–36	"	6	3	"	2	"	6
"	37	"	7	4	"	3	"	7
"	38	"	8	5	"	4	"	8
"	39	"	9	6	"	5	"	9
"	40	"	10	7	"	6	"	10
"	41	"	11	8	"	7	"	11
"	42	"	12	9	"	8	"	12
"	43	"	13	10	"	9	"	13
"	44	"	14	11	"	10	"	14
"	45	"	15	12	"	11	"	15
"	46	"	16	13	"	12	"	16
"	47	Lk. 1 to v. 38		14	"	13	1 COR.	1
"	48	" 1 to v. 39		15	"	14	"	2
"	49	"	2	16	"	15	"	3
"	50	"	3	17	"	16–17	"	4
EXODUS	1	"	4	18	"	18	"	5
"	2	"	5	19	"	19	"	6
"	3	"	6	20	"	20	"	7
"	4	"	7	21	"	21	"	8
"	5	"	8	22	"	22	"	9
"	6	"	9	23	"	23	"	10
"	7	"	10	24	"	24	"	11
"	8	"	11	25	"	25–26	"	12
"	9	"	12	26	"	27	"	13
"	10	"	13	27	"	28	"	14
11–12 to v. 21		"	14	28	"	29	"	15

MARCH

	Morning				Evening		
Ex. 12	V. 22	LUKE	15	1	JOB	30	1 COR.	16
"	13	"	16	2	"	31	2 COR.	1
"	14	"	17	3	"	32	"	2
"	15	"	18	4	"	33	"	3
"	16	"	19	5	"	34	"	4
"	17	"	20	6	"	35	"	5
"	18	"	21	7	"	36	"	6
"	19	"	22	8	"	37	"	7
"	20	"	23	9	"	38	"	8
"	21	"	24	10	"	39	"	9
"	22	JOHN	1	11	"	40	"	10
"	23	"	2	12	"	41	"	11
"	24	"	3	13	"	42	"	12
"	25	"	4	14	PROV.	1	"	13
"	26	"	5	15	"	2	GAL.	1
"	27	"	6	16	"	3	"	2
"	28	"	7	17	"	4	"	3
"	29	"	8	18	"	5	"	4
"	30	"	9	19	"	6	"	5
"	31	"	10	20	"	7	"	6
"	32	"	11	21	"	8	EPH.	1
"	33	"	12	22	"	9	"	2
"	34	"	13	23	"	10	"	3
"	35	"	14	24	"	11	"	4
"	36	"	15	25	"	12	"	5
"	37	"	16	26	"	13	"	6
"	38	"	17	27	"	14	PHIL.	1
"	39	"	18	28	"	15	"	2
"	40	"	19	29	"	16	"	3
LEV	1	"	20	30	"	17	"	4
"	2–3	"	21	31	"	18	COL.	1

APRIL

	Morning				Evening		
LEV.	4	PSALMS	1–2	1	PROV.	19	COL.	2
"	5	"	3–4	2	"	20	"	3
"	6	"	5–6	3	"	21	"	4
"	7	"	7–8	4	"	22 1 THESS.	1
"	8	"	9	5	"	23	"	2
"	9	"	10	6	"	24	"	3
"	10	"	11–12	7	"	25	"	4
"	11–12	"	13–14	8	"	26	"	5
"	13	"	15–16	9	"	27 2 THESS.	1
"	14	"	17	10	"	28	"	2
"	15	"	18	11	"	29	"	3
"	16	"	19	12	"	30 1 TIM	1
"	17	"	20–21	13	"	31	"	2
"	18	"	22	14	ECCLES.	1	"	3
"	19	"	23–24	15	"	2	"	4
"	20	"	25	16	"	3	"	5
"	21	"	26–27	17	"	4	"	6
"	22	"	28–29	18	"	5 2 TIM	1
"	23	"	30	19	"	6	"	2
"	24	"	31	20	"	7	"	3
"	25	"	32	21	"	8	"	4
"	26	"	33	22	"	9 TITUS	1
"	27	"	34	23	"	10	"	2
NUM.	1	"	35	24	"	11	"	3
"	2	"	36	25	"	12 PHIL.	1
"	3	"	37	26	SONG	1 HEB.	1
"	4	"	38	27	"	2	"	2
"	5	"	39	28	"	3	"	3
"	6	"	40–41	29	"	4	"	4
"	7	"	42–43	30	"	5	"	5

MAY

		Morning				Evening		
NUMBERS	8	PSALMS	44	1	SONG	6	HEB.	6
"	9	"	45	2	"	7	"	7
"	10	"	46–47	3	"	8	"	8
"	11	"	48	4	ISAIAH	1	"	9
"	12–13	"	49	5	"	2	"	10
"	14	"	50	6	"	3–4	"	11
"	15	"	51	7	"	5	"	12
"	16	"	52–54	8	"	6	"	13
"	17–18	"	55	9	"	7	JAMES	1
"	19	"	56–57	10	"	8–9 to v. 7	"	2
"	20	"	58–59	11		9 v. 8, 10 v. 4	"	3
"	21	"	60–61	12	"	10 v. 5	"	4
"	22	"	62–63	13	"	11–12	"	5
"	23	"	64–65	14	"	13	1 PETER	1
"	24	"	66–67	15	"	14	"	2
"	25	"	68	16	"	15	"	3
"	26	"	69	17	"	16	"	4
"	27	"	70–71	18	"	17–18	"	5
"	28	"	72	19	"	19–20	2 PETER	1
"	29	"	73	20	"	21	"	2
"	30	"	74	21	"	22	"	3
"	31	"	75–76	22	"	23	1 JOHN	1
"	32	"	77	23	"	24	"	2
"	33	" 78 to v. 37		24	"	25	"	3
"	34	" 78 v. 38		25	"	26	"	4
"	35	"	79	26	"	27	"	5
"	36	"	80	27	"	28	2 JOHN	1
DEUT.	1	"	81–82	28	"	29	3 JOHN	1
"	2	"	83–84	29	"	30	JUDE	1
"	3	"	85	30	"	31	REV.	1
"	4	"	86–87	31	"	32	"	2

JUNE

	Morning					Evening		
DEUT.	5	PSALMS	88	1	ISAIAH	33	REV.	3
"	6	"	89	2	"	34	"	4
"	7	"	90	3	"	35	"	5
"	8	"	91	4	"	36	"	6
"	9	"	92–93	5	"	37	"	7
"	10	"	94	6	"	38	"	8
"	11	"	95–96	7	"	39	"	9
"	12	"	97–98	8	"	40	"	10
"	13–14	"	99–101	9	"	41	"	11
"	15	"	102	10	"	42	"	12
"	16	"	103	11	"	43	"	13
"	17	"	104	12	"	44	"	14
"	18	"	105	13	"	45	"	15
"	19	"	106	14	"	46	"	16
"	20	"	107	15	"	47	"	17
"	21	"	108–109	16	"	48	"	18
"	22	"	110–111	17	"	49	"	19
"	23	"	112–113	18	"	50	"	20
"	24	"	114–115	19	"	51	"	21
"	25	"	116	20	"	52	"	22
"	26	"	117–118	21	"	53	MATT.	1
27–28 to v.	19	119 to v.	24	22	"	54	"	2
28 to v.	20	v. 25 to	48	23	"	55	"	3
"	29	v. 49 to	72	24	"	56	"	4
"	30	v. 73 to	96	25	"	57	"	5
"	31	v. 97 to	120	26	"	58	"	6
"	32	v. 121 to	144	27	"	59	"	7
"	33–34	v. 145 to	176	28	"	60	"	8
JOSHUA	1		120–122	29	"	61	"	9
"	2		123–125	30	"	62	"	10

JULY

	Morning					Evening			
JOSHUA	3	PS.	126–128	1	ISAIAH	63	MATT.		11
"	4	"	129–131	2	"	64	"		12
	5–6 to v. 5	"	132–134	3	"	65	"		13
"	6 v. 6	"	135–136	4	"	66	"		14
"	7	"	137–138	5	JER.	1	"		15
"	8	"	139	6	"	2	"		16
"	9	"	140–141	7	"	3	"		17
"	10	"	142–143	8	"	4	"		18
"	11	"	144	9	"	5	"		19
"	12–13	"	145	10	"	6	"		20
"	14–15	"	146–147	11	"	7	"		21
"	16–17	"	148	12	"	8	"		22
"	18–19	"	149–150	13	"	9	"		23
"	20–21	ACTS	1	14	"	10	"		24
"	22	"	2	15	"	11	"		25
"	23	"	3	16	"	12	"		26
"	24	"	4	17	"	13	"		27
JUDGES	1	"	5	18	"	14	"		28
"	2	"	6	19	"	15	MARK		1
"	3	"	7	20	"	16	"		2
"	4	"	8	21	"	17	"		3
"	5	"	9	22	"	18	"		4
"	6	"	10	23	"	19	"		5
"	7	"	11	24	"	20	"		6
"	8	"	12	25	"	21	"		7
"	9	"	13	26	"	22	"		8
	10–11 to v. 11	"	14	27	"	23	"		9
	11 v. 12	"	15	28	"	24	"		10
"	12	"	16	29	"	25	"		11
"	13	"	17	30	"	26	"		12
"	14	"	18	31	"	27	"		13

AUGUST

	Morning					Evening			
JUDGES	15	ACTS	19	1	JER.	28	MARK	14
"	16	"	20	2	"	29	"	15
"	17	"	21	3	"	30–31	"	16
"	18	"	22	4	"	32	PSALMS	1–2
"	19	"	23	5	"	33	"	3–4
"	20	"	24	6	"	34	"	5–6
"	21	"	25	7	"	35	"	7–8
RUTH	1	"	26	8	"	36, 45	"	9
"	2	"	27	9	"	37	"	10
"	3–4	"	28	10	"	38	"	11–12
1 SAM.	1	ROMANS	1	11	"	39	"	13–14
"	2	"	2	12	"	40	"	15–16
"	3	"	3	13	"	41	"	17
"	4	"	4	14	"	42	"	18
"	5–6	"	5	15	"	43	"	19
"	7–8	"	6	16	"	44	"	20–21
"	9	"	7	17	"	46	"	22
"	10	"	8	18	"	47	"	23–24
"	11	"	9	19	"	48	"	25
"	12	"	10	20	"	49	"	26–27
"	13	"	11	21	"	50	"	28–29
"	14	"	12	22	"	51	"	30
"	15	"	13	23	"	52	"	31
"	16	"	14	24	LAMEN.	1	"	32
"	17	"	15	25	"	2	"	33
"	18	"	16	26	"	3	"	34
"	19	1 COR.	1	27	"	4	"	35
"	20	"	2	28	"	5	"	36
"	21–22	"	3	29	EZEKIEL	1	"	37
"	23	"	4	30	"	2	"	38
"	24	"	5	31	"	3	"	39

SEPTEMBER

	Morning					Evening		
1 SAM	25	1 COR.	6	1	EZEK.	4	PS.	40–41
"	26	"	7	2	"	5	"	42–43
"	27	"	8	3	"	6	"	44
"	28	"	9	4	"	7	"	45
"	29–30	"	10	5	"	8	"	46–47
"	31	"	11	6	"	9	"	48
2 SAM	1	"	12	7	"	10	"	49
"	2	"	13	8	"	11	"	50
"	3	"	14	9	"	12	"	51
"	4–5	"	15	10	"	13	"	52–54
"	6	"	16	11	"	14	"	55
"	7	2 COR.	1	12	"	15	"	56–57
"	8–9	"	2	13	"	16	"	58–59
"	10	"	3	14	"	17	"	60–61
"	11	"	4	15	"	18	"	62–63
"	12	"	5	16	"	19	"	64–65
"	13	"	6	17	"	20	"	66–67
"	14	"	7	18	"	21	"	68
"	15	"	8	19	"	22	"	69
"	16	"	9	20	"	23	"	70–71
"	17	"	10	21	"	24	"	72
"	18	"	11	22	"	25	"	73
"	19	"	12	23	"	26	"	74
"	20	"	13	24	"	27	"	75–76
"	21	GAL.	1	25	"	28	"	77
"	22	"	2	26	"	29	"	78 to v. 37
"	23	"	3	27	"	30	"	78 v. 38
"	24	"	4	28	"	31	"	79
1 KINGS	1	"	5	29	"	32	"	80
"	2	"	6	30	"	33	"	81–82

OCTOBER

	Morning					Evening		
1 KINGS	3	EPH.	1	1	EZEK.	34	PS.	83–84
"	4–5	"	2	2	"	35	"	85
"	6	"	3	3	"	36	"	86
"	7	"	4	4	"	37	"	87–88
"	8	"	5	5	"	38	"	89
"	9	"	6	6	"	39	"	90
"	10	PHIL.	1	7	"	40	"	91
"	11	"	2	8	"	41	"	92–93
"	12	"	3	9	"	42	"	94
"	13	"	4	10	"	43	"	95–96
"	14	COL.	1	11	"	44	"	97–98
"	15	"	2	12	"	45	"	99–101
"	16	"	3	13	"	46	"	102
"	17	"	4	14	"	47	"	103
"	18	1 THESS.	1	15	"	48	"	104
"	19	"	2	16	DAN.	1	"	105
"	20	"	3	17	"	2	"	106
"	21	"	4	18	"	3	"	107
"	22	"	5	19	"	4	"	108–109
2 KINGS	1	2 THESS.	1	20	"	5	"	110–111
"	2	"	2	21	"	6	"	112–113
"	3	"	3	22	"	7	"	114–115
"	4	1 TIM.	1	23	"	8	"	116
"	5	"	2	24	"	9	"	117–118
"	6	"	3	25	"	10		119 to v. 24
"	7	"	4	26	"	11		v. 25 to 48
"	8	"	5	27	"	12		v. 49 to 72
"	9	"	6	28	HOSEA	1		v. 73 to 96
"	10–11	2 TIM.	1	29	"	2		v. 97 to 120
"	12	"	2	30	"	3–4		v. 121 to 144
"	13	"	3	31	"	5–6		v. 145 to 176

NOVEMBER

Morning					Evening			
2 KINGS	14	2 TIM	4	1	HOSEA	7	PS.	120–122
"	15	TITUS	1	2	"	8	"	123–125
"	16	"	2	3	"	9	"	126–128
"	17	"	3	4	"	10	"	129–131
"	18	PHILEM	1	5	"	11	"	132–134
"	19	HEB.	1	6	"	12	"	135–136
"	20	"	2	7	"	13	"	137–138
"	21	"	3	8	"	14	"	139
"	22	"	4	9	JOEL	1	"	140–141
"	23	"	5	10	"	2	"	142
"	24	"	6	11	"	3	"	143
"	25	"	7	12	AMOS	1	"	144
1 CHR.	1–2	"	8	13	"	2	"	145
"	3–4	"	9	14	"	3	"	146–147
"	5–6	"	10	15	"	4	"	148–150
"	7–8	"	11	16	"	5	Lk	1 to v. 38
"	9–10	"	12	17	"	6	"	1 to v. 39
"	11–12	"	13	18	"	7	"	2
"	13–14	JAMES	1	19	"	8	"	3
"	15	"	2	20	"	9	"	4
"	16	"	3	21	OBADIAH	1	"	5
"	17	"	4	22	JONAH	1	"	6
"	18	"	5	23	"	2	"	7
"	19–20	1 PETER	1	24	"	3	"	8
"	21	"	2	25	"	4	"	9
"	22	"	3	26	MICAH	1	"	10
"	23	"	4	27	"	2	"	11
"	24–25	"	5	28	"	3	"	12
"	26–27	2 PETER	1	29	"	4	"	13
"	28	"	2	30	"	5	"	14

DECEMBER

	Morning						Evening		
1 CHR.	29	2 PETER	3	1	MICAH	6	LUKE		15
2 CHR	1	1 JOHN	1	2	"	7	"		16
"	2	"	2	3	NAHUM	1	"		17
"	3–4	"	3	4	"	2	"		18
	5–6 to v. 11	"	4	5	"	3	"		19
"	6 v. 12	"	5	6	HAB.	1	"		20
"	7	2 JOHN	1	7	"	2	"		21
"	8	3 JOHN	1	8	"	3	"		22
"	9	JUDE	1	9	ZEPH.	1	"		23
"	10	REV.	1	10	"	2	"		24
"	11–12	"	2	11	"	3	JOHN		1
"	13	"	3	12	HAGGAI	1	"		2
"	14–15	"	4	13	"	2	"		3
"	16	"	5	14	ZECH.	1	"		4
"	17	"	6	15	"	2	"		5
"	18	"	7	16	"	3	"		6
"	19–20	"	8	17	"	4	"		7
"	21	"	9	18	"	5	"		8
"	22–23	"	10	19	"	6	"		9
"	24	"	11	20	"	7	"		10
"	25	"	12	21	"	8	"		11
"	26	"	13	22	"	9	"		12
"	27–28	"	14	23	"	10	"		13
"	29	"	15	24	"	11	"		14
"	30	"	16	25	" 12–13 to v. 1		"		15
"	31	"	17	26	"	13 v. 2	"		16
"	32	"	18	27	"	14	"		17
"	33	"	19	28	MAL.	1	"		18
"	34	"	20	29	"	2	"		19
"	35	"	21	30	"	3	"		20
"	36	"	22	31	"	4	"		21

Index

A

A.D. (Anno Domini), 9
Aaron
    death, 79
    helps build a golden calf, 76
    Moses and Aaron, 70-71
    serves as high priest, 77
    superiority of Christ over Aaron,
        266
Abba, 240
Abednego, 165
Abel, 29
Abiathar helps David, 102
Abijah *(King)*, 127
Abimelech, self-appointed judge,
    89
Abimelech *(King)*, 47-48
Abinadab, 108
Abishag, 117
Abner, 106-107
Abraham (Abram)
    as forefather of Christianity,
        Judiasm, and Islam, 43
    circumcision of males in
        household, 40
    death, 46
    gives Melchizedek a tenth of
        everything, 38
    Hagar and Abraham's child
        (Ishmael), 39
        Hagar and Ishmael sent to
            wilderness, 43
    journey to Canaan, 36
    justified through faith, 239
    Keturah and Abraham, 69
    lies about relationship to Sarah,
        37
    name change, 39
    offers Isaac as a sacrifice, 43-44
    pleads for Sodom, 41
    promises from the Lord, 38
        birth of Isaac, 40, 43
        "Promised Land," 36
        three visitors, 40-41
    rescues Lot, 38
    Sarah and Abraham's child
        (Isaac), 40, 43

    sends servant to find Isaac a
        wife, 45-46
    separates from Lot, 37-38
Absalom
    David and Absalom
        Absalom overthrows David,
            113-114
        David mourns Absalom's
            death, 115
        reunion, 112
    death, 115
    Joab stabs Absalom, 115
    kills Ammon, 112
Abyss, 284
accuracy of Scripture, 9, 17
Accuser, *see* Satan
Achan, 84
Acts (Book of)
    author, 225
    contents, 235
    growth of church, 236
Adam
    Adam and Eve
        banished from Eden, 29
        Cain and Abel, 29-30
        creation of Eve, 27
        eat forbidden fruit, 28
        punished for disobedience,
            28-29
    creation of, 27
    naming the animals, 27
Adonai (definition), 69
Adonijah, 118
adultery
    as sin, 243
    excommunication of immoral
        brothers, 244
    Jesus speaks the woman caught
        in adultery, 184-185
Ahab
    king of Israel, 124
    Queen Jezebel and King Ahab,
        130
Ahasuerus, *see* Xerxes
Ahaz *(King)*, 128
Ahaziah
    king of Israel, 125
    king of Judah, 127
Ahithophel, 113-114

Ai (location), 84
Aitken Bible, 10
Amalekites, Saul battles them, 98
Amaziah *(King)*, 127
American Standard Version, 10
Ammon, 112
Ammonites, 42
    Saul leads Israelites against,
        96-97
Amon, 128
Amos, 168
Ananias, 229-230
Andrew, one of the Twelve, 181
angels
    appear to Joseph, 177
    cherubim, 163
    Gabriel, 166
    Michael, 166
    seraphs, 158, 163
    superiority of Christ to, 265-266
    visit shepherds to tell of Jesus'
        birth, 178
Anna, 178
Anno Domini (A.D.), 9
anointing with oil, customs/
    traditions, 96
antichrist
    1 John (Book of), 274
    number of the beast, 286
    Revelation (Book of), 285
Antioch
    Jewish leaders teach on
        circumcision, 232
    Paul and Barnabas teach the
        Gentiles, 230
Antiochus IV Epiphanes, 174
    Daniel's vision about, 166
apocalypse, 294
    four horsemen of the
        apocalypse, 283
Apocrypha, accepted by Council of
    Trent, 10
apostles
    choose seven "deacons," 228
    go before the Sanhedrin,
        227-228
    see also the Twelve
Arabs, as Ishmael's descendents, 43
ark (Noah's), 31-32

Ark of the Covenant, 77, 95
    Abinadab stores it, 108
    brought to Jerusalem, 108-109
    contents, 267
    crossing the Jordan River, 83
    Philistines take it, 95
    Ten Commandments, 77
Armageddon, 288
"armor of God," Ephesians
    (Book of) 256
Artaxerxes *(King)*
    allows Nehemiah to return to
        Judah, 136
    gives supplies to the temple,
        135
Asa *(King)*, 127
Asaph, David's choir leader, 147
ascension, 225-226
Assyria (Assyrians)
    captures Israel, 129
    Israel falls to Assyria, 157
    Sennacherib, 159
Athaliah *(King)*, 127
authority, submission to, 272
Azariah (Uzziah), 127

B

B.C (Before Christ), 9
B.C.E. (Before the Common Era), 9
Baal, worship and prophets of, 130
Baasha *(King)*, 124
Babylon
    captures Judah, 129
    Daniel in, 164
    Tower of Babel, 33
baker, Joseph interprets dream, 60
Balaam, 78
    teaching of Balaam, 281
banquet, Parable of the Great
    Banquet, 204
baptism
    Holy Spirit, 179
        Pentecost, 226-227
    of Jesus, 180
    water, 179
Barnabas
    John Mark and Barnabas, 232
    Paul and Barnabas
        Barnabas reassures Paul of
            conversion, 230
        disagree and separate, 232
        first journey, 231-232
        go to Antioch, 230
        Jerusalem church's decision
            on circumcision, 232
baths, traditions/culture, 110

Bathsheba
    David and Bathsheba
        birth of Solomon, 112
        David orders killing of
            Uriah, 110-111
        David sends for her, 110
        David sends for Uriah, 110
        first child, 111-112
        Nathan confronts David, 111
    Nathan warns Bathsheba, 118
    Uriah and Bathsheba, 110
the beast, 285-286
Beatitudes, 200
Before Christ (B.C.), 9
Before the Common Era (B.C.E), 9
believers, 230
    as "living stones", 271
    being "yoked" with nonbeliev-
        ers, 249
    challenges based on the new
        covenant, 267
    edification of the body, 247
    excommunication of immoral
        brothers, 243-244
    increase after Jesus' death, 227
    Jesus prays for all future
        believers, 218
    judgement of, 248
    speaking in tongues, 247
    strong and weak Christians, 244
    unity among the body
        division among the body,
            242-243
        Ephesians (Book of), 255
        2 Peter (Book of), 273
Belteshazzar (Daniel), *see* Daniel
benefits of reading the Bible, 6-8,
    19
Berea/Thessalonica, Paul and Silas'
    visit, 233
Bethel, 55-56
Bethlehem, 177
Bibles
    accuracy of Scripture, 9, 17
    Aitken Bible, 10
    atlases, 21
    benefits of reading, 6-8, 19
    best-selling book, 3
    books of the Bible, 293-296
        Epistles, 294
        Gospels, 294
        historical books, 293-296
        law-related, 293
        prophets (books of), 293-294
    choosing, 11-13
    events between Old and New
        Testaments, 174
    New Testament, 10
    Old Testament, 9-10

one-year reading schedule, 302-
    313
paraphases vs. translations, 11
quiz, 4-6, 13
relevancy for today, 16-17
resources, 297-298
    reference materials, 298-299
translations, 10-11, 298
Bildad, 143
birthright, Esau sells his to Jacob,
    47
blind, healings of the, 189, 195-196
Boaz
    as Naomi's kinsman-redeemer,
        91
    Ruth and Boaz, 90-92
"Book of Jashar," Israel's military
    history, 106
books of the Bible, 293-296
    canon, 10
    Epistles, 294
    Gospels, 294
    historical books of the Bible,
        293-296
        covenant/secular
            relationships, 295-296
        New Testament, 294
    law-related, 293
    number of books, 10
    prophets (books of), 293-294
born again, 183
boy in Nain, healing of, 194
bread
    bread and wine, significance,
        217
    five loaves and two fish, Jesus
        feeds 5,000, 192-193
    loaves of bread, customs/
        traditions, 192

C

C.E. (Common Era), 9
Caiaphas, Jesus tried before him,
    218-219
Cain
    kills Abel, 29
    marked by God, 30
    sacrifices to God, 29
    wife, 30
Caleb
    Joshua and Caleb spy on
        Canaan, 78
    leader of the tribe of Judah, 86
Calvary (Golgatha), 220
Canaan
    Abraham's journey to, 36
    Caleb and Joshua spy on
        Canaan, 78

Canaanites, 32
  defeat the Israelites, 84
  mythology, 128
  relationship with Israelites, 86
centurion's servant, healing of, 188
Cephas, *see* Peter
cherubim, 163
chief priests
  Caiaphas, Jesus' trial, 218-219
  increased hatred toward Jesus,
    215-216
  Judas Iscariot tries to return
    money, 219
  plot with Judas against Jesus,
    216
Christians, *see* believers
church
  apostles choose seven
    "deacons," 228
  division in the church, 242-243
    Ephesians (Book of), 255
    2 Peter (Book of), 273
  evaluation of seven churches,
    281
  growth after Jesus' death, 227
    Acts (Book of), 236
  Jerusalem church, 232
  spiritual gifts, 245-246
  women's part in worship/
    church, 247
circumcision
  Abraham's household, 40
  Jerusalem church's decision on,
    232
  Jesus' circumcision at the
    temple, 178
  Joshua circumcizes troops, 83
  Moses and Zipporah's son, 70
  symbolism, 40
  Timothy, 232
cistern, 58
citizenship, heavenly citizenship,
  257
City of David, *see* Jerusalem
Colossians (Book of), 258-259
  author, 258
  false doctrines, 258-259
  superiority of Christ, 258-259
commandments, *Ten Commandments*, 75, 77
commentaries, 21
commission, *Great Commission*, 224
concordances, 21-22
Corinth, Paul and Silas' journey,
  233
1 Corinthians (Book of)
  author, 242
  dietary restrictions, 244-245
  divisions in the church,
    242-243

excommunication of immoral
    brothers, 243-244
  marriage, 244
  orderly worship, 245
  purpose of letter, 242
  rapture, 248
  speaking in tongues, 247
  spiritual immaturity, 243
  strong and weak Christians,
    244-245
  unity among body of believers,
    and spiritual gifts, 245-246
  women's part in worship/
    church, 247
2 Corinthians (Book of), 249-250
Cornelius, 230
Council of Carthage, 10
Council of Trent, 10
covenants
  Laban and Jacob, 54
  new covenant through Jesus,
    266-267
creation
  Adam and Eve, 27
  and eternity, 25
  days of creation, 26-33
    length of days, 26
  God rests on seventh day, 27
  use of first-person plural
    pronoun, 26
Crossing the Jordan (euphemism
  for dying), 83
crucifixion of Jesus, 220-221
  Golgotha (Calvary), 220
  Jesus' final breath, 221
  Jesus' side pierced, 221
  Joseph of Arimathea and
    Nicodemus place Jesus in the
    tomb, 221-222
  sign on Jesus' cross, 221
  Simeon of Cyrene, 220
  soldiers cast lots for Jesus'
    clothing, 221
  thief asks Jesus to remember
    him, 221
cupbearers, Joseph interprets
  cupbearer's dreams, 60
customs/traditions
  almond trees, 160
  animal manure, 163
  anointing with oil, 96
  baths, 110
  bucklers, 147
  bulls, significance, 76
  elder family members, 38
  firstborn, 65
  goatskins, 209
  hairiness, significance in
    culture, 113
  intermarriage, 136

loaves of bread, 192
  mules, 118
  Persian hangings, 139
  pitching tents, 87
  Roman citizenship, 231
  roofs of homes, 188
  socializing between Hebrews
    and Egyptians, 62
  today vs. biblical times, 16-17
  washing feet, 217
  weddings, 190
Cyprus, 232
Cyrus, king of Persia, 134

D

Damascus, Saul of Tarsus on road
  to Damascus, 229
Daniel, 167
  as Belteshazzar, 165
  in exile in Babylon, 164
  interprets Nebuchadnezzar's
    dream, 164-165
  length of the Great Tribulation,
    286
  three friends in the fiery
    furnace, 165-166
  thrown in lions' den, 166
  visions and prophecies, 166
Darius *(King)*, 166
David *(King)*, 115
  Abiathar helps David, 102
  Abishag takes care of David,
    117-118
  Abner defects to David's side,
    107
  Absalom and David
    Absalom overthrows David,
      113-114
    Ahithophel counsels
      Absalom, 113-114
    David mourns Absalom's
      death, 115
    reunion, 112
  Adonijah plots to overtake
    David, 118
  advises Solomon, 118
  appoints Joab as head of forces,
    106
  Ark of the Covenant brought to
    Jerusalem, 108-109
  author of Psalms, 145
  Bathsheba and David, *see*
    Bathsheba
  cares for Mephibosheth, 109
  children, 111-112
  dances before the Lord, 108-109
  death, 118

establishes Jerusalem as capital, 107-108
fakes insanity, 101
flees Jerusalem, 113
flees to Nob, 101
goes to Gath, 101-102
Goliath and David, 99-100
Jonathan and David, 101-102
lives among the Philistines, 102
Michal and David, *see* Michal
Nathan confronts David, 111
receives news of Saul's death, 106
Samuel anoints him as king, 98-99
Saul and David, *see* Saul
unites Israel and Judah, 107-108
wants to build temple, 109-110
deacons, 228-229
Dead Sea Scrolls
description of Sarah, 37
discovery, 9
debates about Jesus, 199-201
Deborah, prophetess, 87-88
dedication of Solomon's temple, 120-121
deeds/ (faith and deeds), 269-270
Delilah, Samson and Delilah, 90
Demetrius, rallies tradesmen against Paul, 233-234
demon-possessed man, healing of, 189, 195
demons, 189
see also Satan
denominations (Christian), differences among, 15-16
destruction, way of eternal life vs. way of destruction, 202
Deuteronomy (Book of), 80
Devil, *see* Satan
dictionaries, 21
dietary restrictions, 244-245
Dinah, 55
disabilities, *see* healings
disciples
Great Commission, 224
Jesus prays for all future disciples, 218
see also Jesus; the Twelve
division in the church, 242-243
Ephesians (Book of), 255
2 Peter (Book of), 273
divorce
Jesus' teachings on, 201
not remarrying, 244
reconciling, 244
Doeg, tells Saul David's whereabouts, 101

E-F-G

Ecclesiastes (Book of), 152-154
Eden, *see* Garden of Eden
Edomites, 168
Egypt, God brings plagues on Egypt, 71-72
Ehud, 87
Elah *(King)*, 124
Eli, 94-95
Elihu, 143
Elijah
Elijah and Elisha, 130
Jesus' mention of, 130
the Transfiguration, 214
Eliphaz, 143
Elisha, 130-131
Elizabeth
Mary visits Elizabeth, 176
Zachariah and Elizabeth
birth of John, 176
Gabriel visits Zachariah, 175
Elkanah, Hannah and Elkanah, 93-94
end times
signs, 215
ungodly behavior, 262
enemies
dealing with, Jesus' teachings on, 201
Israel's enemies, prophecies against, 158-159
Enemy, *see* Satan
Ephesians (Book of), 255-256
Ephesus, Paul and Silas' journey, 233-234
Ephriam, 61, 65
Epicureans, 233
Epistles, 294
Esau
Edomites, 168
Jacob and Esau
gives up birthright, 47
Isaac blesses Jacob instead of Isaac, 48-49
receives peace offering from Jacob, 54
reunites with Jacob, 55
Esther *(Queen)*
chosen as queen, 139
intervenes for the Jews, 140
raised by Mordecai, 139
receives Haman's property, 141
visits Xerxes, 140
eternal life
for everyone who accepts Jesus, 241-242

way of eternal life vs. way of destruction, 202
eternity, and creation, 25
Euphrates River, Garden of Eden, 27
Eutychus, healing of, 234
Eve
Adam and Eve
banished from Eden, 29
Cain and Abel, 29-30
eat forbidden fruit, 28
punished for disobedience, 28-29
creation of, 27
Satan (serpent) tempts her, 27
Everlasting Father
names of Jesus, 158
excommunication
of immoral brothers, 243-244
Ezekiel, 164
cherubims, 163
makes a model of Jerusalem, 163
seraphs, 163
visions
dry bones, 164
the temple, 164
windstorm, 162-163
Ezra
prays for safety, 135
reads the Law of Moses, 137-138
weeps and prays for people, 135-136

faith
Abraham justified through faith, 239
faith and deeds, 269-270
prayer, 269
refining faith, and trials, 271
righteousness through faith in Jesus, 239
the false prophet, Revelation (Book of), 286
false prophets
and Paul, 249
Jesus' teachings on, 202
warnings against (in Book of)
1 John, 274
2 John, 275
2 Peter, 273
Jude, 276
fasting, Jesus' teachings on, 201
favoritism, 269
Feast of Tabernacles (Sukkot), 134
Feast of Weeks (Pentecost), 226-227
Field of Blood, 219
fiery furnace, 165
fig tree, withered, 193

figurative vs. literal language, 17-18
firstfruits, 247
five loaves and two fish, Jesus feeds
5,000, 192-193
Flood, The, 32
forgiveness
  parables on, prodigal son,
    206-207
  as atonement for sin, 239
    accepting Jesus as the Son of
      God, 199-201
    leaving behind sin and
      accepting Christ, 240
    righteousness through faith
      in Jesus, 239
    salvation for all who accept
      Jesus, 241-242
    sufficiency of Jesus' sacrifice,
      266-267
four horsemen of the apocalypse,
283
freedom, and dietary restrictions,
244-245

Gabriel (angel), 166
  visits Mary, 176
  visits Zachariah, 175-176
Galatians (Book of), 253-254
Garden of Eden, 27
  Adam and Eve
    ate forbidden fruit, 28
    banished from Eden, 29
    creation of, 27
    punished for disobedience,
      28-29
  modern-day location, 27
  Satan tempts Eve, 27
  Tree of Life, 27
  Tree of the Knowledge of Good
    and Evil, 27-28
Gath (location), 101-102
Gehenna, 207
gender/pronoun issues, 18
Gentiles
  "ingrafted branches," 242
  Paul and Barnabas teach in
    Antioch, 230
  relationships with Jews, Peter's
    vision, 230
  salvation for everyone who
    accepts Jesus, 241-242
Geshem, 137
Gethsemane (Garden of), 218
Gibeonites, 85
Gideon, 88
Gilead (location), 58
Gnostics, 258
goatskins, customs/traditions, 209
godlessness of men, 238

golden calf, Israelites build, 76
Golgotha (Calvary), 220
Goliath, David and Goliath, 99-100
Gomer, 167
Gomorrah, 41-42
Good Samaritan (Parable of), 205
Goshen (location), 64
gospels, 173, 210, 294
  John, vs. the others, 179
grace
  and sin, 239
  vs. mercy, 256
Great Commission, 224
great tribulation, 283, 286
greed
  as sin, 243
  Jesus' teachings on, 201
guards at Jesus' tomb, 223
Gutenberg Bible, 10

H

Habakkuk, 169
Hades (Hell), 207
Hagar
  Abraham and Hagar, 39
  Ishmael and Hagar sent to
    wilderness, 43
Haggai, 169
  Zachariah and Haggai, 135
hairiness, significance in culture,
113
Ham (Noah's son), 32
Haman, 139-141
hangings, Persian customs/
  traditions, 139
Hannah
  dedicates Samuel, 94
  Elkanah and Hannah, 93-94
healings, 188
  by apostles, 227
  by Jesus, 188
    blind people, 189, 195-196
    boy in Nain, 194
    centurion's servant, 188
    demon-possessed
      individuals, 189, 195
    Jairus' daughter, 194
    Lazarus, 194-195
    lepers, 189
    paralyzed man, 188
  by Paul
    Eutychus, 234
    demon-possessed man, 233
  by Peter, 227
Hebrews (Book of), 268
  author, 265
  challenges for Christians, 267

faithful men/women of the
  past, 267
  Jesus in the order of
    Melchizedek, 266
  new covenant through Jesus,
    266-267
  perseverance, 268
  sufficiency of Jesus' sacrifice,
    266-267
  superiority of Christ, 265-266
Hell, 209
  Bible references, 207-208
  Jesus' teachings on, 208
Hellenization, 174
Herod *(King)*
  arrested Christians, 230
  imprisoned Peter, 230
  orders death of male children,
    178
  put James to death, 230
Herod Antipas *(King)*
  Jesus tried before Herod, 220
Hezekiah *(King)*, 128
historical books of the Bible
  covenant relationship/secular
    relationship, 295-296
  New Testament, 294
  Old Testament, 293
holiness, 271
Holy City (new Jerusalem), 290-291
Holy of Holies (Most Holy Place),
  77
Holy Spirit
  baptism in the Holy Spirit, 179
  comes at Pentecost, 226-227
  Jesus promises it, 218
  misunderstandings about it in
    Ephesus, 233
homosexuality, 42
  as sin, 243
  excommunication of immoral
    brothers, 244
Hosea, 167
Hoshea *(King)*, 126
humility
  before God, 270
  God rewards, 269
  vs. hypocrisy (parable), 204
husband/wife relationship, 272
  Ephesians, 256
Hushai, 113-114
hypocrisy vs. humilty (parable on),
204

I

Iconium (location), 231
idolatry, 128

Ezra weeps and prays for the people, 136
Israelites build a golden calf, 76
Rachel steals father's idols, 53
reign of Solomon, 118
images of God (Psalms), 146-147
immorality
adultery, 243
excommunication of immoral brothers, 243-244
homosexuality, 42, 243
"ingrafted branches," Gentiles as, 242
intercession, *see* prayer
intercultural marriages, customs/traditions, 136
interfaith marriages, avoiding Old Testament, 46
Iraq, biblical location, 27, 36
Isaac
Abraham sends servant to find Isaac a wife, 45-46
blesses Jacob instead of Esau, 48-49
King Abimelech and Isaac, 47-48
offered as a sacrifice, 43-44
Rebekah and Isaac, 46
Isaac lies about relationship to Rebekah, 47-48
Jacob and Esau, 46-47
Isaiah, 157-159
God increases Hezekiah's life expectancy, 128
prophecies
about Jesus, 158
against Israel's enemies, 158-159
God's people, 159
Ish-Bosheth, 106-107
Ishmael
Abraham's death, 46
Arabs as descendants of, 43
Hagar and Abraham's child, 39
Hagar and Ishmael sent to wilderness, 43
Ishmaelites, 58
Israel (Jacob)
twelve tribes of Israel, 86
see also Jacob (Israel)
Israel, 157
as the "Promised Land," 36
captured by Assyria, 129
Judah and Israel
David unites Israel and Judah, 107-108
God tells Solomon kingdom will split, 122
split under Rehoboam, 122

kings of Israel, 124-126
military history, "Book of Jashar," 106
prophecies against enemies, 158-159
spiritual renewal, 138
Israelites
Ark of the Covenant returned, 95
bury Saul and his sons, 103
descendants of Jacob, 168
enslaved by Pharoah, 68
God tells them they must wander another 40 years, 79
grumble against Moses, Caleb, and Joshua, 78
idolatry, 86-87
build a golden calf, 76
during reign of Solomon, 118
Joshua and the Israelites
Achan disobeys Joshua's command, 84
attack Jericho, 84
attack the city of Ai, 84
circumcision performed and Passover observed, 83
cross the Jordan River, 83
Joshua appointed as leader, 79
make a treaty with Gibeonites, 85
march around Jericho, 83-84
settlement of Promised Land, 86
sun stands still, 85
Moses and the Israelites
building/funishing tabernacle, 77
God provides manna, 74
in the Desert of Sinai, 75
Israelites begin to grumble, 74
led out of Egypt, 73
Moses told to lead them out of Egypt, 69-70
parting of the Red Sea, 73
Pharaoh and the Israelites, 71-73
Philistines and Israelites, 97-98
relationship with Canaanites, 86
Samuel warns them to obey God, 96-97
want a king, 96

J-K

Jacob (Israel)
accepts God as his God, 49
blesses family, 65-66
burial, 66
death, 65-66
discovers truth about Joseph, 64
dream, 49-50
Esau and Jacob, see *Esau*
flees to Mesopotamia with Rebekah, 49
God blesses him at Bethel, 55-56
Israelites as descendants of, 168
"Jacob's ladder," 49
Laban and Jacob
make a covenant, 54
Jacob receives part of Laban's livestock, 52
works for Laban, 50
Leah and Jacob, 50-51
mourns Joseph's "death," 58
name change (Israel), 55
promises from the Lord, 49
Rachel and Jacob, 50-51
twelve tribes of Israel, 86
wrestles with God, 55
"Jacob's ladder," 49
Jairus' daughter, healing of, 194
James (Book of), 268-271
James (son of Alphaeus), one of the Twelve, 181
James (son of Zebedee), one of the Twelve, 181
Jehoahaz
king of Israel, 125
king of Judah, 128
Jehoash *(King)*, 125
Jehoiachin *(King)*, 129
Jehoiakim *(King)*, 129
Jehoram *(King)*, 127
Jehoshaphat
Elisha's prophecy, 131
king of Judah, 127
Jehovah (name of God), 69
Jehu *(King)*, 125
Jephthah, 89
Jeremiah (Book of Jeremiah), 161
advises King Zedekiah, 160
author, Lamentations (Book of), 161
called by God to be a prophet, 159-160
God's message through Jeremiah, 160
Nebuchadnezzar asks that he not be harmed, 160

people try to kill Judah, 160
"the weeping prophet," 159-161
told to observe a potter at work, 160
two visions, 159-160
writes to the exiles in Babylon, 161
Jericho, Joshua and the Israelites, 82-84
Jeroboam
king of Israel, 124
rebels against Solomon, 122
Jeroboam II *(King)*, 125
Jerusalem
Ark of the Covenant brought to Jerusalem, 108-109
David establishes it as capital, 107
David flees Jerusalem, 113
destruction, Lamentations (Book of), 161-162
Ezekiel makes a model of, 163
Ezra
returns to Jerusalem, 135
weeps and prays for people, 135-136
Jesus rides into Jerusalem, 215
Joseph and Mary find Jesus in the temple, 178-179
new Jerusalem (Holy City), 290-291
Paul returns after second journey, 234
temple rebuilt (Zerubbabel's temple)
attack from enemies, 135
celebrating the Feast of Tabernacles, 134
completion of the temple, 135
some return to rebuild temple, 134-136
Zachariah and Haggai encourage people, 135
walls destroyed, 136
walls rebuilt, 137
attack from enemies, 135
completion of walls, 137-138
enemy attacks and other opposition, 137
Jerusalem church's decision on circumcision, 232
Jesus, 176
accepting him as the Son of God, 199-201
and the Twelve
chooses the Twelve, 181
disciples argue about who is greatest, 217

feeding of 5,000, 192-193
Jesus calms the storm, 191
Jesus promises Holy Spirit, 218
Jesus walks on water, 192
Jesus washes their feet, 217
Last Supper, 217
withered fig tree, 193
arrested, 218
as atonement for sin, 239
accepting him as the Son of God, 199-201
leaving behind sin and accepting Christ, 240
righteousness through faith in Jesus, 239
salvation for all who accept Jesus, 241-242
sufficiency of his sacrifice, 266-267
as "the chief cornerstone," 255
ascension, 225-226
baptism by John the Baptist, 180
being in Christ, benefits, 240
birth
angels visit shepherds, 178
born in Bethlehem, 177
circumcision at the temple, 178
Gabriel visits Mary, 176
Magi visit Jesus, 178
myths, 177-178
significance, 179
clears the temple, 215
crucifixion, 220-222
final week (before crucifixion), 216
healings
blind, 189, 195-196
boy in Nain, 194
demon-possessed man, 189, 195
Jairus' daughter, 194
Lazarus, 194-195
lepers, 189
man born blind, 195-196
paralyzed man, 188
the centurion's servant, 188
John the Baptist
prepares the way for Jesus, 179
Jonah, reference to, 168
Joseph and Mary, 176-179
Judas and chief priests plot against Jesus, 216
leaving behind sin and accepting Christ, 240

Mary pours perfume on His feet, 216
miracles
calms the storm, 191
changes water to wine, 190
feeds 5,000, 192-193
healings, 188-189, 194-195
money for taxes, 193
multiples the fish in Peter's net, 191
number recorded in the Bible, 196
walks on water, 192
withered fig tree, 193
names of Jesus, 158
nature of, 185
on trial
before Caiaphas, 218-219
before Herod, 220
before Pontius Pilate, 219-220
before Sanhedrin, 219
taken to Annas, 218
opposition to Jesus increases, 215-216
Peter and Jesus
Jesus multiples the fish in Peter's net, 191
Jesus rebukes Peter, 214
money for taxes, 193
Peter acknowledges Him as the Christ, 214
Peter denies Jesus three times, 219
Peter walks on water, 192
Peter warned about testing, 217
post-resurrection appearances, 222-224
prays for himself, the disciples, and all future believers, 218
prays in Gethsemane, 218
promises the Holy Spirit, 218
prophecies about
Isaiah, 158
Micah, 169
victory over Satan, 28
rejected in Nazareth, 182
resurrection
guards questioned about Jesus' body, 223
news spreads, 225
post-resurrection appearances, 222-224
rides into Jerusalem, 215
righteousness through faith in Jesus, 239
salvation for all who accept Jesus, 241-242

sends word to John the Baptist in prison, 196
Sermon on the Mount, 200-202
speaks at synagogue in Nazareth, 182
speaks with the woman caught in adultery, 184-185
sufficiency of his sacrifice, 266-267
superiority of Christ
    Colossians (Book of), 258-259
    over Aaron, 266
    over angels, 265-266
    over Moses, 266
talks with the woman at the well, 183-184
tells Nicodemus he must be born again, 183
temptation in the wilderness, 180-181
the Transfiguration, 214
the Word of God becomes flesh, 179
Jethro (Reuel), 69
Jewish calendar, Feast of Weeks (Pentecost), 226
Jews
    and Samaritans, 184
    Esther saves the Jews, 141
    Haman plots to kill all Jews, 139-140
    intermarriage, 136
    relationships with Gentiles, Peter's vision, 230
    salvation for all who accept Jesus, 241-242
    see also Israel; Israelites
Jezebel (Queen), and King Ahab, 130
Joab, 115
    Abner and Joab, 106-107
    kills Uriah, 111
    stabs Absalom, 115
Joash *(King)*, 127
Job (Book of Job), 141-143
Joel, 168
John
    author
        1 John (Book of), 274-275
        2 John (Book of), 275
        3 John (Book of), 275
        Revelation, 280
    one of the Twelve, 181
    Peter and John imprisoned, 227
    Peter and John run to see empty tomb, 222
    the Transfiguration, 214

John (Book of) vs. the others, 179
John Mark, 218
    Barnabas and John Mark, 232
John the Baptist
    baptizes Jesus, 180
    birth, 176
    criticizes the Pharisees and Sadducces, 180
    Gabriel visits Zachariah, 175
    life and ministry, 179-180
    receives word from Jesus while in prison, 196
Jonah, 168
Jonathan
    David and Jonathan, 101-102
    eats honey, 97-98
    Saul tries to kill Jonathan, 101
Joram *(King)*, 125
Jordan River, 83
Joseph, 57-58
    brothers go to Egypt for grain, 61-62
    children, 61, 65
    death/burial, 66
    dream, 57-58
    forgotten by new Pharaoh, 67-68
    interprets baker's and cupbearer's dreams, 60
    Jacob discovers truth about Joseph, 64
    Potiphar and Joseph, 59
        famine, 64
        interprets Potiphar's dream, 60
        Joseph given charge over Egypt, 61
        Joseph imprisoned, 59
        Potiphar's wife, 59
    Reuben's defense of, 58
    reunited with his brothers, 63-64
    sold into salvery by brothers, 58-59
    tests his brothers, 63
Joseph (and Mary), 177-179
Joseph of Arimathea, 221
Joshua, 85
    Caleb and Joshua spy on Canaan, 78
    death, 86
    God's encouragement, 81
    Israelites and Joshua
        Achan disobeys Joshua's command, 84
        appointed to lead Israelites into Promised Land, 79
        attack the city of Ai, 84

instructions when attacking Jericho, 84
    make a treaty with Gibeonites, 85
    march around Jericho, 83-84
    sends spies into Jericho, 82-83
    settlement of Promised Land, 86
    sun stands still, 85
    succeeds Moses, 81
Josiah *(King)*, 128
Jotham *(King)*, 128
joy, in the midst of suffering, 239
Judah
    blessed by Jacob, 65
    pleads with Joseph to spare Benjamin, 63
Judah (location), 157
    Cyrus releases some captives to go back and build temple, 134-136
    destruction of, Jeremiah's vision, 160
    Israel and Judah
        David unites Israel and Judah, 107-108
        God tells Solomon kingdom will split, 122
        split under Rehoboam, 122
    Jeremiah's prophecies about inhabitants, 160
    kings of Judah, 127-129
    Nehemiah returns to, 136-137
Judas (son of James), one of the Twelve, 181
Judas Iscariot
    commits suicide, 219, 226
    criticizes Mary, 216
    kisses Jesus, 218
    one of the Twelve, 181
    plots with chief priests against Jesus, 216
    tries to return money to chief priests, 219
the Judgement
    of believers, 248
    nonbelievers, 207-209
judging others, Jesus' teaching on, 202
judges, 87-90
Judges (Book of), 87, 90
Judiasm, 43

King James Version (KJB), 10
Kingdom of God (parables), 203
kinsman-redeemer, 91

L

Laban
  Jacob and Laban
    Laban gives Jacob part of livestock, 52
    Jacob and family leave Laban, 53-54
    Jacob works for Laban, 50
    make a covenant, 54
Lamentations (Book of), 161-162
language in the Bible, 17-18
Laodica (Church at), 281
Last Supper, 217
Latin translation (Vulgate), 10
Lazarus, 194-195
Leah and Jacob, 50-51
lepers, healing of, 189
Levi (Matthew), 181
Levites, 205
Leviticus (Book of), 79
Lewis, C. S., 199
literal vs. figurative language, 17-18
The Living Bible (TLB), 11, 298
"living sacrifices," 242
Lord's Prayer, 204
Lord's Supper, 245
Lot
  captured in battle, 38
  escape from Sodom and Gomorrah, 41-42
  family escapes from Sodom, 42
  journey to Canaan, 36
  rescued by Abraham, 38
  separates from Abraham, 37-38
  wife turns into pillar of salt, 42
Luke, author of Acts, 225
Lydia, 232
Lystra/Derbe, Paul and Silas' journey, 232

M

Maccabees, 166, 175
Magi, 178
major prophets, *see* prophets, major
Malachi, 170
Malta, Paul's shipwreck on Malta, 235
Manassah, 61, 65
Manasseh *(King)*
  death of Isaiah, 159
  king of Judah, 128
manna, Moses and the Israelites, 74

marriage, 244
  husband/wife relationship, 272
    Ephesians (Book of), 256
  intercultural marriages, customs/traditions, 136
  interfaith marriages, avoiding being "yoked" with nonbelievers, 249
  Old Testament, 46
Martha, 194-195
Mary (Lazarus' sister)
  Jesus resurrects Lazarus, 194-195
  pours perfume on Jesus' feet, 216
Mary (mother of Jesus)
  Gabriel visits Mary, 176
  Joseph and Mary, 177-179
  visits Elizabeth, 176
Mary Magdalene
  Jesus' post-resurrection appearance, 222
Matthew (Levi), one of the Twelve, 181
Melchizedek
  Abraham offers a tenth of everything, 38
  Jesus like Melchizedek, 266
Menahem *(King)*, 126
Mephibosheth, 109
mercy
  parables on, 206-207
  vs. grace, 256
Mere Christianity, 199
Meshach, 165
Messiah, *see* Jesus
Micah, 169
Michael (angel), 166
Michal
  David and Michal
    marries David, 100-101
    protects David from Saul, 101-102
    criticizes David's dancing, 109
    returned to David, 107
  given to another man, 107
Midian, 69
Miletus, Paul and Silas' journey, 234
millennium, 288
minor prophets, 168-170
Miriam, 77, 79
Moabites, 42
money, Jesus' teachings on, 201
Mordecai
  asks Esther to intervene for Jews, 140
  raises Esther, 139

  reveals plot to kill Xerxes, 139
  tells Esther to hide fact that she's Jewish, 139
  Xerxes promotes Mordecai, 141
Moses
  Aaron and Moses, 70-71
  burning bush, 69-70
  death, 80
  found by Pharaoh's daughter, 68
  given the Ten Commandments, 75
  Israelites and Moses, 74
    building/furnishing the tabernacle, 77
    God provides manna, 74
    in the Desert of Sinai, 75
    Israelites begin to grumble, 74
    led by God out of Egypt, 73
    parting of the Red Sea, 73
    wander in the wilderness another 40 years, 79
  kills Egyptian, 68
  Miriam slanders Moses, 77
  Mount Sinai, 75-76
  Pharaoh and Moses, 70-72
  superiority of Christ over Moses, 266
  Transfiguration (New Testament), 214
  Zipporah and Moses, 69-70
Most Holy Place (Holy of Holies), 77
Mount Sinai, 75-76
mules, customs/traditions, 118

N

Naaman, 131
Nadab *(King)*, 124
Nahum, 169
Naomi
  Boaz as her kinsman-redeemer, 91
  Ruth and Naomi, 90-92
NAS *(New American Standard)* version, 11, 298
Nathan
  tells David of the Lord's plans, 109-110
  warns Bathsheba, 118
Nathanael, one of the Twelve, 181
Nazareth
  Jesus teaches in, 182
  Mary and Joseph travel to/from Nazareth, 177-178

Nebuchadnezzar *(King)*
    asks that Jeremiah not be
        harmed, 160
    Daniel interprets his dream,
        164-165
    promotes Daniel, 165
Nehemiah
    rebuilds Jerusalem walls,
        137-138
    reforms priesthood, 138
    returns to Judah, 136
nephilim, 30
New American Standard (NAS)
    version, 11, 298
new covenant, 266-267
New International Version (NIV),
    10-11
new Jerusalem, 290-291
New King James Version (NKJV), 11,
    298
New Living Translation (NLT), 298
*New Revised Standard Version
    (NRSV)*, 11, 298
New Testament
    canon identified, 10
    Epistles, 294
    events between Old Testament
        and New Testament, 174-175
    Gospels, 294
    historical books of the Bible,
        294
    number of books, 10
    references to hell, 207-208
    structure, 20
    time period written, 10
    translations, 10-11
Nicodemus
    helps place Jesus in the tomb,
        221
    Jesus tells him that he must be
        born again, 183
Nicolaitans, 281
Ninevah, 168
Noah, 31-32
Nob (location), 101
Numbers (Book of), 79-80

O

Obadiah, 168
Obed, 91
oil, anointing with oil, 96
Old Testament
    canon identified, 10
    Dead Sea Scrolls, discovery of, 9
    events between Old Testament
        and New Testament, 174-175
    historical books of the Bible, 293

law-related books, 293
number of books, 10
Pentateuch translated into
    English, 10
structure, 20
time period written, 9
translations, 9-10
Omri *(King)*, 124
Onesimus (Philemon's slave), 263

P

parables
    a rich man, 204
    about "the kingdom of
        heaven," 203
    good Samaritan, 205
    great banquet, 204
    Jesus' use of, 203
    lost coin, 206
    lost sheep, 206
    on prayer, 204
    persistent widow, 204
    Pharisee and tax collector, 204
    prodigal son, 206-207
    sower, 202-203
    ten virgins, 205
    unused talents, 204
    workers in the vineyard, 204
paralyzed man, Jesus heals, 188
paraphrases vs. translations, 11
Passover
    final week of Jesus' life on earth,
        216
    first Passover, 72
    Joshua and troops observe
        before entering Promised
        Land, 83
    meaning of term, 72
patience, importance of, 270
Patmos, modern-day location, 280
Paul (Saul of Taursus)
    and false prophets, 249
    author (Book of)
        Colossians, 258
        1 Corinthians, 242
        2 Corinthians, 248
        Ephesians, 255
        Galatians, 253
        Philemon, 263-264
        Philippians, 257
        Romans, 238
        1 Thessalonians, 259-260
        2 Thessalonians, 260
        1 Timothy, 260-262
        2 Timothy, 262-263
        Titus, 263

Barnabas and Paul, 230-232
boasts about his hardships,
    249-250
confrontation with Peter, 254
defense of his ministry, 248-249
discredits rumors in Jerusalem,
    234
heals demon-possessed man,
    233-234
heals Eutychus, 234
love for the Corinthians, 249
meets Timothy, 232
prophesied over, 234
Roman citizenship, benefits of,
    231
shipwreck on Malta, 235
Silas and Paul
    journeys, 232-234
    Paul recruits Silas, 232
    return to Jerusalem, 234
    send Timothy to
        Thessalonica, 259
suffering for Christ's sake, 257
third journey, 235
"thorn in the flesh," 249
warns Corinthians, 250
see also Saul of Tarsus (Paul)
peace, in the midst of suffering,
    239
Pekah *(King)*, 126
Pekahiah *(King)*, 126
Peniel (location), meaning, 55
Pentateuch, translation into
    English, 10
Pentecost (Feast of Weeks)
    Holy Spirit comes, 226-227
    time of year, 226
Pergamum (church of), 281
perseverance
    Hebrews (Book of), 268
    importance of, 269-270
Persian customs/traditions,
    hangings, 139
persistent widow (parable of), 204
1 Peter (Book of), 271-272
2 Peter (Book of), 273-274
Peter
    acknowledges Jesus as the
        Christ, 214
    author of 1 and 2 Peter, 272
    confrontation with Paul, 254
    eats with Cornelius, 230
    heals beggar, 227
    imprisoned by King Herod, 230
    Jesus and Peter
        attempts to protect Jesus
            from soldiers, 218
        Jesus multiples the fish in
            Peter's net, 191

Jesus' post-resurrection
appearance, 224
money for taxes, 193
Peter denies Jesus three
times, 219
Peter rejects that Jesus will
suffer, 214
Peter walks on water, 192
Peter warned about testing,
214
Jesus' post-resurrection
appearance, 224
John and Peter
imprisoned, 227
run to see empty tomb, 222
miraculously escapes from
prison, 230-231
one of the Twelve, 181
testifies to crowd at Pentecost,
226-227
the Transfiguration, 214
word spreads about Peter, 227
Pharaoh
Israelites and Pharaoh
Pharaoh enslaves Israelites,
68
first Passover, 72
Pharaoh sends troops after
the Israelites, 73
releases Israelites, 72
Moses before Pharaoh, 70-72
orders killing of male Hebrew
children, 68
Pharaoh's daughter finds Moses,
68
Pharisees, 179
John the Baptist criticizes them,
180
Nicodemus' encounter with
Jesus, 183
Pharisee and tax collector
(parable of), 204
question the man born blind,
195-196
Philadelphia (Church of), 281
Philemon (Book of), 263-264
Philip, 181
Philippi, Paul and Silas' journey,
232
Philippians (Book of)
author, 257
God meets all our needs, 258
heavenly citizenship, 257
suffering for Christ, 257
Philistines, 97
David lives in the land of the
Philistines, 102
Israelites and Philistines,
Israelites led by Saul, 97-98

Samson and the Philistines,
89-90
take the Ark of the Covenant, 95
Phillip
chosen as one of seven deacons,
228
daughters, 234
Ethiopian eunuch and Phillip,
228-229
Pilate
allows Joseph to have Jesus'
body, 221-222
Jesus tried before Pilate, 219-220
places guard at Jesus' tomb, 222
sign on Jesus' cross, 221
plagues
God brings plagues on Egypt,
71-72
seven plagues, Revelation (Book
of), 287-288
Pontius Pilate, *see* Pilate
Postexilic Period, 134
postmillennialism, interpretation
of Revelation, 290
Potiphar
Joseph and Potiphar, 59
famine, 64
interprets Potiphar's dream,
60
Joseph given charge over
Egypt, 61
Joseph imprisoned, 59
Potiphar's wife, 59
prayer
effectiveness of, 40
importance, James (Book of), 271
Jesus' teachings on, 201
Lord's Prayer, 204
parables on, 204
praying always, 260
reasons for, 40
predestination, 241
premillennialism, interpretation of
Revelation (Book of), 290
priesthood, 205
Nehemiah reforms priesthood,
138
sufficiency of Jesus' sacrifice,
266-267
Prince of Peace, *see* Jesus
Priscilla and Aquila, 233
prodigal son (parable of), 206-207
Promised Land
God's promise to Abraham, 36
Joshua and the Israelites
Joshua appointed leader, 79
prepare to enter the land, 83
settlement of Promised
Land, 86

prophecies
about Jesus, 158-159
against Israel's enemies,
158-159
God's people, 159
of Daniel, 166
Satan's defeat, 28
time frame, 159
prophets
books of, 293-294
false prophets (warnings
against)
1 John, 274
2 John, 275
2 Peter, 273
Jude, 276
major
Daniel, 164-166
Ezekiel, 162-164
Isaiah, 157-159
Jeremiah, 159-161
minor, 168-170
Proverbs (Book of), 152
a woman of noble character,
152
author, 149
benefits of wisdom, 149
pitfalls of folly, 149
popular/common, 150-151
Psalms (Book of)
Asaph, 147
author, 145
common/popular, 148-149
honesty of, 147-148
images of God, 146-147
Selah, meaning, 149
Sons of Korah, 147
Purim (holiday), 141

Q-R

Rachel
death, 55
Jacob and Rachel, 50-51
steals father's idols, 53
Rahab, 82-83
rapture, 289
Paul tells the Thessalonians to
be ready, 259-260
Paul's discussion in 1
Corinthians (Book of), 248
reading schedule (one-year),
302-313
Rebekah
flees to Mesopotamia with
Jacob, 49
Isaac and Rebekah, 46-48
Red Sea, 73

reform movement, 10
Rehoboam
    Judah and Israel split, 122
    king of Judah, 126
    succeeds Solomon, 122-129
resources, 297-299
resurrection
    guards questioned about Jesus'
        body, 223
    Jesus' post-resurrection
        appearances, 223
        to Mary Magdalene, 222
        to Peter, 224
        to Thomas, 223-224
    news spreads, 225
    of boy in Nain, 194
    of Jairus' daughter, 194
    of Lazarus, 194-195
    see also rapture
Reuben, 58
Reuel (Jethro), 69
Revelation (Book of), 279-280
    144,000 protected by a seal, 283
    Abyss, 284
    an angel and scroll, 285
    author, 280
    closing, 291-292
    dragon (Satan) thrown in Abyss,
        288-289
    evaluation of seven churches,
        281
    four horsemen of the
        apocalypse, 283
    great tribulation, 283, 286
    group in white robes, 283-284
    harvest, 287
    heavenly throne, 282
    interpretations, 290
    judgement, 289
    new Jerusalem, 290-291
    number of the beast, 286
    one-thousand-year period, 289
    rider on white horse, 288
    seals, 283
    seven (number), significance,
        282
    seven plagues, 287-288
    seventh seal opened, 284
    seventh trumpet, 285
    the lamb and the sealed
        144,000, 287
    the scroll and the lamb, 282
    the two beasts, 286-287
    "two witnesses," 286-287
The Revised Version, 10
rich young man, Jesus' encounter
    with, 212
riches
    and spiritual prosperity, 269
    Jesus' teachings on, 201

righteousness
    Jesus' teachings on, 201
    of God, and godlessness of men,
        238
    through faith in Jesus, 239
Roman citizenship, benefits of, 231
Romans (Book of)
    Abraham justified through
        faith, 239
    author, 238
    becoming "living sacrifices,"
        242
    being in Christ, benefits, 240
    closing chapters, 242
    "ingrafted branches," Gentiles
        as, 242
    Jesus as atonement for our sin,
        239
    leaving behind sin and
        accepting Christ, 240
    made alive in Christ, 240
    opening, 238
    predestination, 241
    righteousness of God and
        godlessness of men, 238
    salvation for all who accept
        Jesus, 241-242
    sanctification, 240
Rome, Paul's third journey, 235
Ruth, 90-92

S

Sadducees, 180
salvation
    and circumcision, 232
    by grace, 255
    faith and deeds, 269-270
    for all who accept Jesus,
        241-242
    Jesus as a sacrifice once and for
        all, 267
Samaritans
    and Jews, conflict between, 184
    good Samaritan (parable), 205
Samson, 89-90
1 Samuel (Book of), 106
2 Samuel (Book of), 106, 115
Samuel
    anoints David as king, 98-99
    anoints Saul as king, 96
    death, 102
    encourages Israelites to
        rededicate themselves to the
        Lord, 95
    God speaks to Samuel about
        Eli's family, 94
    Hannah dedicates Samuel, 94

    rebukes Saul regarding the
        Amalekites, 98
    Saul and the witch of Endor,
        103
    Saul makes sacrifices to God
        without Samuel, 97
    sons, 96
    warns Israelites to obey God,
        96-97
Sanballat, 137
Sanhedrin
    apostles go before the
        Sanhedrin, 227-228
    Jesus tried before Sanhedrin,
        219
Sarah (Sarai)
    Abraham lies about relationship
        to Sarah, 37
    death, 45
    demands Hagar and Ishmael
        sent to wilderness, 43
    description of, in Dead Sea
        Scrolls, 37
    Hagar and Abraham's child
        (Ishmael), 39
    journey to Canaan, 36
    laughs at promise of children,
        40
    name change, 39
Sardis (Church of), 281
Satan
    prophecies about his defeat, 28
    tempts Eve, 27
    tempts Jesus in the wilderness,
        180-181
    tests Job, 142
    thrown into the Abyss, 288-289
Saul
    anointed as king, 96
    battle against the Philistines, 97
    commits suicide, 103
    David and Saul, 98
        David marries Michal,
            100-101
        David plays the harp for
            Saul, 99
        David spares Saul's life, 102
        Saul jealous of David, 100
        Saul tries to kill David,
            101-102
    death, David receives news, 106
    disobeys God regarding the
        Amalekites, 98
    Ish-Bosheth (son), 106-107
    Jonathan and Saul
        Saul tries to kill Jonathan,
            101
    Jonathan eats honey, 97
    makes sacrifices to God, 97

rebuked by Samuel, 98
sons killed in battle, 103
the witch of Endor, 103
victory over Ammonites, 96-97
Saul of Tarsus (Paul)
  Ananias helps Saul, 229-230
  name change, 232
  on the road to Damascus, 229
  persecution of Christians, 228
second coming
  Paul tells the Thessalonians to
    be ready, 259-260
  Peter answers skeptics, 274
  Scripture references, 216
  see also rapture; Revelation
    (Book of)
seeing God, 275
Selah, 149
Semites, 32
Sennacherib, 159
Septuagint (Old Testament
  translation), 9
seraphs (angels), 158, 163
Sermon on the Mount, 200-202
serpent, *see* Satan
seven (number), significance, 282
sexual immorality
  excommunication of immoral
    brothers, 243-244
  sex outside marriage, 244
Shadrach, 165
Shallum *(King),* 125
Sheba (Queen of Sheba), 121
sheep, lost sheep (parable), 206
Sheol (Hell), 209
shepherds, angels visit shepherds,
  178
shrines, 123
signs of end times, 215
Silas, Paul and Silas
  journeys, 232-234
  Paul recruits Silas, 232
  return to Jerusalem, 234
  send Timothy to Thessalonica,
    259
Simeon, 178
Simeon of Cyrene, 220
Simon (the Zealot), one of the
  Twelve, 181
sin
  and grace, 239
  excommunication of immoral
    brothers, 243-244
  Jesus as atonement for our sin,
    239
    accepting him as the Son of
      God, 199-201
    leaving behind sin and
      accepting Christ, 240

righteousness through faith
  in Jesus, 239
salvation for all who accept
  Jesus, 241-242
sufficiency of his sacrifice,
  266-267
one person affecting many, 84
Sodom, 41-42
Solomon
  and his harem, 122
  author of Proverbs, 149
  becomes king, 118
  builds temple, 118, 120-121
  David advises Solomon, 118
  God blesses Solomon, 119
  God tells Solomon kingdom
    will split, 122
  Jeroboam rebels against
    Solomon, 122
  makes judgement about infants,
    119-120
  palace, 121
  Queen of Sheba visits Solomon,
    121
  Rehoboam succeeds Solomon,
    122-129
  second child of David and
    Bathsheba, 112
  wealth, 121
  wisest man on earth, 120
Son of God, *see* Jesus
Song of Songs (Book of), 155-156
Sons of Korah, 147
souls, 283
sower (parable of), 202-205
speaking in tongues
  edification of the body, 247
  Holy Spirit comes at Pentecost,
    226-227
Spirit, *see* Holy Spirit
spiritual gifts, 247
  and unity among believers, 245-
    246
  speaking in tongues, 247
spiritual immaturity, 243
Spurgeon, Charles, 19
Stephen, 228
Stoics, 233
storm, Jesus calms the storm, 191
strong and weak Christians, and
  dietary restrictions, 244-245
study Bibles vs. basic Bibles, 11
study tools, 21-22
submission to authority, 272
suffering
  and faith in Jesus, 239
  for Christ's sake, 257
  Paul boasts about his hardships,
    249-250

refining our faith, 271
rejoicing in, 269
suicide
  Ahithophel, 114
  biblical perspective, 114
  Judas Iscariot, 219, 226
  Saul, 103
Sukkot (Feast of Tabernacles), 134
Susa, modern-day location, 138
synagogues, worship in, vs.
  temples, 182
synoptic gospels, *see* Gospels

T-U-V

tabernacle, 77
talents, parable of unused talents,
  204
Tamar, 112
tax collector, the Phari*see* and tax
  collector, 204
temple
  curtain torn when Jesus died,
    221
  Ezekiel's vision, 164
  Jesus clears the temple, 215
  Joseph and Mary find Jesus in
    the temple, 178-179
  rebuilding of (Zerubbabel's
    temple), 134-135
  Solomon builds temple, 118,
    120-121
temptation
  Eve, 27
  Jesus, 180-181
  vs. testing, 43
Ten Commandments, 75, 77
testing
  testing the spirits, 275
  vs. temptation, 43
Thaddaeus, one of the Twelve, 181
theophany, appearance of God in
  human form, 165
1 Thessalonians (Book of), 259-260
2 Thessalonians (Book of), 260
Thessalonica/Berea, Paul and Silas'
  journey, 233
Thomas
  Jesus' post-resurrection
    appearance, 223-224
  one of the Twelve, 181
Thyaria (church at), 281
Tibni *(King),* 124
Tigris River, 27
1 Timothy (Book of), 260-262
2 Timothy (Book of), 262-263

Timothy
  circumcision of, 232
  sent to Thessalonica, 259
  Paul meets Timothy, 232
Titus (Book of), 263
TLB (*The Living Bible*), 11
Tobiah, 137
tolerance, 243-244
tomb of Jesus, 222-223
tongues, speaking in tongues
  edification of the body, 247
  Holy Spirit comes at Pentecost,
    226-227
Torah, 20
Tower of Babel, 33
traditions/customs, *see* customs/
  traditions
Transfiguration, 214
translations, 10-11
  abbreviations, 298
  vs. paraphrases, 11
Tree of Life, 27, 291
Tree of the Knowledge of Good and
  Evil, 27-28
Trinity, explanation, 180
Troas, Paul and Silas' journey, 234
trusting God, Jesus' teachings on,
  202
the Twelve
  Jesus and the Twelve, 217
    apostles fall asleep in
      Gethsemane, 218
    choosing of the Twelve, 181
    Jesus calms the storm, 191
    Jesus feeds 5,000, 192-193
    Jesus multiples the fish in
      Peter's net, 191
    Jesus prays for himself, the
      Twelve, and all future
      believers, 218
    Jesus promises Holy Spirit,
      218
    Jesus walks on water, 192
    Jesus washes their feet, 217
    Last Supper, 217
    number killed for faith (of
      original 12), 223
    Sermon on the Mount,
      200-202
    the Twelve argue about who
      is greatest, 217
    withered fig tree, 193
twelve tribes of Israel, 86
Tyndale, William, 10

unity
  among body of believers, 255
  and spiritual gifts, 245-246

division among the body,
  242-243
    2 Peter (Book of), 273
    Ephesians (Book of), 255
Ur, modern-day region, 36
Uriah, 110-111
Uzzah, 108
Uzziah (Azariah, *King*), 127

Vashti (*Queen*), 138-139
versions of the Bible, 9-11, 298
virgin birth, 176
Vulgate, Latin translation, 10

W-X-Y-Z

washing the disciples' feet, 217
water
  Jesus changes water to wine,
    190
  Peter walks on water, 192
water baptism, 179
weak and strong Christians, and
  dietary restrictions, 244-245
weddings, customs/traditions, 190
wife/husband relationship, 256,
  272
  Ephesians, 256
wine
  Jesus changes water to wine,
    190
  wine and bread, significance,
    217
wisdom, 152
  benefits of wisdom, 149
  drawbacks of human wisdom,
    152-153
  reading Proverbs, 150
women
  part in worship/church, 247
  woman caught in adultery,
    Jesus speaks with, 184-185
  woman at the well, Jesus talks
    with, 183-184
works, faith and deeds, 269-270
worry, Jesus' teachings on, 201-202
worship
  in temples vs. synagogues, 182
  orderly worship, 245
  women, part in worship/
    church, 247
wrath of God, 238
Wycliffe, John, translated Bible
  into English, 10

Xeres (Ahasuerus), 138
  chooses Esther, 139
  disposes Vashti as queen, 138

Esther visits, 140
gives Esther Haman's property,
  141
Haman advises Xerxes, 140-141
looks for new queen, 139
Mordecai reveals plot to kill
  Xerxes, 139
promotes Mordecai, 141
Xerxes has Haman killed, 141

Yahweh (YHWH), 69

Zacchaeus, 211
Zachariah (prophet), 135
Zealots, 182
Zechariah (Elizabeth's husband),
  169
  Elizabeth and Zachariah
    birth of John, 176
    Gabriel visits Zachariah, 175
Zachariah (*King*), 125
Zedekiah (*King*)
  Jeremiah advises him, 160
  king of Judah, 129
Zephaniah, 169
Zerubbabel leads return to
  Jerusalem to rebuild the temple,
  134
ziggurats, 33
Zimri (*King*), 124
Zipporah
  Moses and Zipporah, 69
    circumcision of son, 70
Zophar, Job's friend, 143